Teachers and the Law

Diverse Roles and New Challenges

THIRD EDITION

A. Wayne MacKay, C.M., Q.C.
Lyle (Chip) Sutherland
Kimberley D. Pochini

emond

Toronto, Canada
2013

Emond Montgomery Publications Limited
60 Shaftesbury Avenue
Toronto ON M4T 1A3
http://www.emond.ca/highered

Printed in Canada.
Reprinted September 2018.

We acknowledge the financial support of the Government of Canada.
Nous reconnaissons l'appui financier du gouvernement du Canada.   Canada

Acquisitions and development editor: Mike Thompson
Supervising editor: Jim Lyons
Copy editor and typesetter: Nancy Ennis
Proofreader: Andrew Gordon
Indexer: Paula Pike
Text designer: Tara Wells
Cover designer: Stephen Cribbin & Simon Evers
Cover image: Getty Images

Library and Archives Canada Cataloguing in Publication

MacKay, A. Wayne, 1949-
    Teachers and the law : diverse roles and new challenges / A. Wayne MacKay,
Lyle (Chip) Sutherland, Kimberley D. Pochini. — 3rd ed.

Includes index.
ISBN 978-1-55239-523-3

    1. Teachers— Legal status, laws, etc.—Canada.   2. Students—Legal status,
laws, etc.—Canada.   I. Sutherland, Lyle I.   II. Pochini, Kimberley D.   III. Title.

KE3850.M34 2013   344.71'078   C2012-908016-0
KF4175.M34 2013

Dedication

Wayne rededicates this book to his father, Alexander MacKay, who served for many years as the chair of the Pictou County School Board as well as municipal councillor, and his mother, Evaline (McCullough) MacKay, who provided a model of caring education in the home. Both Wayne's parents are deceased. He also dedicates this book to his children, Erin, Amanda, Alexa, and Jordi MacKay, as well as to his granddaughters, Laelle, Cassidy, and Sadie, who continue to benefit from a Canadian education system to which their mother and grandmother respectively, Laurie Ann MacKay (Wayne's first wife), devoted her professional career.

Wayne also dedicates this third edition to his late aunt, Mae (MacKay) MacLean, who was his second mother, and who died in 2011 at the age of 88. She provided a model of how to live life well. Finally, he acknowledges the love and support of his wife, JoAnn Martell-MacKay, who handles the important practical things in life.

Chip is pleased that 21 years later he can dedicate the third edition of this book again to his parents, Lyle (Sr.) and Mary Sutherland, who devoted their professional careers to children and education; and to his children, Kate and Will, who are reaping the benefits of the education system, thanks to people like his parents.

Kimberley would like to thank her parents, Jane and Kairens MacDonald, for their support throughout her own education and during the drafting of this book. She would also like to thank the dedicated and skilled teachers she had as a student in rural Pictou County.

Brief Contents

Contents

Chapter 3   Teachers as Educational State Agents

Chapter 4   Teachers as Guardians of Equality

Chapter 5   Teachers as Agents of the Police

Chapter 6   Teachers as Social Welfare Agents

Preface to the Third Edition

This third edition of *Teachers and the Law* is more comprehensive than its predecessors and has been thoroughly updated. During the writing of this edition, the groundbreaking Supreme Court of Canada decision *Moore v. British Columbia* was released, clarifying and potentially expanding the rights of students with special needs within our education system. A new *Copyright Act* was proclaimed as law, with positive and important implications for schools. The evolving rights of teachers within the employment context have been updated, including the privacy rights of teachers in the ever-changing Internet world. The ongoing challenges of balancing the rights of students, teachers, and parents with the important demands of a safe and inclusive school environment are explored throughout this book. The importance of this is emphasized by the tragic mass killing at Sandy Hook Elementary School in the United States in December 2012. The important role of parents in the education of their children and the need for parents and teachers to work together is emphasized throughout the book.

The growing challenges of bullying and cyberbullying and their implications for the diverse roles of teachers are explored in many different chapters. Understanding the modern technological world and its pervasive implications for teaching are addressed throughout the book's chapters and in a stand-alone and completely new Chapter 8. The revolution in communications that is "social media" is addressed in terms of cyberbullying and the need to bridge the growing gap between the young and the old in this evolving domain. In *A.B. v. Bragg Communications*, the Supreme Court of Canada acknowledges the significant harm of cyberbullying and allows a young woman to pursue defamation anonymously for a false and hurtful

Facebook page aimed at ridiculing and embarrassing her. Chapter 8 also includes a comprehensive review of the new *Copyright Act* passed in 2012, as well as several recent Supreme Court of Canada decisions relating to copyright and how it affects schools.

In addition to these new challenges facing teachers, this edition also updates and expands on the more traditional roles of teachers discussed in the previous editions—as parents, educational state agents, police agents, social welfare agents, and employees. A new role for teachers as "guardians of equality" is also explored at length within its own chapter, Chapter 4. Included within this chapter are discussions about the accommodation of Canada's multicultural identity, the needs of First Nations students, and addressing the needs of an inclusive, welcoming, and non-discriminatory school climate. The legal implications of celebrating Canada's growing diversity and the role of teachers in this aspect of schooling are explored in many different contexts.

Particular attention is paid to the growing roles of courts and human rights tribunals in shaping both educational policies and practices. Legislatures and school boards are still the critical institutional players in respect of schools, but the roles of lawyers, administrative agencies, and judges continue to grow. This does not mean that teachers need to acquire law degrees to be effective, but an understanding of the general legal framework for education is an increasing prerequisite for good teaching. This theme is developed in the eight chapters that follow. Our goal is not to convert teachers to lawyers, which would not be positive for the quality of education, but rather to improve on the many talents that teachers bring to their various and important roles in shaping the lives of our children. At the end of the day, law and education are not enemies but natural allies in the pursuit of a meaningful education for Canada's youth.

A Note from the Publisher

The publisher wishes to thank the following people for providing their feedback and suggestions or for other assistance during the development of this book: Derek J. Allison (Western University), Yvette DeBeer (Lakehead University), Nancy Dill and colleagues (SIAST), Frances Helyar (Lakehead University), Michael Parr (Schulich School of Education, Nipissing University), Frank Peters (University of Alberta), Glynn Sharpe (Nipissing University), William Smale (Trent University), Doug Thom (Lakehead University), and Shirley Van Nuland (UOIT).

Additional teaching resources are available to accompany this book. For more information, visit the book's website at **emp.ca/teachers3e.**

About the Authors

This third edition comes 7 years after the second edition. This is half the time that elapsed between the first and second editions (14 years), yet much has happened in the world of education law since the first edition was published over two decades ago in 1992.

A. Wayne MacKay

Wayne MacKay has continued to write extensively in this area and has had two career departures from teaching law at Dalhousie University. The first saw him as executive director of the Nova Scotia Human Rights Commission from 1995 to 1998, where he was immersed in the area of individual rights and systematic change. He then moved on to become president of Mount Allison University in Sackville, New Brunswick from 2001 to 2004, where he gained considerable insight and knowledge about the challenges facing front-line administrators of education. In the spaces between these career departures, he continued to teach at Dalhousie Law School, where he still teaches his pioneering seminar in education law as well as courses in constitutional law and human rights and a new course on privacy law. He completed a major review of the education system in New Brunswick and produced the 2006 report on this, entitled "Connecting Care and Challenge: Tapping Our Human Potential—Inclusive Education: A Review of Programming and Services in New Brunswick." More recently, he chaired a Nova Scotia task force and produced its report, "Respectful and Responsible Relationships: There's No App for That—The Report of the Nova Scotia Task Force on Bullying and Cyberbullying" (February 29, 2012). He is also the first holder of the Yogis and Keddy Chair in Human Rights Law at Dalhousie University.

Lyle (Chip) Sutherland

Chip Sutherland is currently practising law with the firm Pink Larkin, a boutique labour and administrative law firm in Halifax, Nova Scotia, who count among their clients the Nova Scotia Teachers Union. His practice is split between health law, regulatory work in the media field, administrative tribunal advocacy, and entertainment law. Most recently he co-authored the Canadian edition of *All You Need to Know About the Music Business*, 8th ed. (New York: Simon and Shuster, 2013) with world-renowned entertainment lawyer Donald Passman.

Kimberley D. Pochini

Kimberley Pochini has acted as in-house counsel to the largest health authority in Nova Scotia and, more recently, as counsel to the Newfoundland and Labrador Human Rights Commission, where a significant part of her practice involved education-based human rights issues. Kimberley is currently practising with the firm of Patterson Law in Truro, Nova Scotia, where her practice focuses on litigation and advice in the areas of labour and employment, health, education, and municipal law.

Kimberley Pochini would like to thank her law firm, Patterson Law, which provided many of the research resources required for her contributions to producing this edition of the book. As well, all three authors would like to thank Alison Morgan, an articled clerk with Patterson Law, who provided assistance with the research and drafting of Chapter 7 of the book, and Kelsey McLaren, an associate at Pink Larkin, who provided much-needed help in sifting through the new changes in the *Copyright Act* and recent case law.

1

Introduction to the Legal Framework

The field of education law has expanded rapidly over the past several decades. As the larger size of this book's third edition suggests, there have been many new legal developments since we published the second edition in 2006. Although this expansion may present new and exciting challenges for lawyers and educational administrators, it has been a troublesome development for some teachers. The *Canadian Charter of Rights and Freedoms*,[1] now 30 years old, continues to play a significant role in shaping the educational environment. More and more, educational administration and policy must navigate these legal currents.

Teachers are arguably the most important component in any educational structure. When the classroom door is closed, the responsibility for educating today's youth rests squarely on their shoulders. In spite of their vital role in the proper functioning of the educational system, teachers have traditionally been victimized by outdated expectations with regard to their legal roles and responsibilities, both inside and outside the classroom. The emergence and development of education law issues in the past 30 years has also created more confusion for teachers.

The law, generally, can be mystifying. Historically, judges and lawyers have not made the necessary efforts to demystify the law and legal processes. Lawyers are often guilty of resorting to legal jargon instead of using plain language to explain legal principles. Through the numerous lectures and seminars we have conducted across the country, and the many years we have spent representing school boards and parents, we have been able to gain, to some extent, a better understanding of the mysteries of the law as seen through the eyes of teachers. Although, increasingly, teachers and administrators are writing legal handbooks for teachers, we think it is important that lawyers also provide legal information. Some areas of law—for example, constitutional law—are complex. As the field of education law has grown in size and complexity, so too have the roles and responsibilities of teachers. Rather than explore legal issues within the traditional legal framework of negligence, criminal law, and labour law, for example, we have divided this book into chapters that focus on the roles and responsibilities of teachers. The legal issues are woven into this discussion.

Before embarking on our exploration of a teacher's many roles, we first take a brief tour through the Canadian legal system, highlighting the areas that affect education. We also examine the role and status of teachers as seen through the eyes of the law.

Constitutional Basis of Law

Canada's Constitution is divided, essentially, into two parts: the *Constitution Act, 1867*[2] and the *Constitution Act, 1982*.[3] The latter includes section 35, which addresses Aboriginal rights, and the Charter. The 1867 Act, in section 91, sets out a list of powers exclusively exercised by the federal government and, in section 92, a list of powers exclusively exercised by the provincial government. We can draw examples of this division of powers from our daily experiences—that is, the federal government has exclusive authority over matters such as banking, national defence, criminal law, copyright, patents, navigation and shipping, and telecommunications. The provinces have exclusive authority over matters of a "merely local or private nature," property and civil rights, and particular items such as the court system, hospitals, and municipal governments.

Education has historically enjoyed a special status because it is defined by a separate section in the *Constitution Act, 1867*. Section 93 specifically assigns the legislative authority over education to the provinces. Section 93 exclusively permits the provinces to make laws that relate to education, subject to certain protections for denominational schools. For this reason, education has long been considered the "jewel" of the provinces and, historically, the federal government has not sought to interfere in the educational sphere. One exception to this observation is the federal power over the education of Aboriginal peoples. In previous years, the federal government also exercised authority over educational systems in the Yukon and Northwest Territories, but this is no longer the case.

Aboriginal and treaty rights are constitutionally guaranteed in section 35 of the *Constitution Act, 1982*, and there has been considerable judicial interpretation of what these rights mean in a modern context.[4] Whether there is an Aboriginal right to education and what its content might be are questions that have not yet been decided. A report by the Royal Commission on Aboriginal Peoples highlighted the importance of education to an improved relationship with First Nations. In the Western provinces, there may be potential claims to a treaty right to Aboriginal education. The creation and proper funding of these schools remain a major challenge. Although the federal government has responsibility for Aboriginal education, the provinces educate Aboriginal students who choose to attend off-reserve schools. Education in Canada's northern territories raises particular issues of cultural sensitivity as well. Traditional public education methods may not always be culturally appropriate in some communities and a more customized approach must be adopted. Recently, the federal government created a national panel on First Nations Elementary and Secondary Students on Reserve. In February 2012, this panel released a report, "Nurturing the Learning Spirit of First Nations Students."[5] Hopefully, this will provide a first step to more meaningful education for Canada's Aboriginal peoples. Ultimately the solutions must come from the Aboriginal communities themselves, which must be both consulted and involved.

Since 1982, the most important constitutional development in education law has been the entrenchment of the Charter in the *Constitution Act, 1982*. As part of the Constitution, the Charter is the supreme law of Canada and any legislation that is inconsistent with it is inoperative. Throughout this book, we examine the various aspects of the Charter as they relate to education. In general terms, one of the most dramatic effects of the Charter is that it continues to shape national standards in education.

Before the enactment of the Charter, education (other than in denominational schools) was strictly within the purview of the provinces, and educational rights and privileges were defined by provincial education acts. Even with respect to Aboriginals, the federal education jurisdiction was largely delegated to the provinces and local territorial councils. There was also considerable power left in the hands of local school boards. The Charter, however, establishes rights and freedoms for every Canadian citizen regardless of residence. As the courts hear cases that involve the impact of constitutional rights on education, the provinces are being forced to adjust their legislation to comply with the standards of the Charter as interpreted by the courts. Ontario must now pay attention to what the courts are saying in Alberta and Saskatchewan (and vice versa) if it hopes to avoid similar challenges in its own courts. Although education is a provincial matter, court decisions based on the Charter have acted as a nationalizing influence.

Specific Sources of School Law

There are various sources of education law, each with differing scope and degrees of legal force. The Charter exerts the strongest possible legal force and has the widest possible scope; however, it touches on only certain aspects of education law. With the exception of denominational school rights (section 29) and minority language education rights (section 23), the provisions of the Charter are not aimed specifically at education, though their impact is felt in all areas of education law.

The provinces provide the most comprehensive sources of education law through their respective education statutes. These statutes codify the law of the province and cover most aspects of administration, from the powers and responsibilities of the minister of education to the duties of students. They define school districts and outline the powers and duties of school boards, teachers, and principals. Although every province's education statutes deal with similar subjects, the varying approaches from province to province reflect the unique historical development of the various provinces.

In addition to the education acts of each province, there are statutes that regulate specific aspects of education.[6] Laws of more general application—such as labour standards, human rights codes, and occupational health and safety legislation—also have an impact on schools.

A second source of law created by the provinces is known as "subordinate legislation" or "regulations." These laws are expressly authorized in every provincial or territorial education act and may be passed by a minister of education or the Cabinet without a vote by the members of the legislature. Regulations have the same legal force as statutes, but are usually more detailed and technical in scope. In January 2013, in Nova Scotia the terms "bullying" and "cyberbullying" were defined in the updated regulations, while in Ontario these terms were defined in the education statute. Regulations are attractive to governments as a means of implementing educational policies without having to debate the issues in the legislature. All provincial education statutes give the minister and the provincial Cabinet broad powers to make regulations that affect many aspects of education.

The next source of law, located a step down on the legal hierarchy, are the bylaws or policies implemented by school boards. These policies may be developed by either the education departments or the boards; most often, they are developed by both bodies. The policies are guidelines that school administrators and school boards may enact to govern their own activities, but they carry less weight in a courtroom. In other words, a parent may complain to a school board that a certain school policy is not being followed; however, this will rarely serve as the sole basis for legal action. A policy has legal force only if it can be tied to another source of law. Individual schools may also develop their own policies, but these are still further down the chain of authority.

The final and major source of education law in Canada is the common law, or judge-made law. This body of law is composed of the decisions of judges who hear cases across the country and it is in a state of constant evolution. As parents have become more familiar with the protections afforded by the Charter, there has been a surge of judge-made law in the field of education. This takes the form of interpretation of statutes and constitutional provisions as well as interpretation of the decisions of other judges. Some commentators have attributed this phenomenon to a new "rights consciousness" on the part of parents. Judges are therefore becoming prominent figures in the field of education and, in spite of attempts by the provinces to adapt their education processes to reflect the protected rights and freedoms in the Charter, judges and lawyers still play an important role in teachers' lives.

Related Sources of Education Law

Education touches many aspects of contemporary life; consequently, it is affected by many different, though related, sources of law. Not the least of these is the criminal law, which has undergone significant changes in the past few decades. The entire juvenile justice system was overhauled in 1984 through the creation of the *Young Offenders Act*, and then again in 2003 with the passage of the *Youth Criminal Justice Act*. These acts have radically changed the way that the legal system deals with children and youth. The *Criminal Code* was amended in 1988 to better protect children from sexual abuse. These broad protections have caused a great deal of concern among teachers. Although teachers are certainly interested in the welfare of their students, they must also be aware of the danger of falling victim to damaging allegations of sexual or other forms of physical abuse. The newest addition to these laws is the *Safe Streets and Communities Act*, which was passed in 2012. Known commonly as the "omnibus crime bill," or Bill C-10, it affects multiple pieces of legislation relating to criminal justice. One significant aspect of this bill is to shift focus from rehabilitation to protection of society, and the criminal punishments teachers see given to their students may be more severe.

As the workplace becomes more complex, labour law has also proven to be an important area for teachers. In most provinces, the working conditions of teachers are regulated by distinct collective bargaining legislation. The major differences between these statutes and general labour relations legislation are the limitations on the right to strike found in some teachers' collective bargaining acts.

Copyright law has emerged as a concern for teachers in the form of the *Copyright Act*, which does not fully protect the use of materials for educational purposes. However, the 2013 version of the *Copyright Act* is more positive for schools. Teachers with the best educational intentions may find themselves violating copyright laws by making unauthorized copies in some circumstances. Copyright law is created by the federal Parliament and thus affects schools in every province. We examine copyright law and its related issues in Chapter 8 of this book.

Family law issues increasingly arise in schools as governments become more involved in regulating family relationships. Provincial child-protection statutes have been amended to focus on the best interests of the child, and there has been a strong movement toward detecting and prosecuting child abusers. This means that teachers must be aware of the warning signs of abuse and familiarize themselves with the mandates of local social service agencies. Every province's children's services legislation makes it mandatory for professionals who work with children to report suspected child abuse or neglect. Failure to do so may result in prosecution. Mental health issues and concerns about suicide prevention also implicate health departments and there is a need for the various departments to work together in providing more integrated services to students.

Bullying and cyberbullying have become increasingly major issues relating to education. Because of the widespread nature of bullying and the acknowledgement of the significant damage that it causes to children, it is imperative that teachers be aware of these matters. The Senate Report on Cyberbullying and the Report from the Nova Scotia Task Force on Bullying and Cyberbullying, *Respectful and Responsible Relationships: There's No App for That*, for example, are important resources for teachers. Human rights legislation and the *Criminal Code* are also possible sources for teachers who feel that bullying could amount to harassment in either human rights or criminal terms.

We discuss these various sources of law in more detail as they arise in the context of the specific roles played by teachers. Because education law is connected to other legal spheres, teachers must have a general understanding of the larger framework of Canadian law.

Legal Procedures and Related Matters

Canada's legal system was grafted onto British common law traditions and is similar to the legal systems in other Commonwealth countries. The preamble to the *Constitution Act, 1867* describes the Canadian governmental system as "similar in principle to that of the United Kingdom." Each province has a "superior court," with the inherent or historical jurisdiction to deal with any form of legal dispute. This jurisdiction is inherent in the sense that it goes with the court even if the statute is silent on the issue. The superior court may be broken into a trial division and an appeal division, but in all provinces there is a separate appeal court. There are also "inferior courts" created by statute. These courts—for example, family courts and small claims courts—have defined purposes and limited mandates. The final level of appeal is the Supreme Court of Canada, whose decisions are binding on provincial courts. The decisions of the various provincial appeal courts are "persuasive," but not binding on courts outside their province of origin. There are also federal courts whose powers are defined by statute, but school issues are rarely, if ever, raised there.

From the perspective of a parent pursuing an education law issue, the road to final resolution is often long and expensive. The first line of attack is to discuss the problem with the relevant school board authorities and perhaps attend a meeting of the full school board. It is becoming increasingly popular to have lawyers represent the interests of parents at these school board meetings. If parents remain unsatisfied at this administrative level, they may choose to institute legal proceedings in the superior court of the province. It can take as long as two years to prepare a case for court and complete the trial. Considering the expenses involved for both parents and school boards, there is substantial incentive to settle these disputes before going to trial.

If a case proceeds through the trial process, the losing party must decide whether to accept defeat or appeal the ruling. The next step in the litigation process is an appeal to the provincial court of appeal; the appeal can take up to a year to be heard, depending on the court's schedule. If, after the appeal, a party is still dissatisfied, he or she may appeal to the Supreme Court of Canada. If the issue is deemed to be of sufficient national importance, the Supreme Court of Canada may choose to hear the appeal. In the same vein, if the court decides that the issue is not of sufficient national importance, it may decline to hear the case. The majority of cases are declined. To take a case from trial to the Supreme Court of Canada can take as long as seven years and cost hundreds of thousands of dollars. This means that the courts are not easily accessible to average Canadians.

Given the high cost and significant time involved in bringing matters before the courts, remedies are often sought through mediation or particular administrative structures. Some education statutes include administrative structures that allow parents, students, and teachers to appeal decisions to a statutorily created administrative board. There are also specialized labour boards, where teachers may pursue employment-related matters. A common administrative route for resolving rights disputes in schools is bringing a complaint before the human rights commission. Most of the legal costs of pursuing a human rights complaint are borne by the commission and not the complainant. Unfortunately, these administrative procedures can also take a long time, and are usually subject to review or appeal in the courts. The wheels of justice grind slowly.

Legal Role and Status of Teachers

Against this tapestry of interwoven sources of law, we now turn to the status of teachers. The question of a teacher's legal status has been a neglected issue for many years. Perhaps this explains why the law's intervention into educational policy continues to cause such a stir throughout the teaching community. Traditionally, teachers have been largely immune from examination under the legal microscope; however, as the law becomes increasingly involved in education, teachers are also swept into the legal process.

If one were to ask any teacher what he considers his role and legal status in the classroom to be, he would probably reply, "I stand in the place of a parent for the purpose of teaching children." Ask a teacher about the standard of care that is expected of her, and she would probably answer, "I must exercise the care of a reasonable and prudent parent." Ask another teacher about the appropriate scope of her discipline and she would tell you that she is to exercise the discipline of "a kind, firm, and judicious parent." Teachers are inundated with role references based on parental delegation of authority. This is the common-law origin of the status of a teacher.

The theory of parental delegation is drawn from the historical doctrine of *in loco parentis*. This is a Latin phrase meaning "in the place of a parent." Historically, this doctrine served as the basis for a teacher's legal authority. In the early 1900s, for example, parents were often left to their own devices to form community school boards and build their own schools. Parents were thus able to prescribe the manner in which their children were to be taught and they bore the primary responsibility for hiring and firing teachers. Most commentators agree that teachers in that era had little autonomy or privacy. Furthermore, the fact that the one-room school contained students from grades 1 to 12 meant that it was possible for the same teacher to teach the same child for 10 or more years, while simultaneously teaching several children from the same family. This is the model of education that existed when many education statutes were first drafted.

Although the doctrine of *in loco parentis* may well have been operative in the early part of the past century, it has been eroded almost to the point of extinction in the past several decades. Although the doctrine may still have some life in the common-law duties of teachers, it has largely been supplanted by statute.

Without recourse to developments in case law, we need only look at the realities of the school setting to realize that *in loco parentis* has little or no place in today's schools. Although the one-room schoolhouse and community school boards may once have provided a setting for parents to delegate their inherent authority to teachers, the post-1960 world of centralized school authority and legislative regulation leaves little room for similar delegation. Parents are now separated from teachers by a vast maze of administrative and governmental structures. Discretion has been replaced with legislation and regulations that often leave both parents and teachers with a sense of powerlessness.

In addition to their former status of *in loco parentis*, teachers, as agents of the state, have also exercised an additional legal role under the common law principle of *parens patriae*. This principle has been defined as follows:

> The sovereign as *parens patriae* has a kind of guardianship over various classes of persons who, from their legal disabilities, stand in need of protection, such as infants, idiots and lunatics.[7]

The provinces hire teachers in a *parens patriae* capacity to act as state agents for the purpose of providing education to children.

Given that teachers have exercised their role under both the *in loco parentis* and *parens patriae* principles, which of these principles is the primary basis for the present legal status of teachers? Even in the early 1900s, state authority was the predominant basis for teachers' legal authority. This is most clearly seen in the areas of compulsory education and corporal punishment. If a parental delegation were the primary basis for a teacher's authority, then parents would be able to revoke or define that delegation. In cases that involved compulsory education, parents attempted to revoke the delegation of authority to teach their children by refusing, for various reasons, to send their children to provincial schools. They were told by the courts (in most cases) that the government's compelling interest in the education of children should prevail. The role of the state in protecting the child trumped that of the parent.

In cases that involved corporal punishment, parents attempted to "define" their *in loco parentis* delegation by restricting the use of force on their children. If *in loco parentis* were the primary basis for a teacher's authority, then a teacher could be found to have "assaulted" the student, in circumstances where the parents had expressly instructed that their child not be touched. As early as 1910, the courts have upheld the statutory role of teachers to use reasonable force by way of correction to maintain order and discipline in the classroom. In fact, this statutory authority has been, and continues to be, contained in section 43 of the *Criminal Code* as a specific defence available to teachers on a charge of assaulting a student. This section has also survived a constitutional challenge based on the Charter.[8]

When we combine the growth of statutory authority with the historical evolution of the school setting, it is simply not realistic to suggest that in today's schools teachers may rely on the doctrine of *in loco parentis* as a primary source of authority. This was confirmed by the Supreme Court of Canada in *Ogg-Moss v. The Queen*.[9] This case involved an assault charge against a counsellor in a facility for mentally disabled adults. In his discussion of the application of section 43 of the *Criminal Code*, Chief Justice Dickson examined the history and application of the *in loco parentis* doctrine. He concluded that the courts will be reluctant to imply a delegation of parental authority and that *in loco parentis* has little, if any, relevance in institutional settings. Today, teachers' primary source of authority comes from the state and is regulated by statute and related rules.

Modern-Day Roles of Teachers

Today's teachers face many complex and varying roles. Certainly, many teachers would welcome a return to the traditional *in loco parentis* model of teaching, when it was possible simply to rest on their judgment as a parent. In today's schools, the teacher is required to act not only as a parent but also as a police officer, social worker, and professional educator. It is no wonder that many teachers are confused and frustrated in their present circumstances and, in particular, with the conflicting signals sent to them by government officials, school administrators, and the courts. The chapters that follow attempt to identify and demystify these roles. In particular, they focus on the law's effect on each of the modern teacher's roles. In many cases, the law has served to create and enhance a particular role for teachers, and in other cases, it has simply served to shift the boundaries of existing roles.

In preparing this book we have relied to a considerable extent on our legal experience representing both parents and school authorities. However, the primary basis for the particular definition of the roles of teachers was drawn from extensive seminars and lectures across the country—seminars where teachers have had the opportunity to voice their concerns and to ask questions. This interaction has allowed us to focus on the issues that cause the greatest concern among teachers. In a real way, teachers and administrators have shaped the structure of this book. For the purpose of analysis, we have divided this book into eight chapters. The purpose of this chapter is to introduce the legal framework within which schools operate.

Chapter 2 deals with the parental role of teachers. Although *in loco parentis* may no longer be a major doctrine for defining the legal status of teachers, its effects still linger in certain quasi-parental roles. Chapter 2 includes a discussion of negligence and liability for teachers, as well as a discussion of corporal punishment. It examines the sexual abuse provisions of the *Criminal Code* and points out the dangers that these provisions present for teachers. We also briefly touch on the matter of educational malpractice in Canada.

Chapter 3 focuses on teachers as educational state agents. This is an area of immense growth in the law. Chapter 3 includes a discussion of the duties of teachers as defined in the education statutes, as well as the impact of the Charter and provincial human rights codes on teachers' actions in the classroom. We also discuss the right to an education, the validity of religious instruction in schools, and other constitutionally entrenched rights enjoyed by parents and students—for example, freedom of expression and freedom of association. Finally, we move on to another equally difficult area: making and enforcing school rules.

Chapter 4, new to the third edition, focuses exclusively on equality issues. Teachers have a unique and pivotal role in practising and educating their students about the Charter's equality rights as one of the foundational principles of Canadian society. Chapter 4 discusses human rights tribunals as an alternative route to equality, using the recent landmark example of *Moore v. British Columbia*.[10] Here we tackle the challenging issue of special education, focusing on inclusive education, reasonable accommodation, and the importance of appropriate and meaningful education. Other equality issues, including sex, age, race, multiculturalism, and sexual orientation, are also canvassed. Chapter 4 also looks at the disturbing issues of bullying, cyberbullying, and school violence that have become almost omnipresent in today's society. Far too often, their victims are among the most vulnerable students in the schools.

Chapter 5 centres primarily on criminal law and the teacher as a state agent for the police. This involves an examination of the *Youth Criminal Justice Act*, the juvenile justice system in Canada, and the roles played by teachers in that system. We look at various case law examples as well as pressing legal issues, such as search and seizure, detention, and the questioning of students. Chapter 5 also explores the difficult balance between order and students' rights in our schools.

Chapter 6 deals with the teacher as a social welfare agent. Increasingly, teachers are required to assume a social welfare responsibility for students. The most prominent example of this role is the requirement to report any suspected child abuse to the proper authorities. The social welfare role has been expanded in recent years. Where they are available, guidance counsellors are expected to provide more assistance to students than mere advice on course selection. They may provide personal counselling, advocacy, and a host of other services. Teachers are often caught in the middle of family disputes and are required to act as mediators. Teachers may also be seen as resources for the various social agencies in the community. It is not unusual for a teacher to become extensively involved with the parents, social workers, and group homes that affect the lives of particular students. Chapter 6 also examines the teacher's role as paramedic. The legal parameters of this expanding social welfare role are not well understood.

Chapter 7 examines the role of the teacher as an employee. Whereas the earlier chapters deal primarily with teachers in relation to the needs of others, Chapter 7 focuses on teachers' rights and obligations. The school is a complex workplace with a myriad of administrative structures and potential labour relations problems. Teachers are subject to strict collective bargaining procedures and various disciplinary proceedings. They may also experience lifestyle restrictions as a result of their career choice. Chapter 7 examines the labour and employment rights and duties of teachers. It also explores teachers' rights under the Charter, including new and evolving rights to privacy.

Chapter 8, also new to this edition, explores the growing need of teachers to come to grips with the ever changing world of technology. We explore the practical implications of the 2013 *Copyright Act* for teachers, as well as other issues related to technology. Technology is now a vital aspect of good teaching and a necessary component of the competent teacher's tool kit. Although there are many positive aspects to technology, its darker underbelly, cyberbullying, is explored in this chapter and throughout the book.

In the Epilogue to the text, we examine the new challenges faced by the "omnicompetent" teacher. In addition to the challenges of technology just discussed, there is the complex and ever changing world of social media. The task of bridging the gap between students and adults is a major one. We therefore conclude by reinforcing the need for legal awareness.

We hope that our delineation of each of these roles provides some answers to the troubling questions that teachers face everyday as they are required to make difficult decisions in response to the diverse situations that arise in the classroom. By exploring the varied roles of teachers, we also hope to provide a framework for discussion. We are not attempting to answer all the questions that may arise in the day-to-day operation of the classroom. By providing a framework for discussion, we hope that teachers, administrators, and provincial policy makers will share their experiences and create a more comfortable teaching environment—one with clearer expectations about the roles that teachers should play in the school.

In the chapters that follow, it is important to keep in mind that our purpose is to identify and discuss some of the teacher's roles rather than to dissect them in a comprehensive legal fashion. This book is designed to be a practical reference for teachers—to assist their understanding of the complex legal issues they face. We have not attempted to survey each issue exhaustively, but have carefully researched the concepts underlying each one. Where a comprehensive work by another author addresses a specific topic, we make reference to that work in our endnotes for our readers' convenience and further exploration. It is our hope that this book will provide a useful framework for the exploration of important legal issues and demystify the law as it relates to teachers.

NOTES

1   *Canadian Charter of Rights and Freedoms*, part I of the *Constitution Act, 1982*, R.S.C. 1985, app. II, no. 44 (the Charter). All references to the *"Canadian Charter of Rights and Freedoms"* and to "the Charter" in this book are to the above-cited legislation.

2   *Constitution Act, 1867* (U.K.), 30 & 31 Vict., c. 3.

3   *Constitution Act, 1982*, Schedule B to the *Canada Act 1982* (U.K.), 1982, c. 11.

4   For examples of the Supreme Court of Canada's interpretation of these rights, see *R. v. Marshal*, [1999] 3 S.C.R. 456; refusing reconsideration, [1999] 3 S.C.R. 533. See also *Delgamuukw v. British Columbia*, [1997] 3 S.C.R. 1010.

5   "Nurturing the Learning Spirit of First Nation Students," The Report of the National Panel on First Nation Elementary and Secondary Education for Students on Reserve, http://firstnationeducation.ca/wp-content/themes/clf3/pdfs/Report_02_2012.pdf.

6   See *Teaching Profession Act*, R.S.Y. 2002, c. 215; *Northwest Territories Teachers' Association Act*, R.S.N.W.T. 1988, c. N-3; *Teaching Profession Act*, R.S.B.C. 1996, c. 449; *Teachers' Pension Plans Act*, R.S.A. 2000, c. T-1; *Teaching Profession Act*, R.S.A. 2000, c. T-2; *Teachers' Dental Plan Act*, S.S. 1984-85-86, c. T-6.1; *Teachers' Federation Act*, R.S.S. 1978, c. T-7; *Teachers' Life Insurance (Government Contributory) Act*, R.S.S. 1978, c. T-8; *Teachers Superannuation and Disability Benefits Act*, S.S. 1994, c. T-9.1; *Teachers' Pension Act*, C.C.S.M. c. T20; *Teachers' Society Act*, C.C.S.M. c. T30; *Teachers' Pension Act*, R.S.O. 1990, c. T.1; *Teaching Profession Act*, R.S.O. 1990, c. T.2; *Teachers Pension Act*, R.S.N.B. 1973, c. T-1; *Teachers' Collective Bargaining Act*, R.S.N.S. 1989, c. 460; *Teachers' Pension Act*, S.N.S. 1998, c. 26; *Teaching Profession Act*, R.S.N.S. 1989, c. 462; *Teachers' Superannuation Act*, R.S.P.E.I. 1988, c. T-1; *Teacher Training Act*, R.S.N. 1990 c. T-1; *Teachers' Association Act*, R.S.N.L. 1990, c. T-2; *Teachers' Collective Bargaining Act*, R.S.N.L. 1990, c. T-3; *Teachers' Pensions Act*, S.N.L. 1991, c. 17.

7   *Jowitt's Dictionary of English Law*, 2nd ed. (London: Sweet and Maxwell, 1977).

8   *Canadian Foundation for Children and Youth v. Canada*, 2004 SCC 4, [2004] 1 S.C.R. 76.

9   *Ogg-Moss v. The Queen*, [1984] 2 S.C.R. 171 (1984), 11 D.L.R. (4th) 549.

10   *Moore v. British Columbia (Education)*, 2012 SCC 61.

2
Teachers as Parents

This chapter deals with those circumstances in the school setting that most often require a teacher to adopt a parental role with her students. In the introduction, we discussed the limits of the *in loco parentis* doctrine and its inapplicability to the modern school. Although *in loco parentis* may no longer define a teacher's legal status, it has left its mark on the school environment and certainly on the hearts and minds of most teachers. This is most evident in the field of negligence. As MacKay and Dickinson indicate in *Beyond the Careful Parent*,[1] there have been revisions and updates, but the starting point for the standard of care in schools is still the careful parent.

Liability for Accidents at School

Negligence in the school setting is always of concern to teachers. Teachers frequently ask, "When can we be sued?" Before examining the principles of negligence in the school in any detail, it is important to set out the framework in which negligence law operates. Cases that involve accidents at school fall into the common-law category of "tort law." Torts may be briefly described as civil (as opposed to criminal) wrongs. The law of torts has been in a state of constant evolution since the early 1900s. The same tort principles that apply to society in general apply, with only slight modifications, to schools. There are two branches of tort law: negligence and intentional torts. We turn first to negligence, which is the more significant branch for our purposes.

Negligence Principles

Negligence cases involve a basic four-step analysis:

1. Was a duty of care owed to the injured person?
2. What standard of care does the situation require?
3. Was this standard of care breached?
4. What damages, if any, did the injured person suffer that were caused by the breach of the standard of care?

Regardless of the facts and the parties involved, a court usually asks these four questions when it determines liability for negligence.

The term "negligence" is a familiar one. It is clearly negligent to drive on the wrong side of the road or to give a loaded gun to a two-year-old child. Both these actions fall below the accepted standard of care that all people owe to those around them, and both actions are likely to cause harm. A central concept of the law of negligence is that a person should be able to predict when his actions might create risks that could cause harm to others. People should not create these risks. If they must create them, they should adopt preventive measures to diminish the chance of harm to others. This is the underlying philosophy of negligence. It is the responsibility of the courts to hold parties accountable in cases where they have created risks or not taken reasonable measures to prevent risk of harm to others.[2]

Duty of Care

When a court speaks of the "duty of care" to others, it is really stating that all people have a responsibility to take reasonable measures to avoid causing harm to others where the injury is "reasonably foreseeable." For example, everyone knows that when operating a car they must be careful to avoid causing accidents that involve other vehicles or pedestrians. Another vehicle on the road or a pedestrian crossing the street is "reasonably foreseeable"— that is, a reasonable person expects to encounter other traffic, and perhaps pedestrians, while driving a car. With this in mind, a reasonable person drives in a way that minimizes the risk of accidents.

Some other examples of the duty of care are not as obvious. Should a tavern owner, for example, be responsible for injuries caused to a patron who has been served too many drinks? The Supreme Court of Canada has decided that it is reasonable in some circumstances to impose a duty of care on a tavern owner who allows a patron to become severely intoxicated and then leave the bar. In a case where a drunken patron left a tavern and was later struck by a car along the highway as he stumbled home, the court determined that it was appropriate to impose a duty of care on the owner of the bar.[3]

It is important to note that the imposition of a duty of care does not require a person to take steps to eliminate the possibility of harm, only to take reasonable steps to minimize the risk of injury. Consider the example of an outdoor hockey rink bordered by a pedestrian sidewalk. It is foreseeable that a puck might hit a pedestrian. The owner of the rink owes a duty to pedestrians to minimize the risk of injury from flying pucks. This duty probably does not require the owner to prohibit hockey games or completely enclose the rink. A reasonable person would probably erect boards and a net; consequently, this represents the standard of care the owner must meet.

Teachers and school authorities have special common-law duties of care imposed on them because of the nature of their work. Society entrusts them with the care of large numbers of children, which is a weighty responsibility. The duty exists inside and outside the classroom. It may begin before school hours and remain in effect after school hours. In short, teachers must take care to ensure that students are not exposed to any unnecessary risk of harm. When students are under the charge of teachers, a duty of care arises that may lead to legal liability. A teacher's common-law duty of care can be expanded and refined by statutes, such as the relevant education statutes in force in Canada's provinces and territories. Additional duties of care may also be created or modified by government in regulations and policies.

Standard of Care

Although the law imposes a consistent duty of care on teachers, the standard of care it imposes on them varies according to circumstances. Any number of factors can be involved in determining the appropriate standard of care in a particular case. A court's primary task is to establish what a reasonable person would do in circumstances similar to those in which the teacher finds himself. It is difficult, therefore, to provide any precise guidelines by which a teacher may gauge his conduct. In essence, the question is one of good judgment. Teachers and school administrators can help each other by monitoring each other's conduct and holding frank discussions about appropriate conduct in various circumstances.

Many schools and school boards have policies or guidelines that provide teachers with some basis for determining whether their conduct is appropriate. These could include guidelines that set out the number of teachers required on playground supervision and define the playground areas for which each teacher is responsible. Policies may also restrict the number of children that physical education teachers allow to participate in potentially dangerous activities, such as archery, and require that they assign "spotters" to all gymnastic equipment. One of the complaints of principals is that teachers are sometimes late in getting to their classrooms. If a child suffers injury while misbehaving before a teacher arrives in the classroom, the teacher could be the subject of scrutiny by the courts.

It is in the area of standard of care that the ghost of *in loco parentis* haunts educators most prominently. The courts have determined that a teacher's standard of care is that of a "careful parent."[4] Teachers are expected to use the same degree of caution that careful or prudent parents would use in caring for their own children. Perhaps in a one-room schoolhouse with 10 or 15 students, a teacher may reasonably be held to the standard of a careful or prudent parent. In today's schools, where teachers are often responsible for 30 or more students (or for hundreds in the playground), it is simply unrealistic for the courts to continue to impose a standard of care that parents would exercise over their own child.

This criticism of the careful-parent rule has been raised frequently, both in and out of court, over the past several decades. It has been targeted as a paternalistic and outmoded standard that places an extremely heavy burden on teachers. Furthermore, the careful-parent rule offers very little guidance for teachers in the assessment of their conduct and their attempts to avoid negligence. It also allows the courts wide latitude to contort the standard, which makes it difficult for lawyers to predict the outcome of a negligence suit. In spite of these criticisms, the courts have repeatedly upheld the careful-parent rule, which is apparently a fact of life for teachers.

In spite of the uncertain standard set by the courts, the case law provides some examples of the factors that should be considered by teachers in determining appropriate conduct in a particular situation. A complete review of these cases is beyond the scope of this book; however, cases have cited some of the following factors:

1. the age of the student or students;
2. the nature of the activity (is it inherently dangerous, or did the student do something unforeseeable to make it dangerous?);
3. the amount of instruction received by the student;
4. the student's general awareness of the risks involved;
5. the approved general practice and, in particular, any school policies regarding this practice;
6. the foreseeable risk of danger; and
7. previous accidents in similar circumstances.

There is no scientific method for determining the standard of care in any given situation. One of the best methods of ensuring that a teacher is exercising an appropriate standard of care is for the teacher to discuss potentially dangerous situations with colleagues. Often school accidents are precipitated by similar "near misses." Some creative staff-room discussion about close calls may save everyone a lot of anguish down the road. Most important, these conversations may prevent a student from suffering a serious accident.

Breach of Standard of Care

Once a court has determined what it feels is the appropriate standard of care in the circumstances, it then determines whether a teacher has breached this standard. In other words, it determines whether the teacher's actions conform to its view of what a careful parent would have done in the circumstances. The law does not expect anyone to be perfect; it simply expects people to act reasonably. Teachers should act reasonably to minimize the occurrence of accidents. They cannot insure against accidents, but must do their best to prevent them.

The court must also consider whether the student has contributed to her own misfortune. This will rarely apply to very young children or children with special needs, who should be subjected to more restrictive supervision. However, a teenage student may be found to be "contributorily negligent," thereby reducing the teacher's liability. Most provinces have statutes that deal with contributory negligence and allow the courts to apportion the amount of liability that should be attached to each party.[5] For example, students who ignore appropriate instruction in physical education classes may be found as much as 70 percent negligent for voluntarily engaging in a dangerous activity—using a gymnastics springboard to "dunk" a basketball is a time-honoured favourite among high school students. This could be considered contributory negligence, although the school would be partially liable for inadequate supervision.

The issue of contributory negligence illustrates a dynamic tension that pervades all aspects of a teacher's duties, and particularly a teacher's responsibility for negligence. On the one hand, a teacher must supervise and protect the students within her charge; this demands a certain degree of paternalism. On the other hand, one of the teacher's most important educational goals is to produce independent and self-reliant children who are capable of looking after themselves. In this respect, the teacher faces the same dilemma as the parent: how do you protect the child from the many risks of the outside world without smothering her inherent spirit of adventure and need for independence? An English judge who refused to find a teacher negligent for leaving handicraft knives easily accessible addressed this issue. (The presence of the knives later resulted in injuries from student horseplay.) The judge stated, "It is better that a boy should break his neck than allow other people to break his spirit."[6] This quotation is admittedly a drastic statement, but the principle is well taken. It provides a stark illustration of the teacher's need to strike a balance between protecting students adequately and giving them enough freedom to develop their independence.

Damages Caused by the Breach

The fourth step in the analysis of a negligence case considers whether the injured person suffered ascertainable damages, as recognized by law, that were caused by the breach of the standard of care. In most cases, the injured person receives money as compensation for damages suffered as a result of the injury. The law also makes provisions for other remedies, such as injunctions—that is, court orders that direct the parties to maintain or discontinue a certain course of action. We discuss the importance and availability of injunctions as Charter remedies in Chapter 3, Teachers as Educational State Agents, under the heading "Remedies." Injunctions rarely arise in school negligence cases. A school board may choose to alter its policies or conduct as a result of losing a case in negligence (for example, by implementing more detailed safety procedures); however, a court rarely orders a board to do so.

The principle that damages must be sustained before an action can be successful reflects the commonsensical notion "no harm, no foul." The harm, however, does not necessarily mean actual physical harm; it can take the form of nervous shock or emotional distress, provided that there is substantial evidence of these conditions. Aside from the judicial requirement of damages, there is a practical economic component to this principle. Litigation is an expensive process, and there is no point in pursuing a court action in cases where the recovery would be so minimal that the legal fees would not be covered. Even if litigation succeeds and a court orders the losing party to pay the winning party's costs, the amount the winning party receives for costs rarely compensates him for more than one-third of the actual costs incurred. Thus, the damages claim must be large enough to make the litigation worthwhile.

The practical necessity for substantial damages in a school negligence case should reduce a teacher's fear of being sued when a child suffers minimal injuries. For instance, if a teacher is not paying proper attention in the playground and a child engages in a dangerous activity but simply skins her knee, there is no need to be overly concerned about a lawsuit. There may be some in-school repercussions through discipline procedures, but court action is highly unlikely.

A child may, however, sustain severe injuries in the most innocuous situations. At a seminar we attended, one teacher described a situation where a five-year-old child severely cut his arm while sliding headfirst down a large slide in the playground. The area at the foot of the slide consisted of gravel and rocks. Although the boy's cut was not severe enough to result in any legal action, the possibility of a serious head or neck injury in the same situation is staggering. This is merely one example of the kinds of situations where teachers must be vigilant. An ounce of prevention is worth a pound of cure.

Vicarious Liability

Cases that involve the negligence of teachers, principals, or other school employees usually result in a court's finding that the relevant school board is liable under the doctrine of "vicarious liability." If a teacher or other employee of a school board is negligent, she is personally liable for the damages sustained by the injured person. However, the school board that employs her, which is usually in a better financial position to compensate the victim, is often the principal object of the lawsuit—that is, the primary defendant. Under the doctrine of vicarious liability, courts often find school boards, as employers, legally responsible for the negligence of their employees.

The doctrine of vicarious liability originates in the law of master and servant. Initially, an employer was liable only for acts that resulted from orders. The doctrine of vicarious liability has now expanded to apply to all torts committed by an employee while acting in the course of employment and extends well beyond actions that an employer expressly mandates. The rationale behind expanding the doctrine of vicarious liability is to provide a reasonable allocation of loss. It is the school board, not the teacher, that can afford to compensate victims of negligence and the school board is consequently in a better position to carry insurance for these accidents. School boards also have an economic incentive to prevent accidents and to discipline their employees for unreasonable conduct.

For the doctrine of vicarious liability to apply, employees must be acting in the course of their employment. The concept "course of employment" is elusive. In recent times, courts have held that most actions of employees have occurred in the course of their employment. Courts have even held that actions expressly forbidden by an employer have fallen within the doctrine.

In fact, the Supreme Court of Canada has relied on the doctrine of vicarious liability to find that an employer may be liable for the actions of an employee that constitute sexual harassment.[7] Given that sexual harassment would not usually be considered as part of the "course and scope" of someone's job, these cases illustrate the courts' willingness to apply a broad scope to the concept of vicarious liability. This is particularly true with respect to human rights.

If an employee is on a "frolic of his own" and is, in effect, acting as a stranger in relation to his employer, no liability attaches to the employer. Actions that are a means of carrying out the job—albeit negligently or even in breach of express rules—still occur in the course of employment. For example, if a truck driver hit a pedestrian at a crosswalk, the trucking company cannot escape liability by claiming that the driver is not employed to hit pedestrians. "Driving" is the central means of carrying out the job. The following may provide a useful formulation of the test for actions that occur in the course of an employee's employment:

> The test is whether a wrongful act is a mode of performing the general duties of the servant's employment: whether the servant was about his master's business at the time.[8]

Beauparlent v. Board of Trustee of Separate School Section No. 1 of Appleby[9] is a case from the 1950s in which the court held that the actions of teachers were outside the scope of their employment. In this case, teachers decided to transport nearly 70 students to a concert in a nearby town. The concert was held in honour of a priest's birthday. The court concluded that the outing was not connected to the students' course of studies. The teachers transported the students to the concert in a stake body truck provided by a citizen in the community; it had not been inspected for safety. On the way to the concert, chains on the back of the truck gave way, and several children sustained serious injuries when they were thrown onto the highway. No board permission had been obtained for the trip, and the court found the school board not liable for the accident because the teachers were acting outside the scope of their authority. Courts today may adopt an approach that is more sympathetic to injured students, although recent judgments have been inconsistent as to the application of vicarious liability.

Vicarious Liability for Sexual Assault

In a more recent case, *H. (S.G.) v. Gorsline*,[10] a teacher sexually abused a student in 1978–1979 when the student was in grades 7 and 8. The student reported the abuse in 1993, and the teacher was convicted on criminal charges. The student then filed an action for damages against the teacher and the school board. The court found the school board was not vicariously liable because the teachers' duties mandated by the school board did not significantly contribute to the risk of sexual abuse. Simply providing the opportunity for abuse to occur was not enough to incur liability.

In another case,[11] the Newfoundland and Labrador Trial Division found a school board vicariously liable for a teacher's sexual assault on a student (in the form of fondling). In this case, the assault happened on school property during a class the student was taking from the teacher. The court noted the following:

> The basis for vicarious liability is that in certain circumstances, the board, like any agency which introduces into the community an enterprise which may present a risk of harm, may be liable for that risk.[12]

In finding the school board liable, the court noted that the relationship between the school board and the actions of the teacher were sufficiently connected to result in vicarious liability, saying:

> It was the employer's mandate as a school board which placed in the hands of its teachers significant power and authority over the students: quite properly to carry out their teaching roles, but also enhancing the risk of something going wrong if that power was abused. It was the school board which gave [the teacher], as a trusted professional employee, the authority to set up the circumstances wherein this offence was committed.[13]

In two decisions released on the same day in 1999, the Supreme Court of Canada came to two different conclusions regarding vicarious liability for the sexual abuse of children. In *Bazley v. Curry*,[14] an employee sexually abused a child in a residential school for children with emotional problems. The court found that the school was vicariously liable for the actions of its employee. The court found that the assaults against the child took place in circumstances that resulted from the mandate created by the school, which required employees to bathe, dress, and tuck children into bed at night.

In *Jacobi v. Griffiths*,[15] a boys' and girls' club employee sexually assaulted a brother and sister. The assaults did not take place at the club, but at the employee's home and in a van on the way to a sporting event. Though the trial court found the club vicariously liable, the BC Court of Appeal overturned the ruling, holding that the club had no authority over the victims at the times of the abuse, and that the employee had not abused the authority created by his position with the club. The Supreme Court of Canada dismissed the victims' appeal, ruling that vicarious liability could not be imposed in the circumstances of the case, because the club did not know of the employee's actions and had not authorized such actions as taking the children to his home. The court noted that the mandate of the club was to develop relationships between children, not to develop relationships between children and persons in authority. The goal of the club was not to develop parent-type relationships.

The obvious economic reality of these cases is that courts are tempted by the deep pockets of the school board's insurance company. Serious permanent injuries, particularly in the case of children, can result in large damage awards. Where the cost of a child's future care may be significant, the courts may be inclined to hold the board liable to provide the child with access to the board's insurance policy. It is important that the injured child not be denied proper compensation.

A spontaneous class outing to a local restaurant in a teacher's car can expose the teacher to personal liability. It is advisable to seek approval for such trips from either the principal or (preferably) the school board itself. Teachers who transport students in their own vehicles, for any reason, should check with their insurance company to ensure that they have adequate personal coverage. The financial risk of transporting students in this manner may not be covered in a standard insurance policy.

Courts are likely to find activities directly related to education programs and performed by school board employees to be within the course of their employment. A school board was held to be vicariously liable in a case where a 14-year-old student was instructed to poke the fire in a schoolroom so that a teacher could have a hot lunch.[16] The student's pinafore caught fire and she was injured. Fortunately, we do not have open fires or pinafores in today's classrooms. The point, however, is that the courts have historically taken a broad approach to defining the scope of an education program and teacher's employment. School boards are increasingly found liable for the acts of their employees in ever-broadening circumstances.[17]

In a recent incidence of problematic behaviour by teachers outside the classroom, two teachers from the elite Ottawa private school Ashbury College are in front of a disciplinary board, accused of misconduct following the sexual assault of one of their students by another classmate on a field trip to Boston. Although the case is being pursued using the disciplinary measures within the education system, rather than by civil litigation, this type of action could form the basis for a negligence suit against the teachers and their school board. The teachers are before the disciplinary hearing because of their actions or inactions following the report by their student that he had been sexually assaulted. One teacher is accused of discouraging the child from going to the police and both teachers are accused of failing to immediately notify the student's parents. Although the teachers are denying the allegations, and the disciplinary hearing is scheduled to sit two more days in February 2013, in a negligence action this could be found to breach the standard of care of a careful and prudent parent.[18]

Insurance

As mentioned earlier, one of the primary purposes for expanding the doctrine of vicarious liability is to allocate losses in a reasonable manner. It is obvious that school boards are in a much better economic position than teachers to obtain adequate insurance to cover the losses suffered across their school network. It is more economically efficient for boards to carry a single policy than for individual teachers or administrators to take out independent insurance policies. Teachers are therefore reasonably protected from the financial repercussions of their conduct in the schools. Of course, if a teacher's negligence shows a complete disregard for her responsibilities or particularly bad judgment, she may be a candidate for discipline and possible dismissal by her board.

From the above discussion of insurance and vicarious liability, it is obvious that teachers are well protected in the area of negligence. However, from a practical point of view, teachers should always remember that litigation is an uncomfortable process in which they are the object of the court's scrutiny. A teacher, even if not financially responsible for the case, will still be sued as a defendant and thus subject to fact-finding processes before and during trial. Where an accident has resulted in severe injuries to a child, it is terribly disturbing to be forced to relive the accident under the scrutiny of lawyers and judges. To protect students from harm and themselves from litigation, all teachers should be on the lookout for potentially dangerous situations.

Application of Negligence Principles in the School

We now turn to a review of some of the specific opportunities for accidents to occur in a school. As we indicated, negligence cases are fact-specific. Many more opportunities exist than can be covered in the space available in this book.

The Classroom

Teachers are rarely sued for their actions or inactions while in the classroom, although that is where they spend most of their time. Most accidents occur in school hallways, in playgrounds, or on field trips. The major exceptions to this generalization relate to physical education and industrial arts; teachers of these subjects can attract lawsuits while performing the main task for which they are employed. Science teachers may also attract lawsuits as a result of supervising labs where potentially dangerous equipment or activities are stored or conducted.

A teacher has a duty to supervise his students while in the classroom but, as mentioned earlier, it is when the teacher is absent from the classroom that accidents are most likely to occur. There is surprisingly little case law in Canada involving classroom accidents; however, there are several US cases that provide guidance. In one case, a teacher left her special education class unattended for about five minutes and instructed a neighbouring teacher to supervise the class.[19] One of her students injured another in a scuffle. The neighbouring teacher heard only the usual noise of a play period in the adjoining room. The Louisiana court took note of the fact that the teacher was absent for only a few minutes and found no liability on the part of the teacher.

In another US case, one grade 4 student accidentally injured another during calisthenics after the teacher stepped out of the room.[20] The children were performing the exercises by following a recording. The court stated that the injury was not a reasonably foreseeable result of the teacher's absence and was not caused by the absence, but rather by the actions of another student. The court concluded that the accident would have occurred whether or not the teacher was present. Thus, even if the teacher were negligent, there was no causal connection between the teacher's acts and the student's injury. The breach of care must be the "proximate cause" of the damages in order for liability to ensue. There must be some direct link between the negligent acts of the teacher and the damages caused to the student.

These cases should not be read as justifying absence from the classroom. The reasons for a teacher's absence, its duration, the type of accident, and the nature of the class are all factors that could lead to a finding of negligence in a Canadian court. A teacher who is five minutes late getting to class and fails to provide for supervision, for example, could be creating a liability situation. Teachers should be cautious about noon-hour supervision in this regard. Students tend to become unruly during lunch, when school rules are much less clearly defined or enforced. This is particularly important for teachers in Manitoba, where courts have held noon-hour supervision to be a necessarily incidental part of the terms of employment under their collective agreement.[21]

Playgrounds and Other Outside Areas

When a child is injured outside a school, a question arises as to whether an adequate system of supervision was in place and, if it was, whether the teachers responsible for supervision adequately performed their duties. If the inadequacy of the system was the cause of the accident, the principal or other person responsible for supervision of school premises will be liable. In one Ontario case, a school board was sued when a thrown snowball cut the back of a student's head.[22] The incident occurred after school hours, sometime between 3:30 p.m. (dismissal time) and 3:45 p.m. No teachers were supervising the playground at the time. It was the policy of the school for students to leave school buildings and school grounds immediately upon dismissal. Students riding buses were kept in the main lobby of the school until they were ready to board. The lawsuit was brought against the school board for not having an adequate system of supervision after school hours, not against a particular teacher. The court dismissed the case, holding that the school board's policy of not having teacher supervision was reasonable.

There have been circumstances in which courts have found the system of supervision set up by school boards to be inadequate and have imposed liability on the boards. In *Tommy George v. Board of School Trustees, School District 70 (Port Alberni)*,[23] a five-year-old boy was injured when a school bus being parked at the school grounds to load passengers struck him. In this case, the kindergarten was housed in a portable unit, separate from the main school building. It was not hooked up with the main PA or bell system. In the rest of the school, there was a bell and a PA announcement that let the children know when they could leave the classroom to board the school buses. The principal would wait until the school buses were all in place before making the announcement. The teacher in this case was not held to be negligent because she was responsible for 15 or 16 young children, and could not be expected to get them all out of the classroom and also keep them under supervision until they were in the parking lot. In the court's view, the teacher was following her usual routine and had no reason to suspect there was any unusual danger. The bus driver was held 40 percent contributorily negligent for failing to properly check his mirrors, and the school board was held 60 percent contributorily negligent for having an inadequate system of communication in the school.

There is a tragic 2004 New Brunswick case in which a young student was killed in front of his mother when he attempted to board the school bus at his home. A public inquest held in the spring of 2005 resulted in several recommendations to improve school safety, but did not find fault with the driver's actions.

Of course, a teacher will be held liable if his failure to provide proper supervision results in an injury to a student. The Supreme Court of Canada, in *Board of Education for the City of Toronto v. Higgs*,[24] held there was no liability in a case where a bully injured another student. The court was not satisfied that increased supervision could have prevented the injury. The court indicated that the known mischievous tendencies of the bully increased the range of foreseeable risks. There was no discussion about whether teachers have the duty to inform themselves about the various tendencies of the children in the playground. Certainly having more information available to teachers would expand the range of foreseeable risks, and thus expand the likelihood of liability.

In *Little (Litigation Guardian of) v. Chignecto Central Regional School Board*,[24] the Nova Scotia Supreme Court found that neither the school board nor an educational assistant were liable for the broken leg a student sustained while playing football on school property at lunchtime. In dismissing the lawsuit, the court found that the plaintiff—that is, the party bringing the lawsuit—failed to prove that the defendant school board had not met the high standard for student safety set by the *Education Act*, section 38(2)(e) of which specifies that the principal of a public school must

> ensure that reasonable steps are taken to create and maintain a safe, orderly, positive and effective learning environment.

Liability was denied in spite of the fact that the student, a boy with attention deficit disorder, received the injury when the educational assistant who was serving as supervisor was not watching the ongoing football game.

The court found that the school discipline policy met the standards of a reasonably careful and prudent parent in its provision of guidance to students, staff, and parents. As well, a school rules brochure, which delineated areas of supervision of the playground, was given to all playground supervisors as well as to students. Evidence from the plaintiff and other students indicated that they were aware that contact sports were against the rules. With respect to the conduct of the supervisor, the court found that she was circling her area of responsibility and, while unable to see the game for a brief period of 30–60 seconds, was herself visible to the students playing the game. In refusing to find liability, the court stated:

What was required of the school board was a policy related to safety that was clear, known and enforced by staff and communicated to the students. The enforcement of the policy required a physical presence of a supervisor within the visibility of the students and with the capacity of the supervisor to adequately survey what was transpiring. All of these components existed here and given my factual findings, the mere thirty second to sixty second departure by Ms. Manicom, while still visibly present to the students, did not constitute negligence.[25]

This statement is helpful because it emphasizes the guidance a policy may offer and how it can have an important impact on a finding of liability. The clarification of acceptable standards in the form of statutes, regulations, or policies is important for risk management and levels of comfort for teachers.

A court will not find a teacher liable for inadequate supervision of school grounds unless it can be shown that the teacher should have foreseen the incident in sufficient time to prevent injury. Therefore, when, out of several hundred students, a small group of boys was tossing acorns, the four supervising teachers were not liable for failing to see and stop the conduct before one boy was hit in the eye.[27] The principal made it a practice after this case to announce on the first day of school his rule against throwing any objects on school grounds. Such a practice makes it easier to verify the exact date of the announcement if the need arises later in court. Perhaps the safest course is to distribute a written statement of school rules to teachers, other staff, parents, and students. There are some other compelling reasons for distributing school rules, which we discuss in Chapter 3.

Before School Begins

Where students habitually arrive at school early, those charged with the duty to provide supervision of school grounds may have to ensure that this supervision is in place for early arrivals. The responsible person is usually a principal or other administrator, rather than a teacher. When a student was injured before school by a paperclip shot from an elastic band, the court found the principal negligent for failing to provide an adequate system of supervision and for failing to set rules for the students.[28] The court noted that because the students were expected to arrive early, the principal's responsibility arose before classes began. Parents should not, however, be unilaterally entitled to add to the duties of the school by dropping their children off early.[29]

Even though school board regulations may not expressly require pre-school supervision, such a duty may arise because students are beyond parental protection and control once they arrive at school. In addition, when a school permits students to arrive early, it creates a teacher–student relationship, and the associated responsibilities are assumed by the teacher. These conclusions were reached by an Australian court in *Geyer v. Downs*,[30] where an eight-year-old student was injured when playing unsupervised on school grounds before school began. Although a teacher will rarely be responsible for providing a system of supervision, she may be liable for negligent supervision of her assigned area. The major responsibility for pre-school supervision appears to rest with the principal of the school or the school board.

It is advisable for school boards to establish clear hours of supervision both before and after school and communicate these hours to parents. If a child consistently appears at school early, the principal should raise the issue with the parent. Although teachers should not be expected to act as pre-school babysitters, school administrators should be clear about when supervision will and will not be offered, and there must be some flexibility. Many schools have implemented "safe arrival" programs, usually sponsored by parent organizations at the school, and these may be used to track arrivals and communicate with parents.

After School Ends

Similar problems of responsibility for supervision arise at the end of the day. What responsibility, if any, does a school official have once a child leaves the school? In most cases, it is reasonable to assume that children will be able to make their way home safely from school, although this may not be the case when the children are quite young. The foreseeability of harm is increased if a teacher ignores a parent's specific instructions about the child's departure.

In recent years, the transfer of custody from the school to the parent has become more complex. Where buses are involved, a safe transfer of children to the bus is the school board's responsibility. In a city school where children walk home, the teacher may be required to exercise greater responsibility. A working parent may require that a child go to an after-school program on certain days and to the family's home on other days. Because these instructions may be difficult for a young child to follow, a teacher may be expected to provide guidance. In any event, the ultimate responsibility rests with parents to ensure that a reasonable system is in place. A teacher should not be expected to ensure that a parent is home before sending a child home for lunch, but if the child specifically expresses doubt, a teacher may be obliged to inquire further.

Similarly, a teacher should not be expected to babysit students for long periods after school; however, emergencies, such as snowstorms, can extend the time during which school authorities are responsible for students. In the British case *Barnes v. Hampshire County Council*,[31] five-year-old children who were always met by parents at an appointed time were released early. A child whose parent had not yet arrived wandered onto a nearby highway and was struck by a car. The court held that the early release created a risk that some children might not be met by a parent and would try to make their own way home. Because it was foreseeable that a child might be injured, the school authorities were held to be negligent. The fact that the release occurred only five minutes ahead of schedule did not matter because exact timing was crucial to the particular system on which the parents and school authorities had agreed.

In *Parks v. School District #39 (Vancouver)*,[32] an elementary school student was injured when she collided with a student from a nearby high school who skateboarded through the elementary school grounds on his way home from school. The plaintiff suffered a gash on her shin that required medical attention. She was successful in obtaining compensation for her injuries from the high school student, but not from the elementary school. The court stated:

> In order to succeed in this action against the School Board, the [plaintiff] has to prove on a balance of probabilities that Trafalgar School, as a prudent parent, either: a) failed to put in place a reasonable and adequate system of supervision, or b) failed in carrying out that system of supervision in a reasonable manner.[33]

The court found that the system for supervision at the elementary school was adequate, and that supervision was conducted in a reasonable manner; therefore, no fault lay with the school for the accident. The court may have been influenced by the fact that the case was not brought against the school until the plaintiff was 21 years old, at which point there was little evidence of injury remaining.

Bullying

In an age where bullying has attracted a lot of public attention, it is easy to predict that there will be bullies in schools. Accordingly, schools may be liable if measures are not taken to reduce the risk to victims. If bullying is a foreseeable risk, then failing to reduce the risk may be negligence.

Legal actions against teachers for student-on-student bullying have been rare in Canada in the past, but an increased focus on bullying and its negative effects on children and youth may result in an increase in these types of legal actions.

In *Hentze (Guardian ad litem of) v. Campbell River School District No. 72*,[34] the BC Court of Appeal upheld the lower court's ruling that a teacher's lunchtime supervision of a playground was negligent. The case was brought on behalf of a student who was injured while roughhousing with older, bigger students. The teacher who was supervising the playground had turned her back on the playground to speak with a group of students. During this time, the plaintiff was injured. The court made the following statement regarding the duty of teachers:

> The law does not, of course, require that school authorities keep students under constant supervision at all times. The standard is that of the reasonably careful and prudent parent. How the standard is to be applied in any given case will depend upon many factors, including the nature and size of the area to be supervised, the number and ages of the students involved, and the nature of the activity or activities that are in progress.[35]

Although this case was not about bullying per se, it is clear that the court has established that the behaviour of school personnel is open to scrutiny by the courts. Australian courts have rendered several decisions involving liability for bullying in schools. In one New South Wales case, the court found that the school knew of the ongoing bullying and did not take the necessary steps to eliminate the behaviour.[36] This case was not about foreseeability of harm, because the school had previous awareness of the bullying behaviour. The victim in this case had been shoved up against walls, choked unconscious, and had a tooth knocked out, all by the same older student. The victim's mother had complained repeatedly to the school, but the school's only response involved giving the older boy detentions and sending notes home to his parents.

One group of Canadian scholars has suggested that a reduction of bullying in schools will only be achieved once lawsuits against schools increase.[37] McKinlay et al. suggest that more frequent use of legal remedies will increase school boards' interest in addressing this very serious issue.[38] The important issue of bullying is further addressed in later chapters of this text.

School Violence and Risk Assessment

Violence in schools, as in society in general, is an unfortunate reality. Everyone recalls the horrors of Columbine High School in 1999, when two students shot and killed 12 students and a teacher and injured 24 others before committing suicide. A week after Columbine, a 14-year-old student at a high school in Taber, Alberta, opened fire, killing one student and injuring another. At Virginia Tech in 2007, one student shot and killed 32 students and injured 17 others before turning the gun on himself. Most recently, in December 2012, the world was shocked when a gunman shot and killed 20 children and 6 teachers at Sandy Hook Elementary in Newtown, Connecticut.

Although such tragedies may not always be preventable, school boards are well advised to add training to address both prevention of and response to such situations to their professional development and disaster planning. In the wake of the Virginia Tech massacre in particular, that university came under significant scrutiny for what was ultimately seen as an institutional failure to address the shooter's long history of mental illness. Investigation by a state-appointed review panel after the shootings revealed that a number of members of the university community had significant concerns about the student, but no one person or group had access to all of the information about the student.[39] Another important issue that arose as a result of the review was the question of how quickly and effectively campus administrators tried to warn the university community after first receiving notice of a shooter on campus.[40] The duty to warn and associated liability is a complex legal issue with no clear answer, but school officials and teachers would be as remiss in not planning for this scenario as they would for any other reasonably foreseeable crisis.[41]

Vocational (Shop) Classes and Science Labs

One need only consider the tragic death of a student at an Ottawa high school in 2011 to acknowledge the importance of safety in the vocational classroom setting. In that terrible incident, an 18-year-old student was killed in an explosion in an auto-shop class.[42] Four other people were also injured in the blast, which occurred when the student attempted to cut into an oil drum.[43] The school board was charged under provincial occupational health and safety legislation for a number of alleged violations, including failure to take reasonable precautions to protect the workplace, failure to provide instruction or supervision, and failure to properly acquaint a supervisor with hazards associated with the handling of equipment at the shop. At this time the investigation is still ongoing. In fall 2012, the provincial coroner announced that an inquest into the student's death would be held.[44]

When dealing with the possibility of accidents in classes involving cooking, woodworking, auto repair, or chemical experiments, common sense dictates a greater than average degree of supervision. For example, where a classroom has gas stoves with open flames, school authorities could be found negligent for failing to supply a guard to prevent students from being burned, because this type of accident can be reasonably anticipated. By extension, a school would be expected to provide proper protection and give adequate warnings in the use of all forms of equipment in home economics classes, shop classes, and chemistry labs.

A general rule for teachers of all such classes is to give proper instructions to students about all equipment and to maintain proper supervision throughout the class. In one case, a student was "flicking" a chisel near a sanding wheel, and as a result of contact between the two, the chisel was driven into his leg. The court found that the sanding wheel was not inherently dangerous, sufficient supervision was maintained, and therefore the student was solely responsible for his own injury.[45]

In one BC case, a 16-year-old student in grade 11 was injured while moving sheets of plywood during his woodworking class.[46] The sheets of plywood were stored in an unused boys' washroom across the hall from the classroom. The student required a three-quarter inch mahogany plywood sheet to finish a project he was working on. The shop teacher escorted the student across the hall and explained how the student could safely remove the sheet of plywood from the storage area. He told the student to get help from another student when moving the plywood. The student ignored these instructions, and his left knee was crushed when the sheets of plywood fell on top of him.

The court accepted the teacher's testimony with regard to the instructions given to the student. The school board's lawyers led evidence to establish the teacher's general practice and habits in instructing students on safety precautions. The court found the teacher to be conscientious and held that the instructions given in this particular instance were sufficient to meet the standard of care required of him.

In a more recent case, a 15-year-old student in grade 10 had two of his fingers partially amputated as a result of an accident in a woodworking class.[47] The student, who had a cast on his wrist at the time of the accident, had been asked by the shop teacher to supervise another student who had never used an electronic jointer. The student attempted to push a piece of wood through the jointer, and the machine jammed. The court noted that the school and its woodworking teachers were generally safety conscious;

however, it found the school vicariously liable for the accident, ruling that the teacher knew or ought to have known that the machine was malfunctioning and dangerous. The court further noted that the teacher should not have asked the student to supervise a classmate. The court found the student himself partially responsible because he had disregarded the safety instructions he had been taught previously about what to do if the machine jammed and ignored the teacher's direction not to use the machine while his arm was in a cast.

The lesson to be learned from these cases is that all vocational teachers should establish routine safety procedures and perhaps supply students with written safety manuals containing adequate instructions. In this way, if there is any question about whether an injured student received particular instructions, the court will have evidence of the good safety habits of the teacher involved.

The age and ability of the students in any class, particularly a vocational class, can add to the standard of care that a court will expect a teacher to meet. If the students suffer from physical or mental disabilities, the range of foreseeable risks is likely to increase. This is true both for a class of students with disabilities or for a single student with special needs integrated into a typical classroom. In *Dziwenka v. The Queen*,[48] the Supreme Court of Canada held a woodworking teacher to a particularly high standard of care when a deaf student was injured by a power saw. The student's lack of hearing put him at greater risk around power tools, and the teacher was required to exercise a higher standard of care with respect to this child.

When dealing with a science experiment that could pose a danger to students, a teacher should explain appropriate safety precautions and provide safety equipment. In *James v. River East School Division No. 9*,[49] a student was injured when chemicals splattered in her face. She was not wearing safety glasses, and the procedure for the chemistry experiment required her to look into the vessel to determine the progress of the chemical reaction. The teacher was held liable for failing to instruct the students adequately with respect to potential hazards and, in particular, with respect to the possibility of splattering. The court also held that the procedure itself was negligent because it required the student to look into the vessel. The procedure had been followed in the past without incident; however, this did not afford an excuse. Although past practice may be used as a defence against a claim of negligence, if the practice itself is found to reflect negligence, it provides no defence. A practice does not cease to be negligent simply because it is frequently repeated.

Although most teachers would assume that woodworking shops, science labs, and physical education are inherently the most dangerous classrooms, the possibility of accidents in other classrooms must always be taken into account. In one Ontario case, a grade 8 student suffered an eye injury as a result of an accident with a sewing machine in a family studies class.[50] The students, including the boy who suffered the injury, were given an assignment to sew a piece of broadcloth. None of the students had any previous sewing experience. The teacher instructed the students to stop the machines if they had a problem and to come to her for assistance. The injured boy experienced "bunching" or "sewing on the spot." The teacher had not instructed the class specifically about bunching and had not instructed the class to stop sewing when bunching occurred. As a result of the bunching, the needle in the sewing machine shattered and caused permanent injury to the student's right cornea.

The court held that it was reasonably foreseeable that a needle could break from sewing on the spot and that it could shatter and strike a user in the eye, even though this was an unusual occurrence. The court confirmed the standard of care to be exercised by the teacher in providing supervision was that of a careful or prudent parent. In these circumstances, the court held the teacher liable and the school board vicariously liable for not providing adequate instruction. The teacher was dealing with first-year sewers. A reasonably intelligent student who experienced bunching for the first time would not automatically recognize the problem and call for the teacher's assistance. The court held that the teacher should have been more precise in her safety instructions. The court also concluded that the student did not act completely reasonably in the circumstances and found the student to be 10 percent responsible for the accident.

Sports

Injuries commonly occur during school sports activities, although most do not give rise to school liability. Accidents may occur even when no one has been negligent, and a school cannot be an insurer of the safety of all of the students under its care all of the time. There is an inherent risk of injury in most athletic activities, and only if a student is exposed to unreasonable risk will a teacher or school be considered negligent.[51] Because of the strenuous nature of activities carried on in a gymnasium, the injuries that result from accidents are often serious, and the chance of substantial compensation in court is increased.[52] This may explain the relatively large number of cases involving physical education that are brought before the courts.

Traditionally, the standard that courts have applied in determining whether a physical education teacher has been negligent is that of the careful parent. This, for example, was the standard that the court used in *McKay v. Board of Govan School Unit No. 29*[53] in finding a school liable for injuries sustained by a student who was performing on parallel bars. The student's lack of experience in the manoeuvres was a critical factor in determining that he had not received an appropriate level of care and attention. The Supreme Court of Canada, in *Myers v. Peel County Board of Education*,[54] re-affirmed the traditional "careful parent" standard as the enunciation of the rule to be applied.

In light of the specialized training of the instructors and the complexity of athletic activity, the careful parent standard may no longer be appropriate for physical education instructors. In *Thornton v. School Dist. No. 57 (Prince George) et al.*,[55] a decision of the Supreme Court of Canada, a 15-year-old student was rendered quadriplegic as a result of doing a somersault from a springboard. The physical education teacher was found negligent for not realizing that the addition of a box for jumping created a dangerous situation. He had also failed to stop the exercise earlier in the class to determine the cause of a similar accident in which a student broke his wrist. The teacher had been working on school reports rather than supervising the athletic activities going on in the gymnasium. In spite of the high damage award against the school board, the teacher continued to teach in the same school system.

In *Thornton*, both the trial judge[56] and the BC Court of Appeal[57] held that a teacher has the duty to meet the standard of care of a reasonably skilled physical education instructor, rather than that of a careful parent. The Supreme Court of Canada was not required to address that issue on appeal because it concluded that the teacher was negligent by either standard.

The BC Court of Appeal set out a four-point test that has been cited in numerous subsequent cases.[58] There is no negligence on the part of a physical education instructor who permits a student to engage in an exercise if

1. the exercise is suitable to his age and condition (mental and physical);
2. he is progressively trained and coached to do it properly and avoid danger;
3. the equipment is adequate and suitably arranged; and
4. the performance, having regard to its inherently dangerous nature, is properly supervised.[59]

In *Myers v. Peel County Board of Education*,[60] a 15-year-old boy was severely injured while attempting a dismount from suspended rings. At trial,[61] the judge applied the standard of the reasonably competent physical education teacher that the BC Court of Appeal used in *Thornton*, but the Ontario Court of Appeal[62] and the Supreme Court of Canada reaffirmed the careful parent standard as the appropriate test.

In applying the careful parent standard, the Supreme Court of Canada said that the test for determining the standard in a particular case would vary depending on the number of students, the nature of the activity, the students' ages, the degree of skill and training, the nature and condition of the equipment used, the competency and capacity of the students, and "a host of other matters."[63] By taking all of these factors into account in determining the careful parent standard, the court has suggested that a physical education teacher may be held to a higher standard than a classroom teacher because of her more detailed knowledge of the competency and capacity of the students, the nature of the activity, and the equipment used.

Emergencies

Although physical education teachers are more frequently confronted with emergency situations than regular classroom teachers, all teachers must be prepared to respond to emergencies. *Moddejonge v. Huron County Board of Education,*[64] a case in which two young girls drowned on a field trip, provides a dramatic illustration of this. The teacher-coordinator of the school's outdoor education program was unable to swim. During one outing, he took five girls (at their request) to a nearby swimming hole for a brief swim. The teacher pointed out that there was a dangerous drop-off in the lake, and he warned them to stay away from it. However, a breeze carried two of the girls out to the drop-off, where they encountered trouble. One of the girls was a non-swimmer. A third student came to their rescue, saving one of the girls, but failing to save the other and herself drowning during the rescue attempt. The teacher-coordinator, who could not swim, had to return to camp to seek assistance from another supervising teacher. It was not difficult for the court to conclude that the teacher-coordinator's conduct fell below that of a careful parent. What is surprising is that the teacher-coordinator was found to be acting in the course of his employment, and the school board was found to be vicariously liable.

A teacher who provides emergency aid must do so competently. This underscores the need for teachers who are in charge of field trips or high-risk in-school activities to be trained to cope with emergencies. A basic understanding of first aid and life-saving techniques, such as CPR, is a minimum, but there is often no such school requirement. The elimination of all outings may be a safe legal response, but it is not a good educational one. Fear of legal liability should not prevent teachers from challenging their students in creative ways.

Emergency situations may necessitate medical action either at the hands of a supervising teacher or on her authorization. Obtaining parental consent may be impractical, if not impossible. Most provincial health acts or regulations permit medical treatment without proper consent in order to save life, limb, or vital organs. There is a legal presumption that a child consents to life-saving procedures. If a parent objects to such procedures (for example, a Jehovah's Witness may object to blood transfusions), special problems arise; however, a thorough discussion of these issues is beyond the scope of this book. Whenever possible, it is advisable for schools to get medical consents before embarking on a field trip. Another medical matter that may involve teachers is the issue of allergic reactions. This matter is addressed in Chapter 6, Teachers as Social Welfare Agents, under the heading "Teachers as Paramedics."

The *Criminal Code* also has a role to play when teachers administer emergency medical treatment. Sections 216 and 217 prohibit a teacher, whether acting as a rescuer or not, from undertaking acts dangerous to life. However, a teacher may raise a defence of necessity under section 8(3) of the *Criminal Code* in circumstances where actions considered dangerous may be necessary to save a child's life (speeding in a car to the hospital, for example).

A teacher could face a charge of criminal negligence under sections 219, 220, and 221 of the *Criminal Code* where his actions are so extreme as to show "wanton or reckless disregard for the lives or safety of other persons." Criminal charges may arise where death or serious bodily injury results from the negligence. However, most cases are pursued in the civil, rather than the criminal, arena. Charges of criminal negligence against teachers are extremely rare in Canada.

If a teacher takes reasonable measures to cope with an emergency, a successful lawsuit against her is unlikely. It is wise for teachers who may be exposed to potentially dangerous situations to have proper training in emergency procedures. Remember that the standard expected is not that of perfection, but rather that of the careful parent.[65] Courts have continually reinforced this standard, but applied it with creativity in different factual settings.

Liability for Corporal Punishment in Schools

In technical legal terms, any touching without consent is an assault. In real terms, legal action is only likely where the touching results in some physical or emotional damage to the person touched. An assault can lead both to a civil action based on the intentional torts of assault and battery and to a civil action based on a claim in negligence. There may also be a criminal sanction for an assault against another person. Thus, a teacher could face legal action in both civil and criminal courts for the same actions in some circumstances.

There is a defence under section 43 of the *Criminal Code* to what otherwise might be categorized as an assault, and this same kind of defence has been considered in civil actions as well as criminal trials. Section 43 states the following:

> Every schoolteacher, parent or person standing in the place of a parent is justified in using force by way of correction toward a pupil or child, as the case may be, who is under his care, if the force does not exceed what is reasonable under the circumstances.[66]

One of the most striking features of section 43 is that it identifies school teachers separately from "persons standing in the place of a parent." If teachers truly stood *in loco parentis*, there would be no need to identify them in a separate category in section 43. This section provides further evidence of the demise of the *in loco parentis* doctrine as an operative source of authority for teachers.

Historically, there was substantial debate about whether section 43 violated children's Charter guarantees of equality under the *Canadian Charter of Rights and Freedoms* ("the Charter") and whether it discriminated against children on the basis of their age, because the same behaviour used against an adult would constitute assault.[67] In 2004, the Supreme Court of Canada seemingly put this issue to rest in *Canadian Foundation for Children, Youth and the Law v. Canada (Attorney General)*,[68] when a children's rights group brought the issue all the way to the Supreme Court of Canada. The majority of the court upheld section 43 as constitutional. There was a strong dissent from Justice Arbour, who argued that the section was too vague to be useful because it was insufficiently clear about what behaviour constituted "reasonable force."

However, Chief Justice McLachlin, speaking for the majority, found that with proper interpretation the section provides sufficient guidance as to the dimensions of reasonable force. She specified that the section is not a defence for striking a child under age 2 or over age 12, for striking a child with a disability, for striking a child in the head, or for using an object (such as a belt or a ruler) to strike a child. As well, she emphasized that force can be used against a child only "by way of correction," as opposed to in anger or frustration. In sum, she noted that any force applied against a child must be only "minor corrective force of a transitory and trifling nature."[69] The court also found that section 43 was not a violation of section 7 (protecting an individual's right to life, liberty, and security of the person), or section 12 (protecting an individual against cruel and unusual punishment) of the Charter. In reference to the section 12 question, Justice McLachlin noted that discipline that is "reasonable in the circumstances" cannot, by its very definition, be cruel and unusual.

Before this 2004 ruling, eight provinces and territories had amended their education statutes and regulations to prohibit corporal punishment. Before these amendments, many school boards had policies prohibiting corporal punishment. Currently, the education acts of Alberta and Manitoba still allow corporal punishment, though many school districts within these provinces have created their own district-wide bans on the practice.

Although corporal punishment may no longer form the basis of day-to-day correction in the school setting, there are recent cases where the courts have been called on to review a teacher's disciplinary actions in the criminal law context. In one New Brunswick case, the provincial court was called on to consider a case in which a school principal spanked a nine-year-old student who had a long history of discipline problems.[70] The principal testified that he gave the girl one "firm slap" on the buttocks when she refused to do work assigned to her, talked back to the teacher, and disrupted other children from doing their work. Before this incident, the province of New Brunswick had amended its *Schools Act* to include section 70(2), which states, "A teacher shall not discipline any child by administering corporal punishment." The judge found the *Schools Act* was not relevant to the case because it applied in the civil context only. In this instance, the teacher had been charged in the criminal context and was thus able to rely on section 43 as a defence. The court stated:

> Just as the Courts must carefully ensure that no one unlawfully physically abuses a child for any reason, by the same token they must hasten to protect those who are doing their best at the very difficult job of teaching those same children. The alternative is chaos. Section 43 of the Code exists for a very sound purpose, and both administrative educators and Crown prosecutors would do well to follow its guidelines.[71]

The teacher was acquitted of the charge.

In *R. v. Dimmel*,[72] a case that preceded the *Canadian Foundation for Children* case, a teacher was acquitted of assault because he invoked the section 43 defence after he had "shaken some sense" into a student who was being openly defiant.

In the recent case of *R. v. Burtis*,[73] an Alberta teacher was found guilty of assaulting a student with special needs. The court found that the teacher had repeatedly pinched or pulled the student's ears. The teacher had argued she was attempting to correct the child's behaviours, which included targeting the ears of his classmates. The court found that the defence under section 43 was not available to this teacher, because she had not shown that the force was applied for corrective purposes or that it was reasonable in the circumstances.

What may be a more practical and defendable application of section 43 is provided in *R v. Sweet*.[74] In this case, three teachers had reason to believe that three students, including the accused, had been smoking marijuana in one of the classrooms. They asked the three students to stand against the wall and wait for the vice-principal, who had been called to deal with the incident. Two students complied with the request; the accused student refused. The teachers refused to let the accused student leave, and he tried to push his way past one of the teachers. The student was stopped by one teacher and, in an attempt to escape, the student elbowed the teacher in the mid-section and bit his left hand.

The student was charged with assault. At trial, he argued that he was justified in using force to avoid detention because the detention was unlawful under the Charter. The judge dismissed these arguments. He reasoned that the actions of the teachers in using force to keep the students in place were reasonable, whether or not the students had actually been smoking marijuana. The judge also noted that section 43 permits force by teachers where there is a reasonable and probable, although mistaken, belief that a student has committed a breach of discipline.

In *R. v. Haberstock*,[75] a teacher slapped the face of a student whom he thought had called him names from the window of a departing school bus on a Friday afternoon. He administered this punishment on the following Monday morning. Even though he admitted that he had punished the wrong student, the Saskatchewan Court of Appeal dismissed the charge, finding that the teacher had made a reasonable mistake. The lower court had found the teacher guilty of assault on the basis that punishment for an activity in which the student had not engaged could not be regarded as "for correction." It appears that teachers, for better or for worse, have been well protected by the courts in these cases.

In spite of judicial affirmations of section 43, we do not recommend that teachers resort to physical force as a means of correction. Even though the courts have ruled that section 43 exists as a defence to a criminal prosecution, a teacher may also experience work-related discipline if the district has a policy prohibiting corporal punishment. As well, a teacher who uses physical force as a means of discipline opens himself to potential civil liability for negligence, or the intentional tort of assault. If a teacher incorrectly administers discipline, there is a potential for a civil action by the student. If, for example, in the *Sweet* case (discussed above), the teacher had attempted incorrectly to restrain the student and had broken the student's arm, there could have been civil liability. Of course, the use of such force may be necessary in extreme circumstances, and a teacher has the right to defend herself. However, regardless of the state of the law, teachers should always seek other options to avoid physical confrontations with students.

Sexual Interference and Invitation to Sexual Touching: The Teacher's Liability

In today's schools, perhaps one of the most dangerous aspects of the "parental role" of teachers involves the *Criminal Code* provisions on sexual interference and invitation to sexual touching. Teachers, particularly male teachers (historically and statistically) in elementary schools, who think of themselves as standing in the place of a parent can be in for a severe shock if they run up against the criminal law. The *Criminal Code* makes it an offence (punishable by imprisonment for up to ten years) to touch, directly or indirectly, any part of the body of a young person for a sexual purpose. The relevant sections of the Code are reproduced below:

Sexual interference

151. Every person who, for a sexual purpose, touches, directly or indirectly, with a part of the body or with an object, any part of the body of a person under the age of 16 years

(a) is guilty of an indictable offence and liable to imprisonment for a term not exceeding ten years and to a minimum punishment of imprisonment for a term of forty-five days; or

(b) is guilty of an offence punishable on summary conviction and liable to imprisonment for a term not exceeding eighteen months and to a minimum punishment of imprisonment for a term of fourteen days.[76]

Invitation to sexual touching

152. Every person who, for a sexual purpose, invites, counsels or incites a person under the age of 16 years to touch, directly or indirectly, with a part of the body or with an object, the body of any person, including the body of the person who so invites, counsels or incites and the body of the person under the age of 16 years,

(a) is guilty of an indictable offence and liable to imprisonment for a term not exceeding ten years and to a minimum punishment of imprisonment for a term of forty-five days; or

(b) is guilty of an offence punishable on summary conviction and liable to imprisonment for a term not exceeding eighteen months and to a minimum punishment of imprisonment for a term of fourteen days.[77]

Sexual exploitation

153(1) Every person commits an offence who is in a position of trust or authority towards a young person, who is a person with whom the young person is in a relationship of dependency or who is in a relationship with a young person that is exploitative of the young person, and who

(a) for a sexual purpose, touches, directly or indirectly, with a part of the body or with an object, any part of the body of the young person; or

(b) for a sexual purpose, invites, counsels or incites a young person to touch, directly or indirectly, with a part of the body or with an object, the body of any person, including the body of the person who so invites, counsels or incites and the body of the young person.

Punishment

(1.1) Every person who commits an offence under subsection (1)

(a) is guilty of an indictable offence and liable to imprisonment for a term not exceeding ten years and to a minimum punishment of imprisonment for a term of forty-five days; or

(b) is guilty of an offence punishable on summary conviction and liable to imprisonment for a term not exceeding eighteen months and to a minimum punishment of imprisonment for a term of fourteen days.

Inference of sexual exploitation

(1.2) A judge may infer that a person is in a relationship with a young person that is exploitative of the young person from the nature and circumstances of the relationship, including

(a) the age of the young person;

(b) the age difference between the person and the young person;

(c) the evolution of the relationship; and

(d) the degree of control or influence by the person over the young person.

Definition of "young person"

(2) In this section, "young person" means a person 16 years of age or more but under the age of eighteen years.[78]

Any criminal offence contains two elements: the *actus reus* and the *mens rea*. The *actus reus* is the actual criminal act; the *mens rea* is the intention on the part of the accused to commit this act. For example, in a murder case, the act of stabbing the deceased is the *actus reus*. The accused's intention to kill the deceased is the *mens rea*. In order to obtain a conviction for murder, the Crown (prosecuting lawyer) must prove both the *actus reus* and the *mens rea* beyond a reasonable doubt. If the Crown is unable to prove the *mens rea* but able to prove the *actus reus* of stabbing, the accused might be convicted of manslaughter.

Whenever the police learn that an *actus reus* of an offence has been committed, they are entitled to launch an investigation. In the case of sexual interference, every time a teacher touches a young person, he has, on a strict reading of the *Criminal Code*, committed the *actus reus* of the criminal offence and may be subject to investigation and possible prosecution. The job of the police and the Crown is to amass and present evidence that the touching was done "for a sexual purpose." This is a substantial task because there must be proof "beyond a reasonable doubt" of a sexual intention before a judge can convict a person accused of committing this offence. However, all teachers are painfully aware of the fact that a criminal conviction is quite minor compared with the devastating effect of an allegation becoming public through an investigation in the community.

Legislators have further made it difficult for teachers by amending evidentiary sections of the *Criminal Code*. The Code now provides that a conviction may be obtained on the basis of the testimony of a child alone, without corroborating evidence—that is, without the testimony of another witness to back up the child's story. Prior to this amendment, it was necessary to have some other objective physical evidence of assault before the court could rely on the testimony of a child.

In addition, the law draws no distinction between a complaint made recently and a complaint made months or years after an assault allegedly occurred. Section 715.1 of the Code also allows videotaped evidence, in which a child (that is, someone under the age of 18) describes the acts complained of, to be admitted into court. This relieves the child of the ordeal of narrating disturbing events on the witness stand. Typically, Crown-appointed social workers question child witnesses on videotape to reduce the stress and trauma of the courtroom setting.

The Supreme Court of Canada first considered the constitutionality of section 715.1 in *R. v. L. (D.O.)*.[79] In this case, an accused argued that section 715.1 violated the Charter's principles of fundamental justice and his right to a fair trial. The accused was the grandfather of a child who was nine years old when the sexual abuse began. The trial judge found no violation of the accused's rights under the Charter, admitted the videotape, and convicted the accused. The Court of Appeal overturned the conviction, declaring section 715.1 unconstitutional. The Supreme Court of Canada overturned the

Court of Appeal and reinstated the conviction. In discussing the legislative history of section 715.1, Justice L'Heureux-Dubé noted:

> Children require special treatment to facilitate the attainment of truth in a judicial proceeding in which they are involved. These special requirements stem not so much from any disability of the child witness, but from the fact that our ordinary criminal and courtroom procedures have been developed in a time when the participation of children in criminal justice proceedings was neither contemplated nor plausible.[80]

The Supreme Court of Canada re-examined section 715.1 in *R. v. F. (C.)*.[81] In this case, a six-year-old reported sexual touching by her father. The police videotaped the child's statements soon after the alleged incident. At trial, the child indicated that the statements she made on the videotape were true, but she then made contradictory statements during cross-examination. The trial judge admitted the tape, finding it to be of significant evidentiary value, and convicted the accused. The Court of Appeal overturned the conviction and ordered a new trial, saying that the trial judge erred in allowing the inconsistent statements on the videotape. The Crown appealed to the Supreme Court of Canada, which reinstated the conviction. With respect to section 715.1, the court stated:

> It is a common experience that anyone, and particularly children, will have a better recollection of events closer to their occurrence than he or she will later on. ... It follows that the videotape which is made within a reasonable time after the alleged offence and which describes the act will almost inevitably reflect a more accurate recollection of events than will testimony given later at trial. Thus the section enhances the ability of a court to find the truth by preserving a very recent recollection of the event in question.[82]

Although there were inconsistencies between the statement on the videotape and the child's answers to questions on cross-examination, the court found that the trial judge had not erred in considering the child's videotaped statement. In support of this finding, the court stated:

> There are several factors present in s. 715.1 which provide the requisite reliability of the videotaped statement. They include: (a) the requirement that the statement be made within a reasonable time; (b) the trier of fact can watch the entire interview, which provides an opportunity to observe the demeanor, and assess the personality and intelligence of the child; (c) the requirement that the child attest that she was attempting to be truthful at the time that the statement was made. As well, the

child can be cross-examined at trial as to whether he or she was actually being truthful when the statement was made. These *indicia* provide enough guarantees of reliability to compensate for the inability to cross-examine as to the forgotten events.[83]

These sexual touching provisions may seem excessively harsh and drastic in their implications for teachers; however, the problems of child abuse in Canadian society are such that Parliament felt it necessary to take these measures. We agree that the protection of children from sexual abuse is extremely important, and the law has not always risen to the challenge.[84] The question is how to properly balance teachers' rights and child protection.

The problem for teachers is obvious. Any touching of a child can be called into question by the child's mere allegation that the touching was improper. With the renewed energy devoted by schools and social agencies to educating children to come forward when they have been improperly touched, the dangers of potentially false allegations are increased. This is predominantly a problem for male teachers in both elementary and secondary settings given that, historically and statistically, these offences are committed primarily by men. One of the popular myths among many teachers is that male teachers need only be careful about how they handle female students. We have often had teachers describe the extreme care taken whenever they are alone in a classroom with a female student. However, many of the cases that involve children under 13 concern male teachers touching male students, and there have also been a number of recent cases involving female teachers and male students. All teachers must, therefore, be conscious of how they deal with both male and female students.

Even innocent touching has the potential to lead to a traumatic court experience. In *R. v. C.B.*,[85] a teacher was charged with sexual assault when a student alleged that the teacher had touched her left shoulder, and then moved his hand to her left breast. The judge observed that it would not be unusual for this teacher to put his hand on the student's chair or shoulder when offering assistance in class. He held that the act of touching a student's shoulder was not prudent in today's school setting. He found that the touching of a student's breast would be inappropriate and subject to criminal charges. In this case, the teacher was acquitted, primarily because the trial judge preferred the teacher's evidence over the student's when he denied ever touching her breast. The relative credibility of the victim and the accused is often at the heart of such cases where there is no other corroborating evidence.

In another case, *R. v. P.L.S.*,[86] a teacher testified that he encouraged children in his class by roughing their hair, patting them on the neck or back, and placing his hand on their shoulder while complimenting them on their work. He would also squeeze the knees of boys by way of encouragement, but testified that he would never touch girls in this manner. He also claimed that he would put his hand on the neck, elbow, or back of students as a reprimand to guide them back to their seats. He might also have tapped them on the thigh while they were standing at his desk, urging them to think more quickly.

The teacher was convicted at trial of sexual assault. The trial judge accepted the cumulative evidence of the children and parents as establishing a sexual intent. The Court of Appeal overturned the conviction because it found that the trial judge erred in examining the cumulative effect of the touching in looking at the accused's intention. The court concluded that the physical contact took the form of pats or taps, and was more accidental or incidental than sexual in nature. There was no evidence of force or threats, and most of the incidents were accompanied by reprimands or compliments in respect of students' work. A reasonable observer would not view these incidents as sexual assault, according to the Court of Appeal.

The difficulty of predicting what the courts will do in this area of the law is emphasized by the fact that the Supreme Court of Canada ordered a new trial in this case.[87] There is no indication that a new trial was ever conducted; however, regardless of the outcome, the trauma of being convicted at trial and proceeding to the Court of Appeal and the Supreme Court of Canada would certainly leave its mark on both the complainants and the accused. No teacher wishes to place himself in this situation. It is almost impossible to teach at the elementary level without physical contact with students. That is, however, clearly where the law is directing teachers to head. The only advice we have to offer is this: be extremely cautious whenever touching children and avoid any unnecessary contact. Teachers must not conduct themselves as would a parent with regard to touching of students, but must instead acknowledge their positions as professionals whose actions can be scrutinized under the microscope of the law. We can only hope that the law will not prevent teachers from touching their students when such conduct is appropriate and non-sexual. The educational value may justify the risk in some cases. Teachers in elementary classes should not be prevented from hugging a student when it is reasonable and appropriate to do so. Schools must be caring as well as safe.

In *R. v. Conway*,[88] a teacher was charged with sexual interference and sexual assault after he allegedly touched a kindergarten student's buttocks. Another teacher testified that she observed the accused holding the child in his arms while touching the child's buttocks. The same teacher also testified that, on a previous occasion, she had witnessed the accused rubbing a child's back. The accused testified that he picked up the child after almost stepping on her inadvertently. The court found the testimony presented by the witness and the accused compelling, but found that the witness's testimony did not provide proof of the teacher's guilt beyond a reasonable doubt. The accused was a 27-year veteran teacher with an unblemished record and a reasonable explanation for his actions. He was acquitted of the charges of sexual assault and sexual interference.

In the secondary school setting, the dangers are perhaps more obvious. Generally, there is not the same need for touching students and therefore educational problems in restricting touching are minimal. One of the more prevalent problems apparent from the case law is that of "consensual" sexual relationships between high school students and teachers. Although the vast majority of teachers agree that this is certainly inappropriate conduct, and teachers' associations and school boards claim that it is grounds for discipline and possible revocation of a teacher's licence, it is clear that there are still teachers who choose to engage in this activity. In *R. v. Palmer*,[89] a male high school teacher was involved in two incidents with female students. The teacher was popular in the school for offering special assistance to vulnerable and at-risk students. He invited one of these 16-year-old students to his house one evening and engaged in intimate sexual activity. He invited her to go to bed with him, but she refused and he took her home.

In the second incident, the same teacher was approached by a grade 10 student who actively pursued an intimate relationship with him. The teacher and student agreed that they would have a sexual relationship but would deny this relationship to anyone who asked. Eventually, the student told her friends of the relationship, and rumours began to circulate around the school. The student was called to the principal's office and denied the relationship, saying that the rumour was entirely her fabrication. The teacher was charged under section 153 of the *Criminal Code.*

Section 153 is identical to the sections applicable to sexual touching, with the exception that it applies to children over the age of 16 and persons in a position of trust or authority over the child. Teachers obviously fall into the category of persons in a position of trust and authority. The teacher in *R. v. Palmer* was given a 15-month jail term upon conviction. The court stated that the actions of the teacher were not only illegal, "but they grossly derogated from his responsibility to direct and nurture the growth of students both in psychological and physical development."[90] The court further stated:

> In his position of trust, a teacher, like a parent or step-parent, is in a position of dominance over a young person. The teacher has natural advantages of age, experience, finances, and probably as important as

all these, a psychological cloak or perception that he is a confidant or a helper to the students who, almost by definition, need that help.[91]

In one BC case, a teacher received a sentence of eight months in prison, and one year of probation, for his admitted sexual touching of a student with her consent.[92] The relationship between teacher and student lasted for seven months and progressed over time to include sexual intercourse. The accused had no prior criminal record and presented numerous character witnesses who were stunned by this turn of events. In determining the appropriate sentence, the court noted:

> The sexual touching of a young person by a person in a position of trust is a very serious offence. It is an offence that this court and society in general finds abhorrent. It is particularly troubling to the community when a teacher breaks that special trust placed in him to educate and serve as a role model for young people.[93]

In another similar case, a teacher permitted sexual advances by a 15-year-old student that developed into sexual intercourse on at least six occasions.[94] The court pointed out that parents must be able to trust their children in the care of teachers and not worry about any improper sexual conduct. Teachers who are faced with students who have crushes on them must remind themselves that any intimate activities are unacceptable and contrary to the law. In this case, the court did not sentence the teacher to imprisonment because it was convinced by the evidence presented that the teacher had not initiated the conduct, was remorseful, and was capable of rehabilitation. The court was convinced that a similar incident would not occur in the future. The teacher was sentenced to one year's probation. The court stated that incarceration would have been the only appropriate sentence to impose if the teacher had been the instigator of the conduct. We prefer the view that the conduct is reprehensible regardless of who is the instigator.

The BC case of *Noyes v. South Caribou School District No. 30*[95] represents the more serious end of the spectrum. This case involved a teacher who had sexual relations with students in numerous different schools before finally being charged. He suffered severe legal consequences, both in criminal court and in the form of dismissal from his job. After he was criminally charged, the school district suspended him without pay, pursuant to its authority under the BC *School Act*. His attempt to use section 7 of the Charter (which guarantees the fundamental freedoms of life, liberty, and security of the person) in his argument that he should have been suspended with pay was unsuccessful. The court held that the protections guaranteed by section 7 were not intended to protect a person's livelihood.

One recent civil case illustrates another major area of concern for teachers who choose to engage in sexual contact with students. In *A.B. v. C.D.*[96] a former student successfully sued a teacher who had previously plead guilty to sexual touching (under section 153) when she was his student and peer tutor. While unsuccessful in her suit against the school district, which she alleged was negligent in not preventing the abuse, the young woman was successful in obtaining a significant award of more than $100,000 against her former teacher. The court found that she had established damages, including for pain and suffering, future lost income, costs associated with counselling she sought after the incidents, and costs for future care.

Not only are the possible legal, financial, and career consequences of engaging in sexual contact with students grave, but the psychological damage to students can be devastating and long-term. This is clearly a high-risk and abhorrent activity for teachers in both personal and legal terms.[97]

Duty to Prevent Sexual Abuse

A relatively new area of the law has emerged that is a combination of both negligence and criminal law. In *Lyth v. Dagg et al.*,[98] a 22-year-old plaintiff brought an action against a teacher with whom he had been sexually involved when he was 16 years old. The teacher was charged and criminally convicted; as well a civil court awarded monetary compensation to the plaintiff for emotional trauma. This case is somewhat unique in that the plaintiff also sued the school board for failing to meet its duty of care. The trial judge summarized the allegation in the following way:

> The allegation is that the School District knew or ought to have known that [the teacher] had a propensity to engage in sexual activity with male students and therefore it failed to discharge its duty of care to students enrolled in the school when it permitted exposure of adolescent male students to a teacher with that propensity.

The court heard evidence that three years before the initial assault on the plaintiff, two students had approached the vice-principal of the school and warned that the teacher posed a potential danger for male students. They alleged that they had been to his cabin for the weekend and that he had made sexual advances toward them. The vice-principal confronted the teacher with the allegations. The teacher denied them outright and warned that his lawyer would become involved if the allegations were pursued.

The court found that there was a duty of care on the vice-principal and the school district to protect students from this type of abuse, particularly where there is some advance warning. In the circumstances, however, the judge was satisfied that the vice-principal had made the appropriate inquiries and taken reasonable steps to ascertain whether any real danger existed. In other words, the court found that the school district had met the appropriate standard of care.

In a more recent case discussed earlier in this chapter, *H. (S.G.) v. Gorsline*,[99] a student was sexually assaulted by her physical education teacher in 1977 and 1978, while she was in junior high school. She came forward in 1993, and the accused teacher was convicted and sentenced to imprisonment. She then filed civil actions against the teacher and the school board. The court awarded her $110,000 in compensation to be paid by the teacher, but dismissed her action against the school board. The student appealed, but the appeal was dismissed. The Court of Appeal upheld the trial judge's findings that the teacher's actions were not substantially connected to his duties as assigned by the school board. They also agreed with the trial judge's concern that holding school boards vicariously liable for the actions of teachers could result in boards feeling pressure to place rules and restrictions on relationships between teachers and students that could be harmful to the education system. The Supreme Court of Canada declined to hear an appeal in this case.[100]

Overall, it appears that courts are reluctant to impose vicarious liability for sexual abuse by teachers on school boards. However, specific circumstances may result in the courts finding that the abuse perpetrated by a teacher was "reasonably foreseeable." In such a case, they could hold a school board liable for its failure to protect students.

In recent years, there have been numerous cases surrounding abuse of students at residential schools.[101] The plaintiffs in these cases tend to be groups of students who have experienced abuse, sometimes over significant periods of time, and the defendants are typically the government or religious institutions. These cases are complex, and an in-depth examination is beyond the scope of this book. For a more detailed look at the ongoing effects of Aboriginal residential schools, see James Miller's *Shingwauk's Vision: A History of Native Residential Schools*.[102]

Religion

As schools become increasingly diverse, issues relating to religion arise with greater frequency. The personal and familial nature of religion and the right to practise that religion unfettered is sometimes at odds with the education system's duty to provide a secular environment for learning for a diverse population.[103]

Schools that historically were heavily influenced by Christianity as the basis of faith for the vast majority of students have grappled with increasing diversity with varying degrees of success. Issues such as morning prayers, Christmas concerts, and religion classes loom large in today's classrooms.

One question that sits at the intersection of parental rights and the educational duties of schools relates to the extent to which schools can provide education surrounding religion. In a recent decision of the Supreme Court of Canada, the court was asked to consider the implementation of an Ethics and Religious Culture (ERC) program in Quebec schools.[104] The program replaced previous Catholic- and Protestant-based programs of religious and moral instruction. Two parents, S.L. and D.J., sought a ruling that the school board's refusal to exempt their children from the ERC program was an infringement of their freedom of religion and conscience, as protected by the Charter. The majority of the court found that, although the parents involved sincerely believed they had an obligation to pass the tenets of Catholicism on to their children, there was no proof that the ERC program would interfere in their ability to pass their faith on to their children.

The majority decision noted:

> [37] ... Having adopted a policy of neutrality, the Quebec govern-
> ment cannot set up an education system that favours or hinders any
> one religion or a particular vision of a religion. Nevertheless, it is up to
> the government to choose educational programs within its constitu-
> tional framework. In light of this context, I cannot conclude that expos-
> ing children to "a comprehensive presentation of various religions
> without forcing the children to join them" constitutes in itself an
> indoctrination of students that would infringe the appellants' freedom
> of religion.

The parents attempted to argue that exposure to various religious beliefs would be confusing for their children. The majority responded by citing an earlier decision of the Supreme Court of Canada, *Chamberlain v. Surrey School District No. 36*,[105] in which Chief Justice McLachlin provided the following commentary:

> Children encounter [some cognitive dissonance] every day in the public
> school system as members of a diverse student body. They see their
> classmates, and perhaps also their teachers, eating foods at lunch that
> they themselves are not permitted to eat, whether because of their
> parents' religious strictures or because of other moral beliefs. They see
> their classmates wearing clothing with features or brand labels which
> their parents have forbidden them to wear. And they see their class-
> mates engaging in behaviours on the playground that their parents

have told them not to engage in. The cognitive dissonance that results from such encounters is simply a part of living in a diverse society. It is also a part of growing up. Through such experiences, children come to realize that not all of their values are shared by others.

Exposure to some cognitive dissonance is arguably necessary if children are to be taught what tolerance itself involves.[106]

The majority in *S.L.* went on to note:

[40] Parents are free to pass their personal beliefs on to their children if they so wish. However, the early exposure of children to realities that differ from those in their immediate family environment is a fact of life in society. The suggestion that exposing children to a variety of religious facts in itself infringes their religious freedom or that of their parents amounts to a rejection of the multicultural reality of Canadian society and ignores the Quebec government's obligations with regard to public education.

One could certainly argue that, in determining the religious teachings to which children will be exposed, school systems, and by extension, teachers, have to some degree stepped into the role of parent.[107]

Educational Malpractice

Given parents' increased consciousness of their children's rights and the general tendency toward increased use of litigation, educational malpractice has become a popular topic of discussion among educators and academics. Although the catchphrase "educational malpractice" has been in our language for several decades, Canadian courts have shown little interest in it as a phenomenon. We think it is unlikely that the courts will adopt it in the future except in the most exceptional circumstances.

The tort of educational malpractice was considered in two US cases, considered by many to be the benchmark cases on the subject. In the first of these cases, *Peter W. v. San Francisco School District*,[108] the plaintiff argued that the school did not educate him properly. He claimed to have graduated without basic reading skills because the school did not note his reading disabilities and continued to assign him to classes where he was unable to read the materials. He also argued that the school permitted him to graduate from high school despite his inability to read beyond a grade 8 level. The California Court of Appeal found that he did not have a proper "cause of action" (valid case) because he had failed to establish the necessary duty of care. The court appeared mainly concerned with policy issues, particularly the concern that to allow this claim would encourage large numbers of other parents and children to bring their claims to court.

In *Donohue v. Copiague Union Free School District*,[109] the New York Court of Appeal refused to accept educational malpractice as a claim. The court found the plaintiff's claim that the school had failed to adequately evaluate his mental abilities, although theoretically capable of satisfying the elements of a negligence claim, was not the proper subject of a court case for policy reasons. The court noted that to allow the plaintiff's lawsuit to succeed would interfere with schools' responsibility for the administration of education.

The 1996 case *Gould v. Regina (East) School Division No. 77*[110] was one of the first cases in Canada where the court discussed the tort of educational malpractice at length. The school district was seeking to strike out the parents' and student's claim of educational malpractice. The plaintiff's parents claimed that the school district failed to meet its obligations to provide their daughter with an appropriate education. The court, in finding that the parents did not have a cause of action, stated:

> It is surely not the function of the courts to establish standards of conduct for teachers in their classrooms and to supervise the maintenance of such standards. Only if the conduct is sufficiently egregious and offensive to community standards of acceptable fair play should the courts even consider entertaining any type of claim in the nature of educational malpractice.[111]

In another Canadian case, *Haynes (Guardian ad litem of) v. Lleres*,[112] a grade 9 student who received a "C" in his French immersion social studies course brought an action alleging negligence by his teacher for her failure or refusal to teach a large portion (approximately 30 percent) of the prescribed curriculum. The defendant sought to have the claim struck for failure to disclose a cause of action. Although the plaintiff and his guardian had argued the cause of action lay in tort law, the court concluded that the claim was based in educational malpractice or negligent instruction, and ruled that policy reasons prohibited the claim.

A 1999 case from the BC Court of Appeal considered the impact of the American cases on the Canadian educational scene. In *Rumley v. British Columbia*,[113] the court considered the tort of educational malpractice in the context of a provincial school for deaf persons. Former students who claimed that they were abused sexually, physically, and psychologically and that they were denied access to a proper education to meet their needs brought the lawsuit. The plaintiffs alleged that the school misrepresented the type and quality of education it could provide. The court considered the limited history of educational malpractice, noting that courts in the United States and England consistently refused to recognize it as something that can be recognized and enforced in the courts.

The court stated that the general rule in Canadian case law is not to recognize the tort of educational malpractice; however, the possibility remained that a court might recognize the tort in extreme situations. The court refused to strike out the claim, thus allowing the case to move forward to trial, but the judge warned the plaintiffs that they would fight an uphill battle in attempting to have their claim recognized as an exception to the general rule. There has yet been no decision on the matter because of other legal issues.[114]

In 2000, the matter of educational malpractice arose in another Canadian case—this time in Alberta, where the plaintiffs were a group of Aboriginal peoples who were placed in residential schools as children.[115] The plaintiffs alleged educational malpractice (and advanced other claims) for the abuse they suffered while they were students at the school. The defendants denied that educational malpractice was a cause of action, but the court found that the facts presented in the plaintiff's documentary material were egregious enough to allow them to proceed to trial. There has not yet been a final decision in this case.

Although in the past courts were reluctant to allow cases involving the tort of educational malpractice to proceed, there may well be occasions in the future where courts allow plaintiffs the chance to prove these cases at trial. These will likely be the most extreme cases, where the government bears a high standard of care, as indicated above by the two cases dealing with residential and provincial schools.

Some scholars feel that recent case law suggests that Canadian courts are moving, albeit slowly, toward recognition of instructional negligence, or educational malpractice.[116] In *North Vancouver School District No. 44 v. Jubran*,[117] a case in which a student was bullied by other students because he was (wrongly) perceived to be gay, the court found the school liable for administrators' failure to mitigate the long-term bullying. The court accepted evidence that numerous teachers and administrators had knowledge of the bullying and the fact that it had gone on for some time, and found that the school board's attempts to address the bullying were inadequate. The court found that the school had a duty to provide a healthy environment for students and that the failure to assist Jubran constituted a failure to meet that obligation. Note that this case was pursued as a human rights complaint, rather than a tort action, but the analysis would be equally applicable to both.

In *Wiggins v. British Columbia*,[118] the plaintiff attempted to argue that the minister of education had a duty to closely oversee the administration of school boards and was therefore responsible for the decisions and policy implementation of the board. McDade[119] takes the position that the court's refusal to find governments liable for policy decisions in relation to matters of education limits the possible scale of any potential class action suits and potential educational malpractice claims.

Most recently, the BC Court of Appeal found that a physical education teacher failed to provide progressive instruction to students prior to a game of field hockey.[120] The student was injured and the court considered damages for the loss of future earnings associated with his head injury. McDade argues:

> The *Hussack* case is interesting so far as on the surface, at least, it seems to award damages for a chain of events that starts with instructional negligence, but the case's reliance on a critical element of physical injury and resultant medically quantifiable damages follow the typical tort model of injury resulting in monetary relief. It does represent an incremental step towards the tort of educational malpractice, but at its core, it is a reinforcement of the very old and traditional notion that teachers have a legal duty to ensure the safety of their students.[121]

Regardless of the current state of the law, we feel that a more appropriate attack on the issue of educational malpractice from a parental standpoint would involve a proactive rather than a reactive stance. The courts are clearly disinclined to award monetary damages to children after the fact. That is, a court will not recognize a cause of action when parents come to court with an 18-year-old child, arguing that they should be given large sums of money as compensation for their child's improper education.

The courts will be more inclined to entertain an action by parents in the early stages of their child's education, where they advance their claim to an appropriate education pursuant to the Charter and the duties of school boards under the provincial education acts or human rights legislation. Actions of this nature can already be seen in some of the Charter challenges to special education provisions, as in *Wynberg*.[122] Parents who feel that their child is not receiving appropriate educational services have a much better chance of success by pursuing the matter when their child is young than by coming to court ten years later and looking for monetary damages to compensate for what they feel was an inappropriate education.

Although still a difficult case to make out in courts, except perhaps in the most extreme of cases, the tort of educational malpractice may become more or a reality than a possibility in years to come. The creation of liability out of Charter rights and statutory duties is an emerging trend. The role of teachers as state agents is a complex and growing one that has greatly expanded since the first edition of this book in 1992. The traditional common law of negligence is also expanding to meet the realities of contemporary society. For example, aspects of providing a safe school environment, such as providing nut- or dairy-free settings for students with severe allergies, could produce liability for negligence.[123] We provide more discussion on this topic in Chapter 6, Teachers as Social Welfare Agents, under the heading "Teachers as Paramedics."

Summary

This chapter outlined the aspects of a teacher's role that identifies teachers with parents. It is clear from the discussion of *Criminal Code* offences that it is sometimes dangerous for teachers to see themselves as acting in a parental role. At the same time, the common law of negligence continues to impose the standard of the careful and prudent parent on teachers. This does not mean that teachers should equate themselves with parents in the school setting.[124] The reality is that society now views teachers as agents of the state for the purpose of delivering a service to children, and teachers must see themselves in this light. Teachers have a range of legal and professional responsibilities that distinguish them from parents. In Chapter 3, we move on to an examination of teachers' substantial role as educational state agents.

NOTES

1   A.W. MacKay and G. Dickinson, *Beyond the Careful Parent: Tort Liability in Education* (Toronto: Emond Montgomery, 1998).

2   For further information on negligence law, see P.H. Osborne, *Law of Torts*, 4th ed. (Toronto: Irwin Law, 2011) or L.N. Klar, *Tort Law*, 4th ed. (Toronto: Thomson Carswell, 2008).

3   *Jordon House Limited v. Menow*, [1974] S.C.R. 239 (1973), 38 D.L.R. (3d) 105.

4   The careful-parent rule was first set out in *Williams v. Eady* (1894), 10 T.L.R. 41 (C.A.). For a recent consideration of the rule, see *Hussack v. School District No. 33 (Chilliwack)*, 2009 BCSC 852 (CanLII).

5   See *Negligence Act*, R.S.B.C. 1996, c. 333; *Contributory Negligence Act*, R.S.A. 2000, c. C-27; *Contributory Negligence Act*, R.S.S. 1978, c. C-31; *Tortfeasors and Contributory Negligence Act*, C.C.S.M., c. T90; *Negligence Act*, R.S.O. 1990, c. N.1; *Contributory Negligence Act*, R.S.N.B. 2011, c. 131, c. C-19; *Contributory Negligence Act*, R.S.N.S. 1989, c. 95; *Contributory Negligence Act*, R.S.P.E.I. 1988, c. C-21; *Contributory Negligence Act*, R.S.N.L. 1990, c. C-33; *Contributory Negligence Act*, R.S.N.W.T. 1988, c. C-18; *Contributory Negligence Act*, R.S.Y. 2002, c. 42.

6   *The Times* (London), January 27, 1955, reproduced in G.R. Barrell, *Legal Cases for Teachers* (London: Methuen, 1970), 245.

7   *Robichaud v. Canada (Treasury Board)*, [1987] 2 S.C.R. 84, 40 D.L.R. (4th) 577.

8   H.C. Cosgrove, "The Teacher and the Common Law," in A. Knott, K. Tronc, and J. Middleton, eds., *Australian Schools and the Law*, 2nd ed. (St. Lucia, Aust.: University of Queensland Press, 1980), 71.

9   *Beauparlent v. Board of Trustees of Separate School Section No. 1 of Appleby*, [1955] 4 D.L.R. 558 (Ont. H.C.).

10 *H. (S.G.) v. Gorsline* (2004), 23 C.C.L.T. (3d) 65, 2004 CarswellAlta 688, 2004 ABCA 186, 29 Alta. L.R. (4th) 203, [2005] 2 W.W.R. 716, 329 W.A.C. 46, 354 A.R. 46 (C.A.); affirming (2001), 285 A.R. 248 (Q.B.), additional reasons at [2001] 11 W.W.R. 405 (Alta. Q.B.); leave to appeal refused (2005), 2005 CarswellAlta 62 (S.C.C.). See also *B.(A.) v. D.(C.)* 2011 BCSC 775 (Carswell), where the court came to a similar conclusion about a relationship between a grade 12 student and a teacher. The court found the teacher liable for sexual battery, but ruled that there was no act or omission by the school board that led to the sexual relationship between the two.

11 *John Doe v. Avalon East School Board* (2004), 2004 CarswellNfld 378, 244 Nfld. & P.E.I.R. 153 (Nfld. T.D.).

12 Ibid., at para. 51.

13 Ibid., at para. 62.

14 *Bazley v. Curry*, [1999] 2 S.C.R. 534, 1999 CarswellBC 1264.

15 *Jacobi v. Griffiths*, [1999] 2 S.C.R. 570.

16 *Smith v. Martin and the Corporation of Kingston*, [1911] 2 K.B. 775 (Ont. C.A.).

17 An example of how far the courts are willing to stretch the scope of vicarious liability may be found in *Moddejonge v. Huron County Board of Education* (1972), 25 D.L.R. (3d) 661 (Ont. H.C.).

18 Allison Jones, "Teachers Defend Response to Ottawa Students' Sexual Assault," *Globe and Mail*, January 29, 2013, http://www.theglobeandmail.com/news/national/teachers-defend-response-to-ottawa-students-sex-assault/article7990744.

19 *MacDonald v. Tenebonne Parish School Board*, 253 So. 2d 558 (La. C.A. 1971).

20 *Segerman v. Jones*, 259 A.D. (2d) 794 (Md. C.A. 1969).

21 *Snowlake Local Association No. 45-4 of the Manitoba Teachers' Society v. School District of Snowlake No. 2309*, [1987] 2 W.W.R. 348 (Man. Q.B.); [1987] 4 W.W.R. 763 (Man. C.A.); leave to appeal refused 86 N.R. 400 (S.C.C.).

22 *Mainville v. Ottawa Board of Education and MacLean* (1990), 75 O.R. (2d) 315 (Sm. Cl. Ct.).

23 *Tommy George v. Board of School Trustees, School District 70 (Port Alberni)* (1986), School Law Commentary, Case File No. 2-4-6 (B.C.S.C.).

24 *Board of Education for the City of Toronto v. Higgs*, [1960] S.C.R. 174 (1956), 22 D.L.R. (2d) 49.

25 *Little (Litigation Guardian of) v. Chignecto Central Regional School Board* (2004), 227 N.S.R. (2d) 103 (S.C.).

26 Ibid., at para. 28.

27 *Dyer v. Board of School Commissioners of Halifax* (1956), 2 D.L.R. (2d) 394 (N.S.S.C.).

28 *Titus v. Lindberg*, 38 A.L.R. (3d) 818 (N.J.S.C. 1967).

29 See G.R. Barrel, *Teachers and the Law* (London: Methuen, 1978); for case authority, see *Mays v. Essex County Council*, cited in Barrel, at 303-306.

30 *Geyer v. Downs* (1977), 17 A.L.R. 408 (Aust. C.A.).

31   *Barnes v. Hampshire County Council*, [1969] 3 L.E.R. 746 (H.L.).

32   *Parks v. School District #39 (Vancouver)* (2003), 2003 CarswellBC 83 (Prov. Ct.).

33   Ibid., at para. 40.

34   *Hentze (Guardian ad litem of) v. Campbell River School District No. 72*, [1994] B.C.J. no. 1876 (Q.L.) (C.A.).

35   Ibid., at para. 14.

36   *Cox v. New South Wales*, [2007] NSWSC 471.

37   See J. McKinlay, R.J. Konopasky, A. Konopasky, A.W. MacKay, and T. Barrett, "Bullying: Finding Schools Liable Changes Everything," in R. Flynn, ed., *Rights and Reason: Shifting Tides in Education* (Proceedings of the 22nd Annual Conference of CAPSLE, St. John's, Newfoundland) (Toronto: CAPSLE, 2012).

38   Ibid.

39   Virginia Tech Review Panel, "Mass Shootings at Virginia Tech, April 16, 2007," Report of the Review Panel, Presented to Governor Kaine, Commonwealth of Virginia (August 2007).

40   Ibid.

41   For an evaluation of the legal analysis surrounding the issue of violence in the educational setting, see Kimberley Pochini, "Managing Risk of Violence in the Post-Secondary Educational Environment" (2008), 18 *Education and Law Journal* 146.

42   See CTV News, "Student Dies After Explosion at Ottawa High School," May. 26, 2011, http://www.ctvnews.ca/student-dies-after-explosion-at-ottawa-high-school-1.648880.

43   See CBC News Ottawa, "Ottawa School Explosion Death Leads to Charges," January 25, 2012, http://www.cbc.ca/news/canada/ottawa/story/2012/01/25/ottawa-eric-leighton-charges-school-board.html.

44   See CTV news, "Inquest Called for Death of Eric Leighton," October 1, 2012, http://ottawa.ctvnews.ca/inquest-called-for-death-of-eric-leighton-1.978476.

45   *Ramsden v. Hamilton Board of Education* (1942), 1 D.L.R. 70 (Ont. S.C.).

46   *Peter Kelamis v. Board of School Trustees of School District No. 39 (Vancouver)* (1987), School Law Commentary, Case File No. 2-5-7 (B.C.S.C.).

47   *Jahangiri-Bojani (Guardian ad litem of) v. North Vancouver School District No. 44*, 2001 BCSC 1371.

48   *Dziwenka v. The Queen*, [1972] S.C.R. 419.

49   *James v. River East School Division No. 9*, [1976] 2 W.W.R. 577 (Man. C.A.).

50   *Donald Brown v. Essex County Roman Catholic School Board, Joseph Carty and Mary Scipione* (1990), School Law Commentary, Case File No. 5-5-7 (Ont. S.C.).

51   H. Appenzeller, *Physical Education and the Law* (Charlottesville, VA: Michie Co., 1978), provides a good summary of the basic principles relevant to negligence and physical education as well as examples of the outlandish cases for which the United States is known. J. Barnes, *Sports and the Law in Canada*, 3rd ed. (Toronto: Butterworths, 1996) is the best-known comprehensive Canadian book on the topic. See also R. Corbett, H. Findlay, and D. Lech, *Legal Issues in Sport: Tools and Techniques for the Sport Manager* (Toronto: Emond Montgomery, 2008).

52   There are a number of factors considered. See A.W. MacKay, *Education Law in Canada* (Toronto: Emond Montgomery, 1984), 124-126, and A.W. MacKay and G. Dickinson, supra note 1.

53   *McKay et al. v. Board of Govan School Unit No. 29 et al.*, [1968] S.C.R. 589 (1968), 64 W.W.R. 301.

54   *Myers v. Peel County Board of Education*, [1981] 2 S.C.R. 21 (1981), 17 C.C.L.T. 269.

55   *Thornton v. School Dist. No. 57 (Prince George) et al.*, [1978] 2 S.C.R. 267 (1978), 83 D.L.R. (3d) 480.

56   *Thornton, Tanner et al. v. Board of School Trustees of School District No. 57*, [1975] 3 W.W.R. 622, 57 D.L.R. (3d) 438 (B.C.S.C.).

57   *Thornton et al. v. Board of School Trustees of School District No. 57 (Prince George)* (1976), 73 D.L.R. (3d) 35 (B.C.C.A.).

58   See *MacCabe v. Westlock Roman Catholic Separate School District No. 110*, [1998] A.J. no. 1053 (Q.L.) (Q.B.) for an example of a more recent case that applies this standard.

59   Supra note 56, at 58.

60   Supra note 53, at 279.

61   *Myers v. Peel (County) Board of Education* (1977), 2 C.C.L.T. 269 (Ont. H.C.).

62   *Myers v. Peel (County) Board of Education* (1978), 5 C.C.L.T. 271 (Ont. C.A.).

63   Supra note 53.

64   Supra note 17.

65   This legal position was enunciated in *Board of Education for Toronto v. Higgs et al.*, [1960] S.C.R. 174 (1959), 22 D.L.R. (2d) 49, which involved the reaction of a supervising teacher to an accident on an icy playground.

66   *Criminal Code*, R.S.C. 1985, c. C-46, s. 43.

67   For a discussion of some of the issues surrounding corporal punishment in the classroom (before the *Canadian Foundation for Children* case, infra note 68), see A.M. Watkinson, *Education, Student Rights and the Charter* (Saskatoon: Purich Publishing, 1999).

68   *Canadian Foundation for Children, Youth and the Law v. Canada (Attorney General)*, 2004 SCC 4, [2004] 1 S.C.R. 76.

69   Ibid., at para. 40.

70   *R. v. Graham* (1994), 387 A.P.R. 81 (N.B. Prov. Ct.); affirmed (1995), 160 N.B.R. (2d) 306 (Q.B.).

71   Ibid., at para. 44.

72   *R. v. Dimmel* (1981), 55 C.C.C. (2d) 239 (Ont. Dist. Ct.).

73   *R. v. Burtis*, 2012 ABPC 12 (CanLII).

74   *R. v. Sweet* (1986), School Law Commentary, Case File No. 1-8-1 (Ont. Dist. Ct.).

75   *R. v. Haberstock* (1971), 1 C.C.C. (2d) 433 (Sask. C.A.).

76   *Criminal Code*, R.S.C. 1985, c. C-46, s. 151; R.S.C. 1985, c. 19 (3d Supp.), s. 1; S.C. 2005, c. 32, s. 3; S.C. 2008, c. 6, s. 54.

77   Ibid., s. 152.

78   Ibid., s. 153.

79   *R. v. L. (D.O.)*, [1993] 4 S.C.R. 419.

80   Ibid., at para. 37.

81   *R. v. F. (C.C.)*, [1997] 3 S.C.R. 1183.

82   Ibid., at para. 19.

83   Ibid., at para. 44.

84   One illustration of the previous inadequacy of the *Criminal Code* is illustrated by *R. v. Cadden* (1989), 70 C.R. (3d) 340 (B.C.C.A.). In this case, a teacher was charged with sexual assault against five young boys (aged 9 and 10). Evidence indicated that the teacher invited the boys to crawl under his desk in the classroom (during class) and perform various sexual acts on him. The teacher did not actually touch the students; he simply gave verbal instructions about what he wanted them to do. The case went to the BC Court of Appeal because the defence argued that there could be no sexual assault without actual touching by the accused. Words alone, the defence argued, do not constitute an assault. The Court of Appeal held that the combination of the words and gestures used by the teacher constituted a threat to invade the bodily integrity of the victims and, therefore, constituted an assault within the meaning of the *Criminal Code*. There is no question that the court had to stretch the meaning of the former *Criminal Code* in order to convict the accused in this case.

85   *R. v. C.B.* (1988), 73 Nlfd. & P.E.I.R 141 (Nfld. Prov. Ct.). In this case the accused was charged with sexual assault (under section 271(1)(a)), rather than with sexual interference.

86   *R. v. P.L.S.* (1990), 84 Nfld. & P.E.I.R. 181 (Nfld. C.A.). This case involved a charge of sexual assault (under section 271(1)(a)).

87   *R. v. S. (P.L.)*, [1991] 1 S.C.R. 909.

88   *R. v. Conway* (2003), 32 C.C.E.L. (3d) 142 (Ont. Ct. J. (Prov. Div.)).

89   *R. v. Palmer* (1990), School Law Commentary, Case File No. 5-2-7 (Ont. Dist. Ct.).

90   Ibid.

91   Ibid.

92   *R. v. C. (M.)*, 2000 BCPC 64.

93   Ibid., at para. 28.

94   *R. v. R.B.T.* (1990), School Law Commentary, Case File No. 5-9-6 (B.C. Co. Ct.).

95   *Noyes v. South Caribou School District No. 30* (1985), 64 B.C.L.R. 287 (S.C.).

96   *A.B. v. C.D.*, 2011 BCSC 775 (CanLII).

97   For more discussion of this topic, see R.G. Keel and N. Tymochenko, *An Educator's Guide to Managing Sexual Misconduct in Schools* (Aurora, ON: Aurora Professional Press, 2003). See also B. Bowlby and J.W. Regan, *An Educator's Guide to Human Rights* (Aurora, ON: Aurora Professional Press, 1998). Also, we note the possibility of sexual harassment findings in the human rights setting.

98   *Lyth v. Dagg et al.* (1988), 46 C.C.L.T. 25 (B.C.S.C.).

99   Supra note 10.

100   Ibid.

101   See *Rumley v. British Columbia*, [1998] B.C.J. no. 2588 (Q.L.) (S.C.) for an example of a residential school case dealing with children with disabilities; also see *Blackwater v. Plint*, [2001] B.C.J. no. 1446 (Q.L.) (S.C.), a case where Aboriginal students claimed abuse at the hands of their teachers and sought compensation from the church system. See also *Bazley v. Curry*, supra note 14. As well, see Keel and Tymochenko, supra note 97.

102   J. Miller, *Shingwauk's Vision: A History of Native Residential Schools* (Toronto: University of Toronto Press, 1997).

103   See, for example, *Multani v. Commission scolaire Marguerite-Bourgeoys*, 2006 SCC 6, [2006] 1 S.C.R. 256, in which the Supreme Court of Canada upheld the right of a Sikh elementary student to wear his kirpan (a ceremonial dagger) to school under his clothes.

104   *S.L. v. Commission scolaire des Chenes*, 2012 SCC 7, [2012] 1 S.C.R. 235 ("*S.L.*").

105   2002 SCC 86, [2002] 4 S.C.R. 710.

106   Ibid., at paras. 65-66.

107   For an interesting consideration of the issue of parental rights and education, see Paul Clarke, "Parental Rights, the Charter and Education in Canada: The Evolving Story" (2010), 19 *Education and Law Journal* 203.

108   *Peter W. v. San Francisco Unified School District*, 60 Cal. App. (3d) 131 (1976).

109   *Donohue v. Copiague Union Free School District*, 407 N.Y.S. (2d) 874 (1978).

110   *Gould v. Regina (East) School Division No. 77* (1996), [1997] 3 W.W.R. 117 (Sask. Q.B.).

111   Ibid., at para. 47.

112   *Haynes (Guardian ad litem of) v. Lleres*, [1997] B.C.J. No. 1202 (Prov. Ct.).

113   *Rumley v. British Columbia* (1999), 1999 CarswellBC 2581, 180 D.L.R. (4th) 639 (C.A.); appeal dismissed by the Supreme Court of Canada, 2001 SCC 69, [2001] S.C.R. 184.

114   See *Rumley v. British Columbia*, 2001 SCC 69, 2001 CarswellBC 2166, on the issue of whether the plaintiffs met the requirements of certification of a class proceeding, and *Rumley v. British Columbia*, 2002 BCSC 1300, 2002 CarswellBC 2064, on the issue of contents of the statement of claim submitted by the applicants.

115   *Indian Residential Schools, Re*, [2000] 9 W.W.R. 437, 2000 CarswellAlta 526 (Q.B.).

116   For an interesting and in-depth analysis, see Sonia Ben Jaafar, "Fertile Ground: Instructional Negligence and the Tort of Educational Malpractice" (2002), 12 *Education & Law Journal* 1. See also J.D. McDade, "The Evolving Tort of Educational Malpractice," a paper submitted to Wayne MacKay's 2012 Education Law Class, Schulich School of Law, Dalhousie University (submitted to *Education & Law Journal* for publication).

117   *North Vancouver School District No. 44 v. Jubran*, 2005 BCCA 201, [2005] B.C.J. No. 733.

118   *Wiggins v. British Columbia*, 2009 BCSC 121.

119   Supra note 116.

120   See *Hussack v. Chilliwack School District No. 33*, 2011 BCCA 258.

121   Supra note 116.

122   *Wynberg v. Ontario*, [2005] O.J. no. 1228 (S.C.J.); reversed on appeal, 2006 CarswellOnt 4096, 82 O.R. (3d) 561 (C.A.).

123   A.W. MacKay and T.L. Flood, "Negligence Principles in the School Context: New Challenges for the 'Careful Parent'" (1999-2000) *Education & Law Journal* 371.

124   This is particularly true in respect of matters of educational malpractice, where teachers are among the few professionals not held to a "professional" rather than a "parental" standard of expertise: see supra note 116.

3
Teachers as Educational State Agents

This chapter reviews the predominant role of teachers in the schools—that of educational state agents. The major role of the modern teacher is to deliver public education in accordance with education statutes and regulations. In Chapter 2, Teachers as Parents, we reviewed the legal status of teachers and concluded that teachers no longer operate under the *in loco parentis* doctrine, but are now more properly considered to be agents of the state. They are employees of the state and not simply delegates of parents. This distinction became particularly important in light of the impact of the *Canadian Charter of Rights and Freedoms* in the educational sphere. In this chapter and the one that follows, we discuss the impact of the Charter in some detail, particularly with respect to making and enforcing school rules and delivering special education services.

State Agent Defined

Most education acts across Canada provide some definition of the duties of teachers and their role in delivering educational services to children. The difficulty with the statutory definitions of teachers' authority is that they are usually very broad and open-ended. Another difficulty is that, until recently, these definitions had remained largely unchanged over the past 50 years in many provinces. The old provisions in Ontario and Nova Scotia provide good examples of this phenomenon.

Nova Scotia's 1918 *Education Act*, in force until 1995, set out

> (a) to teach diligently and faithfully all the branches required to be taught in the school, and to maintain proper order and discipline therein; ...
>
> (d) to inculcate by precept and example a respect for religion and the principles of Christian morality and for truth, justice, love of country, loyalty, humanity, benevolence, sobriety, industry, frugality, chastity, temperance and all other virtues.[1]

The contemporary Nova Scotia *Education Act* sets out these duties in section 26(1), which requires teachers to

> (a) respect the rights of students;
>
> (b) teach diligently the subjects and courses of study prescribed by the regulations that are assigned to the teacher by the school board;
>
> (c) implement teaching strategies that foster a positive learning environment aimed at helping students achieve learning outcomes;
>
> (d) encourage students in the pursuit of learning; ...
>
> (f) acknowledge and, to the extent reasonable, accommodate differences in learning styles;
>
> (g) participate in individual-program planning and implement individual program plans, as required, for students with special needs;
>
> (h) review regularly with students their learning expectations and progress; ...
>
> (k) take all reasonable steps necessary to create and maintain an orderly and safe learning environment;
>
> (l) maintain appropriate order and discipline in the school or room in the teacher's charge and report to the principal or other person in charge of the school the conduct of any student who is persistently defiant or disobedient;
>
> (m) maintain an attitude of concern for the dignity and welfare of each student and encourage in each student an attitude of concern for the dignity and welfare of others and a respect for religion, morality, truth, justice, love of country, humanity, equality, industry, temperance and all other virtues;
>
> (n) attend to the health, comfort and safety of the students;
>
> (o) report immediately to the principal the existence of any infectious or contagious disease in the school or the existence of any unsanitary condition in the school buildings or surroundings, and perform such duties as are from time to time prescribed by or under the Health Protection Act;

(p) take all reasonable steps to secure full and regular attendance at school of the students under the teacher's supervision;

(q) keep accurate attendance records and report absent students to the principal as prescribed by the regulations;

(r) communicate regularly with parents in accordance with policies established by the school board;

(s) keep such records as are required by the school board or the Minister and permit the inspection of those records by the board, the superintendent or superintendent's representative, the principal, the supervisor and the Minister or Minister's representative or, upon their request, provide the records to them;

(t) assist in the development and implementation of the school improvement plan;

(u) maintain their professional competence;

(v) serve, to the extent reasonable, on committees established within the school to improve student achievement and success;

(w) implement programs and courses as prescribed by the public school program; and

(x) perform such other duties as are prescribed by this Act or the regulations.[2]

Ontario's 1927 *Public Schools Act*, in force until 1990, prescribed the duties of teachers in section 100:

(a) to teach diligently and faithfully the subjects in the public school course of study as prescribed by the regulations, to maintain proper order and discipline in the schools; to encourage the pupils in the pursuit of learning; to inculcate by precept and example, respect for religion and the principles of Christian morality and the highest regard for truth, justice, loyalty, love of country, humanity, benevolence, sobriety, industry, frugality, purity, temperance, and all other virtues;[3]

The current Ontario *Education Act* sets out the duties of teachers in section 264(1):

(a) to teach diligently and faithfully the classes or subjects assigned to the teacher by the principal;

(b) to encourage the pupils in the pursuit of learning;

(c) to inculcate by precept and example respect for religion and the principles of Judeo-Christian morality and the highest regard for truth, justice, loyalty, love of country, humanity, benevolence, sobriety, industry, frugality, purity, temperance and all other virtues; ...

(e) to maintain, under the direction of the principal, proper order and discipline in the teacher's classroom and while on duty in the school and on the school ground.[4]

Although there have been some changes over the years, it is striking that there are still many similarities between the roles defined for teachers in the 1920s and the roles defined today. Although teachers in Nova Scotia may take comfort from the fact that "chastity" and "sobriety" have been removed from the present Act, the remainder of the definition is certainly far from comforting. The legislation illustrates that teachers have good reason to be confused about their role in the school. In 1970, John MacDonald undertook a study of the teaching profession in Canada in *The Discernable Teacher*.[5] In the course of this study, he described what he called the "omnicapable model" of teachers:

> The conventional description of the teacher invites teachers to refer themselves to an omnicapable model, at once intelligent and effectively warm, knowledgeable and tolerant, articulate and patient, efficient and gentle, morally committed and sympathetic, scholarly and practical, socially conscious and dedicated to personal development, fearless and responsible.[6]

These comments illustrate that expectations placed on teachers constitute an almost superhuman standard. This standard is arguably the product of the combined authority of the *in loco parentis* doctrine and the power conferred on teachers by statute. The combination of the two sources of authority provides a powerful, almost omnipotent, legal status that may have spilled over into the definition of a teacher's role. In today's school setting, this is a dangerous model for teachers to follow. At the very least, it is inaccurate and misleading for teachers. It is more appropriate in today's schools for teachers to think of themselves as state agents, who are small but vital components of a larger educational structure. The statutory definitions of teachers' duties promote and enhance the omnicapable myth and create unrealistically high expectations for teachers.

Unfortunately, academic criticism does not change legislative reality. The reality is that statutory duties exist, and teachers should at least be aware of their potential impact. Perhaps a better definition of the teacher's role and duties may be found in the professional codes of conduct provided by teachers' associations in each of Canada's provinces and territories. These guidelines for conduct provide a more workable definition on which teachers may rely in determining their role as state agents. The scope of this book does not permit an examination of each of the codes of conduct; however, we encourage readers to review the code of conduct in force in their area as a valuable reference. Aside from providing possible role definitions, the teachers' associations in every province have the power and authority to implement disciplinary proceedings in cases where a teacher breaches the code of conduct. It is, therefore, advisable for all teachers to be aware of the provisions of their respective codes of conduct.

Application of Section 32 of the Charter

Since its entrenchment in 1982, the *Canadian Charter of Rights and Freedoms* ("the Charter") has significantly affected the education community. There are a number of important sections in the Charter that directly influence education as well as how teachers, as state agents, deal with and relate to students. In this section, we examine the general application of the Charter as well as how specific sections of the Charter affect teachers. Section 32(1)(b) states that the Charter applies to "[t]he legislature and government of each province in respect of all matters within the authority of the legislature of each province."

The Charter applies only to government action and government actors; it cannot intrude on relationships between private individuals. There is no question that the Charter applies to the education legislation of each province.[7] It is now generally accepted that the Charter also applies to public school boards and their employees.[8] Some lower courts and tribunals have found that the Charter does apply[9] in this way. Although the Supreme Court of Canada has yet to make a definitive statement regarding the application of the Charter to school boards, it has applied the Charter to the educational activities of several school boards.[10] There has been some discussion in the case law about whether the Charter applies to all school-board activities or only to those activities that reflect "government action." For example, the Charter applies to special education services, but it might not apply to a school board's contract for services with a local landscaping company. This has been expressed as differentiating between "the nature and the quality of the actor" and the "nature and quality of the action or activity."[11]

The Supreme Court of Canada has performed a comprehensive review of the application of the Charter in the context of universities. In *McKinney v. University of Guelph*,[12] *Harrison v. University of British Columbia*,[13] *Stoffman v. Vancouver General Hospital*,[14] and *Douglas/Kwantlen Faculty Assn. v. Douglas College*,[15] the Supreme Court of Canada released four concurrent decisions that related to mandatory retirement. Although the court addressed a number of important issues, the most important for our purposes focus on the application of the Charter.

The Supreme Court of Canada spent a good deal of time addressing the application of the Charter to university bodies. There were some difficult questions to be addressed because universities are partially controlled by the government and are dependent on government funding, but they also act independently of the government in many respects. The majority of the Supreme Court of Canada consistently found that the Charter did not apply to universities because there was insufficient government control to justify its application. Justice La Forest qualified this by stating that the court's decision in these cases did not eliminate the possibility that universities could be found to be part of the government for the purposes of the Charter; rather Justice La Forest concluded that the universities in the cases before the court were not part of the government because of the manner in which they were currently organized and governed. The court was also reluctant to apply the Charter in the context of a carefully designed collective bargaining structure. Both parties to the collective agreement had consented to the current employment terms, and the imposition of Charter principles might distort this balance.

More recent case law suggests that the Charter does apply in the context of student discipline. In *Pridgen v. University of Calgary*,[16] the Alberta Court of Queen's Bench considered an application for review of a university discipline panel. The panel made a finding of non-academic misconduct and imposed a probationary period on a number of students who made negative comments about a professor on Facebook. Two of the students, twin brothers, sought the court's review of the discipline, arguing that their right to free expression guaranteed in section 2(b) of the *Canadian Charter of Rights and Freedoms* was infringed. The court found that the students' Charter rights to free speech were infringed and, accordingly, quashed the decision of the disciplinary committee.

An education statute specifically addresses elementary- and secondary-level programs and services, and children are required by compulsory attendance laws to go to school until they reach the age of 16 in most provinces. Children are not required to attend university. A school board delivers an educational service that is controlled through provincially developed and approved curriculums. By contrast, universities are entitled to set their own curriculums. In many provinces, school boards are publicly elected in a manner similar to the election of municipal councils, and they have taxing powers in some instances. For these reasons, we conclude that, although there may be some outstanding questions with regard to a school board's ostensibly non-governmental activity, courts will generally hold school boards to be subject to the Charter. Whenever core educational services to children such as special education and access are affected, the nature and quality of the school board as a government actor and the action it takes will fall under Charter scrutiny.[17]

In *R. v. M. (M.R.)*,[18] the Supreme Court of Canada, although not addressing the matter specifically, assumed that the Charter applied to school personnel. This case dealt with a student being searched for drugs by the school's vice-principal, in the presence of a police officer.

The more difficult question to answer is whether the Charter applies to teachers. In *O.T.F. v. Ontario (Attorney General)*,[19] the court held that the Charter did not apply to the collective bargaining arrangements of teachers. However, when teachers act as state agents pursuant to their statutory duties, it is clear that they are caught in the net of government action for the purpose of Charter application.[20] This does not mean that teachers should fear that they will be sued personally based on the Charter. The nature of the remedies in the Charter dictates a broader scope of action against school boards or the provincial attorneys general than against individual teachers.[21]

The Nature of Charter Rights and Litigation

The Charter is indeed a unique legal document. Because it is also a constitutional document, it is difficult to change.[22] The Charter contains a list of rights and freedoms that are to be enjoyed by all Canadians, including children. It is unclear at what age children attain independent Charter rights, but the preamble of the *Youth Criminal Justice Act*[23] specifies that young persons have the rights and freedoms set out in the Charter and the *Canadian Bill of Rights*.[24] The Act defines "young person" as a person between the ages of 12 and 18, suggesting that anyone over the age of 12 has the ability to exercise her Charter rights. The main goal of the Charter is the balancing of the rights of the individual against the rights of society as a whole. In a democratic society, where the majority rules, there is a danger that the rights of the individual may be overlooked and overcome by the forces of the state. The Charter is aimed at addressing this potential imbalance. Unlike the *Canadian Bill of Rights*, the Charter is constitutionally entrenched; it is the entrenchment of the Charter that has led the courts into taking an active role in interpreting the document.

The Charter affects education in two significant ways. First, it provides parents with a tool for challenging both the process and the substance of school board decisions. Before the Charter, parents were restricted to administrative law remedies that dealt primarily with procedural irregularities, such as inadequate notice of school decisions or a board's failure to obtain adequate public input.[25] The broad discretion enjoyed by school boards in delivering educational services prior to the Charter has now been eroded.

Second, the Charter is the supreme law of Canada and applies to all Canadians. Decisions of the Supreme Court of Canada are binding on all provinces. Therefore, if a Charter issue in education makes its way to the Supreme Court of Canada, the court's decision will apply to every province irrespective of whether the province took any part in presenting the case. Under section 93 of the *Constitution Act, 1867*, the provinces have always had exclusive jurisdiction over education. The presence of the Charter now makes it necessary for educators to be aware of issues and conflicts in all areas of the country. If, for example, a case involving the religious rights of students arises in Ontario and is decided by the Supreme Court of Canada, it may dictate how students must be treated all across Canada. Of course, some provincial differences remain, such as the existence of denominational schools in some provinces and not in others.

Before discussing the content of the rights and freedoms contained in the Charter, it is vital to explain the steps involved in Charter litigation. In many ways, Charter rights and freedoms are defined by the method and procedures used to enforce them. First and foremost, it is important to remember that Charter issues are resolved in the courts, which follow a traditional adversarial approach to litigation. This is a lengthy and very expensive process.[26]

There are four essential steps to any Charter litigation:

1. The court must determine that the Charter applies to both the plaintiff and the defendant.
2. The plaintiff must establish that the defendant has breached the plaintiff's rights on the basis of evidence formally presented to the court.
3. The defendant has the opportunity to rely on section 1 of the Charter to limit the rights claimed by the plaintiff.
4. The court must determine an appropriate remedy.

We examine each one of these steps in the following sections.

Application of the Charter to Plaintiff and Defendant

The first step for a plaintiff in Charter litigation is to establish that the defendant is a government actor, pursuant to section 32(1)(b) of the Charter. We discussed this issue above in the context of education, under the heading "Application of Section 32 of the Charter." School boards, school administrators, and teachers are considered government actors for the purpose of applying the Charter to the educational services provided to children. There is also the question of whether the person claiming the rights has legal standing to make the particular claim. Generally, anyone who is brought before the court by another party (such as the Crown in a criminal case or a plaintiff in a civil case) has legal standing. If a party wishes to bring a claim to court—for example, if a parent wishes to make a claim against a provincial department of education—a court will grant legal standing only if the plaintiff can prove (1) there is a serious issue to be tried, (2) she has a genuine interest in the issue or is directly affected by it, and (3) there is no other reasonable and effective way in which the issue can be brought before the court.[27] If a person's rights have been violated, a court will usually allow that person to have standing.

The plaintiff must also be claiming a right that is contained in the Charter. The language of the Charter is intended to encompass a wide range of rights and freedoms. The exact nature of the rights being protected is therefore not always clear on the face of the document. There is a strong argument, for example, that section 7 of the Charter, which guarantees every Canadian the right not to be deprived of "life, liberty and security of the person," except in accordance with the principles of fundamental justice, creates a constitutional right to an education. It is important to note, however, that the Supreme Court of Canada has not yet ruled definitively on this matter. Justice Wilson, in *R. v. Jones*,[28] defined the term "liberty" in the following manner:

> I believe that the framers of the constitution in guaranteeing "liberty" as a fundamental value in a free and democratic society had in mind the freedom of the individual to develop and realize his potential to the full.[29]

Clearly, this broad and purposive definition could encompass many aspects of an individual's rights, including the right to an education. We examine the constitutional right to an education in more detail in Chapter 4, Teachers as Guardians of Equality.

Breach of Rights

Once the court is satisfied that the defendant is, in fact, a government actor and the plaintiff is claiming a right that may be included in one or more sections of the Charter, it is then up to the plaintiff to establish a denial of the right in issue.

Because the Charter is enforced through the usual process of courtroom litigation, the plaintiff has the "burden" of proving her case on a "balance of probabilities." This means that the plaintiff must demonstrate that "more likely than not" her rights under the Charter have been violated. The degree of difficulty in proving this violation will vary with the particular facts of the situation and the rights involved.

Some of the sections of the Charter contain internal limits that increase the difficulty in proving a denial of rights. For example, section 8 guarantees that everyone has the right to be secure against "unreasonable" search or seizure. It is not enough for a plaintiff simply to show that he was searched; he must also show that the search was unreasonable before a court can find that the search was a breach of the Charter. Essentially, the plaintiff has the burden, first, to show that his complaint falls within the scope of one of the sections of the Charter, and second, to prove on a balance of probabilities, through the introduction of evidence in court, that his rights have been violated. The task of gathering, organizing, and leading this evidence in court can be lengthy and difficult, thus generating the extensive legal bills mentioned earlier.

Section 1 of the Charter

Unlike the US Constitution, the Canadian Charter, while protecting individual rights and freedoms, is also an instrument of balance and compromise. This balance is expressed throughout the Charter; however, it appears most explicitly in section 1:

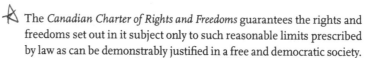 The *Canadian Charter of Rights and Freedoms* guarantees the rights and freedoms set out in it subject only to such reasonable limits prescribed by law as can be demonstrably justified in a free and democratic society.

This section mandates that all of the rights and freedoms set out in the Charter are subject to "reasonable limits" that are prescribed by the government in some legal form in an effort to accommodate the interests of all Canadians. In the educational context, it is this section that allows school boards to exercise some of the discretion they enjoyed before the entrenchment of the Charter in 1982. This section is an expression of common sense for most Canadians, who recognize that for every right there is a corresponding responsibility on some person or agency. Section 1 allows the government to seek a balance between competing priorities.

Chief Justice Dickson dealt with the scope of section 1 in detail in *R. v. Oakes*.[30] It is unnecessary for our purposes to delve into the details of the criteria used to test a section 1 limit. Essentially, the court set out two major criteria and three subcriteria to define whether a limitation meets the section 1 test. The first criterion is whether the objective of the legislative provision being reviewed is pressing and substantial. The second criterion is whether the means adopted to pursue this objective are proportional. To determine this, the court considers (1) whether there is a rational connection between the objective and the provision in question; (2) whether the provision is minimally impairing, and (3) the proportionality between the benefit to be gained from attaining the objective and the detriment to the individual of infringing the right.[31] For school boards, this elaborate section 1 analysis can be avoided simply by asking the questions: "Why do we need this particular rule or policy? What is its effect on the students? Is it unfair or arbitrary?" and "Can the objective be achieved by intruding less drastically on rights?" If, after asking these questions, a school board is satisfied that the rule or policy is reasonable, it is in a good position to convince a court of its reasonableness.

Another major stumbling block for school boards is the requirement that a section 1 limit must be "prescribed by law." This does not necessarily mean that the limit is set out somewhere in legislation, although that would clearly meet the test.[32] In the school context, "prescribed by law" can mean school board policies and school rules that limit Charter rights should, where possible, be in written form and publicized in some way.[33] Justices Wilson and Lamer and Chief Justice Dickson indicated in *Irwin Toy* that a limitation must set "an intelligible standard" that provides a clear and discernable limit.[34]

In a Charter courtroom battle, where the plaintiff has proven a violation, the judge will then turn to the defendant school board and, before listening to arguments about reasonable limits, will ask to see where these limits have been articulated in some form. If there are no written limits, the courts are less likely to entertain arguments under section 1. Thus the importance of written rules is clear; schools and school boards should put their rules in writing and make them available to staff and students if they expect to be able to defend them as reasonable in a court of law. While written limits are not essential in every case, they are certainly a highly desirable practice.

A further significant feature of section 1 is that it effectively shifts the burden of proof from the plaintiff to the defendant. This shift can often determine the outcome of a case. The Supreme Court of Canada has established that the burden of showing reasonable limits rests squarely on those seeking to enforce these limits.[35] In essence, this means that if a judge is satisfied that there has been a violation of a Charter right, but is uncertain about whether the government's limits are reasonable, the plaintiff will be successful. Indeed, the language of section 1 indicates that the state must "demonstrably justify" the limitation on Charter rights.

More important, even if there is a valid section 1 limit, it may not be recognized by the courts unless it is in proper form. This requirement represents a blow to many school boards and administrators who often rely on ad hoc policy making. In areas where Charter violations may arise, proactive decisions and policy making will have to replace the previous ad hoc procedures. This should be a prime motivating factor for school boards and school administrators to get together with legal counsel to discuss the policies and practices of the school board and set them out in a clear and accessible, and preferably written, form. Many school boards already engage in this process, and many schools have taken a proactive approach in anticipating Charter challenges.

Remedies

The ultimate goal of any litigation is to obtain an appropriate remedy from a court. In the usual course of civil litigation, this remedy is monetary compensation. The Charter has a much broader remedial scope. There are three remedies contained in the Charter. The first is set out in section 24(2), which allows a court to exclude any evidence in a criminal proceeding that has been gathered in a manner that violates rights under the Charter. For example, a principal who searches a student for narcotics in an unreasonable manner that violates the Charter may find that a court excludes any evidence uncovered during the search from consideration in the case.[36] We discuss this idea in more depth in Chapter 5 under the heading "A School's Investigative Role." Section 24(2) would not be applied in a school board context to a disciplinary hearing that concerns students or teachers because a disciplinary hearing panel would be unlikely to meet the requirements of a court of "competent jurisdiction," whereas the courts would clearly meet this standard.[37]

The second remedy is found in section 52(1) of the *Constitution Act, 1982*. Section 52(1) states that the Constitution, which includes the Charter, is the supreme law of Canada and that any law inconsistent with it is, to the extent of the inconsistency, of no force or effect. This section allows individuals the opportunity to have a court strike down a piece of legislation or declare the legislation inoperative to the extent that it is inconsistent with a provision in the Charter. For example, in special education cases, the court may prescribe specific services to be provided without striking down the entire *Education Act*. This remedy is vital to the integrity of the Charter as a document that sets standards for government action. Because the Constitution is the supreme law of Canada, if the Supreme Court of Canada strikes down a section of an education act of one province, all other provinces must take a close look at their own legislation to determine whether they have a similar problem. In our experience, it is surprising how many provinces fail to adequately recognize their vulnerability in this regard.

The third, and perhaps most dramatic, remedy is contained in section 24(1) of the Charter. This section states:

> Anyone whose rights or freedoms, as guaranteed by this Charter, have been infringed or denied may apply to a Court of competent jurisdiction to obtain such remedy as the court considers appropriate and just in the circumstances.

Because the Charter forces the courts to scrutinize unique situations, the drafters of the Constitution realized that they must grant the courts flexible and substantial remedial powers.[38] This is accomplished by section 24(1). In the usual course of litigation, the courts are restricted in their remedies by statutory provisions and principles of common law. Remedies provided by statutes and common law may also apply in some cases involving Charter challenges. Section 24(1), however, allows superior courts to step outside the usual restrictions that are imposed on them and devise extraordinary remedies.[39]

Plaintiffs frequently rely on section 24(1) of the Charter in education cases to obtain "interlocutory and interim injunctions." These injunctions are granted before trial to preserve or create a particular status quo for the parties involved. In many jurisdictions, it can take years to get to trial. This is problematic when the situation demands an immediate remedy to avoid irreparable harm to the plaintiff. The courts have developed a system whereby they will hear the parties on an interim or interlocutory basis to decide how the situation should be handled until trial. For instance, if a defendant plans to demolish a house and a plaintiff is suing for ownership of that house, it is vital that the plaintiff obtain an interlocutory injunction to stop the defendant, or a future trial will be pointless.

Parents and students are increasingly coming to the courts on an interlocutory basis to have the courts decide Charter issues in education. To obtain an interlocutory injunction, a plaintiff must show (1) "a serious issue to be tried," (2) the probability of "irreparable harm" if the injunction is not granted, and (3) the balance of convenience in the plaintiff's favour. To accomplish the third objective, the plaintiff must demonstrate that the injunction should be granted because the plaintiff's harm would be greater than any possible harm to the defendant.[40] In many cases, and in particular education cases, an interlocutory injunction will provide a final remedy because by the time the case reaches trial, the issue has become moot. In *Tuli v. St. Albert Board of Education*,[41] for example, a grade 12 student obtained an injunction from the Alberta Court of Queen's Bench that allowed him to wear his kirpan (ceremonial dagger) in school. The Human Rights Board of Inquiry later found that there had been no discrimination, but, by that time, the injunction had lasted long enough for the student to finish high school.

In another case, an Ontario student obtained an injunction to allow him to bring his same-sex partner to his Catholic high school prom.[42] After attending the prom, the student did not pursue the issue further because he had accomplished his goal with the injunction.

Even where an issue is not moot at the time of trial, it is possible that the position of a school board may have been prejudiced to such an extent that there is little likelihood of success. In *Elwood v. Halifax County Bedford District School Board*,[43] the parents of a seven-year-old child with special needs obtained an injunction in October to allow their son to remain in an inclusive setting until trial, which was scheduled for June. The integration of the child over this period of months helped the parents gather evidence about the benefits of inclusion, evidence that they might not otherwise have been able to obtain. The school board decided to settle the case rather than take it to trial.

The possibility that a plaintiff may obtain an injunction is one of the most important reasons for school boards to communicate with legal counsel to ensure that their policies and practices are consistent with the Charter. An injunction hearing can be held in most areas on less than seven days' notice and, as illustrated above, can disrupt an entire school year. School boards are particularly at risk if they are caught off guard and have not turned their minds to the possibility of a Charter challenge. Courts may be sympathetic to the argument advanced by parents that their child will suffer irreparable harm if his education is affected in some way.[44] The battle will generally centre on whether there is a serious issue to be tried, though the courts have indicated that the standard to be applied in determining the seriousness of the issue is reasonably easy to meet.[45] If school boards address Charter issues and take a proactive stance in clearly setting out their policies and practices, they have a much better chance of defending an application for an injunction than if they are unprepared.

Teachers' Role

It is perhaps obvious from this discussion that Charter issues are largely institutional ones that affect school board policy making and government regulation more than the individual habits of teachers. However, as in all aspects of education, the teacher often makes the frontline decisions regarding students. When a child presents with a "special need" in the classroom, most teachers' first response is to find a suitable education strategy right away, rather than seek an institutional remedy. Furthermore, teachers are in the best position to bring particular situations to the attention of superintendents and school board officials. Because teachers ultimately must implement the policy set out by school boards on many of these issues, it is wise for teachers to become more involved as a collective force in structuring policies and procedures. Consequently, it is a good idea for teachers to familiarize themselves with the principles set out in the Charter. It is also wise for teachers to familiarize themselves with the Charter in order to use it to model and teach good citizenship to their students.

Students' Rights Under the Charter

One of the thorny problems of applying the Charter to schools is determining who is entitled to exercise Charter rights. Is it the student who claims the rights, or the parents who claim them on behalf of the student? There are obvious restrictions on the ability of students to exercise some of their rights; however, there are many rights that they may exercise independently of their parents. For example, the preamble to the *Youth Criminal Justice Act*[46] provides that young persons have rights and freedoms, including those stated in the Charter. This legislation applies to young persons from ages 12 to 18.

One obvious restriction on the independent exercise of rights by students is that seeking legal redress for a violation requires significant financial resources. Parents must usually support their children's pursuit of any legal remedy financially. However, there are situations—for example, those involving freedom of religion—where parents' and students' interests may diverge. Throughout this section, we attempt to identify some of these situations, which can pose a difficult problem for teachers who may be forced to balance competing interests.

As we examine some of the various Charter rights that apply to education, it is important to know at the outset that we have not addressed two of the larger Charter issues in education, which are beyond the scope of this book. Minority language educational rights, protected by section 23 of the Charter, are an elaborate set of guarantees for protecting French- and English-speaking minorities in Canada.[47] This section has been extensively litigated in the past 30 years; however, this is an institutional issue and of minor consequence for individual teachers. In essence, it is up to the provincial governments to determine how they are going to provide minority language education to children of parents qualified under the definitions of section 23.

The second issue that we omit is denominational schools, which are protected by section 93 of the *Constitution Act, 1967* and section 29 of the Charter. Again, this is a large institutional issue that is primarily of concern to provincial legislators. An examination of these two important Charter issues is beyond the scope of this book because these issues do not significantly affect the various roles of the teacher. The implications of denominational schools for the human and employee rights of teachers are discussed in Chapter 7, Teachers as Employees, under the heading "Freedom of Religion." Religious rights of individual students are discussed below.

Fundamental Freedoms: Section 2 of the Charter

Section 2 of the Charter states:

> Everyone has the following fundamental freedoms:
> (a) freedom of conscience and religion;
> (b) freedom of thought, belief, opinion and expression, including freedom of the press and other media of communication;
> (c) freedom of peaceful assembly; and
> (d) freedom of association.

Freedom of Religion

Freedom of religion in the school system has been one of the more widely litigated Charter issues to date. One of the first issues to come to court under section 2(a) of the Charter was whether schools could conduct religious exercises in the morning. In *Zylberberg v. Sudbury Board of Education*,[48] a group of parents of non-Christian students challenged a school board policy that required morning reading of the Lord's Prayer in a grade 2 classroom. The school policy allowed any parents who did not wish their child to take part in the reading to have their child excluded from the class during exercises. The parents challenged this practice, arguing that it was unfair and harmful to their children to force them to be excluded during morning exercises. The parents claimed that the practice should be declared unconstitutional.

At the trial level, the court held that although the reading of the Lord's Prayer was a violation of section 2 of the Charter, it was justified as a reasonable limit under section 1. The court's conclusion was based on its perception of a Christian basis of the public school system (not to be confused with the denominational system) and the fact that the students could be excluded from religious exercises at the request of their parents. The Ontario Court of Appeal disagreed with this reasoning and overturned the trial court's decision. The Court of Appeal determined that the practice was "coercive" and that children at the grade 2 level could not appreciate the "voluntariness" of the practice of allowing them to be excluded from the classroom. The excluded children would likely feel singled out and different. The school board accepted the ruling and did not appeal the case to the Supreme Court of Canada.

In *Corporation of the Canadian Civil Liberties Association et al. v. Ontario (Minister of Education) and Elgin County Board of Education*,[49] a declaration was sought by the Civil Liberties Association, representing a group of parents in the Elgin County area, that the religious instruction provided by the school board was unconstitutional. There was lengthy evidence presented to the court to explain the religious instruction and its various aspects, which included discussions of religions other than Christianity. The court concluded, however, that the primary purpose of this religious instruction was the indoctrination of the Christian faith. Part of the evidence was a fill-in-the-blank question on one of the tests in the school that stated, "Jesus Christ is the _____ way to God." The word to be inserted was "only." The Court of Appeal determined that this program was coercive and therefore violated section 2(a) of the Charter. The court felt that compelling religious observance through the indoctrination of children could not be protected by section 1 of the Charter as a reasonable limit.

The Supreme Court of Canada has recently considered the issue of religious instruction. As discussed in Chapter 2, Teachers as Parents, in *S.L. v. Commission scolaire des Chenes*,[50] several parents challenged a school board's refusal to exempt their children from an Ethics and Religious Culture program. The majority of the court noted:

> [37] ... Having adopted a policy of neutrality, the Quebec government cannot set up an education system that favours or hinders any one religion or a particular vision of religion. Nevertheless, it is up to the government to choose educational programs within its constitutional framework. In light of this context, I cannot conclude that exposing children to "a comprehensive presentation of various religions without forcing the children to join them" constitutes in itself an indoctrination of students that would infringe the appellants' freedom of religion.
>
> • • •
>
> [40] Parents are free to pass their personal beliefs on to their children if they so wish. However, the early exposure of children to realities that differ from those in their immediate family environment is a fact

of life in society. The suggestion that exposing children to a variety of religious facts in itself infringes their religious freedom or that of their parents amounts to a rejection of the multicultural reality of Canadian society and ignores the Quebec government's obligations with regard to public education.

In light of these decisions, teachers who are providing religious instruction or observing any religious exercises in their classrooms should undertake a careful review of these practices. The clear signal sent by the Ontario Court of Appeal in *Elgin County*[51] is that any religious instruction that leans toward indoctrination is coercive and violates the Charter. This view is reinforced in the recent Supreme Court of Canada decision from Quebec. Many metropolitan school boards have opted to have religious exercises in the morning that involve readings from various religious faiths. The emphasis is on history and the development of religion as opposed to indoctrination. This may be the wisest course for the future in both legal and educational terms. In Ontario, regulations under the *Education Act* specifically prohibit the presentation of religious instruction during the school day, except in denominational schools.[52] A number of other provinces now follow a similar policy. In some provinces, such as Newfoundland and Labrador, Saskatchewan, and Alberta, special religious rights were included in the Terms of the Union by which the province joined Confederation. The extent of these rights has not yet been fully tested.

Another significant religious issue that has come to the courts in several provinces is that of Sikh students wearing kirpans (ceremonial daggers). Whereas the issue of religious instruction and exercises involves a school's promotion of religion, the issue of kirpans involves an individual's desire to exercise his personal religious beliefs. The Supreme Court of Canada heard an appeal dealing with a school district's decision to forbid a student from coming to school wearing a kirpan.[53] The Quebec Court of Appeal had ruled that the refusal, although a Charter violation, was justified by section 1 as a reasonable limit.[54] The Supreme Court of Canada disagreed. The majority decision found that although the refusal to allow the student to wear his kirpan was motivated by a pressing and substantial objective—that is, safety—it was not a minimal impairment of the student's rights. The majority noted that the risk associated with the kirpan was low, particularly when one considered the conditions imposed by the lower court (that is, that the kirpan be worn under clothing and sewn into a sheath). Further, the Supreme Court found that there were numerous other objects in the school environment that could be used as weapons, including scissors, pencils, and baseball bats. The court noted that not a single incident of a kirpan being used as a weapon in schools had been reported. In response to the argument that some other students might find it unfair that a Sikh student could wear a kirpan when they are prohibited from having knives at school, the majority noted that this was an opportunity for schools to teach students about religious tolerance as a cornerstone of democracy.

The next major issue involving freedom of religion that arises in schools concerns forms of dress as an expression of religious belief. One such example occurred in Quebec, where a secondary school refused to allow a student who was a recent convert to Islam to wear a hijab (head scarf). The issue never reached the courts because the student transferred to another school, where she was permitted to wear the hijab. However, there was much public attention focused on the issue, and the Quebec Human Rights Commission ultimately published a discussion paper about it. In the paper, the commission noted that although the hijab is seen by some as a means of oppressing women in extremist societies, in Quebec, people must assume that a person wearing a hijab has made a choice to do so. Therefore, an outright prohibition would be a violation of the Quebec *Charter of Human Rights and Freedoms*. As a result, schools must reasonably accommodate a student's right to wear a hijab unless restrictions are based on safety concerns, such as might arise in physical education classes or science labs.[55]

In 2007, in the wake of significant public debate over accommodation of religious beliefs, the government of Quebec established a Consultation Commission on Accommodation Practices Related to Cultural Differences (commonly known as the Bouchard-Taylor Commission). The commission made a number of recommendations in 2008, most surrounding promotion of multiculturalism and better integration strategies for immigrants, most of which were not adopted by the government. Subsequently the Quebec government proposed Bill 94 (*An Act to establish guidelines governing accommodation requests within the Administration and certain institutions*), which required persons seeking government services to show their face. The legislation would have particular effect on women who wear niqabs, burkas, and other head-covering clothing, and ignited a firestorm of controversy from those who claimed that the bill was unfairly targeting Muslim women. Interestingly, although the bill was first introduced in 2010, more than two years later, it has not yet been proclaimed.

A case that drew significant interest in Europe involved a United Kingdom school's refusal to allow students to wear a jilbab (a strict form of Islamic dress for women, consisting of a full-length shapeless garment that covers the body) as a part of their school uniform.[56] The case proceeded to the House of Lords, the majority of whom found that the school's refusal did not infringe on the student's religious rights. As one author noted in a published case comment:

> The *Begum* case and the questions it raises can be seen as a microcosm of the increasing social and legal dilemma facing Britain and indeed much of Western society as longstanding tensions between the proper place of the "divine and the secular" in the classroom are joined by clashes grounded in differences within and among Christian and non-Christian religions. What is at stake in such cases as *Begum* is the social and legal ground where "family values" intersect with the classroom. As Laura Lundy suggests, the classroom today is the theatre where "family values" meet "the public domain." The question remains: Will family values and public interest either "clash" or "cohabitate," especially when religious beliefs and cultural practices are at stake?[57]

With the growing multiculturalism of Canadian society, issues of religious and cultural accommodation in our schools are critical. In this regard, religion is often used as a proxy for culture and, in the post-9/11 world, the accommodation of both the religion and culture of Islam are controversial.[58] Apart from the above issues of religious apparel such as the niqab or burka, there are also questions of whether prayer rooms should be provided for Muslim prayers to Mecca. These issues are particularly pronounced in larger urban areas such as Toronto, Montreal, and Vancouver.

In an interesting article, Justice Peter Lauwers of the Ontario Superior Court of Justice explores the challenges of pluralism in modern Canada.[59] He suggests that too often Canada has exhibited convergence pluralism, whereby new groups and cultures are absorbed into the mainstream. In that sense Canada has resembled the American melting pot model. Justice Lauwers advocates accommodation pluralism of the kind advocated by Canadian philosopher Charles Taylor—a variant of pluralism more consistent with the cultural mosaic that Canada has traditionally claimed.

The extent to which Canada rises to the challenges of accommodating our growing diversity helps to define the identity of the nation. It also provides a contrast with how such issues are handled in the United Kingdom, France, and the United States. This is particularly true with respect to the growing Muslim population in all these countries. Schools provide one of the early and most significant venues for striking the proper balance between accommodating religious and cultural differences and advancing Canadian core values.

Accommodation of diversity does not always involve cultures beyond Canadian borders. Since the first arrival of the Europeans in what is now Canada, the treatment of First Nations peoples has been problematic. The tragic experiences of First Nations students in residential schools have now been recognized as a shameful chapter in Canadian history and, in 2010, resulted in an apology from Prime Minister Stephen Harper. A recent report that was jointly sponsored by the federal government and the Assembly of First Nations calls for significant changes in the education of First Nations students, including a better accommodation of their unique heritages and cultures.[60]

Another interesting example of freedom of religion exercised by students in a school setting was raised in *Kingston v. Board of Trustees Central Okanagan.*[61] This case involved the indefinite suspension of students who refused on religious grounds to attend coeducational gym classes. In a successful application for an interim injunction to return their children to school, the parents established that compulsory participation in coeducational gym classes might be in violation of their rights to religious freedom under section 2 of the Charter. This point was not finally determined because the case did not proceed to trial.

This case raises an interesting potential for student–parent conflict. It is easy to imagine a situation in which parents, on the basis of their religious beliefs, prohibit their children from participating in coeducational gym classes. The children might not agree with the restriction. It is conceivable that where the parents have made an arrangement with the school to have their children excluded, a rational 17-year-old student could approach a gym teacher and ask that she be allowed to attend the gym class in spite of her parents' request. The teacher is then faced with a direct conflict between the student's independent exercise of her religious rights and the parents' claim over the religious beliefs of their child. This is a difficult issue to resolve. It might be settled at a meeting of school administrators, the parents, and the student, but could ultimately be resolved in a court.

In Canada and the United States, a number of parents have argued for the right not to send their children to the public schools on the basis of religion. In *R. v. Jones,*[62] a parent was charged with three counts of truancy under Alberta law. He defended the charges by arguing that the requirement that his children attend public school, and even the requirement that he must apply for an exemption from attendance, violated his religious beliefs and was an infringement of his section 2(a) Charter rights to freedom of religion and section 7 rights to life, liberty, and security of the person. The Supreme Court of Canada held that the province had a right to place reasonable limits on the parent's rights because of the "compelling" interest of the province in the education of the young.[63] The court found the requirement that people who wish to educate their children at home must apply for certification from the province, although an infringement of individual religious freedom, was justified under section 1, because such a require-ment constituted a minimal intrusion on religion.[64] It is clear from modern case law that courts have upheld the idea that education is important without requiring the provinces to prove repeatedly why education is a pressing and substantial objective sufficient to override Charter rights to freedom of religion.

Freedom of Expression

In Canadian law, the right to freedom of expression comes from section 2(b) of the Charter. A large volume of case law in the Supreme Court of Canada has helped to clarify the extent of this right. It is important to keep in mind the section 1 limits that accompany these Charter rights. The Supreme Court of Canada has protected the widest possible definition of expression, includ-ing hate propaganda and speech with violent content; but expression with violent form (such as intentional damage to property—for example, breaking the window of a politician's car) is not protected. Governments have been successful in justifying limits on freedom of expression. In *R. v. Keegstra*,[65] a case about a teacher who was dismissed for giving anti-Semitic lectures and who was convicted of unlawfully promoting hatred against an identifiable group, the Supreme Court of Canada upheld a Canadian law that criminal-ized the dissemination of hate propaganda. The court ruled that the distri-bution of such material directed at an identifiable group significantly impaired the rights of persons in that group to participate in society.

There has been minimal case law regarding the issue of freedom of ex-pression for students in Canada. *Lutes*,[66] in which a grade 9 student asked the court to suspend implementation of his in-school detention until the issue could be addressed at trial, is one of the few cases on student freedom of expression in Canada. The student was given a detention for singing the banned song "Let's Talk About Sex." Although the judge considered the Charter applicable, the court decided not to grant an injunction. In other words, the student had to serve his lunchtime detentions before the trial and, if he won at trial, the school would compensate him for that lost time. Although this case appears to endorse students' rights to freedom of expres-sion in schools, it is important to remember that this case never actually reached the trial stage.

The above cases do not express a definitive Canadian stance because they are lower court decisions. No high court in Canada has yet made a statement about student rights to freedom of expression. It is helpful to look to US case law to see the direction in which Canadian law may turn. The leading US case on expression in the schools was for many years *Tinker v. Des Moines*

Independent Community School District.[67] This case involved a group of high school students who were suspended for wearing black armbands to protest the Vietnam war. The US Supreme Court found that these suspensions violated the free speech provisions of the First Amendment and asserted that students do not "shed their constitutional right to freedom of speech at the schoolhouse gate." There is no reasonable limits clause in the US constitution; however, the US Supreme Court discussed the limits on the students' freedom of speech. The issue was whether the actions of the students created a "material and substantial disruption." The compelling logic of this type of test makes it likely that Canadian courts could adopt a similar test.

Another US case, although dated, is also instructive. In *Bethel School District No. 403 v. Fraser,*[68] the US Supreme Court considered whether a school district's disciplinary action against a student for making a lewd speech at a school assembly violated his First Amendment rights. The school met with the student to allow him an opportunity to explain his behaviour, and, after he admitted his conduct, suspended him for several days and removed his name from a list of candidates for graduation speaker. The student and his parents sought the court's review of the disciplinary decision. Although the lower courts found that the student's rights to free speech had been violated, the Supreme Court held that school districts have the right to maintain order and discipline, noting "[t]he First Amendment does not prevent the school officials from determining that to permit a vulgar and lewd speech as Respondent's would undermine the school's basic educational mission."[69]

In 2007, the US Supreme Court placed significant limits on the protections offered to students in the *Tinker* decision. In *Frederick v. Morse*[70] ("*Morse*"), a student was disciplined by the school principal after holding up a sign at a school function that read "Bong Hits 4 Jesus." Principal Morse took the position that the ten-day suspension she imposed on the student was justified on the basis that the sign was a violation of school policy against the promotion of drug use. The Supreme Court, in a 5–4 decision, upheld the discipline. The majority found that, although students have some rights to political speech in school, the right does not extend to pro-drug messages that might impact the school's anti-drug stance. US and Canadian legal commentators have suggested that this decision undercuts the substantial disruption test from *Tinker*, potentially further limiting freedom of speech for American students.[71]

VIOLENT EXPRESSION AND CENSORSHIP

Teachers may become concerned with freedom of students' expression in the content of class assignments or on the school playground. When students are free at work or at play, their actions may startle or shock their teachers. A number of years ago, the national media took an interest in one Nova Scotia primary student who was suspended twice in one year for pointing at a classmate and pretending to shoot by saying "Bang"; the first time the student pointed with his finger and the second time he pointed with a chicken finger at lunch.[72] Obviously, the immediate physical danger posed by this type of behaviour is low, but fear of violence is high in light of widely publicized school shootings, beatings, and bullying in both Canada and the United States.

The Supreme Court of Canada has stated that part of a teacher's duty is to be aware of his role in transmitting values, something that occurs subtly but constantly.[73] A unanimous court held that teachers must be seen to uphold the values that Canada's education systems seek to transmit. However, when the content of children's expression is violent in school, competing rights emerge. Ultimately, school officials and teachers need to find a balance between a student's right to freedom of expression (including the right to express violent ideas and create violent images) and the generally presumed right of the rest of the school community to be free from exposure to that expression and to inhabit a safe school. Two critical questions need to be answered. Where a child's expression contains violent content, is the child's right to free expression being respected? And where limits are necessary to preserve a safe school environment, are they justifiable in a free and democratic society, as required by section 1 of the Charter?[74]

Although there is no question that maintaining a safe school environment is an important objective, debate continues to rage over whether the means used to achieve it (often censorship) is actually useful in preventing violent behaviour. If censorship is applied, students will learn to hide what they feel for fear of provoking punishment. As well, censorship does not teach students about why violent content is a cause for concern. Moreover, censorship fails to recognize that if violent content is an early warning sign for future violent behaviour, prohibiting children from voicing their feelings may not be a proactive way to address safety concerns.

These comments should certainly not be taken as a minimization of the real concerns about violence in schools in an era that has witnessed Columbine, Taber, Red Lake, Virginia Tech, and Sandy Hook.[75] Teachers have an obligation to maintain a safe classroom and to be alert to signs of violence. We are not suggesting that all violent content is benign and should be tolerated.[76] Clearly, the burden on school officials under the Charter framework (to justify outright censorship of free expression) is a heavy one, but some kind of balance must be achieved.

The consequences of censoring violent content worsen as children grow older and as incidents of violence raise greater safety concerns. In 2000, an Ontario high school student who was a long-time victim of school bullies, identified only as E.B.J.,[77] wrote and presented a story to his drama class. The story, entitled "Twisted," was about "a boy who's been harassed and tortured all his life until he was at the brink of insanity." In the story, the bullied student sought revenge by planting explosives throughout the school. E.B.J. was arrested and spent more than a month in jail (including Christmas and his 16th birthday) during pre-trial custody. After finding no evidence that the student had actually planned any revenge, the Crown withdrew the charges against the student, who was suspended from school.

The Upper Canada District School Board's Eastern Region Safe School Committee recommended that the student be placed in an alternative educational setting and, until that placement could be effected, that the student be placed on home instruction. The student's family launched a civil lawsuit against the school board.[78] The court ruled there was sufficient evidence to support a conclusion that the involuntary home schooling constituted irreparable harm to the student. It did not, however, award the requested relief—money for private school tuition. The judge instead sought further evidence from the parties about available public school alternatives.

It is arguable that censorship is not the best strategy for addressing issues that arise when a student expresses violent ideas or creates violent images. We maintain that expressions of violent content, provided that there is no evidence of real physical threat, can be seen as an opportunity to generate intelligent dialogue in response to controversial expression. Careful and ongoing monitoring of the situation will, of course, be required.

DRESS CODES

The imposition of dress codes can give rise to complaints that students' rights to freedom of expression are being violated. We have often heard questions from teachers about T-shirts that display profane language, shorts, miniskirts, leggings, halter tops, and hats in schools. In *Devereux v. Lambton County R.C. Separate School Board*,[79] the Ontario High Court considered whether a school board policy requiring students to wear uniforms infringed the students' right to free speech. The judge in the case found that dress was not a significant part of a student's freedom of expression. The court ruled that to hold otherwise would "trivialize" the right to freedom of expression.

Although no legal action ensued, in spring 2012, there was wide media coverage of a dispute between a Nova Scotia school board and a student who came to school wearing a T-shirt with the slogan "Life is Wasted Without Jesus." Initially the student was suspended for five days for his refusal to stop wearing the shirt.[80] Following widespread media coverage and public debate, the school board reversed its decision and allowed the student to continue wearing the shirt. The school board further determined that this was a valuable opportunity for learning and planned learning sessions, with speakers from the Human Rights Commission and the Departments of Education and Justice, to spark discussions regarding religious tolerance. It is interesting that the student who originally wore the controversial T-shirt was removed from school by his father for the school discussions on religious tolerance.

Generally speaking, schools and teachers have a relatively wide range of discretion to restrict student expression in the school setting, particularly in cases that relate to dress. A more difficult problem arises in circumstances where a student chooses to have an extravagant hairstyle—for example, a spiked, red Mohawk.[81] Although it is possible for students to change their clothes after school and wear whatever clothing they wish, they cannot necessarily change their hairstyle. A school board may have a difficult time suspending students on the basis of their hairstyle choices.

STUDENT PUBLICATIONS

Where a student wants to run a student newspaper in a high school and the school is reviewing the material with an eye toward censorship, the school personnel should tread carefully, but should act appropriately, keeping in mind the "material and substantial" disruption test. Again, several US cases are instructive. In one 1986 US case,[82] a court acknowledged that schools may limit lewd or offensive speech as a means of inculcating values and providing appropriate role models for students. In 1988, another US court indicated that school administrators had the right to regulate written speech by students in the context of school curriculum or classroom activities.[83]

In *R. v. Burko*,[84] a Canadian pre-Charter case, the court found that the *Petty Trespass Act* prevailed over the rights of former students to distribute literature in school hallways. Since the Charter, it is clear that schools should carefully consider the methods they choose to balance a student's right to freedom of expression with the school's need for order and discipline. Some provinces, including Ontario, claim the authority to limit the distribution of unauthorized student publications. Section 24 of regulation 298, passed under the *Education Act* of Ontario, states:

> No advertisements or announcements shall be placed in school or on school property or distributed or announced to the pupils on school

property without the consent of the board that operates the school except announcements of school activities.

Schools must keep in mind whether distribution of the item will negatively affect proper order and discipline within the school.[85] This leads us back to the useful test of "material and substantial disruption."

ACCESS TO IDEAS

The question of access to ideas has been a hot-button issue in many school districts. The issue often revolves around the right of a school board or administrators to remove books from a school library or a school curriculum because of "objectionable" content. In the US case *Board of Education v. Pico*,[86] the school board removed a number of books from the school library and curriculum following administrators' attendance at a conservative conference. They claimed the books they removed were anti-American, anti-Christian, anti-Semitic, and "just plain filthy."[87] A group of plaintiffs brought a lawsuit on behalf of students, claiming that their First Amendment rights were curtailed by the defendants' actions. The majority of the court found that students had a First Amendment right to receive information as a component of their rights to free speech, a free press, and political freedom. Justice Brennan, for the majority of the court, stated, "Local school boards have broad discretion in the management of school affairs, but such discretion must be exercised in a manner that comports with the transcendent imperatives of the First Amendment."[88] Although the court acknowledged the necessity for school boards to have the right to amend the curriculum and to control school libraries, the majority noted that the board's discretion could not be exercised in a political manner and careful consideration of the First Amendment was required in making any such decisions. It will be interesting to see whether recent changes in the composition of the US Supreme Court alter this historical protection of students' rights.

A similar issue arose in one Canadian case,[89] when the Surrey School Board refused to authorize several books for elementary school classroom instruction because of the books' depiction of same-sex parent families. The Supreme Court of Canada found that the board had acted outside the scope of its mandate in refusing to authorize the use of the books. Chief Justice McLachlin noted, "if the school is to function in an atmosphere of tolerance and respect ... the view that a certain lawful way of living is morally questionable cannot become the basis of school policy."[90] She pointed out that the *School Act*, the board's governing statute, stressed secularism. When looked at in combination with Canada's constitutional commitment (via the Charter) to equality and minority rights, it is clear that the actions of the board, based on the religious beliefs of certain of its members, were not reasonable. It is apparent from these cases that the courts are no longer content to allow school administrators to make decisions without scrutiny to ensure compliance with statutory and constitutional law. The chief justice further stated:

[66] Exposure to some cognitive dissonance is arguably necessary if children are to be taught what tolerance itself involves. As my colleague points out, the demand for tolerance cannot be interpreted as the demand to approve of another person's beliefs or practices. When we ask people to be tolerant of others, we do not ask them to abandon their personal convictions. We merely ask them to respect the rights, values and ways of being of those who may not share those convictions. The belief that others are entitled to equal respect depends, not on the belief that their values are right, but on the belief that they have a claim to equal respect regardless of whether they are right. Learning about tolerance is therefore learning that other people's entitlement to respect from us does not depend on whether their views accord with our own. Children cannot learn this unless they are exposed to views that differ from those they are taught at home.

[67] The Board's concern with age-appropriateness was similarly misplaced. The Board's regulation on appropriate selection criteria requires it to consider the age-appropriateness of proposed supplementary materials. However, here the curriculum itself designated the subject as age-appropriate by stating that all types of families found in the community should be discussed by K-1 students, including same-sex parented families. The Board was not entitled to substitute its contrary view.[91]

THE UNTAMED INTERNET

The Internet has created a vast arena for expressing one's thoughts. This arena, which students often enter outside school hours, can have a substantial impact on students' lives and schooling.

By far one of the most talked-about current issues in education, also addressed at length in other chapters of this book, is cyberbullying (in particular, see Chapter 2, Teachers as Parents, under the heading "Bullying," and Chapter 4, Teachers as Guardians of Equality, under the heading "Bullying, School Violence, and Vulnerable Students"). As this text was being written, a BC teenager tragically took her own life after a long period of vicious cyberbullying.[92] Less than two weeks later, eight teenage girls were arrested at an Ontario high school for bullying another student.[93] The eight accused faced charges of criminal harassment for behaviour that allegedly included physical and emotional bullying and cyberbullying. It is at least somewhat positive to note that, in the Ontario arrests, police stated that information about the bullying came to them through an anonymous school-based reporting web portal, as well as through in-person reports.[94]

In *R v. W. (D.)*, the court considered when schoolyard taunts and bullying cross the line into criminal acts.[95] The court found one young woman guilty of the offence of criminal harassment against another student at her school after a number of schoolyard threats of violence. Tragically, the victim of this crime committed suicide before the case went to trial.

Bill Belsey, an Alberta educator, provides the following definition of cyberbullying:

> Cyberbullying involves the use of information and communication technologies to support deliberate, repeated, and hostile behaviour by an individual or group, that is intended to harm others.[96]

More recently, the Nova Scotia Task Force on Bullying and Cyberbullying provided the following definition of bullying generally, encompassing cyberbullying therein:

> [B]ehaviour that is intended to cause, or should be known to cause, fear, intimidation, humiliation, distress or other forms of harm to another person's body, feelings, self-esteem, reputation, or property. Bullying can be direct or indirect, and can take place by written, verbal, physical, or electronic means, or any other form of expression.[97]

Belsey reports that a 2002 British survey found that one in four youths, aged 11 to 19, has been threatened by means of computers or cellphones, and some have encountered death threats. Belsey further reports that there are 250,000 cases of bullying in Canadian schools every month.[98] More recent data notes that 60 percent of Nova Scotia students say they have been bullied,[99] while another recent study of Toronto schools reports that 49.5 percent of students surveyed reported being bullied online.[100]

The Nova Scotia Task Force Report noted that cyberbullying was particularly harmful to students because of the speed with which content can spread:

> The immediacy and broad reach of modern electronic technology has made bullying easier, faster, more prevalent and crueler than ever before.
>
> ... [C]yberbullying follows you home and into your bedroom; you can never feel safe, it is "non-stop bullying." ... [I]t invades the home where children normally feel safe, and it is constant and inescapable because victims can be reached at all times and in all places.[101]

The potentially detrimental effects on students are clear. Indeed, the Nova Scotia Task Force was born out of a series of high profile suicides by young school girls, in part linked to cyberbullying. But what can schools do about it? The conduct occurs most often off school grounds, but has a considerable impact on the school environment. The Nova Scotia Task Force recommends that school jurisdiction extend to off-ground and after-hours conduct that has a detrimental effect on the school climate.[102] This extended jurisdiction already exists in the Ontario *Education Act*.

There is a significant challenge for schools to protect students' Charter right to free speech and freedom from unreasonable search, while at the same time providing students with a safe haven to learn and grow. Eric Roher, in a 2002 article,[103] noted that schools are often faced with the question of what their role should be with regard to unauthorized messages and websites on the Internet. In 1999, Canada became the first country in the world to connect every school and public library to the Internet. Over the past decade, increasing numbers of students have gained daily access to the Internet at home and at school.

With respect to freedom of expression in Internet activity that occurs outside the school setting, Roher reviewed US experiences and noted:

> In order for school officials to justify prohibition of a particular expression of an opinion, they must be able to show that their actions were caused by something more than a desire to avoid the discomfort and unpleasantness that accompany an unpopular viewpoint. The courts have held that to prohibit such conduct, it would have to be shown that the conduct would materially and substantially interfere with the requirements of appropriate discipline in the operation of the school.[104]

Because of a lack of case law in Canada, Roher notes that courts have not yet had the opportunity to provide school boards with direction regarding where the balance falls between the rights of students and the duties of school boards. It is safe to assume that the "material and substantial disruption" test from *Tinker v. Des Moines*[105] would apply. Schools may choose to respond proactively, by teaching students about responsible Internet use and providing parents with information about computer use by their children.

Another problem in many homes and schools is that children have computer skills that far outpace that of their parents and teachers. It is incumbent on teachers to be aware of what exists in cyberspace that may affect their classrooms and their students.

Further complicating matters is the anonymity often provided by the Internet. As noted in the Report of the Nova Scotia Task Force on Bullying and Cyberbullying:

Anonymity allows people who might not otherwise engage in bullying behaviour the opportunity to do so with less chance of repercussion. Because senders of electronic taunts or hate mail can't see the reaction of the recipient, they can be oblivious to the hurt they have caused.[106]

A recent decision of the Supreme Court of Canada may have an impact on the issue of anonymity for online bullying. In *A.B. v. Bragg Communications Inc.*,[107] a unanimous court considered the case of A.B., a 15-year-old girl who found that someone had posted a fake Facebook profile using her picture, a slightly modified version of her name, and other information that identified her. The page also included explicit sexual references and humiliating commentary about the girl's appearance. The girl's father sought an order from the courts of Nova Scotia requiring the Internet provider to disclose the identity of the person who published the profile so that the individual could be named in a defamation suit.

The family also asked for anonymity for the young victim from the court to seek the information and for a publication ban on the information contained on the page itself. The Nova Scotia Supreme Court granted the family's request for disclosure from the Internet provider, but denied the request for anonymity and the publication ban on the information contained on the page.[108] The Nova Scotia Court of Appeal reached the same conclusions.[109] The issue for the lower courts was that the girl and her father had not proven that there was evidence of harm to her that could justify the restricted access to the information about parties to the case. The Supreme Court of Canada, however, found that the protection of a child from the effects of cyberbullying was a compelling reason to justify restricting access to information about the name of the child, stating:

> [14] The girl's privacy interests in this case are tied both to her age and to the nature of the victimization she seeks protection from. It is not merely a question of her privacy, but of her privacy from the relentlessly intrusive humiliation of sexualized online bullying. ...
>
> [20] It is logical to infer that children may suffer harm through cyberbullying. Such a conclusion is consistent with the psychological toxicity of the phenomenon described in the Report of the Nova Scotia Task Force on Bullying and Cyberbullying chaired by Prof. A. Wayne MacKay, the first provincial task force focused on online bullying. ...
>
> [24] Professor MacKay's Report is consistent with the inference that, absent a grant of anonymity, a bullied child may not pursue responsive legal action.[110]

The court went on to grant the appeal, allowing A.B. and her father to proceed anonymously in her request for an order requiring Eastlink to disclose the identity of the person who created the fake Facebook page. This is a landmark case in advancement of the rights of victims of cyberbullying.

The legal issue of defamation is a complex one, particularly where the Internet, cyberbullying, and young people are involved. How Canadian courts will address these issues going forward, remains to be seen. As noted by one Canadian author:

> The ultimate test that Canadian courts use is how a reasonable, informed and thoughtful person would receive or react to the defamatory information and whether he or she would take it seriously or at face value. The question that remains is whether a court, in applying this test to a cyber-libel case of cyber-bullying among adolescents, would rule that because of their social immaturity, adolescents are not reasonably thoughtful or old enough to be sufficiently informed to dismiss the libel as untrue. Such a ruling, however, would benefit the victim because it suggests that the libelous statements on the Internet would be interpreted by most young people as true, causing even more damage to the victim's reputation than if he or she were an adult. This arguably places young perpetrators who are not sufficiently mature to realize the consequences of their actions at greater risk of liability.[111]

In *Ross v. New Brunswick School District No. 15*,[112] the Supreme Court of Canada imposed a duty on school boards to make schools discrimination-free zones. Although *Ross* specifically dealt with teachers' freedom of expression, it provides an important statement by the court about the responsibility of school boards in general toward their students. We suggest that teachers' responsibilities include keeping "an ear to the ground" to ensure that students have a safe and welcoming learning environment. Teachers should also use all available opportunities to discuss appropriate use of and interaction through the Internet.

There is also concern that schools may react in an overzealous fashion in an attempt to protect students and staff. One Minnesota student, backed by the American Civil Liberties Union, is suing her school district after a search of her Facebook and email accounts by school officials.[113] The 12-year-old student was punished on several occasions for comments made on Facebook and alleges that she was pressured into providing her passwords to school officials and a deputy sheriff. On one occasion, the inappropriate comment made by the student was about a school employee and, on another, the girl was reportedly discussing sex. The postings were not violent in nature. Further, the comments were not made using school computers or on school property. The lawsuit alleged violations of the student's First Amendment rights (to free speech) and Fourth Amendment rights (against unreasonable search and seizure).

The line between free speech and cyberbullying and other inappropriate forms of Internet communications is a difficult one in any environment, but becomes infinitely more so in an environment heightened by very real concerns about violence and vulnerable young people, and where staff have concerns about the protection of their reputations from online libellous statements from angry students. Even the application of what constitutes a "material and substantial disruption" is not an easy evaluation. This will certainly be an evolving area of education law.[114]

Peaceful Assembly and Freedom of Association

These aspects of sections 2(c) and (d) of the Charter have received a good deal of attention in the field of labour law, but have had little impact on the field of education. That is not to say that they lack the potential for controversy. One of the early cases on freedom of association concerned a sit-in by students at the University of Moncton in New Brunswick.[115] The court held that a group of students who took over the administration building to protest increased tuition fees could not rely on freedom of association to justify their actions because their rights had to be balanced with the rights of others to have unimpeded access to the university.

A more recent example of issues surrounding freedom of association issues in the university setting is the student street protests in Quebec surrounding proposed tuition increases, which ultimately helped to defeat the Charest government and the subsequent, and very unpopular, provincial laws to limit these street protests.

It does not take much imagination to foresee the problems that could arise in the public school context where, for example, high school students wish to form an extreme or militant religious group or other sensitive organization. Again, teachers should simply be aware of the reasonable limits section of the Charter and whether they can justify the denial of any such association. There is also a question of the extent to which schools should lead rather than follow public opinion on sensitive matters. Bill 13, the *Accepting Schools Act, 2012* in Ontario, encourages schools to allow students to form gay–straight alliance groups, certainly a form of free association. A debate was stirred when the Halton Catholic school board rescinded their ban on gay–straight alliances (in response to Bill 13), but still refused to allow such groups in their schools, instead directing new policy that encourages students to form groups called SIDE (safety, inclusivity, diversity, equity).[116]

It may also be that the courts would rely on the *Tinker* "material and substantial disruption" test to apply to the freedom of association issue by analogy.

Freedom of association has always been a bigger issue at universities than at elementary or high schools because of the distinct and active student groups that exist on many university campuses. The issue is now complicated by the question of whether the Charter applies to student activities on a university campus. This remains an open topic.

Enforcing School Rules in the Wake of the Charter

The foregoing discussion focuses on potential Charter problems in the delivery of educational services. There are a host of separate Charter issues that primarily involve school discipline and the making and enforcing of school rules. All levels of the school system hierarchy are involved in the discipline process, from provincial department officials, to school board members and administrators, to the classroom teacher. To understand their role, teachers need to take a bird's-eye view of the entire rule enforcement process. Bob Keel provides a useful review of students' rights and responsibilities in the rule enforcement process in his 1999 book on this topic.[117] The school rule process can be broken down into three phases:

1. making rules,
2. enforcing rules, and
3. penalizing for breach of rules.

Given this breakdown, a school board can be viewed as a microcosm of the larger political structure:

1. rule making is a legislative function;
2. rule enforcing is an administrative function; and
3. penalizing is a judicial function.

All rungs of the school hierarchy are involved in rule making at different levels. Education department officials and school board members spend most of their time formulating policy and drafting rules. School administrators and teachers are the primary rule enforcers and, in some respects, resemble a school police force. We discuss the policing aspect in Chapter 5. School administrators and school board members, as well as committees composed of both, also sit in a judicial capacity and determine the penalty for breach of a particular rule. The compartments are far from watertight because teachers and administrators may also get involved in rule formulation or the assessment of penalties. It is important to consider which of the rule-related functions is relevant to a particular set of facts because there are different Charter considerations for each function.

Rule Making

At the rule-making level, the major Charter concern is the actual content or substance of the rules. Rules that in substance violate principles contained in the Charter may be subject to challenge. We have already looked at many aspects of the Charter that can affect the delivery of education. School rules are similarly subject to scrutiny if they restrict, for example, freedom of expression or freedom of religion. One of the examples we referred to earlier was school dress codes, which might arguably be seen to violate a student's freedom of expression. School officials should look at the school rules in an effort to determine whether they constitute "reasonable limits" within the meaning of section 1 of the Charter. Whether or not there are Charter violations, it is a useful exercise for schools to look at all their rules to determine which ones are reasonable and to revamp those that are not.

As mentioned earlier, the burden of showing that a particular rule is a reasonable limit on a Charter right rests with the state agent who made the rule or who seeks to apply it. In the school context, this means that the school board, school administrator, or teacher must "demonstrably" justify the rule as a reasonable one "in a free and democratic society." This, in essence, involves asking the following questions: Why do we need this particular rule? What is its effect on the students? Is the rule unfair or arbitrary? In addition to answering these questions, the school officials will have to bring some convincing evidence to court to show why the objective of the rule could not be achieved without violating a Charter right. Courts will consider whether the value of achieving the objective is proportional to the Charter violation.

The Supreme Court of Canada has set a further requirement for the operation of section 1: the means used to sanction a particular behaviour must be reasonable and proportional to the ends sought.[118] Another limitation on the use of section 1, which we discussed earlier, is that the rule must be "prescribed by law."[119] What constitutes "law" in a school setting can be debated, but it would embrace school policies in some form. The safest course is to have the rules codified by the school and distributed to both parents and students at the beginning of the school term. This allows students to know when and how their conduct could violate a rule. In many cases, a thoughtful review of rules allows educators to avoid any conflict by "cleaning their own house."

Because teachers have such extensive contact with students, it is vital that they take an active role in the formulation of school rules. We recommend that, as a part of the annual year-end process in June, teachers set aside time to go through the school rules and determine whether any of them need amending or updating. It may also be useful to ask the student council or other representative student groups to be part of the process. Certainly, schools should get into the habit of formulating and distributing a school policy handbook to students at the beginning of each year. Most schools now do this. This will avoid a great deal of conflict with both students and parents, and it is good educational, as well as legal, practice. Fair process should be taught by example as well as precept.

Enforcing Rules

Although rule making is fairly distinct from rule enforcement and punishment, the line between administratively enforcing a rule and judicially setting a sanction is much less clear. The same people often both enforce the rule and deliberate on the penalty for its breach. In society, there is a clear line between the police, who enforce the law, and judges, who handle the sentencing. In the school setting, however, the principal may be the person who makes the rule, enforces it, and penalizes those who break it.

In Chapter 5, we discuss the teacher's role as an agent of the police in detail. The line between an educational state agent enforcing rules and a police agent enforcing the criminal law can often become blurred. This is primarily because many school problems span both areas. The current trend in schools is to rely more heavily on criminal law enforcement in cases where students have clearly broken the law. In the past, the paternal tendencies of educators led them to deal with some of these problems as in-school matters. This practice has now been replaced by a more standard reliance on criminal procedure in most schools. Teachers and administrators must now distinguish between situations in which they are enforcing a school rule and those in which they intend to use the criminal process. This is so because the evidentiary restrictions created by the *Youth Criminal Justice Act*[120] do not apply to school rules. We examine these evidentiary restrictions in detail in Chapter 5 under the heading "A School's Investigative Role." For now, we look at the enforcement of rules through the in-school process.

It is easy to think of school rules whose *content* does not violate the Charter, but whose *application* could violate Charter rights. For example, a rule that no teacher or students may use a cellphone in class is not discriminatory on its face; however, were the rule to be applied only to females or to students in grade 10, there would probably be grounds for an equality challenge. This is a problem of application, and not content. As will be discussed in Chapter 4, zero-tolerance policies that affect students from certain racial or ethnic groups more than other students are also of concern, because they raise questions about the discriminatory application of rules. This was the concern that led the Ontario Human Rights Commission to issue its report on Ontario's *Safe Schools Act, 2000*,[121] which is a part of the province's *Education Act*, and which led to changes in the implementation of that legislation.

The Safe Schools Act and the Youth Criminal Justice Act

Under Ontario's *Safe Schools Act, 2000*, both principals and teachers have the authority to suspend students: principals for up to 20 days and teachers for a single day only. The legislation also expands the authority to expel students to both principals and school boards. However, by far the most significant innovations in the *Safe Schools Act, 2000* were the mandatory suspension, expulsion, and police involvement components. Either suspension or expulsion were mandatory for a large number of infractions. Although there are several factors that may mitigate the use of suspension and expulsion—including a student's lack of ability to control or understand the consequences of her behaviour or the fact that the student's presence at the school constitutes an acceptable safety risk—there were concerns that these factors would not encompass diverse student needs. Many critics argued that these policies disproportionately affect minority students and students with special needs.[122] Another major criticism of the Ontario *Safe Schools Act, 2000* is that it fails to incorporate an Aboriginal perspective, leading to discrimination against Aboriginal students.

Ontario's *Safe Schools Act, 2000*, often called a "zero tolerance" policy, was much maligned by academics and practitioners because of its perceived lack of flexibility.[123] There has been a significant retreat from this law in Ontario and the zero-tolerance approach has been replaced by progressive discipline and more flexibility, as we discuss in Chapter 4.

Although not all provinces followed the statutory route taken by Ontario, many provinces implemented some variation of the approach in their school board policies and procedures. The *Safe Schools Act, 2000* focused on punishment for bad behaviour and isolation via mandatory suspension or expulsion for specified behaviours that are thought to threaten the safety of the school. It is described by some academics as a "throw the book at them" approach to behaviour control. New and more flexible approaches are now used to respond to matters such as school violence and bullying, as we explore in Chapter 4.

The *Youth Criminal Justice Act* also focuses on restoration and accountability, and it provides young people with the right to be informed of and to take part in their cases. If a young person is willing to admit his fault and to make amends to his victim, a court is likely to assign a light sentence. Many school administrators face the problem of what to do when the *Youth Criminal Justice Act* and provincial education legislation collide in the context of student behaviour that breaks school rules as well as criminal laws. Often the two systems of youth accountability operate on parallel streams.

Sarah Colman and Allyson Otten, counsel to the Ontario Principals' Association, address the problems that have haunted Ontario school administrators since the introduction of the *Safe Schools Act, 2000*.[124] They observe that much of the language used to describe student behaviour was "borrowed" from criminal law.[125] They argue that, by using criminal law terms, the Act suggests that the criminal justice system mirrors or determines a school's response to the behaviour. As well, they suggest that the apparent "criminalization" of behaviour results in victim and community assumptions that the school will be able to provide punishment of the criminal variety.

Another problem with the legacy of the *Safe Schools Act, 2000* is that while the school has the ability to mete out serious consequences, it has no corresponding obligation to provide rehabilitation. When schools expel students under the Act, they are supposed to be able to provide strict discipline programs for the expelled student; however, Colman and Otten report that this programming is often not available, especially in rural areas and in urban areas where demand outstrips capability.[126] These problems have been reduced by changes in legislation and a greater focus on mediation and restorative approaches.

One of the biggest criticisms of the *Safe Schools Act, 2000* was the lack of personal and community accountability for the misbehaving student. It is interesting, and troubling, that although the *Youth Criminal Justice Act* has increased the expectations of personal accountability for crimes committed by young offenders, the *Safe Schools Act, 2000* did not contain a similar expectation. Colman and Otten contrast this to the *Youth Criminal Justice Act*, which focuses on accountability as the pathway to extrajudicial measures instead of the traditional route to punishment. They argue that although the *Safe Schools Act, 2000* purports to offer accountability to the school community by means of suspension or expulsion, this is not a viable solution because it offers only a short-term reprieve to teachers and students, and may cause problems in the community as the misbehaving student is left to her own resources.[127]

Colman and Otten note as well that the community, including the victim, may play a role under the *Youth Criminal Justice Act* in determining appropriate reparations through youth justice committees and conferences. The *Safe Schools Act, 2000* made no provision for victim involvement.[128] This lack of policy, when combined with privacy legislation, means that victims may not even be able to find the name of the young offender who abused them or the consequences that the offender suffered as a result of the abuse. Colman and Otten recommend that schools and police services develop joint protocols and learn to understand the processes of each other's guiding statutes.[129] They also encourage the legislature to allow school principals more discretion in considering factors that may mitigate the behaviour of offending students and in determining the punishment or other consequences that are appropriate in the circumstances, particularly where the student acknowledges the wrongdoing.[130] Current education statues across Canada have taken account of many of these criticisms and the era of zero tolerance is largely a thing of the past.

There is an argument to be made that suspending or expelling students from school affects not only the student and her community and family, as a result of the loss of education, higher dropout rates, and increased antisocial behaviour, but also society as a whole. After evaluating the Act, Jennifer Trépanier and John Bell concluded that it contains an "unprecedented level of regulation ... [which] turns the Ontario discipline process on its ear by creating a multi level appeal process, hampering the discretion of decision makers, and creating uncertainty as to its processes."[131] In a follow-up article one year later, the same authors reviewed the first year under the new regime. They indicated that they felt the process had become "more legalistic, adversarial and more complex, and bears too close a resemblance to the criminal justice system."[132] The authors note that such an adversarial system is not suited to the school environment, where issues are better resolved through cooperation and teamwork. Fortunately, these arguments have been heard and the legacy of the *Safe Schools Act, 2000* is largely a matter of history. There is still room for improvement, but both the rules and their enforcement have advanced to a more remedial and progressive model, more in line with the *Youth Criminal Justice Act*.

Fair Process and Procedure

Another potential problem is the procedure by which the rules are enforced. While some provinces have detailed procedural codes, others afford students little in the way of procedural rights. Those provinces that provide minimal procedural rights may fall short of the fundamental justice guarantees contained in section 7 of the Charter. We discuss section 7 in Chapter 4 in respect to special education and inclusion. Section 7 may be used to challenge both the content and the procedure of government action. Thus, it could be used as the basis for a challenge to a rule so vague that it does not provide proper notice of its meaning and effect. Section 7 also imposes a constitutional form of Canadian due process, stating:

> 7. Everyone has the right to life, liberty and security of the person and the right not to be deprived thereof except in accordance with the principles of fundamental justice.

In applying section 7 within the school context, we are assuming that education is encompassed within the phrase "liberty and security of the person." There could also be cases of detention in the school context that would attract section 7 procedural protections. In essence, schools may not deprive a student of his "liberty"—here, the freedom to pursue an education—without following some form of due process. Due process does not involve full court procedures in this context; however, it necessarily involves giving a student advance notice of the rule, the opportunity to state his position in relation to its alleged breach, and the right to know the case against him.[133] Some of these fair-process principles existed before the Charter came into force in 1982.

In *Gianfrancesco v. Junior Academy Inc.*,[134] an eight-year-old student with learning disabilities was expelled from her private school after she allegedly threatened the life of a classmate. The principal suspended the student for one day while she investigated the claim but, after receiving complaints from parents of other students, the principal met for five minutes with the student before deciding to expel her. The expelled student's father brought an action for damages. The court allowed the claim, finding that, although the standards of procedure for a private school might be lower than those for public schools, there still existed an implied duty of procedural fairness. In this case, the court held that the five-minute meeting that the principal held with the student did not amount to a hearing, which the rules of procedural fairness require. These rules did not require a formal oral hearing, but the parents and student had a right to hear and respond to the case before them. Because this case arose in a private school, the Charter did not apply, but the common-law rules of fair procedure still did.

It is important for a classroom teacher to be aware of the potential difficulties in responding to a case that is brought before a school board and to document incidents properly. Challenges under section 7 of the Charter are primarily based on improper documentation of the events and allegations that the student did not have proper notice of the case to be met. These documentation issues raise the problem of maintaining proper student records in the schools. All of the provincial education acts require schools to maintain records that contain all information relevant to the improvement of the instruction of students. A detailed review of student record requirements is beyond the scope of this book because it is an institutional issue for administrators and provincial policy makers to decide. However, teachers should certainly note student behaviour in student files and relay any and all issues to the principal. Today, when concerns about privacy and freedom of information are heightened, use of and access to personal information is subject to growing student scrutiny.[135]

Aside from the Charter, provincial education statutes may require the school to keep proper notation of student behaviour for a potential suspension or expulsion hearing. For example, the Nova Scotia *Education Act* required a student to be persistently disobedient in order to be suspended.[136] Therefore, the school had to provide evidence of dates, times, and details of the incidents of persistent disobedience. As a result of a recent amendment, the Nova Scotia focus is on disruptive and severely disruptive behaviours, but the need for documentation is still there.[137]

Penalizing for Breach of Rules

Although most sanctions can be challenged as infringing a liberty or security interest under section 7 of the Charter, judges will certainly not ban all forms of discipline in schools. Thus, suspensions, fines, and the recording of negative comments in student records are likely to be acceptable, as long as they are enforced fairly and consistently. Similarly, detentions are likely to be acceptable if they are not so lengthy as to constitute cruel and unusual treatment under section 12 of the Charter. Some areas have a statutory maximum (for example, 30 minutes) in their regulations on detentions. The current trend in many schools across the country is away from expulsion and toward in-school suspensions. Rather than holding children after school or during lunch hour, schools have opted for suspensions that last from one to three days as a more effective means of discipline. Some Ontario schools have taken this trend a step further, creating a program called PASS, or positive alternative to school suspensions. This program allows students to serve their suspension in a supervised setting, off school grounds, thus preserving the safety of other students. Nova Scotia has a similar system, as do other provinces. While suspended, students are still expected to engage in schoolwork. Courts will probably find this type of educational policy to be consistent with the Charter.

The critical Charter section with regard to penalizing students for breach of rules is section 12:

> Everyone has the right not to be subjected to any cruel and unusual treatment or punishment.

The first question to be considered is whether section 12 of the Charter applies to schools at all. In the United States, the cruel and unusual punishment provision was not applied to schools.[138] The US Supreme Court restricted a similar provision to apply only in a criminal law context. The historical context and the draft statutes on which the provision was based indicated to the court that its purpose was to protect criminals from abuse. This reasoning is reinforced by the reference in the provision to excessive incarceration and fines as well as by the use of the word "punishment."

It is possible to argue in the Canadian context that section 12 of the Charter has a wider application because it does not have the same origins as the US Eighth Amendment and because it makes no reference to bail or fines that would limit it to the criminal context. It may also be significant that the Charter uses the word "treatment" as well as the word "punishment." "Treatment" has a broader meaning than "punishment," and has fewer criminal connotations. On this basis, it is possible that a Canadian court might find that section 12 prevents school officials from subjecting students to cruel and unusual treatment or punishment. The issue is likely to boil down to a section 1 analysis of whether the treatment or punishment used by the school is "reasonable" in the circumstances.

Most penalties could be administered in a way that violates section 12; however, the section will most probably be applied to penalties that, by their very nature, violate the prohibition against cruel and unusual punishment. The most logical candidate for concern is corporal punishment. Corporal punishment has now largely been removed from schools in most provinces. If not strictly prohibited by legislation, it is prohibited by many school boards. Nonetheless, the authority to use reasonable force for correction is still protected in section 43 of the *Criminal Code.*

A 2004 Supreme Court of Canada case, *Canadian Foundation for Children, Youth and the Law v. Canada (Attorney General)*,[139] addressed the issue of corporal punishment. The court considered the constitutionality of section 43 of the *Criminal Code*, which provides a defence for parents, teachers, and persons standing in the place of a parent who use "force by way of correction toward a pupil or a child." Although the majority of the court upheld the section, the court split on whether section 43 should still apply to teachers (the majority held that it did). Chief Justice McLachlin considerably narrowed the section by "reading in" a number of qualifiers. She explained that the section did not justify hitting children under 2 (because they are not able to comprehend the corrective aspect of the action), hitting children over 12, striking children on the head, or using an object such as a belt or a ruler to strike a child. She also noted that force that is "reasonable in the circumstances" cannot, by definition, be "cruel or unusual." McLachlin C.J. went on to clarify that corporal punishment, as opposed to corrective force, is unreasonable and not protected by section 43. Therefore, it is clear that any provinces or individual boards that allow corporal punishment must change their regulations to meet the standards imposed by this decision. It is noteworthy that the Supreme Court found that section 43 did not violate section 7, 12, or 15 of the Charter. There was a strong dissent from Justice Louise Arbour.

The decision of the court in *Canadian Foundation for Children* illustrates the extent to which the courts remain willing to defer to front-line educators with respect to the discipline of students. The court quickly dismissed arguments based on sections 7 and 12. It found no violation of section 15 without having to resort to the reasonable limits provision in section 1 of the Charter. Surprisingly, the court concluded that removal from children of the option of a criminal assault charge was not a violation of the dignity interest of children. The court is clearly of the view that, in some contexts, adults know better than children what is in children's best interests. This is a debate that will no doubt continue as the Charter continues to evolve.

Generally speaking, the same analysis used in *Canadian Foundation for Children* may be expanded to cover issues under section 12 of the Charter. Any time a teacher is imposing a form of treatment or punishment on a student, one consideration should be whether the discipline is appropriate in the circumstances and whether the child can appreciate the nature of the discipline. Obviously, teachers will have to be especially aware of this when working with children with special needs, because of the potential lack of appreciation by the individual student.[140]

Summary

In this chapter we have discussed the application of the Charter to schools and the broad parameters of some of these Charter rights. It is important for teachers to remember that their predominant role is as an educational state agent and to be aware of the expectations of that role. As this chapter indicates, this role has expanded significantly in recent years, a trend that is likely to continue. The Charter has had a major impact on the operation of schools and requires the balancing of order and student rights. As identified by the Supreme Court of Canada in *R. v. M. (M.R.)*,[141] schools must be involved in teaching Charter rights by example and justify limits on the rights of these in the schools.

NOTES

1   *Education Act*, R.S.N.S. 1918, c. 9, s. 93(1).

2   *Education Act*, S.N.S. 1995-96, c. 1, s. 26(1).

3   *Public Schools Act*, R.S.O. 1927, c. 323, s. 100.

4   *Education Act*, R.S.O. 1990, c. E.2, s. 264(1).

5   J. MacDonald, *The Discernable Teacher* (Ottawa: Canadian Teachers' Federation, 1970).

6   Ibid., at 4.

7   *Mahe v. Alberta*, [1990] 1 S.C.R. 342 (1990), 105 N.R. 321.

8   W.F. Foster and W.J. Smith, *Equality in the Schoolhouse: Has the Charter Made a Difference?* (Toronto: CAPSLE, 2003), 359. For an expansive discussion of Charter rights, see A.M. Watkinson, *Education, Students Rights and the Charter* (Saskatoon: Purich Publishing, 1999). Alberta courts have gone in a different direction in recent years. In *Calgary Roman Catholic Separate School District No. 1 v. O'Malley*, 2007 ABQB 574, the court considered the actions of a school board that sought to remove one of its trustees after a conflict of interest. Justice Clark ruled that the school board was "an essentially autonomous body [with] routine or regular control over the day-to-day operations of schools and the Minister of Education can intervene only in extraordinary circumstances" (at para. 131). Justice Clark ruled that the Charter was, therefore, inapplicable, because the board was not a government actor. He also found that the Charter did not apply to the decision as a "government action," because the case was about internal policies and administration of the board. In 2009, *Hamilton v. Rocky View School Division No. 41*, 2009 ABQB 225, the court concluded that the "method used to hire teachers is part of Rocky View's internal school management decision making and cannot be said to be a decision of the government or an activity in which the government is sufficiently involved to make it an act of the government." An appeal to the Court of Appeal was dismissed (2010 ABCA 217) and the Supreme Court of Canada dismissed a motion for an extension of time to file an application for leave to appeal and further noted that the application for leave to appeal would have also been dismissed (2011 CanLII 50143 (SCC)).

9   *British Columbia Public School Employers' Assn. v. B.C.T.F.* (2004), 2004 CarswellBC 2901, 129 L.A.C. (4th) 245 (Arb. Bd.); see also *J. (E.B.) (Litigation Guardian of) v. Upper Canada District School Board* (2001), 2001 CarswellOnt 3757 (S.C.J.).

10   See *R. v. M. (M.R.)*, [1998] 3 S.C.R. 393, which assumed, without deciding, that the Charter applies to schools. See also *Chamberlain v. Surrey School District No. 36*, [2002] 4 S.C.R. 710.

11   *Re Ontario English Catholic Teachers' Association et al. v. Essex County Roman Catholic School Board* (1987), 36 D.L.R. (4th) 114 (Ont. H.C.).

12   *McKinney v. University of Guelph*, [1990] 3 S.C.R. 229 (1990), 188 N.R. 1.

13   *Harrison v. University of British Columbia*, [1990] 3 S.C.R. 451, [1991] 1 W.W.R. 681.

14   *Stoffman v. Vancouver General Hospital*, [1990] 3 S.C.R. 483, [1991] 1 W.W.R. 577.

15   *Douglas/Kwantlen Faculty Assn. v. Douglas College*, [1990] 3 S.C.R. 570, [1991] 1 W.W.R. 643.

16   *Pridgen v. University of Calgary*, 2010 ABQB 644; affirmed *Pridgen v. University of Calgary*, 2012 ABCA 139.

17   This appears to be the opinion of the judge in *Lutes (Litigation Guardian of) v. Prairie View School Division No. 74* (1992), 101 Sask. R. 232, at para. 2 (Q.B.). In this case, a grade 9 student received a month-long noon-hour detention for singing a rap song during his noon recess. The contents of the song were offensive to a school official who overheard him, and the school punished the student for his actions. The student sought an injunction to prevent the school from enforcing his punishment until a court heard the matter. He argued that the school had violated his Charter right to freedom of expression. Counsel for the school posited that the Charter did not necessarily apply to schools. The judge disagreed, saying that the student had raised a good argument to apply the Charter to the school.

18   *R. v. M. (M.R.)*, supra note 10.

19   *O.T.F. v. Ontario (Attorney General)*, [2000] O.J. no. 2094 (Q.L.) (*sub nom. Ontario Teachers' Federation v. Ontario (Attorney General)*), 132 O.A.C. 218, 74 C.R.R. (2d) 247, 49 O.R. (3d) 257, 188 D.L.R. (4th) 333, 2000 CarswellOnt 1988 (C.A.); affirming [1998] O.J. no. 1104 (Q.L.), [1998] L.V.I. 2921-2, 37 C.C.E.L. (2d) 56, 1998 CarswellOnt 1129 (Gen. Div.); leave to appeal refused, [2000] S.C.C.A. no. 457 (Q.L.), 147 O.A.C. 400, 268 N.R. 195, 80 C.R.R. (2d) 187, 2001 CarswellOnt 495, 2001 CarswellOnt 494 (S.C.C.).

20   See *R. v. M. (M.R.)*, supra note 10.

21   Teachers are also protected against personal lawsuits in the school context by the doctrine of vicarious liability: see A.W. MacKay, *Education Law in Canada* (Toronto: Emond Montgomery, 1984), 133.

22   Amendment requires the assent of two-thirds of the provinces with 50 percent of the population and the consent of both the House of Commons and the Senate (*Constitution Act, 1982*, part V, s. 38).

23   *Youth Criminal Justice Act*, S.C. 2002, c. 1.

24   *Canadian Bill of Rights*, S.C. 1960, c. 44.

25   See *Ward v. Board of Blaine Lake School*, [1971] 4 W.W.R. 161 (Sask. Q.B.).

26   Proceeding with a case through to the Supreme Court of Canada can take over seven years and can easily cost in excess of $250,000. Some administrative agencies can also consider the Charter, but only in the context of other legal issues and, because these agencies have limited remedial power, the significant cases will still proceed through the courts.

27   *Borowski v. Canada (Minister of Justice)*, [1981] 2 S.C.R. 575, at 598.

28   *R. v. Jones*, [1986] 2 S.C.R. 284.

29   Ibid., at 318.

30   *R. v. Oakes*, [1986] 1 S.C.R. 103 (1986), 26 D.L.R. (4th) 200.

31   Ibid., at para 70.

32   Ibid., at para. 62.

33   See A.W. MacKay and L.I. Sutherland, "Making and Enforcing School Rules in the Wake of the Charter of Rights," in Y.L.J. Lam, ed., *Canadian Public Education System: Issues and Prospects* (Calgary: Detselig Enterprises, 1990), chapter 4, at 67; see also *Ontario Film and Video Appreciation Society and Ontario Board of Censors* (1983), 147 D.L.R. (3d) 58 (Ont. Div. Ct.); affirmed (1984), 5 D.L.R. (4th) 766 (Ont. C.A.).

34   *Irwin Toy Ltd. v. Quebec (Attorney General)*, [1989] 1 S.C.R. 927, at 983.

35   See *Hunter et al. v. Southam Inc.*, [1984] 2 S.C.R. 145 (1984), 55 N.R. 241, at 254 (S.C.R.).

36   But since *R. v. M. (M.R.)*, supra note 10, it is unlikely that a court would exclude any evidence obtained by a principal in a search, unless the search was highly unreasonable.

37   *Mooring v. Canada (National Parole Board)*, [1996] 1 S.C.R. 75, [1996] 3 W.W.R. 305, at para. 22.

38   See *Doucet-Boudreau v. Nova Scotia (Department of Education)*, 2003 SCC 62, [2003] 3 S.C.R. 3, 232 D.L.R. (4th) 577, at para. 51.

39   See, for example, *Doucet-Boudreau*, ibid., and *Wynberg v. Ontario*, 2005 CarswellOnt 1242, [2005] O.J. no. 1228 (Q.L.). Note, however, that the power to expand remedial jurisdiction extends only to the superior courts of the provinces, which have inherent powers. These inherent powers are not granted by statute, but by the very nature of the superior courts. Such powers allow a superior court to draw on its residual powers to control its own process and to control the procedure in the case before it.

40   *RJR MacDonald Inc. v. Canada*, [1994] 1 S.C.R. 311, 1994 CarswellQue 120.

41   *Tuli v. St. Albert Board of Education*, unreported decision, April 19, 1985 (Alta. Q.B.); Human Rights Board of Inquiry (December 23, 1986).

42   *Hall (Litigation Guardian of) v. Powers*, [2002] O.J. no. 1803 (Q.L.) (S.C.J.).

43   *Elwood v. Halifax County Bedford District School Board*, unreported decision, October 1986 (N.S.S.C.T.D.); see also J. Batten, "Luke's Case," in *On Trial* (Toronto: Macmillan, 1988), 135-206.

44   See *Bettencourt (Litigation Guardian of) v. Ontario* (2005), 2005 CarswellOnt 106 (S.C.J.), where the court granted an injunction requiring the province to continue to pay for an educational program for two children with autism outside the public school system pending an upcoming trial, because the court found that if the children were removed from the program, they would suffer irreparable harm.

45   *RJR Macdonald Inc. v. Canada*, supra note 40.

46   *Youth Criminal Justice Act*, S.C. 2002, c. 1.

47   For more on this subject, see M. Bastarache, ed., *Language Rights in Canada* (Montreal: Éditions Y. Blais, 2003). See also *Doucet-Boudreau v. Nova Scotia (Department of Education)*, supra note 38.

48   *Zylberberg v. Sudbury Board of Education* (1988), 65 O.R. (2d) 641 (C.A.).

49   *Corporation of the Canadian Civil Liberties Association et al. v. Ontario (Minister of Education) and Elgin County Board of Education* (1990), 37 O.A.C. 93 (C.A.).

50   *S.L. v. Commission scolaire des Chenes*, 2012 SCC 7, [2012] 1 S.C.R. 235.

51   *Elgin County*, supra note 49.

52   *Operation of Schools, General*, R.R.O. 1990, Reg. 298, s. 29.

53   *Multani v.Commission scolaire Marguerite-Bourgeoys*, 2006 SCC 6, [2006] 1 S.C.R. 256.

54   *Singh-Multani c. Marguerite-Bourgeoys (Commission scolaire)* (2004), 2004 CarswellQue
377, [2004] J.Q. no. 1904 (Q.L.) (*sub nom. Multani v. Commission scolaire Marguerite-
Bourgeoys*), 241 D.L.R. (4th) 336 (Que. C.A.); reversing (2002), 2002 CarswellQue 1237
(S.C.).

55   Commission des droits de la personne du Québec, *Religious Pluralism in Québec: A
Social and Ethical Challenge* (Montreal: CDPQ, 1995). For an interesting and recent
treatment on the topic of religious dress in Canadian schools, see W.H. Harris and
A. Ackah, "Freedom of Religion and Accommodating Religious Dress in Schools"
(2011) 20 *Education & Law Journal* 211.

56   *Begum v. Headteacher and Governors of Denbigh High School*, [2006] 2 All E.R. 487 (H.L.).

57   Yola Hamzo Ventresca, "Religious Dress in Schools: Balancing Religious
Accommodation, Family Autonomy, Free Choice and Equality" (2007) 17 *Education &
Law Journal* 245.

58   A. Wayne MacKay, "In Defence of the Courts: A Balanced Judicial Role in Canada's
Constitutional Democracy" (2006) 21 *National Journal of Constitutional Law* 183, at
237-242.

59   P. Lauwers, "The Ambiguities of Liberal Pluralism: A Canadian Perspective" (2007) 37
Supreme Court Law Review (2d) 1.

60   *Nurturing the Learning Spirit of First Nation Students: The Report of the National Panel on
First Nation Elementary and Secondary Education for Students on Reserve* (February
2012).

61   *Kingston v. Board of Trustees Central Okanagan* (1984), 1984 CarswellBC 2025 (S.C.).

62   *R. v. Jones*, supra note 28.

63   Ibid., at para. 23.

64   Ibid., at para. 28.

65   *R. v. Keegstra*, [1995] 2 S.C.R. 381 (1995), 124 D.L.R. (4th) 289.

66   *Lutes*, supra note 17.

67   *Tinker v. Des Moines Independent Community School District*, 21 L.Ed. 2d 733 (U.S.S.C.
1969).

68   *Bethel School District No. 403 v. Fraser*, 106 S. Ct. 3159, 92 L. Ed. 2d 540 (1986).

69   Ibid.

70   *Frederick v. Morse*, 127 S.Ct. 2618, 168 L.Ed. 2d 290 (U.S., Sup. Ct. 2007).

71   M. Arseneault Cooper, "Bong Hits for Jesus ... In Canada" (2008) 18 *Education & Law
Journal* 57.

72   *Toronto Sun*, July 31, 2001, at 4.

73   *Ross v. New Brunswick School District 15*, [1996] 1 S.C.R. 825. These conclusions were
unanimously supported by the justices of the Supreme Court of Canada in the
subsequent case of *Trinity Western University v. British Columbia College of Teachers*,
2001 SCC 31, [2001] S.C.R. 772.

74   A. Wayne MacKay and J. Burt-Gerrans, "Student Freedom of Expression: Violent
Content, Censorship, and the Safe School Balance" (2005) 40:3 *McGill Journal of
Education* 423.

75   Here we are referring to the widely publicized school shootings at Columbine High
School, Littleton, Colorado, and W.R. Myers High School, Taber, Alberta, in April 1999;
Red Lake High School, Minnesota, in March 2005; Virginia Tech, Blacksburg, Virginia,
in April 2007; and Sandy Hook Elementary School, Newtown, Connecticut, in
December 2012.

76   Expression that is harassing or discriminatory can be justifiably limited and teachers are required to address this kind of expression through their duty to maintain a safe and positive school environment. Some speech promoting the hatred of an identifiable group based on colour, race, religion, or ethnic origin may be an offence under sections 318 and 319 of the *Criminal Code*, R.S.C. 1985, c. C-46.

77   Only this young person's initials may be used to identify him because of requirements to protect a youth's identity under the *Youth Criminal Justice Act*, supra note 23.

78   *E.B.J. (Litigation Guardian of) v. Upper Canada District School Board*, [2001] O.J. no. 4174 (Q.L.) (S.C.J.).

79   *Devereux v. Lambton County R.C. Separate School Board*, unreported decision, October 31, 1988 (Ont. Div. Ct.), digested in (1988) School Law Commentary, Case File No. 3-5-12; cited in J. Wilson, *Wilson on Children and the Law* (Toronto: Butterworths), 8.57 (looseleaf).

80   " 'Jesus' T-Shirt Student Taken Out of School by Dad," CBC News online, http://www.cbc.ca/news/canada/nova-scotia/story/2012/05/07/ns-jesus-shirt-student-school.html; see also the *Chronicle Herald*, May 4, 6, and 8, 2012.

81   See *Ward v. Board of Blaine Lake School*, [1971] 4 W.W.R. 161 (Sask. Q.B.), where the court upheld a suspension for hair length.

82   *Bethel School District No. 403 v. Fraser*, 106 S. Ct. 3159, 92 L. Ed. 2d 540 (1986).

83   *Hazelwood School District v. Kuhlmeier*, 108 S. Ct. 562 (1988).

84   *R. v. Burko* (1968), 3 D.L.R. (3d) 330 (Ont. Mag. Ct.).

85   R.W. Weir, *Freedom of Expression and Unauthorized Student Publications* (Toronto: CAPSLE, 2001), 385.

86   *Bd. of Educ. v. Pico*, 457 U.S. 853 (1982).

87   Ibid.

88   Ibid.

89   *Chamberlain v. Surrey School District No. 36*, 2002 SCC 86, [2002] 4 S.C.R. 710.

90   Ibid., at para. 20.

91   Ibid., at paras. 60 and 67.

92   "B.C. Girl's Suicide Foreshadowed by Video," October 12, 2012, CBC News, online, http://www.cbc.ca/news/canada/british-columbia/story/2012/10/11/bc-maple-ridge-suicide.html.

93   "8 Ontario Girls Arrested in High School Bullying Case," October 19, 2012, CBC News online, http://www.cbc.ca/news/canada/story/2012/10/19/london-bullying-arrests-girls-cyber.html.

94   Ibid.

95   *R. v. W. (D.)*, 2002 CarswellBC 641.

96   cyberbullying.org, http://www.cyberbullying.ca.

97   A. Wayne MacKay, Q.C., Chair, "Respectful and Responsible Relationships: There's No App for That": The Report of the Nova Scotia Task Force on Bullying and Cyberbullying, February 29, 2012, at 42-43, online, http://www.cyberbullying.novascotia.ca.

98   As cited in MacKay, ibid.

99   Nova Scotia Cyberbullying Task Force Online Survey, Nova Scotia Department of Education (2011).

100   Faye Mishna, Charlene Cook, Tahany Gadalla, Joanne Daciuk, and Steven Solomon, "Cyber Bullying Behaviors Among Middle and High School Students" (2010) 80:3 *American Journal of Orthophsychiatry* 362.

101   MacKay, supra note 97, at 11. It is noteworthy that this passage was cited with approval by the Supreme Court of Canada in *A.B. v. Bragg Communications Inc.*, 2012 SCC 46, discussed below.

102   Nova Scotia Task Force, supra note 97, Recommendation 31, at 65. See also E. Roher, "Dealing with Off-School Conduct: Cyberbullying, Drug Dealing, and other Activities Outside of School Premises" (2012) 21 *Education & Law Journal* 91.

103   E. Roher, "Problems.com: The Internet and Schools" (2002) 12:1 *Education & Law Journal* 53.

104   Ibid. Roher extends this concept in his article cited at note 102.

105   *Tinker v. Des Moines*, supra note 67.

106   MacKay, supra note 97, at 11.

107   *A.B. v. Bragg Communications Inc.*, 2012 SCC 46.

108   *A.B. (Litigation Guardian of) v. Bragg Communications Inc.*, 293 N.S.R. (2d) 222, 2010 CarswellNS 397 (S.C.); additional reasons at *A.B. (Litigation Guardian of) v. Bragg Communications Inc.*, 297 N.S.R. (2d) 42, 2010 CarswellNS 766 (S.C.).

109   *A.B. (Litigation Guardian of) v. Bragg Communications Inc.*, 301 N.S.R. (2d) 34, 2011 CarswellNS 135, (C.A.).

110   *A.B. v. Bragg Communications Inc.*, supra note 107, at paras. 14, 20, and 24.

111   S. Shariff and L. Johnny, "Cyber-Libel and Cyber-Bullying: Can Schools Protect Student Reputations and Free-Expression in Virtual Environments?" (2007) 16 *Education & Law Journal* 307. See also S. Shariff, *Confronting Cyber-Bullying, What Schools Need to Know to Control Misconduct and Avoid Legal Consequences* (Cambridge: Cambridge University Press, 2009).

112   *Ross v. New Brunswick School District No. 15*, supra note 73.

113   "Minnesota Girl Alleges School Privacy Invasion," CNN U.S. online, http://www.cnn.com/2012/03/10/us/minnesota-student-privacy/index.html.

114   For a comprehensive discussion of cyberbullying as it relates to students' online comments about teachers, see R. Broster and K. Brien, "Cyber-Bullying of Educators by Students: Evolving Legal and Policy Developments" (2010) *Education & Law Journal* 35.

115   *Federation of Students of the University of Moncton v. University of Moncton*, unreported decision, December 22, 1982 (N.B.Q.B.).

116   "Halton Catholic Board SIDE-Steps Gay–Straight Alliances," *The Globe and Mail*, April 5 2011, online, http://www.theglobeandmail.com/news/toronto/halton-catholic-board-side-steps-gay-straight-alliances/article598546.

117   R. Keel, *Student Rights and Responsibilities: Attendance and Discipline* (Toronto: Canada Law Book, 1999).

118   *R. v. Oakes*, [1986] 1 S.C.R. 103 (1985), 24 C.C.C. (3d) 321.

119   The judges in *Ontario Film and Video Appreciation Society v. Ontario Board of Censors* (1984), 5 D.L.R. (4th) 76 (Ont. C.A.) insisted that a policy manual be written and made public before it could be used as a section 1 justification.

120   *Youth Criminal Justice Act*, S.C. 2002, c. 1.

121   *Safe Schools Act, 2000*, S.O. 2000, c. 12, s. 3.

122 Eric Roher, "Will the New Safe Schools Legislation Make Ontario Schools Safer?" (2007) 17 *Education & Law Journal* 203.

123 Ibid.

124 S. Colman and A. Otten, "The Safe Schools Act and the Youth Criminal Justice Act: Different Approaches to Justice for Youth" (2005) 14 *Education & Law Journal* 287.

125 Ibid., at 289.

126 Ibid., at 290.

127 Ibid., at 296.

128 Ibid., at 296-297.

129 Ibid., at 298.

130 Ibid., at 298-299.

131 J.P. Bell and J. Trépanier, *The Safe Schools Act of Ontario: A Lesson for the Rest of the Country—How Not to Do It* (Toronto: CAPSLE, 2001), 369.

132 J.P. Bell and J. Trépanier, *The Safe Schools Act, One Year Later: Lessons Learned* (Toronto: CAPSLE, 2002), 1.

133 See *Goss v. Lopez*, as discussed in G.M. Dickinson and A.W. MacKay, *Rights, Freedoms and the Education System in Canada: Cases and Materials* (Toronto: Emond Montgomery, 1989).

134 *Gianfrancesco v. Junior Academy Inc.*, [2001] O.J. 2730 (Q.L.), 2001 CarswellOnt 2383 (S.C.J.).

135 For further discussion on this important topic, see B. Stokes Vernon, *An Educators' Guide to Freedom of Information* (Aurora, ON: Canada Law Book, 1999).

136 *Education Act*, S.N.S. 1995-96, c. 1, s. 121.

137 Bill 102 revised the wording of section 26(1)(l) of the Act from "is persistently defiant or disobedient" to "engages in severely disruptive behaviour including bullying or cyberbullying." The bill passed first reading in the fall of 2012 and awaits debate in the House.

138 *Ingraham v. Wright*, 430 U.S. 651 (1977).

139 *Canadian Foundation for Children, Youth and the Law v. Canada (Attorney General)*, 2004 SCC 4, [2004] 1 S.C.R. 76.

140 For a clear example of this principle, see *Ogg-Moss v. R.*, [1984] 2 S.C.R. 173.

141 Supra note 10.

4

Teachers as Guardians of Equality

Introduction

Teachers are well placed to promote equality and to act as exemplars for young people. This chapter addresses areas in which teachers can educate and exemplify equality. The case law involving various educational issues provides teachers with some clarity, and in some instances, additional fodder for debate.[1] Teachers must lead by both precept and example and teaching the Charter value of equality is an increasingly important role in an ever-more diverse and multicultural Canada. The need to be truly inclusive is one of the major challenges facing schools today and into the future.

As discussed in previous chapters, the *Canadian Charter of Rights and Freedoms* ("the Charter") has had a dramatic impact across the entire spectrum of education. One of its most significant effects has been in the field of special education, particularly with regard to the inclusion of children with special needs into regular classrooms. Parents of disabled children have seen the Charter as their means for achieving suitable educational placements and programming for their children. The Charter contains two provisions that have an impact on special education: sections 7 and 15:

> 7. Everyone has the right to life, liberty and security of the person and the right not to be deprived thereof except in accordance with the principles of fundamental justice.

• • •

15(1) Every individual is equal before and under the law and has the right to the equal protection and equal benefit of the law without discrimination and, in particular, without discrimination based on race, national or ethnic origin, colour, religion, sex, age, or mental or physical disability.

(2) Subsection (1) does not preclude any law, program or activity that has as its object the amelioration of conditions of disadvantaged individuals or groups including those that are disadvantaged because of race, national or ethnic origin, colour, religion, sex, age, or mental or physical disability.

Section 7 of the Charter has been designated by many commentators as the heart of a constitutional guarantee to education in Canada. Certainly, it is possible to make a strong argument that, in today's society, there is no quality of life, liberty, or security of the person unless a person has a basic education.[2] These arguments are more compelling in the context of the Charter because of its express guarantees of the collective right of citizens to education in the context of denominational schools and the right to minority language education in other sections. It seems inconsistent to constitutionally protect specific types of education without protecting the right to education itself. The section 7 argument has not been extensively or successfully litigated. This may be because it is often combined with equality claims under section 15(1), which has received more attention from the courts. Section 7, however, has been used as a constitutional reinforcement of the statutory and common-law guarantees of fair process. Fair process means, at minimum, the right to be heard before an unbiased decision maker.

Many provincial departments of education have now instituted detailed procedural provisions dealing with both classification and placement of children with special needs. These often include comprehensive appeal procedures.[3] In the past, courts have been reluctant to delve into the merits of the program or placement decision or add much to the procedural structure provided by statute. In one early integration case from Ontario, *Bales v. Board of School Trustees (Okanagan)*,[4] the judge emphasized that fair procedure in an educational context need not involve a full-blown court process. This case involved a dispute between a school board that wanted a mentally disabled child placed in a segregated school for special needs and the parents who wanted their child in the special education class offered by the regular neighbourhood school. The parents were unsuccessful because they failed to demonstrate that the school's placement was unreasonable.

In *B. (J.) v. Nova Scotia (Minister of Education)*,[5] the educational plan for a child with Down's syndrome was the issue between the child's mother and the school board. The mother withdrew the child from school for one year, but registered him the following year because she sought to appeal a placement decision. As a result of the child's removal from school, there was no current educational plan in place for the child when the mother sought her appeal. Without a current educational plan, the minister of education refused to create an appeal board to hear the mother's concerns. The Court of Appeal upheld the school board processes with respect to special education appeals, and declined to require the minister of education to put together an appeal board to hear the matter.

In the groundbreaking integration case, *Elwood v. Halifax County Bedford District School Board*,[6] procedural irregularities and a lack of meaningful parental involvement in the classification and placement of their child were essential to the case, which was eventually settled out of court. As one consequence of this case, a process allowing more parental involvement in decisions about a child's education emerged, which has now been fortified by regulations.

For teachers, the relevant aspect of these procedural guarantees is that parents should always be provided with appropriate information about and notice of the type of classroom setting that they can expect for their child, either in an inclusive or segregated class. In an inclusive setting, the primary responsibility often rests with the classroom teacher in collaboration with special needs experts (such as special education teachers) to determine whether the child can receive an appropriate education in a regular classroom. In recent years, there has been a trend for some parents to request segregated classrooms or funding for private school tuition because they find their child increasingly vulnerable in an inclusive setting.[7] Inclusion is not a panacea for the complex needs of all students, although inclusive schooling has enjoyed substantial success. The failures of inclusive schooling often arise from underfunding and issues of implementation rather than from problems with the concept itself.

Many teachers voice the concern that the ordinary stressors of a classroom of 25 to 30 children do not allow for effective programming for children with special needs. It is up to teachers to properly document the progress of special needs children in their classroom in order to provide the parents and the school board with accurate information on which to base decisions about programming changes. If the matter were to come before the courts, a judge would be very interested in the classroom teacher's view of the child's abilities and needs. Courts are still quite deferential to the expertise of the front-line teachers.

The equality rights embodied in section 15 of the Charter have proved the most effective tool for parents challenging school board authority in the area of special needs education. The Supreme Court of Canada has reviewed this section numerous times, and has provided guidance on its interpretation.[8] In essence, the court has determined that not all forms of discrimination violate section 15. Only discrimination that amounts to prejudice or stereotyping and has an adverse impact on the individual will be subject to Charter scrutiny. An earlier emphasis on human dignity is still relevant but is not as central to equality analysis as before. Therefore, in the context of special education, the matter becomes a "battle of the experts" to determine whether an inclusive or a segregated classroom will have the most beneficial effect on the student. Obviously, both regular classroom and special education teachers have an important role to play in providing evidence of a child's abilities and suitable programming. Most provinces identify the regular classroom as the best option, where feasible, but also emphasize that one size does not fit all students.

It is important to remember that, in any given case, these issues may ultimately be determined in an adversarial litigation process. A parent whose child has been identified as requiring a special program plan, but who desires more extensive or customized supports, must come to court and establish a breach of her child's rights. Part of her case must include evidence of adverse impact. Once the parent demonstrates an adverse impact, it will be up to the school board to establish that any limitation placed on the child's equality rights is reasonable, within the meaning of section 1 of the Charter. To do that, the school board is well advised to have written policies and procedures for dealing with special needs children. Teachers can play a vital role in developing these policies and procedures. Giving some input to parents is also beneficial, and can enhance the fairness of the process.

Human Rights Tribunals as an Alternate Route to Equality: The Landmark Moore Case

In addition to the Charter guarantee of equality in section 15, provincial human rights legislation (which applies to both the public and the private sectors) also prohibits discrimination on a range of grounds, including physical and mental disability. Increasingly, parents are using the human rights commission process to challenge school decisions about their children. This process is more accessible and less expensive because it does not require hiring lawyers. In many provinces, challenges before human rights commissions and the tribunals they appoint are eclipsing court challenges.

The remedies available through the human rights commission process are more limited than Charter remedies, but human rights challenges often provide a context for mediation, restorative approaches, and, ultimately, the settlement of disputes. Increasingly, parents or guardians of children with special needs are seeking redress through provincial human rights processes. One reason for this is likely the prohibitive costs associated with a Charter challenge.

One recent high-profile education law case began in 2005 with a complaint to the BC Human Rights Tribunal.[9] In this case, Frederick Moore filed a complaint on behalf of his son Jeffrey against the BC Ministry of Education ("the province") and the school district ("the district"), alleging discrimination on the basis that instruction was not available to Jeffrey, who required intensive remediation for dyslexia, in the public school system. The complaint was based on the ground that Jeffrey had been denied a "service customarily available to the public" under the BC *Human Rights Code*. It is important to note that the district had previously had a Severe Learning Disabilities program that could have addressed Jeffrey's needs but, on the basis of budgetary concerns, had closed the program prior to Jeffrey's attendance. When he was in grade 4, Jeffrey's parents, on the recommendation of a school psychologist, mortgaged their home to pay for tuition at specialized private schools for the remainder of his education.

The tribunal concluded that discrimination had occurred because the public school system had failed to provide Jeffrey with the necessary supports to allow him meaningful access to education as compared to the general student population. The tribunal found the discrimination was both individual, as against Jeffrey, and systemic, as against students with severe learning disabilities. The tribunal ordered that the Moores be reimbursed for costs associated with the private schools Jeffrey attended, as well as $10,000 in damages for pain and suffering. With respect to the finding of systemic discrimination, the tribunal ordered a wide range of remedies against both the district and the province.

Both the district and the province applied for judicial review of the tribunal decision.[10] The trial judge allowed the application, finding that the tribunal should have compared Jeffrey to other students with special needs, and not to the general student population. Having found that the tribunal applied the wrong comparison, the trial judge set aside the tribunal's decision in its entirety. The Moores appealed the decision to the BC Court of Appeal.

The majority of the Court of Appeal (that is, two of a three-judge panel) dismissed the Moores' appeal, agreeing with the trial judge that the tribunal had erred in comparing Jeffrey to the general student population and not to other students with special needs.[11] The majority found that the "service" under consideration was special education, and not the broader access to education generally.[12] The dissenting judge, Justice Rowles, found that the tribunal was correct in comparing Jeffrey to the general student population because, in her view, the special education services Jeffrey required were the means by which he received meaningful access to education services.[13] The Moores appealed to the Supreme Court of Canada.

In a unanimous decision, the Supreme Court of Canada "substantially allowed" the appeal.[14] The court began its assessment by noting that the preamble to the *School Act* in British Columbia (in effect at the time Jeffrey Moore was in school) stated that "[t]he purpose of the British Columbia school system is to enable all learners to develop their individual potential and to acquire the knowledge, skills and attitudes needed to contribute to a healthy, democratic and pluralistic society and a prosperous and sustainable economy." On this basis, the court stated:

> This ... is an acknowledgement by the government that the reason all children are entitled to an education is because a healthy democracy and economy require their educated contribution. Adequate special education, therefore, is not a dispensable luxury. For those with severe learning disabilities, it is the ramp that provides access to the statutory commitment to education made to *all* children in British Columbia.[15]

One of the most important issues that the court addressed in this decision was the identity of the group to whom it was appropriate to compare the services provided to Jeffrey, in order to determine whether Jeffrey had been discriminated against. In previous human rights cases, the appropriate comparator group for a child with special needs was usually other special needs students with different diagnoses than those of the complainant child. In this case, however, the court veered off the historical path of comparing special needs students with other special needs students. The court agreed with the tribunal and the dissenting judge of the Court of Appeal that the appropriate comparator group was general education students, not only other special education students. The court noted:

> [28] [F]or students with learning disabilities like Jeffrey's, special education is not the service, it is the *means* by which those students get meaningful access to the general education services available to all of British Columbia's students. ...
>
> • • •
>
> [30] To define "special education" as the service at issue also risks descending into the kind of "separate but equal" approach which was majestically discarded in *Brown v. Board of Education of Topeka* ... . Comparing Jeffrey only with other special needs students would mean

that the District could cut all special needs programs and yet be immune from a claim of discrimination. It is not a question of who is or is not experiencing similar barriers.[16]

The court then went on to consider the next steps in the analysis of discrimination, noting:

> [33] [T]o demonstrate *prima facie* discrimination, complainants are required to show that they have a characteristic protected from discrimination under the Code, that they experienced an adverse impact with respect to the service, and that the protected characteristic was a factor in the adverse impact. Once a *prima facie* case has been established, the burden shifts to the respondent to justify the conduct or practice ... . If it cannot be justified, discrimination will be found to occur.[17]

The court first noted that it was clear that Jeffrey's dyslexia was a disability, and that the adverse impact was related to his dyslexia. The next focus for the court was whether Jeffrey was denied access to the same general education available to other students in British Columbia and, if so, whether there was a reasonable basis for that denial.

The court carefully considered the evidence put forth to the tribunal about the special education services provided to Jeffrey, and agreed with the tribunal that the evidence indicated that, simply put, the services were inadequate to support Jeffrey's meaningful access to education. Of specific concern was the fact that district employees acknowledged that Jeffrey required intensive remediation, which was available initially at the district's "Diagnostic Centre." However, after the closure of the Diagnostic Centre, the only option for receipt of these services was to go outside the public school system.[18]

Of interest to teachers is the fact that the tribunal, and thereafter the Supreme Court of Canada, placed significant emphasis on the views of two educational professionals who had worked directly with Jeffrey in the elementary school setting and who had agreed that the Diagnostic Centre would have been beneficial for Jeffrey. The court noted that in spite of the one-on-one attention provided, and the good qualifications of the teachers involved, the services were not sufficient to meet Jeffrey's needs.[19]

The tribunal, and the Supreme Court of Canada, took particular issue with the closure of the Diagnostic Centre in light of evidence that indicated the closure took place without consideration of what would happen to the students who required its services, and without consultation with the educational professionals directly involved in providing services to those students who would be most affected by the closure. The tribunal concluded that the closure of the Diagnostic Centre was based solely on financial reasoning, and the Supreme Court of Canada agreed.[20]

Turning to the justification phase of the analysis, the court noted that "it must be shown that alternative approaches were investigated" and that "the *prima facie* discriminatory conduct must be 'reasonably necessary' in order to accomplish a broader goal."[21] The district's defence focused largely on the budget crisis it was under at the time of the closure. Although accepting that the district was having serious financial issues, the tribunal found that cuts were disproportionate in their effect on special needs programs and, significantly, that the district did not assess other alternatives for students who availed themselves of the services at the Diagnostic Centre. The Supreme Court, in review of the evidence accepted on this point by the tribunal, noted, "In order to decide it had *no* other choice, it had at least to consider what those other choices were."[22]

The Supreme Court overturned the lower courts and upheld the decision of the tribunal with respect to the findings against the district. The court did not, however, accept the findings of the tribunal with respect to the province's liability. Although the court accepted that the budget crisis faced by the district was partially a result of shortcomings in the funding provided by the province, the court ruled that because the tribunal's findings supported the conclusion that it was the district's failure to consider the consequences on students of closing the Diagnostic Centre, there could be no liability assessed to the province.[23] The province was not censured for its budget cuts, although the district was held accountable for how it dispensed the reduced funding.

The Supreme Court upheld the remedies awarded by the tribunal to Jeffrey and his parents (tuition, some transportation costs, and $10,000 in damages for injury to "dignity, feelings and self-respect").[24] The tribunal had also ordered a number of sweeping systemic remedies against the district and province. The Supreme Court did not support these, finding that they were too remote from the scope of the Moores' complaint.[25] This is likely to engender considerable political debate between education departments and school boards in the future.

The impact of this recent Supreme Court of Canada decision remains to be seen, but it is safe to say that it will likely be far reaching in the educational context, particularly where the court has charted a new course with respect to comparator groups when assessing whether a student has experienced differential treatment. *Moore* is a landmark case in equality and education law.

Disability, Special Education, and Inclusion

In an attempt to translate this important legal equality doctrine into the practice of educating special needs children in schools, four important questions emerge:

1. Do all special needs children have access to Canadian schools?
2. What education is appropriate, and who should decide this question?
3. What related services are needed to make access for students with disabilities meaningful?
4. What role do increasingly limited school board resources play in determining a reasonable level of related services? This is perhaps the most critical issue for teachers.

Even the term "special education" is less universally accepted than in the past. A more frequently used term is "inclusive education," which is the international standard set by the recently ratified *Convention on the Rights of Persons with Disabilities* in article 24 of that document.[26] These international commitments, although not directly enforceable in Canada's domestic courts, are increasingly persuasive and used by judges in interpreting the Charter, human rights codes, and regular statutes. This inclusive approach to students with disabilities was also approved by the landmark Supreme Court of Canada decision in *Moore*.[27]

The use of the term "inclusion" is more than a matter of semantics; the concept embraces all forms of diversity in students, not only disability.

> Inclusion is not just about students with disabilities or "exceptionalities." It is an attitude and an approach that encourages all students to belong. It is an approach that nurtures the self-esteem of all students; it is about taking account of diversity in all its forms, and promoting genuine equality of opportunity for all students in New Brunswick. I cannot over emphasize that effective inclusion is for all students and not just one particular group or category.[28]

With respect to the concept of inclusion, it is clear that inclusion must be a manifestation of equality as enshrined in the Charter and is far more than bringing students together in one place. This point is well stated in a Manitoba education study:

> Inclusion is a way of thinking and acting that permits individuals to feel accepted, valued and secure. An inclusive community evolves constantly to respond to the needs of its members. An inclusive community

concerns itself with improving the well-being of each member. Inclusion goes further than the idea of physical location; it is a value system based on beliefs that promote participation, belonging and interaction.[29]

Sometimes terms such as "inclusion," "mainstreaming," "destreaming," and "integration" are used interchangeably. Sometimes this language is even used as political rhetoric, because these words conjure up notions of equality. But, in reality, equality is not an easy political slogan. Equality is often messy and requires tough balancing acts. More than anything, the language of equality is about belonging, about equal "concern, respect, and consideration."[30] Bill Pentney, in a paper prepared for the Canadian Association of Statutory Human Rights Agencies, states it plainly:

> Belonging. Such an achingly simple word. It conjures up some of our deepest yearnings, and for some of us, perhaps our most painful memories. Equality claims begin and end with a desire for belonging, for community. Ideas of equality lie at the heart of the Canadian promise of community.[31]

Thus, the overriding question concerns how inclusive schools need to be to meet the standards set at the international level, the constitutional level in the form of the Charter, and statutory human rights codes. Whether the challenge to school authorities comes in the form of the Charter or human rights codes, the essence of the debate is about what reasonable limits can be placed on the equality of students or what steps to be inclusive constitute reasonable accommodation of students' diverse needs.

Accommodation of students is not an absolute right. Equality claims under the Charter are subject to "reasonable limits," and under human rights codes reasonable accommodation is only up to the point of "undue hardship." There are many factors relevant to determining the limits of reasonable accommodation, but matters such as cost, safety, practical impact on operations, and context are major considerations.

Once a denial of equality and the need to be accommodated is established, there is a high burden on school authorities to justify limiting rights of access. Accommodating students with disabilities has both an individual component and a systemic one. With regard to the former, efforts are made to accommodate the individual within the existing system; in the latter case, efforts need to be directed to changing the system itself to make it more universally inclusive. Both forms of accommodation require a commitment of human and financial resources that move beyond the positive rhetoric about inclusion.

The meaning of these accommodation rights, in practice, is a matter of vigorous debate. This debate occurs in court cases, tribunal hearings, and the judicial reviews of both. Courts, and increasingly tribunals, have focused on two separate and distinct spheres to ensure equality in particular contexts. The first sphere, which has received the most attention, is that of individual accommodation. The second sphere, which is the least developed and least precise in its implications, is systemic or institutional accommodation.[32]

Access to Schools

All children, except those with the most severe disabilities, now have access to public schools. The general right of access was asserted even before the enactment of the Charter in *Carriere v. Lamont Co. School Board*.[33] The pre-Charter position was that children with disabilities were excluded from school because they were a disruptive influence in the classroom. Even after the enactment of the Charter, the courts have upheld the exclusion of an autistic child from a classroom because the child's behaviour was too disruptive.[34] Severely aggressive behaviour can trigger the removal of a child with special needs from school as well. In *Bonnah (Litigation Guardian of) v. Ottawa-Carleton District School Board*,[35] the Ontario Court of Appeal upheld a lower court ruling that a principal, and ultimately a school board, can exclude a child with special needs from school for legitimate safety reasons. The court found that, although a principal is required to consider a student's special needs when deciding whether to remove him from school, the student's special needs in and of themselves cannot undermine the principal's statutory duty to maintain safety in the school.[36] Interestingly, the court ruled that a school board cannot "administratively transfer" a student from one setting to another pending a decision on appeal from the Identification Placement Review Committee (IPRC). The court ruled that, while an IPRC decision is pending, the most the school can do is offer an alternative placement to the parents. If the parents refuse this placement, the child will remain out of school pending the appeal decision.

School administrators and teachers have expressed concern that, in many cases, it is the parents rather than the child who can pose the greater challenge to an orderly school environment. Parents can become agitated and frustrated by the lack of available resources. Understandably, they are concerned about the welfare of their child and obtaining as many resources as possible to meet their child's needs. Teachers often bear the brunt of this frustration.[37] In these situations, it is important to engage school administration and school board resources to mediate this interaction and set appropriate boundaries for parents to participate in shaping the education of their child. Parents do not have unlimited and unfettered access to the school and the classroom.

In their article on special needs and school safety, Nolan, Trépanier, and Ellerker suggest that when students are potential safety risks at school, there are two possible options for placement: home instruction, where the school board provides programming, materials, and some instruction; and home schooling, where the parents assume sole responsibility for the provision of education for their child.[38] There are many disadvantages to placement at home, not the least of which are isolation of the child and the potential inability of the parents to provide a suitable educational program.

In practical terms, the barriers to access to education for children with special needs have largely been broken down. An exception possibly exists for children with extremely challenging behaviour. Although physically disabled children may still experience barriers because of the costs of making old school buildings accessible, progress is ongoing.

Appropriate and Meaningful Education

Establishing the appropriate education for a child with special needs leads us directly into the controversy over inclusion. One of the earliest relevant cases was *Bales*,[39] where the segregated placement of a child was upheld in British Columbia. The case was decided before section 15 of the Charter came into force. In *Hickling v. Lanark-Leeds Roman Catholic School Bd.*,[40] the right of the parents to have their children integrated into a Catholic school, rather than sent to a special class in the Protestant school, was upheld by an Ontario board of inquiry established under the *Human Rights Code*. This ruling was overturned in the courts at both the trial and appeal levels because, once again, the judges deferred to the expertise of the educators.[41]

Perhaps the most groundbreaking case dealing with special education, and specifically the question of inclusion, is *Eaton v. Brant County Board of Education*.[42] In this case, a child with special needs was unable to communicate through speech or alternative forms of communication, was visually impaired, and confined to a wheelchair. In spite of her disabilities, the school board agreed to try the child in a regular classroom in her neighbourhood school with a full-time assistant. After three years, her teachers and assistants were in agreement that the current inclusive setting was not benefiting the child, and might actually be causing harm. The IPRC decided that it would be better to place the child in a special education class. The parents, who wished the child to stay in the inclusive setting, appealed to the Ontario Special Education Tribunal, which unanimously upheld the decision of the IPRC.

The parents then sought a review by the courts. The Ontario Court of Justice (General Division) dismissed the application for review. The Eatons then appealed to the Ontario Court of Appeal, which set aside the order of the tribunal. The school board appealed to the Supreme Court of Canada, which reinstated the decision of the tribunal. The Supreme Court considered section 15 with respect to disability, and ruled that because disability could mean so many different things, it was possible that segregation could provide the most appropriate educational setting in certain circumstances. The court ruled that the presumption that children were entitled to inclusive education was not constitutionally mandated. Every placement decision should be based on the personal characteristics of each child, and must focus on reasonably accommodating those characteristics. Parents, supported by some academic commentators, have interpreted the *Eaton* test as being sufficiently broad to incorporate the "best interests" of the child. This would be considered a more expansive right than merely the duty of "reasonable accommodation."

Eaton eliminated what had been a growing view that there was a presumption in favour of placing all children with special needs in regular classrooms; the school board was thought to bear the burden of proving that such a placement was inappropriate. Since *Eaton*, schools have greater flexibility in showing that a substantially segregated placement is preferable to an inclusive setting in individual cases. This aspect of the *Eaton* decision has led to concerns about its impact on inclusion. Some commentators support the Ontario Court of Appeal decision;[43] however, some parents of special needs children are relieved to have the option of specialized segregated placements.

Since the decision in *Eaton*, instead of relying on presumptions, both parents and school boards must provide information about the most suitable accommodation for the child. Note that a court will make its decision on the basis of what is best for the child, and not simply follow the parents' preference. This "reasonable accommodation" test (as described above) will be applied both where parents wish to have their child included in a regular classroom and where parents seek a segregated and specialized learning environment for their child.

Another decision of some importance comes from the New Brunswick Human Rights Commission. In *Bonnie Cudmore v. Province of New Brunswick Department of Education and School District 2*, the mother of a child with attention deficit hyperactivity disorder (ADHD) filed a complaint that her son was being discriminated against by the Department of Education and the school board, on the basis of a mental disability.[44] After seven years of inclusive education with extensive and ongoing accommodations in Moncton, the mother made the choice to send her child to Landmark East, a private nonprofit school for children with learning disabilities in Nova Scotia. After her son began at the new school, the mother requested that the Department of Education fund this placement. The department notified her that it was not its policy to provide financial support for alternative placements, citing New Brunswick's educational philosophy of inclusive education. The department offered its view that the child could succeed in the public school system, and offered to set up a special education plan. The mother visited several alternative learning centres in the district, but because they did not offer one-on-one attention, she felt that they could not provide the same services as Landmark and refused to consider the programs. When the department still refused to fund the placement, she filed a human rights complaint.

The Board of Inquiry found that attention deficit disorder (ADD) and ADHD were disabilities under the New Brunswick *Human Rights Code*. It determined that school officials tried to accommodate the child, but the mother failed to provide them with pertinent information regarding external factors, such as medication changes, which decreased the school's efficacy in working with the child. The board also noted that factors outside of school often have an impact on student behaviour, performance, and achievement. It found that the mother had not established that the Department of Education and the school district had denied the child a service available to the public based on his mental disability. Moreover, it found that the department and the district had not discriminated against him with respect to any other services on the basis of his mental disability. The mother's complaint was dismissed. This case exemplifies the government's emphasis on accommodation of children within the public school system, rather than on funding private school options.[45] Unlike in *Moore*,[46] there was evidence in this case suggesting that accommodation within the public school system was possible for this particular student.

This case is important for several other reasons. First, it acknowledges that ADD and ADHD are mental disabilities; therefore, persons with these disabilities will be protected from discrimination under provincial and federal human rights codes. Second, it underlines the reality of the relationship between school and parent. In this case, the child's teachers, dating back to kindergarten, were called to testify at the hearing. By the time the case was heard, the child was 14 years old. This illustrates the importance of continuous program planning and documentation over several years, various grade levels, and numerous teachers.

Autism

A firestorm of litigation has surrounded the issue of appropriate education for the growing number of children diagnosed with autism. In the well-publicized *Auton* case,[47] a group of parents of autistic children challenged the government's refusal to fund a specific type of treatment called applied behaviour analysis (ABA), sometimes known as intensive behavioural intervention (IBI). Although the lower courts of British Columbia found that the government had violated the children's section 15(1) equality rights, the Supreme Court of Canada ultimately overturned their decisions.

The Supreme Court of Canada found that ABA/IBI was not a "core medical service" under the *Canada Health Act*;[48] it therefore fell within the discretion of the province to choose whether to fund this treatment. Because the government was not obliged to provide the treatment, the complainants were unable to meet the first step of the section 15(1) analysis for discrimination—that is, they were unable to show that the service was "a benefit provided by law." Although the court could have stopped there, it continued on to evaluate whether the children had been discriminated against, in accordance with step 2 of the test. The first requirement of this step is to establish a comparator group—that is, a group against which the complainants can be compared to see if discrimination existed. The court considerably narrowed the comparator group suggested by the parents. In the end, it found that the province did not discriminate against the complainants by failing to provide a non-core, emerging treatment.

In a more recent case dealing with the right to treatment for autism, *Wynberg v. Ontario*,[49] 35 families with autistic children sued the Ontario government. The families sought a declaration from the court that the government discriminated against their children by failing to provide them with ABA/IBI after age six. This lawsuit differed from *Auton* in that, in *Wynberg*, the Ontario government had already implemented an intensive early intervention program (IEIP), based on ABA principles, for children under age six. Because of long waiting lists, however, many children with autism in this age group did not receive services. In *Wynberg*, the question was not about having a program at all (as in *Auton*), but about gaining access to the program. Justice Kiteley of the Ontario Superior Court found that the children were discriminated against on the basis of age with respect to the IEIP, and on the basis of disability with respect to special education programs and services. The court found that the violation on the basis of age could not be justified under section 1 of the Charter.

The court ruled that the government knew that children were not receiving appropriate special education services in schools, and that it was a duty of the minister of education to ensure that all students with special needs were receiving free and appropriate services and programming. This was a blow to the minister, whose counsel had argued that this responsibility rested with the school board. The court awarded the families the declaration they sought, as well as compensation for past and future ABA. The court's declaration stated that the criteria for the IEIP were discriminatory on the basis of age, and that the minister's failure to provide and fund ABA based on the needs of individual children, including educational services, was a violation of section 15 on the basis of disability. This failure was also held to be a violation of the Ontario *Education Act*.[50] Note that the court found that no section 7 rights existed on the facts of this case.

In response to the ruling, the government suspended the age cutoff for receipt of IEIP services. However, long wait lists for services continued to prevent many from receiving treatment.

The Ontario government successfully appealed the decision.[51] The Ontario Court of Appeal unanimously allowed the appeal and held that the IEIP was not discriminatory and did not contravene the Charter. With respect to the age discrimination claim, the court agreed that there had been differential treatment on the basis of age, but that the parties had not proven that the differential treatment constituted discrimination. Specifically, the Court of Appeal found that there was no evidence to support a finding that autistic children age six and over suffered historical disadvantage as compared to younger autistic children. Accordingly, there could be no discrimination on the basis of age.

With respect to the claim of discrimination on the basis of disability, the Court of Appeal compared children with autism to children with other special needs, and found that the claimants had not proven differential treatment on the failure to provide IEIP programming. In the wake of the decision in *Moore*,[52] this particular ground of appeal might well have been differently decided. The relevant comparator after *Moore* would be the general student body and not other subgroups with special needs.

As noted above, the lower court had ruled that the government had not proven that the cutoff age was a "reasonable limit prescribed by law" in accordance with section 1 of the Charter. The Court of Appeal disagreed. In spite of their finding that the cutoff age was not discriminatory, the Court of Appeal went on to state that the government had shown that IEIP was enacted by the minister of education in response to pressing and substantial objectives. The court found that the age limit was put in place to ensure that the intensive intervention delivered through the IEIP was available to younger children, because research indicated intervention was most effective when delivered in the early years. The court also found that the age limit reflected the government's efforts to balance the needs of younger children for early intervention with the needs of older children, who received school-based programming, and was a reflection of the government's need to allocate scarce resources where they will be most effective. This position is a clear acknowledgment of the "hands-off" approach that courts have traditionally shown with regard to government policy decisions about allocation of limited funds.

Finally, the Court of Appeal found that the intensive nature of ABA/IBI made it impossible to deliver in a school setting. The families involved sought leave to appeal the decision to the Supreme Court of Canada, but leave to appeal was denied.[53]

The decision in *Wynberg* affected not only the 35 families involved but numerous other families as well. A number of injunctions had been sought in the years leading up to this decision by other parents who wanted to keep the funding for their children's ABA/IBI therapy going until the court made a decision in *Wynberg*.[54] In *Bettencourt*,[55] Justice Ferrier of the Ontario Superior Court ordered the province to partially fund a private IBI program for twins whose parents had tried unsuccessfully to integrate them into the public school system. The parents had to remove the two boys and place them in a private school where IBI was provided. Justice Ferrier found that without IBI, the children were unable to learn, and "at this time, the public and separate school systems are either unable or unwilling to provide the required level of support for children with autism."[56]

In April 2005, in the wake of the lower court's decision in *Wynberg*, a group of parents of children with autism commenced what was intended to be a class action suit against the Ontario government and seven school boards (the case was never certified as a class action). The parents alleged that the funding and services provided by the defendants were insufficient to meet the needs of their children; failed to integrate the only effective teaching method (ABA); and, accordingly, were negligent, in breach of sections 7 and 15 of the Charter, a breach of the defendants' fiduciary duties, and misfeasance of public office.

In 2007, following the Court of Appeal's decision in *Wynberg*, the government and school boards brought motions to strike out the plaintiffs' statement of claim.[57] The Superior Court allowed the defendants' motions in part and struck out all of the plaintiffs' claims except for those of breach of section 15 of the Charter. The plaintiffs appealed and the Ontario Court of Appeal largely upheld the decision of the lower court,[58] noting that many of the issues raised by the plaintiffs had already been addressed in *Wynberg*.

There have also been numerous complaints to the Ontario Human Rights Commission regarding the aforementioned issues. In the time that

Wynberg was before the courts, some 240 human rights complaints had been filed with the Commission. These complaints were held in abeyance while the courts decided *Wynberg*.[59] The government engaged in numerous mediations to resolve a number of the complaints. The government, not the school boards, was involved in these discussions and appeared as a party in some instances. Some complaints were ultimately settled through these processes, while others were simply dismissed.

Ontario is by no means the only province with ongoing litigation over funding and provision of autism treatment. A large number of parents in both Canada and the United States have sought declarations from the courts that school systems and provincial health care systems should provide highly specialized treatments for autism. In *D.J.N. v. Alberta (Child Welfare Panel)*,[60] a mother of an autistic child sought funding from child welfare services to augment the special education that her son received in school. The mother requested approximately $15,000 to address her son's needs for speech and occupational therapies, reading programming, social skills training, and computer training. She was denied the funding by the director of child welfare on the basis that he lacked the jurisdiction to grant her request. Her appeal was rejected by the Child Welfare Appeal Panel, which found that the services she sought were the responsibility of the school board. The panel cited the *School Act* as justification for its decision that it lacked jurisdiction to order funding. The Alberta Court of Queen's Bench also denied the mother's appeal, agreeing with the panel that the requested services fell within the school board's mandate, and that nothing in the *Child Welfare Act* required the delivery of these services. Justice Rawlins, however, delivered a rebuke to the government, stating:

> It seems to me to be extremely unproductive for two departments of the same government, both of whom may bear some responsibility for the provision of services to handicapped children, to engage in a war as to whose budget should bear the expense. Ideally, the Ministers of both departments should work together to provide a comprehensive approach to the needs of the handicapped children. It ought not to matter what the service is; if it assists the child and there is available funding in one or more government departments, then the public should get the benefit of one-stop shopping instead of the current unpredictable, costly avenues.[61]

This more holistic approach to meeting students' needs, sometimes referred to as "wrap-around services," is growing in popularity. Integrating the services of various government departments and breaking down the traditional silos has been frequently recommended by various studies.[62]

One theme that has reverberated through many of the autism cases is the cost–benefit analysis. In *Wynberg*, Justice Kiteley heard evidence as to the long-term benefits of providing intensive and early autism treatment. The plaintiffs produced a cost–benefit analysis that suggested that expanding services to all qualified children ages 2–4 would result in a net savings of $172,549,472 over a 60-year period. Further, the plaintiff's expert suggested that this was not a one-time savings but that it "attached to the cohort of autistic children currently aged 2, 3 and 4" and that "every 5 years a new cohort of autistic children will be in this age range and will attract a similar cost savings figure."[63] Unfortunately, funding for these programs is needed now to create savings over the next 50 years; and many current governments are not prepared to invest such huge sums for programming that may not yield immediate and visible results.

It is clear from these cases that section 15(1) is currently the most effective tool for parents to use when arguing special education cases before Canadian courts. However, as we mentioned earlier, discrimination claims before human rights commissions are another route for parents who seek better services for their children.

Related Services

In order for disabled children to benefit from their education, they also need related services that help them to overcome their disabilities. For example, it is essential that transportation and facilities be accessible to children with physical disabilities. Accessibility standards are imposed by human rights codes in most provinces, and resistance to implementation arises only in relation to concerns about costs.[64] Because of the cost factor, these standards are phased in and, as a result, implementation sometimes proceeds very slowly.

One of the major areas of concern in integrating mentally and physically disabled students or providing special education is the administration of drugs or other medical services. Most teachers are not qualified to administer medication or perform medical procedures, and by doing so they expose themselves to considerable legal risk. However, if no qualified staff person is hired to address their medical needs, these students are effectively excluded from school on the basis of their disability. We address the issue of legal liability for teachers and teaching assistants with respect to drug administration and medical procedures in Chapter 6, under the heading "Teachers as Paramedics."

Another area of concern is the limited supply of expert human resources. Speech therapists, audiologists, school psychologists, and resource teachers with specialized training for certain disabilities are in short supply in many districts. This creates longer than necessary waiting times for assessment and treatment.[65]

On a philosophical level, special education, like minority language education and denominational school rights, is perhaps more of an institutional problem than one directly involving teachers. On a practical level, however, it continues to be a major concern for all teachers, not just special education and resource teachers. It is rare today for a classroom teacher not to be faced with the demands of including multiple children with special needs in her classroom. Good school board policies on inclusion and special education necessarily involve frank discussion with teachers in an effort to determine the appropriate level of services for children in inclusive classrooms. Class composition is a vital issue for teachers and one that focuses on a lack of adequate resources. Courts can provide a framework but cannot ultimately answer the service delivery and resource questions.

Balancing Limited Resources: The Limits of Reasonable Accommodation

School boards have scarce resources to meet the many demands placed on the educational system, yet the costs of accommodating the diverse range of students within society are growing, creating a tough balancing act for school administrators and policy makers. Although courts are aware of these challenges, they nevertheless have an obligation to ensure that educational services are provided on the basis of equality in accordance with the requirements of section 15 of the Charter and provincial human rights codes. Courts may consider scarce public resources as a factor in determining whether a limit placed on an equality right in the educational sphere is reasonable within the meaning of section 1 of the Charter; however, this is not always a reliable "reasonable limits" argument. Cost is not a total answer to a Charter equality claim, but may be one component of determining what is reasonable in a free and democratic society. This point was emphasized in a 2004 Supreme Court of Canada decision denying pay equity to women in Newfoundland and Labrador as a result of the financial crisis facing the government of the day.[66] The landmark *Moore* case from the Supreme Court of Canada in 2012 is less sympathetic to budget cuts as an effective response to limits on students' equality rights.[67] The allocation of resources within school systems continues to be a systemic issue that is beyond the scope of this book, but one that affects teachers every day.

Other Equality Issues

Special education focuses attention on physical or mental needs, and is frequently the basis for findings of discrimination against young people in the schools. However, other prohibited modes of discrimination listed in section 15 of the Charter and human rights codes might also give rise to equality challenges. These have been somewhat lost in the shadow of special education. The Supreme Court of Canada has made it clear that the types of discrimination prohibited by section 15 are not exhaustive and may be expanded to include other analogous categories. Types of discrimination not specifically listed in section 15 have been claimed to protect the equality rights of other groups who have formerly faced exclusion and discrimination. Gay, lesbian, bisexual, and transgendered students provide recent, and high-profile, examples of this extension of section 15.

Sex

The prohibition in section 15 against discrimination on the basis of a person's sex opens up the question of whether school policy can validly distinguish between male and female students in the school. This would include matters such as courses offered only to women or sports teams delineated by the players' sex.

Outside the school context, the Ontario Court of Appeal has upheld the right of a teenage girl to play hockey on a boys' all-star team based on section 15 of the Charter.[68] The trial judge accepted the discrimination as justified under section 1 because of the benefits of separating girls and boys in athletic activities. However, the Court of Appeal disagreed with this reasoning, stating that section 19(2) of the Ontario *Human Rights Code* (now repealed), which allowed this type of discrimination in athletic activities, failed to prescribe any limits or guidelines for the distinction. The court held that participation in athletics is important for the development of "health, character and discipline," and is therefore worthy of protection.

By the time this case was decided, the young woman in question had moved beyond that level of hockey, but this case has paved the way for other women who wish to play male-dominated sports. The Canadian Association for the Advancement of Women and Sport and Physical Activity (CAAWS) notes that the issue of women or girls wishing to play for men's or boys' sports teams tends to arise where there is no local female team, or when playing on a male team would create better access to tournaments, resources, and facilities. CAAWS suggests that "the legal opinion has largely been that females have the right to compete for a position on a male team on the same basis as males, as long as they demonstrate sufficient skills and ability to meet the requirements of the team."[69]

In 2010, the Ontario Federation of School Athletic Associations changed its gender equity policy, thus allowing female athletes to play on boys' sports teams.[70] The change resulted from a human rights complaint filed by a female soccer player, Courtney Greer, who wished to play on her school's male soccer team. Previously, the policy had been that girls could only play on boys' teams where the sports activity was not otherwise available to them—that is, where there was no corresponding girls' team.

Similar human rights complaints were raised in 2006 in Manitoba, by twin sisters Amy and Jesse Pasternak, who wished to try out for the High School Men's Hockey League, and who were prevented from doing so by the Manitoba High School Athletic Association, in spite of having the support of their school administrator and the school division superintendent.[71] A Manitoba Human Rights Board found that the two young women had been discriminated against and made a number of orders, including the order that the association remove the requirement that, if a female team existed, female students would not be permitted on male teams.

In *Casselman v. Ontario Soccer Association*,[72] also in Ontario, two teenage girls were denied the right to play on an under-16 boys' team for the league championships because the organizing association did not approve of mixed-sex teams for players past the age of puberty. The prohibition occurred despite the fact that the girls had played with the team for the entire regular season. The board of inquiry allowed the girls' complaint, ruling that the girls were discriminated against on the basis of their sex. The board also noted, as an additional reason for its finding, that there were no girls' teams in the area.

In Nova Scotia schools, sports teams are labelled "boys'," "girls'," and "open." Sports such as basketball are classified as "boys'" and "girls'," and students must play on teams according to their sex; hockey is classified as "girls'" and "open," and football is classified as "open." Girls with the requisite skills, can therefore play hockey on either the girls' or the open team and can play football, but they cannot play on the boys' basketball team because the teams are divided on the basis of the sex of the players. The Nova Scotia Schools Athletic Federation (NSSAF) instituted this policy so that schools would be required to provide both boys' and girls' teams for the more popular sports, and not simply create one team from the strongest players in the school regardless of their sex.

Over the past several decades, there have been significant changes to the curriculum and pedagogy in public schools. More attention is paid to the learning styles of both female and male students, and significant efforts have been made to engage female students in the traditionally male-dominated fields of math and science. Gone are the days when girls were directed toward typing and home economics and boys toward woodworking and drafting. The field of computer science is one area where boys still appear to have an advantage over girls—they appear to learn how to operate computers more quickly and demonstrate better manual dexterity. Overall, however, more young girls than boys are excelling academically and going on to post-secondary education.

Some educators believe that so much focus has been placed on girls that boys are beginning to feel the lack of attention, and problems in school are resulting. However, most research does not support this conclusion. Nevertheless, teachers should be conscious of the manner in which they divide their attention and should attempt to have the same expectations for male and female students. Research suggests that boys and girls do learn in different ways, and equality demands recognition of these differences.

Age

The primary issue in the field of age discrimination is whether age limits for starting and finishing public education are reasonable. In general, schools can set age limits for schooling, but should be prepared to defend them. For young children, problems are most likely to arise in cases where parents feel that their child is particularly gifted and the "appropriate" education should consequently begin at an early age. In *Winnipeg School Division No. 1 v. McCarthur*,[73] parents tried to force a school to admit their child, who was one month short of the required five years of age at the cutoff date. This case came to court before the Charter's enactment, and the parents sought to apply the Manitoba *Human Rights Code*. The court held that human rights legislation did not apply to schools. This is no longer the case. More important, however, it held that the age restrictions in Manitoba's *Education Act* were specific and had been enacted later than the human rights statute; hence, the age limitation prevailed. This illustrates that courts may rely on the "reasonable limits" exclusion in section 1 of the Charter to restrict claims of age discrimination in relation to early school admission.

A school board in Quebec ran into the problem of trying to assess each child individually to determine the appropriate entry age for primary education. The school board developed a policy in which parents could attend meetings of a committee set up by the board to assess a child's abilities and whether it would be appropriate for that child to start school earlier than the prescribed cutoff date. The process involved gathering and bringing evidence before the school board concerning the child's ability, which was a costly exercise. The board soon discovered that because of the associated costs only parents of higher economic means were applying. The board was then faced with a difficult dilemma; its new program, meant to be universal, was effectively excluding lower-income children. It may be that schools should not try to enter into this type of inquiry but should instead rely on the traditional method of setting an arbitrary cutoff date. The courts are likely to defer to a school board's cutoff date, provided that the board can show some reasonable basis for limiting the access of young children.

The more contentious issue with respect to age discrimination in schools is the extension of educational services to adults. Each provincial education statute contains provisions that govern the cutoff age for publicly funded education. Many of these statutes also include special provisions for adults in the education system, including night classes and classes held in local community centres. Concerns also focus on special needs students who require services past the age of 21.

A variation on age discrimination occurs in the North, where Aboriginals often decide to return to school later in life. Given their unique cultural values, a strong argument can be made that an arbitrary "cutoff" age should not apply to Aboriginals, whose special status is reflected in the education acts of the North. As yet, these cases have not made their way to the courts. The argument on behalf of Aboriginals becomes stronger when coupled with the further argument under section 15 that restricting access to schools is a matter of racial discrimination. Aboriginal rights are also guaranteed in section 35 of the *Constitution Act, 1982*. In the face of the information above, an argument can be made that age limits are a good example of structural or systemic race discrimination that is not obvious at first glance. Racial discrimination is most often a problem of latent structural inequality.

Race and Multiculturalism

The systemic nature of racial discrimination makes it difficult to address on a case-by-case basis in the courts. There have been some human rights challenges, but most school-based cases involving racial discrimination do not even proceed to a board of inquiry, let alone the courts. The primary reason that cases are settled out of court is the desire on the part of school boards to avoid the adverse publicity that accompanies a racial complaint. Although race and ethnic origin are explicitly included as prohibited grounds of discrimination under section 15 of the Charter, no student appears yet to have launched a racial challenge using the Charter that has proceeded to trial. However, school board employees, including teachers, have used section 15 challenges in a number of labour cases.[74]

Complaints of racism can be coupled with an argument under section 27 of the Charter, which protects the multicultural heritage of Canadians as follows:

> This Charter shall be interpreted in a manner consistent with the preservation and enhancement of the multicultural heritage of Canadians.

Because section 27 is an interpretive section, it lacks the substantive force of some of the other provisions of the Charter, such as section 15. Most provinces, however, have multicultural policies with respect to education, and they could use the interpretive principles in section 27 to strengthen the application of these provincial policies.

Because of its widespread nature, discrimination may be a problem beyond the power of any one teacher to correct. However, as educational state agents, it is important for all teachers to be aware of potential discrimination in their schools—in particular, latent or systemic discrimination. As Canada's population becomes increasingly multicultural, discrimination will have a growing legal importance. The growing diversity of student populations in Toronto, Vancouver, and other large urban centres emphasizes the importance of an open and inclusive school climate.

On a practical level, teachers should take a close look at the teaching materials they use on an everyday basis to ensure that they are appropriate for the cultural makeup of their particular classroom. Teachers should also be sensitive to their own biases. A lack of cultural diversity within the classroom is problematic for more than philosophical reasons. Research indicates that

> exclusion of the experiences, values, and viewpoints of Aboriginal and racial and ethnocultural minority groups constitutes a systemic barrier to success for students from those groups and often produces inequitable outcomes for them. Such inequities have been linked to students' low self-esteem, placement in inappropriate academic programs, low career expectations, and a high dropout rate.[75]

Teachers must also be aware of the criminal component of racial violence, which places students' safety at risk. One need look only to the terrible murder of Reena Virk[76] to see what can happen when young people react violently to someone who is "different." Although Virk's death was not attributed solely to racism, it is clear that she did not "fit in" and was murdered by a group of her peers because of it. It is plausible that one of the reasons she did not fit in was her race.

Another major concern is the impact of school discipline policies on racial minorities. In 2007, the Ontario Human Rights Commission reached a settlement with the Ministry of Education with respect to the "safe schools" provisions of the *Education Act* and their resultant policies on student discipline, generally known collectively as "zero tolerance."[77] The settlement was effected two years after the commission brought forward a complaint on behalf of students, in which the commission alleged that the policy had a disproportionately negative effect on racial minority students and students with disabilities.[78]

The settlement required the Ministry to agree that schools must consider mitigating factors before expelling or suspending a student and to remove all references in the *Education Act*, regulations, or policies to the concept of "zero tolerance." The commission proposed, and the Ministry accepted, a number of mitigating factors to consider, including (but not limited to):

- whether racial or other harassment was a factor in the misbehavior;
- the impact of a suspension or expulsion on the student's continuing education;
- in the case of a student with a disability, whether the disability was a factor in the behaviour and whether appropriate accommodation had been provided; and
- the safety of other students.[79]

The Ministry subsequently released a policy memorandum enunciating the expectations for school boards for provision of services to students who have been expelled, in order to allow them continued access to education.[80] It is clear that race has historically been a factor in many decisions made by administrators and teachers.[81] It is important for teachers to become increasingly sensitive to race, culture, and ethnicity as Canadian schools become more diverse each year.

Religion as Proxy for Culture: New Challenges of Diversity and Multiculturalism

Although in some respects religion is of little significance in Canadian schools (except denominational schools), in others it has become more important as a proxy for race and culture. This is particularly true in relation to Muslim students in places such as Toronto and also to Sikh students on the West Coast of Canada. The exclusion of students from traditional religious practices such as the Lord's prayer has been explored in Chapter 3.[82] Here, we will briefly explore newer claims to religious equality in the diverse and multicultural Canada where white Protestants are no longer the majority in many schools, especially in large centers like Toronto.

As discussed at length in Chapter 3, the issue of religious dress in schools continues to create a challenge for school districts, teachers, and the courts.[83]

Accommodation of the growing diversity of the Canadian student body is an important challenge facing Canadian schools and teachers on the front lines. This is a new and increasingly important aspect of inclusive education that has many parallels to the inclusion of students with disabilities. In parts of Western Canada, the accommodation of First Nations students in the general public schools and the creation and proper funding of First Nations schools is also a major challenge. It is a vital part of establishing a new relationship between the First Nations and the rest of Canada.[84] This is more a matter of culture than religion, but there still needs to be a celebration and accommodation of differences.

As was dramatically played out in the province of Quebec and discussed in the report of the Bouchard-Taylor Commission,[85] accommodating new cultures and religious traditions into the more traditional bilingual Canada is a significant challenge. As with other human rights issues, the central question is: what amounts to reasonable accommodation? To be consistent with Canada's claims to be a mosaic, we should be accepting but not to the point where core Canadian values such as gender equality are compromised. The need to be appropriately accommodating of new immigrants to Canada and its First Nations is accentuated by current Canadian demographics. Immigrants and indigenous populations are growing, while the traditional English and French populations are in decline. The face of Canada is changing and this must be properly reflected in our schools.

Sexual Orientation

In recent years, the issue of sexual orientation has become a hot-button issue in schools. Teachers often ask us whether they should address this issue in their classrooms, and, if so, how they might go about it. The issue of discrimination on the basis of sexual orientation has come before the courts in several high-profile cases.

In *Jubran v. North Vancouver School District No. 44*,[86] a high school student filed a complaint with the BC Human Rights Commission, alleging that he had been discriminated against on the basis of perceived sexual orientation. The student had been harassed by his peers for several years. His classmates used physical violence and homophobic slurs to taunt him despite the fact that he was not gay. The student and his parents sought support from the school. The human rights tribunal found that although the school had taken action against individual offenders, it had failed to address the harassment and bullying in a systematic fashion and had never taken any proactive steps to address the student's concerns. The tribunal awarded the student $4,500 in damages. The BC Supreme Court overturned the ruling, but the Court of Appeal reversed the lower court's decision, reinstating the tribunal's decision and award. The BC Court of Appeal confirmed that schools can no longer sit back and wait for bullying to occur before they take steps to prevent it. This decision appears to require school boards to address the issue of homophobia in schools and to educate their students about the unacceptability of homophobic behaviour. The Supreme Court declined to hear an appeal of the BC Court of Appeal ruling.[87] It is important to note that gay and lesbian students are among the most frequent targets of bullying and are more susceptible to suicide than other young people.[88]

In Ontario in 2002, another case made headlines when a student named Marc Hall sought an injunction from the courts to allow him to bring his same-sex partner to his Catholic school's senior prom.[89] The court granted the injunction, holding that to exclude the student from his prom would be to restrict his access to a "fundamental social institution." The judge noted the long social history of discrimination against gays and lesbians that did not accord with Charter values of respect for the dignity and worth of all persons. It is clear that the rights of gay and lesbian students to attend school and school functions free of discrimination have been upheld by the courts and human rights commissions.

There appear, however, to be limits on how far the judiciary will go in allowing teachers to disclose their homosexuality in the classroom. In 1998, a Manitoba arbitration board declined to hear and determine a grievance from a teacher who argued that her school district had behaved improperly in denying her the right to disclose her sexual orientation to her students.[90] The teacher felt that if she were able to disclose her lesbianism to her students at a "teachable moment," she would be able to present herself as a positive model for tolerance and show her students that stereotyping of gay and lesbian students is inappropriate. When she requested the permission of her school district to disclose this information, the district informed her that it was inappropriate for any teacher, whether homosexual or heterosexual, to declare her sexual orientation. The teacher filed grievances, arguing that her academic freedom as well as her human rights had been violated. The division rejected her grievances. At the arbitration hearing, the division argued that disclosure of the teacher's sexuality would result in a backlash from parents' groups and a loss of the teacher's effectiveness in the classroom. They also argued that it would be impossible for the teacher to advise 13- and 14-year-old students of her lesbianism and then simply move on to another topic. The arbitration board ruled that because a teacher informing students of her sexuality would be significant in terms of lessons and curriculum, the division had the right to determine whether such a disclosure should be made to students. The teacher's grievances were dismissed because the arbitration board found it had no jurisdiction to rule on this matter.

Bullying, School Violence, and Vulnerable Students

Although the victims of bullying are not exclusively drawn from traditionally protected categories under human rights codes, sex, race, sexual orientation, and disability are often factors. One of the defining features of a bullying relationship is a power imbalance, and the victims in this relationship are often drawn from the ranks of the vulnerable. Human rights codes draw parallels between bullying and harassment, and addressing matters of bullying by referring them to human rights commissions is one of the important recommendations of the Nova Scotia Task Force on Bullying and Cyberbullying.[91] Australia has had considerable success by using the human rights structure to address some forms of bullying and cyberbullying.

In Ontario, the link between bullying and human rights is even more explicit. The *Accepting Schools Act, 2012* enunciates the following definition of bullying:

> "bullying" means aggressive and typically repeated behaviour by a pupil where,
>
> (a) the behaviour is intended by the pupil to have the effect of, or the pupil ought to know that the behaviour would be likely to have the effect of,
>
> (i) causing harm, fear or distress to another individual, including physical, psychological, social or academic harm, harm to the individual's reputation or harm to the individual's property, or
>
> (ii) creating a negative environment at a school for another individual, and
>
> (b) the behaviour occurs in a context where there is a real or perceived power imbalance between the pupil and the individual based on factors such as size, strength, age, intelligence, peer group power, economic status, social status, religion, ethnic origin, sexual orientation, family circumstances, gender, gender identity, gender expression, race, disability or the receipt of special education.[92]

The above section discusses the various categories of people protected under human rights codes; however, these codes include other categories as well. In the big picture, a wide range of students are vulnerable to bullying and cyberbullying and there is no closed list of categories to determine who will be bullied. Being subjected to bullying is a serious problem that detracts from the quality of the school experience and, at its core, displays a lack of respect for the dignity of the victimized student. It is therefore an issue of concern to educators.

As discussed in Chapter 2, Application of Negligence Principles in the School, under Bullying, a group of Canadian scholars has suggested that bullying will be reduced only when lawsuits against schools increase in an attempt to hold them responsible for bullying.[93] Questions as to the legal responsibility of schools remain—for example, to what standard of care would a court hold a school when dealing with bullies? Most important, teachers and administrators want to provide a safe environment for students to learn and grow. This concern increases each time we hear of another student who has taken his own life in an effort to escape from bullying or who has been murdered by her schoolmates. What actions must a school take?

First, it is important to define "bullying," as did Ontario's Bill 13, *Accepting Schools Act, 2012*, above. In its discussion of bullying, the Nova Scotia Task Force on Bullying and Cyberbullying notes:

> Bullying is typically a repeated behaviour that is intended to cause, or should be known to cause, fear, intimidation, humiliation, distress or other forms of harm to another person's body, feelings, self-esteem, reputation or property.
>
> Bullying can be direct or indirect, and can take place by written, verbal, physical or electronic means, or any other form of expression.[94]

This definition goes on to define "cyberbullying" as a form of bullying and holds accountable not only the bullies but also the bystanders who encourage or assist the bullying.

> Cyberbullying (also referred to as electronic bullying) is a form of bullying, and occurs through the use of technology. This can include the use of a computer or other electronic devices, using social networks, text messaging, instant messaging, websites, e-mail or other electronic means.
>
> A person participates in bullying if he or she directly carries out the behaviour or assists or encourages the behaviour in any way.[95]

Debra Pepler and Wendy Craig define bullying as "a form of aggression in which there is an imbalance of power between the bully and the victim."[96]

They note four key factors: a power imbalance, repeated incidents, intent to harm the victim, and the victim's distress.

Pepler and Craig found that the effects on both the victim and the bully are significant and long lasting.[97] Eric Roher reports that people who are bullied are often blamed and ostracized by other children for what happened to them and tend over time to have academic and emotional difficulties, including depression, anxiousness, and insecurity.[98] These characteristics, as we have seen numerous times, can lead to tragic results. The high profile suicide of BC teen Amanda Todd in the fall of 2012 captivated the nation and emphasized the seriousness of the problem.

Bullies also suffer long-term effects from their own behaviour. Pepler and Craig's study shows that a child bully can grow into an adult bully who needs more government services than the average citizen because of criminal convictions, alcoholism, and family breakdowns.[99] The tragic consequences of bullying and cyberbullying are also highlighted in the report of the Nova Scotia Task Force on Bullying and Cyberbullying.

Under the common law, school boards, schools, and teachers have a responsibility to protect students from harm that is reasonably foreseeable. Thus, if a negligence claim were brought against the school and its personnel, the court would evaluate whether a reasonable person in the place of the teacher or school administrator, knowing what they knew about the situation, would have foreseen the harm to the student. If the answer is "yes," then the court may find that the teacher or administrator owed a duty of care to the student. A plaintiff would also have to show that there was a connection between the student's injury and school's actions or inactions.[100]

The common law is not the only source for a duty of care. Provincial legislation creates statutory duties for most school boards, administrators, and teachers. As we saw at the beginning of Chapter 3, teachers in Ontario have a statutory duty, created by the *Education Act*, "to maintain, under the direction of the principal, proper order and discipline in the teacher's classroom and while on duty in the school and on the school ground."[101] Under the regulations attached to the *Education Act*, principals are required to maintain proper order and discipline in the schools and to inform parents when their child has committed an infraction of school rules.

When a bullying case is proven in court, it is likely the school board (rather than the teacher) that will have to pay any compensation the court awards, pursuant to the doctrine of vicarious liability, which we discussed in Chapter 2. It is clear that schools can be held liable for injuries that a student suffers as a result of bullying, as was seen in *Jubran*,[102] where the school board was held accountable through the human rights process, rather than the common-law principles of negligence. Although the amount of money awarded to the student was not substantial, it illustrates the court's position that schools can be held accountable for failing to protect students from their peers.

Roher argues that the courts have, in effect, established a test for deciding whether a school "created a situation of increased violence or vulnerability."[103] He suggests that the plaintiff must prove four components in order to successfully bring a claim:

1. The alleged misconduct placed the student "at substantial risk of serious, immediate and proximate harm."
2. The defendant (usually a teacher or principal) knew of the risk, or the risk was obvious.
3. The defendants acted recklessly in consciously disregarding the known risk.
4. The defendant's actions or inactions "shock the conscience."

According to Roher, the courts apply this test "stringently," so that the acts of violence on which the claim is based must approach the standard of "inhumane."[104] This stringent test has not stopped parents from filing civil lawsuits against school boards, alleging negligence in failure to protect their children from bullying. Many such claims are settled before they proceed to trial.

In May 2004, an Alberta family filed a claim against Calgary school officials, claiming that the school was aware that their son had been repeatedly victimized by a bully, and did nothing to ensure his safety.[105] The bullying culminated in an attack that resulted in serious injuries to the student.

In another case, a family in Kilbride, Ontario, wanted more than just money in reparation for the bullying their son suffered. They sued the Halton District School Board seeking $500,000 in damages, a public apology, and a commitment from the board to develop a systemic plan to combat bullying.[106] The bullying against their son began in grade 4; it included stealing his belongings, throwing ice at him, and shooting him in the leg with a pellet gun. Through to high school, the physical violence continued, but the verbal and psychological violence expanded by means of the Internet, when several of his tormentors from school began posting hateful messages about him.

Some Canadian schools have turned to the criminal law to address the more heinous examples of bullying. Criminal liability may apply to cases involving assault (the application, or threat of application, of force), threats of death or bodily harm, and stalking (or criminal harassment). Roher notes that the criminal courts have indicated concerns about the perceived increase in bullying in schools.[107] One of the issues that courts have struggled with is the question of where schoolyard taunting crosses the line to become the criminal offence of harassment.

In *R. v. D.W.*,[108] the BC Youth Court struggled with this very question. After a 14-year-old student committed suicide, a classmate was charged with three counts of threatening death or bodily harm and one count of criminal harassment. Two other classmates were also charged with uttering threats of death or bodily harm to the deceased student. In finding the first defendant guilty, the court noted that the charge of uttering threats of death or bodily harm does not require intent to carry out the threat, as long as there was an intention to intimidate. The defendant was sentenced to 18 months' probation, including 20 hours of community service. Roher postulates that this decision is an important one because it involved no physical violence, as do the vast majority of criminal convictions for bullying.[109] The court in *R. v. D.W.* ruled that the threat to beat someone up might be sufficient to constitute a threat to commit bodily harm.

From the decisions discussed above, in particular *Jubran*,[110] it appears that school boards and school administrators must implement programs to reduce and prevent bullying in schools. Indeed, many provincial governments have made public commitments to address the issue.

The Nova Scotia Task Force on Bullying recommended a four-pronged approach to the problems of bullying and cyberbulling:

1. anchoring change in law and policy;
2. implementing preventive interventions;
3. educating diverse audiences about the nature and the scope of the problem; and
4. establishing clear accountability lines.[111]

Changes have been made to the legislative and policy framework in Nova Scotia, as has been the case in many provinces. These include holding accountable encouraging bystanders as well as the bullies themselves. Ontario has recognized that jurisdiction over cyberbullying extends beyond the school grounds and after school hours.[112]

With respect to preventive interventions, the Nova Scotia Task Force sets out criteria for selecting effective and evidence-based interventions to reduce bullying and recommends that an anti-bullying coordinator be hired to oversee the responses to the problem. This coordinator has now been hired. The Nova Scotia Task Force also strongly endorses restorative approaches, especially ones that involve young people themselves. Peer responses—for example, the pink shirt initiative in Nova Scotia[113]—have been most effective. The importance of youth engagement in responding to bullying is a major theme of the Nova Scotia Task Force.

Finally, it is vital to educate the diverse audience of students, parents, teachers, and the general public about both the scope and consequences of bullying and cyberbullying. The Nova Scotia Task Force recommends courses in digital citizenship, Internet safety, and related matters for students. There is also a need to educate parents about both technology and the world of social media. The Standing Senate Committee on Human Rights produced both an excellent report on cyberbullying and a practical guide for both students and parents on this topic.[114]

Eric Roher notes that although there is no single prescribed form for anti-bullying programs, the programs that appear to be most successful are those that apply a "whole school" approach, addressing bullying at the school, classroom, and individual levels.[115] Roher suggests a number of steps to minimize the legal liability of schools when dealing with bullying and create a positive learning environment for children.[116] First and foremost, he finds it essential that schools develop programs and policies that are both preventive and responsive. In other words, schools must be prepared to teach children about why bullying is wrong before the bullying occurs and must also be ready to address the behaviour after it happens, as it inevitably will. He suggests that early intervention strategies, such as conflict resolution programs, peer mediation, and restorative justice programs, are good examples of the proactive end of the spectrum.[117] Responsively, schools should have plans for specific consequences and clear courses of action for teachers and administrators to follow. Peer involvement in responding to bullying, as stated above, is very important.

There have not yet been many successful negligence cases brought against teachers and school boards over bullying incidents. However, in the face of ever-rising public awareness, the courts are more likely to find a duty on the part of school administrators and staff to intervene in incidents of bullying. Bullying is a reasonably foreseeable occurrence in today's school culture.[118] The growth of cyberbullying poses new challenges for schools and the courts, particularly with respect to the limits of a school's jurisdiction in addressing behaviour that occurs outside the school setting. It is also a problem with significant human rights dimensions.

Concluding Thoughts on Schools as Guardians of Equality

Equality is one of the defining principles of inclusive schools. Although truly inclusive schools are difficult to achieve, much progress has been made in Canada over the last few decades. In charting the course toward schools that embrace and celebrate diversity, the principles of equality enshrined in the Charter and human rights codes serve as a lighthouse to guide school authorities. Educators and lawyers need to work together to produce better environments in which students can learn that are safe and, as much as possible, free from discrimination.[119]

NOTES

1   A.W. MacKay, "Safe and Inclusive Schooling—Expensive ... Quality Education—Priceless. For Everything Else There Are Lawyers!" (2008) 18 *Education & Law Journal* 21.

2   A.W. MacKay, *Education Law in Canada* (Toronto: Emond Montgomery, 1984), at 37-41.

3   See, for example, *Ministerial Education Act Regulations*, N.S. Reg. 80/97, as amended by N.S. Reg. 157/2005, ss. 53-61.

4   *Bales v. Board of School Trustees (Okanagan)* (1984), 8 Adm. L.R. 202 (B.C.S.C.).

5   *B. (J.) v. Nova Scotia (Minister of Education)* (2001), 198 N.S.R. (2d) 87 (C.A.).

6   *Elwood v. Halifax County Bedford District School Board*, unreported decision, October 1986 (N.S.S.C.T.D.). This case is the subject of "Luke's Case," one of the three chapters in Jack Batten, *On Trial* (Toronto: MacMillan, 1988), 135-206.

7   See *Bonnie Cudmore v. Province of New Brunswick Department of Education and School District 2*, Human Rights Board of Inquiry, file no. HR-003-01 (2004); affirmed 2005 NBQB 90.

8   *Andrews v. Law Society of British Columbia*, [1989] 1 S.C.R. 284; *Law v. Canada*, [1999] 1 S.C.R. 497; and *R. v. Kapp*, 2008 SCC 41 are three landmark cases on section 15 of the Charter.

9   *Moore v. British Columbia (Ministry of Education) and School District No. 44*, 2005 BCHRT 580, 54 C.H.R.R. D/245.

10   *British Columbia (Ministry of Education) v. Moore*, 2008 BCSC 264.

11   *British Columbia (Ministry of Education) v. Moore*, 2010 BCCA 478.

12   Ibid., at para. 171.

13   Ibid., at para. 131.

14   *Moore v. British Columbia (Education)*, 2012 SCC 61.

15   Ibid., at para. 5 (emphasis in original).

16   Ibid., at paras. 28 and 30.

17   Ibid., at para. 33.

18   Ibid., at paras. 41-42.

19   Ibid., at para. 42.

20   Ibid., at paras. 43-44.

21   Ibid., at para. 49.

22   Ibid., at para. 52 (emphasis in original).

23   Ibid., at para. 54.

24   Ibid., at para. 56.

25   Ibid., at para. 57.

26 See A.W. MacKay, "An International Call for Action and Canada's Long and Winding Road to Inclusion: The Canadian Experience" (2010) 40 *Hong Kong Law Journal* 449, Appendix A.

27 *Moore*, supra note 14. In particular, this SCC case is cited with approval in A.W. MacKay, "Author's Summary, Connecting Care and Challenge: Tapping Our Human Potential—Inclusive Education: A Review of Programming and Services in New Brunswick" (2007) 17 *Education & Law Journal* 37. This article is a summary of a year-long study of inclusive education in New Brunswick, conducted by MacKay in 2005-6, which makes 95 recommendations for enhancing the quality of inclusive education.

28 A.W. MacKay, *Inclusion! What Is Inclusion Anyway?* booklet submitted to the New Brunswick Department of Education, July 2007, available online, Government of New Brunswick, http://www.gnb.ca/0000/publications/mackay/mackay-e.asp (MacKay Report).

29 Manitoba Education, Training and Youth, *Follow-up to the Manitoba Special Education Review: Proposals for a Policy, Accountability and Funding Framework* (Manitoba Education, Training and Youth, 2001).

30 *Law v. Canada*, [1999] 1 S.C.R. 497, at 549.

31 Bill Pentney, "Equality Values and the Canadian Promise of Community" (1996) 35 C.H.R.R. No. 6 C/6-C15.

32 For a more detailed analysis of inclusion and its limits in the school context, see A.W. MacKay, "The Lighthouse of Equality: A Guide to Inclusive Schooling," in M. Manley-Casimir, ed., *The Courts, the Charter and the Schools* (Toronto: University of Toronto Press, 2009).

33 *Carriere v. Lamont Co. School Board*, unreported decision, August 15, 1978 (Alta. Q.B.).

34 *Doré v. La Comm. Scholaire de Drummondville* (1983), 4 Can. H.R.R. D/1377 (Que. C.A.).

35 *Bonnah (Litigation Guardian of) v. Ottawa-Carleton District School Board* (2002), 2002 CarswellOnt 1212, 44 Admin. L.R. (3d) 25 (Ont. S.C.J.); affirmed 2003 CarswellOnt 1210, 64 O.R. (3d) 454, 170 O.A.C. 248 (C.A.). See also *Walker Youth Homes Inc. v. Ottawa-Carleton District School Board*, 2004 CarswellOnt 2237.

36 For further discussion on this topic, see E.M. Roher and A.F. Brown, "Special Education and Student Discipline" (2002) 14:1 *Education & Law Journal* 51.

37 See *Angle v. LaPierre*, 2008 ABCA 120, 2008 CarswellAlta 393 (Alta. C.A.), dismissing an appeal of the lower court's finding of defamation against a number of parents for their publications, which the court found constituted personal attacks against a school principal and teachers. R. Keel and N. Tymochenko, in *An Educator's Guide to Parental Harassment* (Aurora, ON: Canada Law Book, 2004), explore the line between legitimate child advocacy and harassment.

38 B.P. Nolan, J.E. Trépanier, and B. Ellerker, "When Special Needs Education and Safety Collide: How School Boards Can Balance the Competing Interests of Special Needs Students and a Safe School Environment" (2005) 14:3 *Education & Law Journal* 235.

39 *Bales*, supra note 4.

40 *Hickling v. Lanark-Leeds Roman Catholic School Bd.*, Ontario Board of Inquiry under the *Human Rights Code* (1986).

41 *Lanark, Leeds Roman Catholic School Bd. v. Ontario Human Rights Comm.* (1989), 57 D.L.R. (4th) 479 (Ont. CA). See also *Robb v. St. Margaret's School*, 2003 BCHRT 4, 2003 CarswellBC 3500 (BCHRT), in which the tribunal found the school had discriminated against the child when they withheld re-enrollment forms between grades 3 and 4, because of her severe learning disability.

42 *Eaton v. Brant County Board of Education,* [1997] 1 S.C.R. 241.

43 A.W. MacKay and V. Kazemierski, "And on the Eighth Day, God Gave Us Equality in Education" (1996) 7:1 *National Journal of Constitutional Law* 1.

44 *Bonnie Cudmore v. Province of New Brunswick Department of Education and School District 2,* 2003 CanLII 64199 (N.B.L.E.B.).

45 A.W. MacKay and J. Burt-Gerrans, "Inclusion and Diversity in Education: Legal Accomplishments and Prospects for the Future" (2003) 13:1 *Education & Law Journal* 77.

46 Supra notes 9 to 14.

47 *Auton (Guardian ad litem of) v. British Columbia (Attorney General),* 2004 SCC 78, [2004] 3 S.C.R. 657.

48 *Canada Health Act,* R.S.C. 1985, c. C-6.

49 *Wynberg v. Ontario,* 2005 CanLII 8749 (ONSC).

50 *Education Act,* R.S.O. 1990, c. E.2.

51 *Wynberg v. Ontario,* 2006 CanLII 22918 (ONCA).

52 Supra note 14.

53 *Wynberg v. Ontario,* 2007 Carswell2148, 153 C.R.R. (2d) 375 (note).

54 See *Kohn v. Ontario (Attorney General),* [2004] O.J. no. 4112 (Q.L.) (S.C.J.); see also *Bettencourt (Litigation Guardian of) v. Ontario,* (2005) 74 O.R. (3d) 550, 2005 CarswellOnt 106 (S.C.J.).

55 *Bettencourt,* ibid.

56 *Ibid.,* at 16. See also *McNabb (Litigation Guardian of) v. Ontario,* 2005 CarswellOnt 99 (S.C.J.), which was decided at the same time as *Bettencourt,* in which an injunction ordering the reinstatement of IBI treatment pending trial was ordered.

57 *Sagharian (Guardian ad litem of) v. Ontario (Minister of Education),* [2007] O.J. no. 876, 2007 CarswellOnt 1432 (S.C.J.).

58 *Sagharian (Guardian ad litem of) v. Ontario (Minister of Education),* [2008] ONCA 411, 2008 CarswellOnt 2888 (C.A.); leave to appeal refused by the Supreme Court of Canada 256 O.A.C. 398 (note).

59 Cited from Education Law eBulletin, April 2007, http://www.cpco.on.ca/LawLibrary/ ShibleyRighton/Shibley Righton LLP Education Law eBulletin - April 2007.pdf.

60 *D.J.N. v. Alberta (Child Welfare Panel),* [1999] A.J. no. 798 (Q.L.) (Q.B.).

61 Ibid., at para. 59.

62 A.W. MacKay, "Connecting Care and Challenge: Tapping Our Human Potential— Inclusive Education: A Review of Programming and Services in New Brunswick," January 2006, available in hard copy and online, Department of Education and Early Childhood Development, http://www.gnb.ca/0000/publications/mackay/mackay-e.asp.

63 *Wynberg v. Ontario,* supra note 49 at 665.

64 In Ontario, the *Accessibility for Ontarians with Disabilities Act, 2005,* S.O. 2005, c. 11 requires that the government work with the disabled community and the public and private sectors to establish standards for accessibility, and requires the development of committees to create these accessibility standards. However, the new Act does not require the implementation of these new standards until 2025.

65 See MacKay, supra note 62.

66 *Newfoundland (Treasury Board) v. N.A.P.E.,* 2004 SCC 66, [2004] 3 S.C.R. 381.

67 *Moore,* supra note 14.

68   *Blainey and the Ontario Hockey Association et al.* (1986), 26 D.L.R. (4th) 728 (Ont. C.A.).

69   See CAAWS, "Girls Playing on Boys Teams," http://www.caaws.ca/e/advocacy/article
.cfm?ID=7.

70   See CBC News, "Gender Equity: Girls on Boys' Sports Teams?," April 26, 2010, http://
www.cbc.ca/news/pointofview/2010/04/gender-equity-girls-on-boys-sports-teams.html.

71   *Pasternak v. Manitoba High School Athletic Association Inc. (No. 2)*, [2006] M.H.R.B.A.D.
No. 2, upheld by the Manitoba Court of Queen's Bench in *The Manitoba High School
Association Inc. v. Pasternak et al.*, 2008 MBQB 24 (CanLII).

72   *Casselman v. Ontario Soccer Association* (1993), 23 C.H.R.R.D. 307 (Ont. Bd. of Inquiry).

73   *Winnipeg School Division No. 1 v. McCarthur*, [1982] 3 W.W.R. 342 (Man. Q.B.).

74   See *Bhaduria v. Toronto (City) Board of Education* (1990), 1990 CarswellOnt 3713 (Bd. of
Inquiry); see also *Ayangma v. Prince Edward Island* (2000), 2000 CarswellPEI 118
(S.C.T.D.).

75   A.W. MacKay, "Human Rights and Education: Problems and Prospects" (1998) 8:1
Education & Law Journal 69; see also A. Wayne MacKay & C. Richard,
"Multiculturalism: Who Needs It?" (1998) 8 *Education & Law Journal* 265.

76   Fourteen-year-old Reena Virk was savagely beaten by a group of teenagers and
drowned by two of her original attackers in November 1997 in Vancouver, BC. Six
teenage girls were convicted of assault causing bodily harm for their roles in the initial
attack. Two other teenagers, Warren Paul Glowatski and Kelly Ellard, were convicted of
second degree murder for their roles in Virk's death.

77   See "Human Rights Settlement Reached with Ministry of Education on Safe Schools—
Terms of Settlement," Ontario Human Rights Commission online, http://www.ohrc
.on.ca/en/human-rights-settlement-reached-ministry-education-safe-schools-terms-
settlement.

78   Ibid.

79   Ibid.

80   See "School Board Programs for Students Who Have Received a Full Expulsion,"
Ontario Ministry of Education Policy/Program Memorandum No. 130, online: Ministry
of Education, http://www.edu.gov.on.ca/extra/eng/ppm/130.pdf.

81   BLAC Report on Education, *Redressing Inequality Empowering Black Learners*, vol. 1
(Halifax: Black Learner Advisory Committee, 1994).

82   See also B. Sokhansanj, "Our Father Who Art in the Classroom: Exploring a Charter
Challenge to Prayer in Public Schools" (1992) 56 *Saskatchewan Law Review* 47.

83   See the Supreme Court of Canada's decision regarding the right of a Sikh student to
wear a ceremonial dagger (the kirpan) to school: *Multani v. Commission scolaire
Marguerite-Bourgeoys*, 2006 SCC 6, [2006] 1 S.C.R. 256. See also W.H. Harris and A.
Ackah, "Freedom of Religion and Accommodating Religious Dress in Schools" (2011)
20 *Education & Law Journal* 211.

84   *Nurturing the Learning Spirit of First Nation Students: The Report of the National Panel on
First Nation Elementary and Secondary Education for Students on Reserve* (February
2012). This panel was created by the federal government of Canada and chaired by
Scott Haldane, CEO of the Y.M.C.A. in Canada. The importance of education to an
improved relationship with First Nations is also emphasized in the earlier Royal
Commission Report on Aboriginal Peoples. Further information about the report of
this commission can be viewed online, http://www.aadnc-aandc.gc.ca/eng/1307458586
498/1307458751962.

85   The Report of the Bouchard-Taylor Commission of Reasonable Accommodation of Minorities can be viewed online, http://accommodements-quebec.ca/documentation/memoires/A-N-Montreal/quebec-community-group-s-network.pdf.

86   *Jubran v. North Vancouver School District No. 44,* [2003] B.C.H.R.T.D. no. 10 (Q.L.); affirmed 2005 BCCA 201.

87   *Board of School Trustees of School District No. 44 (North Vancouver) v. Jubran,* 2005 CarswellBC 2475.

88   S. MacDonald, "Acknowledging the Rainbow: The Need for the Legitimization of Lesbian, Gay, Bisexual, and Transgender Youth in Canadian Schools" (2006) 16 *Education & Law Journal* 183.

89   *Hall (Litigation Guardian of) v. Powers,* [2002] O.J. no. 1803 (S.C.J.).

90   "Disclosure of Sexual Orientation" (1998) 12 *School Law Commentary* 1.

91   A.W. MacKay, Q.C., Chair, *Respectful and Responsible Relationships: There's No App for That,* Report of the Nova Scotia Task Force on Bullying and Cyberbullying, February 29, 2012, recommendation 23, at 47.

92   Bill 13, *Accepting Schools Act, 2012,* S.O. 2012, c. 5.

93   J. McKinlay, R.J. Konopasky, A. Konopasky, A.W. MacKay, and T. Barrett, "Bullying Finding Schools Liable Changes Everything," in R. Flynn, ed., *Rights and Reason: Shifting Tides in Education,* Proceedings of the 22nd Annual Conference of CAPSLE, St. John's Newfoundland (Toronto: CAPSLE, 2012), at 129. This article also suggests that "bullying" may be too soft a term for what is really a much harsher phenomenon involving assaults, threats, intimidation, and harassment.

94   Supra note 91, at 42-43.

95   Ibid., at 43.

96   D. Pepler and W. Craig, "What Should We Do About Bullying: Research into Practice" (1999) *Peacebuilder* 2, 9-10.

97   Ibid.

98   E. Roher, "When Push Comes to Shove: Bullying and Legal Liability in Schools" (2002-3) 12:1 *Education & Law Journal* 319, at 325. See also E. Roher, *An Educator's Guide to Violence in Schools,* 2nd ed. (Aurora, ON: Canada Law Book, 2010).

99   Supra note 96.

100 As *Jubran,* supra note 86, indicates, issues of bullying may also be pursued from a human rights perspective.

101 *Education Act,* R.S.O. 1990, c. E.2, s. 264(1)(e).

102 Supra note 86.

103 Roher, "When Push Comes to Shove," supra note 98, at 335.

104 Ibid.

105 *Calgary Sun,* May 14, 2004, as cited in Roher, "When Push Comes to Shove," supra note 98, at 323.

106 *Ottawa Citizen,* March 21, 2005, as cited in Roher, "When Push Comes to Shove," supra note 98, at 321.

107 Roher, "When Push Comes to Shove," supra note 98, at 336.

108 *R. v. D.W.,* [2002] B.C.J. no. 627 (Q.L.) (Youth Ct.).

109 Roher, "When Push Comes to Shove," supra note 98, at 341.

110 Supra note 86.

111   Supra note 91, chapters 4-7.

112   Eric Roher, "Dealing with Off-School Conduct: Cyberbullying, Drug Dealing, and Other Activities Outside of School Premises" (2012) 21 *Education & Law Journal* 91.

113   See Day of Pink, What's the DEAL.org, http://deal.org/youth-initiatives-database/day-of-pink.

114   *Cyberbullying Hurts: Respect for Rights in the Digital Age*, Report of the Senate Standing Committee on Human Rights, December 2012.

115   Roher, "When Push Comes to Shove," supra note 98, at 343.

116   Ibid., at 344.

117   St. Bonaventure's College, a private school in St. John's, recently made headlines for their implementation of a restorative justice program; see "St. John's School Embraces Restorative Justice," CBC News, http://www.cbc.ca/news/canada/newfoundland-labrador/story/2013/01/02/nl-school-restorative-justice-102.html.

118   S. Findlay, "Bullying Victims Are Taking Schools to Court," *Macleans Magazine*, September 14, 2011.

119   MacKay, "Safe and Inclusive Schooling," supra note 1.

5
Teachers as Agents of the Police

Two possible conflicting roles that teachers may have to adopt are highlighted by the intersection of education and criminal law. Reconciling the roles of teachers and administrators as educational agents and as agents of the police can be difficult. Furthermore, the problem of school violence ensures that resolving these conflicting roles will continue to be a real and pressing problem for educators.

Throughout the discussion of school rules in Chapter 3, Teachers as Educational State Agents, we did not discuss how teachers should handle students in the face of potential criminal consequences. The passage of the *Young Offenders Act* (YOA) in 1984 significantly altered the traditional position of schoolteachers and administrators with respect to young people. The YOA was followed by the *Youth Criminal Justice Act* (YCJA),[1] enacted in 2003. The YCJA built on the provisions of the YOA, making it necessary for teachers to distinguish between enforcing school rules as an educational state agent and enforcing the criminal law as an agent of the police.

Increasingly, the emphasis of provincial governments and school boards on special education and on keeping children in school through creative truancy programs has created a situation in which teachers are faced with the "unwilling child." In earlier times, children in a mainstream classroom were, for the most part, willing participants. The YCJA combined with a growing school board policy of inclusion has created an increasingly difficult classroom situation.

In addition to some provisions of the YCJA, there are a number of *Canadian Charter of Rights and Freedoms* ("the Charter") requirements that teachers must be aware of as police agents. In this chapter, we examine the provisions of the YCJA and some of the sections of the Charter that affect teachers' role as enforcer's of state law. Even the Supreme Court of Canada has had difficulty in drawing the line between teachers as educational state agents and teachers as agents of the police.[2]

The YCJA represented a shift in the philosophy of juvenile justice in Canada. The previous rehabilitative emphasis of the *Juvenile Delinquents Act* (JDA) was replaced by legislation that held young people responsible for their actions, and concurrently recognizes the special guarantees of the rights and freedoms of young people. This new model of juvenile justice has had a significant impact on the manner in which the school system handles young offenders, both in the investigation of offences and in the treatment of offenders after the courts have considered their cases.

The Juvenile Delinquents Act

The JDA of 1908 represented the first codification of a national system of juvenile justice in Canada; however, it may also be viewed as the product of a larger "child-saving" movement[3] that had its origins in the late 19th century. This movement of social reform was a response to the plight of children brought about by the increasing urban and industrialized society of the 19th and early 20th centuries.[4] The critical issue for the proponents of this early legislation was not whether children should be held accountable for their behaviour—criminal or otherwise—but how best to treat the child so that he could become a productive member of society.[5]

These child-saving origins of delinquency legislation are significant because they represent one of two opposing tensions at play when young people are involved in criminal activity—that is, whether the primary focus should be the protection of children from the harshness of society, or the protection of society from the antisocial behaviour of some children. This tension has been a recurring theme throughout the development of juvenile justice and continues to haunt the courts under the current regime. In strict legal terms, the *parens patriae* doctrine justifies the state in extending its protection "over various classes of persons who, from their legal disability, stand in need of protection, such as infants."[6] In addition, the federal government's constitutional authority to enact criminal law[7] provides the basis for the state's general obligation to protect society. The original drafting of the JDA in 1908 was the first attempt to balance the promotion of child welfare simultaneously with the perceived need to prevent and control the criminal misbehaviour of children.

The Young Offenders Act

With the exception of a few minor amendments in the 1930s,[8] the JDA remained unchanged until the mid-1960s. However, in 1960, the federal Department of Justice set up a five-member committee to recommend improvements to the juvenile system; this report, released in 1966, served as the blueprint for the eventual enactment of the YOA 16 years later.[9] An extensive consultation process took place over the 16-year period between the 1966 report and the final draft of the YOA. This process included draft legislation and political party proposals.[10]

These proposals addressed the areas that had been identified as problematic under the JDA—that is, the lack of emphasis on children taking responsibility for their actions, the vagueness of children's civil rights, the growing public hostility toward serious and violent young offenders, the age for criminal responsibility, and society's disillusionment with rehabilitative treatment.[11] Perhaps the most significant problem facing the reformers in the 1970s was the fact that, throughout the history of the JDA, there had never been a consistent and coherent set of policies and standards developed by either the judiciary or the legal profession.[12] This lack of direction may be attributed to the ambivalence toward lawyers and criminal procedure demonstrated by the original drafters of the JDA.[13] In any event, the task facing the drafters of the YOA was to find a middle ground between a paternalistic approach based on rehabilitation and treatment and a punitive approach based on the harshness of the adult criminal system.

The Youth Criminal Justice Act

Parliament first acknowledged the need for reform in the youth justice system in 1998 with the introduction of *A Strategy for Youth Justice Renewal*, which led to the enactment and coming into force of the YCJA on April 1, 2003. At the time, federal opposition parties in Parliament demanded a "get tough" approach to youth crime. Some had even expressed interest in lowering the age of criminal responsibility from 12 to 10, the age it once was under the JDA, and lowering the age at which a person is considered an adult from 18 to 16. However, youth justice system professionals expressed concern that court and custody were being overused under the YOA. Parliament avoided this approach, instead opting to address matters that it believed had not received adequate focus under the YOA.[14]

The YCJA builds on the strengths of the YOA, and addresses many identified weaknesses. Significant changes under the YCJA include a differentiation between violent and non-violent offences, a reduction in the use of incarceration for young offenders before and after trial, a new approach to sentencing, and the encouragement of a range of diversionary responses to non-violent youth offences, known as "extrajudicial measures."

In March 2012, the government passed Bill C-10 into law (the *Safe Streets and Communities Act*).[15] Bill C-10 was known as an "omnibus crime bill" because it made amendments to multiple pieces of legislation relating to criminal justice, including the YCJA. The resultant changes to the YCJA were largely panned by critics, who say that the amendments are a step back in the effort to rehabilitate young offenders in their communities. One significant change as a result of the new legislation is a shift from a focus on rehabilitation to a focus on "protection of society."

Declaration of Principle

The preamble to the YCJA illustrates a departure from the YOA. Although the preamble does not have the same force of law as the numbered sections of the Act, it is an important interpretative tool for courts, giving insight on the intentions of Parliament in enacting the YCJA. The declaration of principle in section 3 of the YCJA is an attempt by Parliament to provide guidance to decision-makers involved in the youth justice process. The YCJA recognizes the intent to prevent crime and the need for meaningful consequences, the differentiation between youth and adults in the criminal justice system, and the need to involve family and community in the rehabilitation and reintegration of youth.[16]

Age Limitation

There are age limits in the YCJA: the Act applies to young people ages 12 to 18. The criminal law considers people over 18 to be adults and handles them under the *Criminal Code*. Children under 12 cannot be charged with a crime because the law assumes they are too young to form the necessary criminal intent. If actions need to be taken to address a particularly violent, dangerous, or destructive child, they are typically taken under provincial child protection statutes.[17] Many feel that the legal sanctions for those under 12 are not adequate as a response to the growing violence at this age level.

Extrajudicial Measures

The YOA introduced youth justice diversion programs, which were termed "alternative measures." These alternative measures provided an option: if a young person accepted responsibility for her offence, the Crown could impose a penalty (for example, an essay on shoplifting) without putting the young person through the court system. These measures were usually available only for first-time offenders and did not result in any form of criminal record. One major problem with alternative measures was that they were discretionary and, consequently, applied inconsistently across the country.

Under the YCJA, alternative measures have been significantly expanded and codified in sections 4–12 to form extrajudicial measures. The provisions governing extrajudicial measures place an obligation on police officers and prosecutors before beginning judicial proceedings to consider the appropriateness of taking no further action, warning or cautioning the youths in question, or referring them to a community-based program. There is a strong presumption under the YCJA, where the offence is not violent or particularly serious, that the appropriate response is an extrajudicial measure, rather than the laying of charges.[18] Depending on the nature of the offence, an extrajudicial measure may be appropriate even for young persons with prior records of offences.[19]

Where a police officer believes an extrajudicial measure cannot adequately address a situation, the officer may choose to employ an extrajudicial sanction,[20] which involves an informal response to the violation. However, there are many requirements that must be met before an extrajudicial sanction may be used—for example, the young person must admit responsibility for the act and consent to being subjected to such a sanction.

Detention Before Sentencing

Parliament's concern with overreliance on incarceration also extends to pre-trial detention. Sections 28–31 of the YJCA incorporate the *Criminal Code* provisions governing pre-trial detention, with exceptions. The YCJA prohibits pretrial detention as a substitute for appropriate welfare or mental health protection. As well, there is a presumption that detention is unnecessary if a young person, after being found guilty in court, cannot be committed to custody as a result of sentencing restrictions under the YCJA. As an alternative to detention, section 31 allows for the placement of young persons in the care of a "responsible" person. The 2012 amendments have, however, made it easier for courts to remand young offenders pending trial where the alleged crime is of a serious nature.

Detention

The principles governing the detention of young persons are set out in detail in sections 38 and 39 of the YCJA, and require consideration of a number of factors. Proportionality is a prevalent theme under the YCJA. A young person's sentence cannot be greater than the punishment that an adult convicted of the same offence would receive, and the sentence must be in proportion to the seriousness of the offence. Generally, under section 39(1) of the YCJA, detention is prohibited unless one of the following criteria is met:

> (a) the young person has committed a violent offence;
> (b) the young person has failed to comply with non-custodial sentences;
> (c) the young person has committed an indictable offence for which an adult would be liable to imprisonment for a term of more than two years and has a history that indicates a pattern of findings of guilt under this Act or the *Young Offenders Act* ... ; or
> (d) in exceptional cases where the young person has committed an indictable offence, the aggravating circumstances of the offence are such that the imposition of a non-custodial sentence would be inconsistent with the purpose and principles set out in section 38.

Section 39(6) requires a court to consider a pre-sentence report and any sentencing proposal made by the young person or her counsel before committing the young person to custody.[21] Teachers can certainly be helpful in the preparation of a pre-sentence report, although they are not obligated to participate. As part of the report, a court may want to see a synopsis of an offender's attendance in school.

Right to Counsel

Section 25 provides an example of the YCJA's emphasis on civil rights for young people because it gives young offenders the right to retain and instruct counsel without delay at any stage of the proceedings; it also enables them to exercise this right personally, without having to involve a parent or guardian. When the YOA was enacted, it was silent about the personal exercise of this right, and the Manitoba Court of Appeal held that a young person did not have the capacity to retain and instruct counsel.[22] Parliament consequently amended the Act to allow young people to retain counsel directly. Section 25(2) requires every young person who is arrested or detained to be informed of his right to retain and instruct counsel without delay. This is reinforced by the terms of the *Convention on the Rights of the Child*, an international human rights convention originating from the United Nations whose tenets have been accepted by Canada.[23] Article 37 of the convention appears below.

> States Parties shall ensure that:
>
>   (a) No child shall be subjected to torture or other cruel, inhuman or degrading treatment or punishment. Neither capital punishment nor life imprisonment without possibility of release shall be imposed for offences committed by persons below eighteen years of age;
>
>   (b) No child shall be deprived of his or her liberty unlawfully or arbitrarily. The arrest, detention or imprisonment of a child shall be in conformity with the law and shall be used only as a measure of last resort and for the shortest appropriate period of time;
>
>   (c) Every child deprived of liberty shall be treated with humanity and respect for the inherent dignity of the human person, and in a manner which takes into account the needs of persons of his or her age. In particular, every child deprived of liberty shall be separated from adults unless it is considered in the child's best interest not to do so and shall have the right to maintain contact with his or her family through correspondence and visits, save in exceptional circumstances;
>
>   (d) Every child deprived of his or her liberty shall have the right to prompt access to legal and other appropriate assistance, as well as the right to challenge the legality of the deprivation of his or her liberty before a court or other competent, independent and impartial authority, and to a prompt decision on any such action.

Although this convention does not legally bind Canada, by signing it, the Canadian government has indicated Canada's intention to meet the standards set by the United Nations for the appropriate treatment of children and young persons. These standards may serve as an expansive source of interpretation for the courts when deciding whether the Crown has met its obligations with respect to young offenders.

Sentencing

Section 42 of the YCJA gives judges a wide range of sentencing options—for example, absolute discharges, fines, restitution, community service hours, treatment orders, and probation. Under sections 42(2)(j)–(k), a youth court may make a probation order containing terms and conditions pursuant to sections 55 and 56 of the Act, including "any other conditions set out in the order that the youth justice court considers appropriate." Judges must be careful to spell out the terms and conditions of probation clearly. If attendance at school is required as a term of probation, clear communication between the school and justice officials is necessary to promote effective cooperation.[24]

In *R. v. P.D.F.*,[25] a probation order was held to be too vague to be enforceable under section 26 of the YOA (now section 137 of the YCJA) because it simply required the youth to "live with mother and obey rules and curfew." Judge Naismith further held that if these terms were "fleshed out" (by a youth court worker, for example), it would amount to an unlawful delegation of a judicial function and consequently be invalid.

Custodial Dispositions

The custodial provisions under sections 42(2)(n)–(q) pose a particular problem for educators because custodial dispositions are disruptive to developing and maintaining a learning strategy for students who may be forced to miss many months of school. One significant and positive change is the requirement that the last third of a young offender's custodial sentence be served under supervision in the community (subject to some exceptions).[26] This is an attempt to do a better job of reintegrating young offenders into the community, with the goal of limiting recidivism. There is a general attitude that imprisonment does little to help put young people back on the right track.[27] The YCJA is more sensitive to this fact than earlier legislation had been, allowing a larger number of alternatives to incarceration. As noted above, under section 39(1), a young offender will not be incarcerated unless she has committed a violent offence, has failed to comply with non-custodial sentences, or has committed a serious offence for which an adult would be imprisoned for more than two years and has a history of having committed other crimes.

One significant concern for educators is that judges do not always take account of the school year when handing out a custodial disposition. Although judges will usually order as short a period of detention as possible in the circumstances, the timing of the sentence may still directly interfere with the school year. A young offender sentenced in November may receive six months, with the last two months served in the community under supervision. This means that the young person would find himself back in school (under community supervision) at the beginning of March. The school is then left to devise a suitable program for him.

Under the YCJA, judges have the power to detain young people found guilty of certain crimes (generally, violent offences) for the purpose of treatment rather than punishment. However, a judge may make such an order only when a young person is suffering from a mental or psychological illness or an emotional disturbance and there are reasonable grounds to believe that the treatment plan will reduce the risk that the young person will repeat the offence or commit another violent offence. Because a young person maintains her right to consent to physical or mental health care unless and until she reaches the point where she lacks capacity to make medical decisions, it is likely that these types of programs would require the consent of the offender. This consent is often difficult to obtain, because rehabilitation programs typically last longer than other custodial sentences.

Interference with Dispositions

Section 136 of the YCJA establishes an indictable offence punishable by imprisonment of up to two years for interfering with the disposition of a youth court. There are no reported cases of convictions for violating this section. In one BC case, however, while sentencing a young offender for her role in an assault, the court ordered that a copy of the section be served on two men who had in the past encouraged her to engage in criminal acts.[28] The court had ordered the offender, as a condition of her release on probation (after serving time in custody), to have no contact with these two men. Thus, it appears that section 136 may be used as a warning to prevent others from attempting to lure young offenders back to criminal activity.

School officials should be aware of the prohibitions in section 136 in order to avoid an accidental breach. The section prohibits anyone from "inducing or assisting" a young person to leave a place of custody unlawfully, or "knowingly harbouring or concealing" a young person. Therefore, if a young person ran away from a group home and showed up at a teacher's house at 3 a.m., looking for a place to stay, it could be a contravention of this section to allow him to stay overnight. It is important to note, however, that the teacher would be guilty of an offence only if she knew the young person was in custody.[29]

Section 136 further prohibits anyone from "inducing or assisting"[30] a young person to breach a condition of a disposition order (court sentence), or "wilfully preventing or interfering with" the performance of a condition contained in such an order. Consider the example of a young offender who is required to attend ten special counselling sessions as a part of a probation order, and a guidance counsellor who feels, after speaking with the young person, that four sessions are sufficient. The guidance counsellor could be subject to criminal sanction if he does not apply to have the order varied pursuant to section 59, but merely allows the sessions to end early. Admittedly, the likelihood of an educator being charged is slim, but it is important to be aware of the law in any event.

A School's Investigative Role

Often, young people who have contact with the criminal law system also experience difficulty with the authority structures in a school setting. For this reason, it is important that education professionals appreciate the implications of the YCJA and be familiar with its basic operation. Previously, most school officials relied on ad hoc and informal procedures when they investigated offences committed by students and were loath to involve any outside legal authorities. Now, under the YCJA, schools must adhere to special safeguards from the outset of any investigation of a young offender.

Section 24(2) of the Charter provides that a court may exclude any evidence obtained in a manner that violates an individual's rights if admission of the evidence "would bring the administration of justice into disrepute." Under the preamble of the YCJA, young people have a "special guarantee" of this evidentiary protection; therefore, authorities must be particularly careful when dealing with young offenders. School officials may well be barred from pursuing a criminal prosecution in cases where informal searches or questioning procedures violate the protections afforded to young people and consequently result in the exclusion of evidence. Lack of evidence commonly results in acquittals in the criminal context. Whether these exclusionary rules would apply to students outside the criminal context is far less clear. Courts may not interpret disciplinary hearings as being part of the administration of justice.

Arrest and Detention

Educators have the capacity to act both as educational state agents and as agents of the police. As mentioned earlier, it is not always clear in any given situation which role they are assuming.[31] Section 10 of the Charter requires police "on arrest or detention" to inform the accused promptly of the reasons for arrest, to inform the accused of his right to retain and instruct counsel, and to provide the opportunity to retain and instruct counsel without delay. Section 25(2) of the YCJA also requires an arresting officer to advise a young person of his right to counsel "without delay" upon arrest or detention. An educator who, in acting as an agent of the police, detains a young person for questioning may be required to comply with the requirements of section 10(b) of the Charter and section 25 of the YCJA.

In *R. v. J.M.G.*,[32] the Ontario Court of Appeal examined a situation in which a principal detained a young person in order to conduct a search for narcotics. Justice Grange assumed that the principal was acting in an educational capacity. He was not clear as to whether a principal should ever adhere to the section 10(b) Charter requirements, but did state that, in "serious" cases, a principal should either comply with the Charter or involve the police. Justice Grange further clouded the issue by claiming that students are in a "constant state of detention" while in school, and therefore it is impossible for them to be detained within the meaning of section 10 of the Charter. This likens the school to a prison,[33] and clearly violates the principle established in the United States that students do not shed their constitutional rights at the schoolhouse gates.[34] The approach of Justice Grange was also unacceptable in that it did not adequately protect the rights of the student, who faces the same consequences whether the investigation is conducted by the principal or the police.

The Supreme Court of Canada was provided the opportunity to resolve this question in *R. v. M. (M.R.)*.[35] In this case, a vice-principal brought students into his office to determine whether they were in possession of narcotics. The Supreme Court held that even if a student feels compelled to go to a principal's office, the student is not under "detention" for the purposes of section 10(b). The court stated:

> [Section 10(b)] was not meant to apply in relations between students and teachers. ... Its application in the school context is inappropriate.[36]

However, if a school official is acting as an agent of the police or if a police officer takes an active role in the student's detention, the situation may fall within the scope of section 10(b). In *R. v. A.B.S.*,[37] Youth Court Justice Crawford found that where students have been detained, as under section 10(b), they have a right to be informed of their Charter rights, including the right to counsel, without delay.

The question of how best to detain a child for investigation while maintaining the integrity of her Charter and YCJA protections still remains. Case law suggests that the courts continue to yield to the discretion of educators in these situations, even though this is inconsistent with the special protections afforded to young offenders under the preamble of the YCJA. Most educators welcome this discretion because they are not prepared to inform children of their "rights" at every detention. We would recommend, however, that school officials take a proactive stance in this area and set guidelines that are consistent with the YCJA protections. If the purpose of the detention is to enforce a school rule, no warnings or opportunities to consult legal counsel are required. However, if criminal proceedings are contemplated, the young person should be informed about the nature of the allegation, and at least be permitted to contact a parent before any further investigation takes place. It is necessary to maintain school order and discipline, but important to acknowledge that schools also serve as a microcosm of society at large. There is, therefore, an educational as well as a legal basis for offering a student the protections guaranteed by the Charter.

Search and Seizure

Section 8 of the Charter guarantees individuals the right to be "secure against unreasonable search or seizure." In *Hunter v. Southam*,[38] Justice Dickson set out four principles governing search and seizure. First, he stated that section 8 creates a "right to privacy" or a "right to be let alone."[39] Second, he found searches without a warrant to be *prima facie* unreasonable—that is, there is a presumption against the validity of the search that the searcher must rebut. Third, he dealt with the general constitutionality of searches in the following manner:

> An assessment of the constitutionality of a search and seizure ... must focus on its reasonable or unreasonable impact on the subject of the search or seizure, and not simply on its rationality in furthering a valid government objective.[40]

Justice Dickson's final principle addressed the balance between crime control and the protection of privacy rights; he concluded that this balance is achieved when "credibility based probability replaces suspicion."[41] The person conducting the search must, therefore, have some grounds beyond mere suspicion before engaging in the search.

In the school context, courts will view students as having a right "to be let alone," and any search will be deemed unreasonable unless a school official can provide a justification based on the impact of the search on the student. This is essentially the same test applied by the US Supreme Court in *New Jersey v. T.L.O. ("T.L.O.")*.[42] In this case, a principal searched the purse of a 14-year-old while looking for cigarettes; he found marijuana and a list of names implicating the student as a narcotics dealer. The court held that the constitutional prohibitions against unreasonable search and seizure applied to school officials; however, it found the search to be constitutionally valid, and therefore reasonable under the circumstances, because it was not excessively intrusive in light of the age of the student. The standard of "reasonableness" applied by Justice White is one that "would not unduly burden the efforts of school authorities to maintain order, nor would it authorize unrestrained intrusions of privacy."[43]

The test for what constitutes a reasonable search of a child by school officials as set out in *T.L.O.* was upheld by the US Supreme Court in their

2009 decision in *Safford Unified School District #1 v. Redding*.[44] In that case, a school principal confronted a 13-year-old middle-school student with an allegation that she had given pain medication to other students. She denied the allegation and agreed to allow the principal to search her belongings. After failing to find anything in that search, the principal had two female staff members search the student's person. They ordered the student to remove her outer clothing, and shake out her bra and underwear to prove that she was not hiding any contraband on her body.

The student's mother filed suit against the school district and three staff members who participated in the search of her daughter. The Supreme Court found that neither the search of the student's bag in her presence nor the search of her outer clothing was excessively intrusive in the circumstances, but requiring the student to shake out her underwear was unreasonable. The court held that the principal's knowledge that the pills in question were common painkillers, coupled with no evidence to suggest that the student had any hidden on her person, was insufficient to warrant the resultant "strip search." In essence, the court affirmed its earlier position in *T.L.O.* that although the standard to search a student remains a "reasonable suspicion" (that is, a lower threshold than the criminal threshold of probable cause), the method of search must be reasonably related to the objective of the search and must not be excessively intrusive when one considers the nature of the alleged infraction and the student's age and sex.

Canadian Supreme Court Justice Cory, in discussing searches within the school setting in *R. v. M. (M.R.)*, noted:

> Teachers and principals are placed in a position of trust that carries with it onerous responsibilities. When children attend school or school functions, it is they who must care for the children's safety and well-being. It is they who must carry out the fundamentally important task of teaching children so that they can function in our society and fulfill their potential. In order to teach, school officials must provide an atmosphere that encourages learning. During the school day they must protect and teach our children. In no small way, teachers and principals are responsible for the future of the country.
>
> ... Current conditions make it necessary to provide teachers and school administrators with the flexibility required to deal with discipline problems in schools. They must be able to act quickly and effectively to ensure the safety of students and to prevent serious violations of school rules.[45]

Justice Cory then adopted the reasonable-standard test as set out in *New Jersey v. T.L.O.* and *R. v. J.M.G.* He expanded on this test, outlining instances that may constitute reasonable grounds for a search by a school official in the school setting:

> The following may constitute reasonable grounds in this context: information received from one student considered to be credible, information received from more than one student, a teacher's or principal's own observations, or any combination of these pieces of information which the relevant authority considers to be credible. The compelling nature of the information and the credibility of these or other sources must be assessed by the school authority in the context of the circumstances existing at the particular school.[46]

The standard established in *R. v. M. (M.R.)* effectively requires school officials to have a "reasonable suspicion" that their search will turn up evidence, rather than "probable cause" that such evidence will be found.[47] Although this appears to violate the fourth principle set out by Justice Dickson in *Hunter*, the importance of crime control in the school system has led the courts to apply similar tests in education cases across Canada.

Personal Searches

Of the three types of searches that commonly occur in the school setting—personal, lockers (and other spaces), and "dragnet" searches—personal searches are the most contentious. The Supreme Court of Canada had the opportunity to review a personal search in the school setting in *R. v. M. (M.R.)*, where a vice-principal searched a student's socks after being informed by another student that the student was in possession of narcotics. The vice-principal found marijuana and the student was charged with possession. A plainclothes police officer was present during the search, but did not participate in any way until he arrested the student for possession. Justice Cory stated that the search by the vice-principal was by inference authorized by the *Education Act*.[48] The court upheld the search as reasonable because the vice-principal had received information from several reliable students implicating the arrested student and because the search was conducted in a minimally intrusive and sensitive manner.[49]

The *R. v. M. (M.R.)* situation clearly fits into the test from *New Jersey v. T.L.O.* and *R. v. J.M.G.* because the principal had a reasonable suspicion and the search was not excessively intrusive. There are, however, situations that may arise that would not be so easily dealt with. First, there is the case where a student is being searched for breach of a school rule (for example, smoking in the washroom) and, in the course of the investigation, a school official discovers grounds for a criminal charge (for example, possession of marijuana). Should evidence obtained in the search be admissible? In *New Jersey v. T.L.O.*, the evidence obtained as a result of this precise fact situation was admitted because the court failed to differentiate between the suspected breach of a school rule and the suspected breach of criminal law. An appropriate solution is to admit evidence obtained through a bona fide search for breach of a school rule, but to exclude evidence obtained by a school official who has engaged in a "fishing expedition," or who has authorized a search that was not reasonably necessary to establish that a school rule had been broken.

There is further potential for trouble in cases where a student does not cooperate in the search or physically resists it. What are the limits on the extent of the search? In *R. v. Morrison*,[50] the Ontario Court of Appeal upheld a strip search of a woman charged with theft and possession of stolen property; however, the search was conducted at the police station in the presence of a female officer and was incidental to a lawful arrest. Unless there is some element of imminent danger or urgency, it does not seem appropriate for school personnel to strip search young offenders. Further, a principal who anticipates that a student will physically resist a search should call the police. A principal certainly has a responsibility to maintain discipline and order in his school, but crime control is the job of law enforcement agencies and should be left to them whenever this is reasonably practical.

Searches of Lockers and Other Places

The second common type of search in schools is the locker search. Although there is some debate over the right of students to "exclusive possession" of their lockers,[51] it is unrealistic to expect the courts to declare lockers out of bounds for school personnel. The crux of the problem is that lockers create an expectation of privacy among students, and some consideration ought to be given to this expectation.[52] In the United States, students have been held to have exclusive possession of lockers in relation to other students, but not in relation to school authorities.[53] The lower expectation of privacy is what is likely to prevail in Canada as well.

In *R. v. S.M.Z.*,[54] the Manitoba Court of Appeal considered a student's expectation of privacy with regard to her locker. The court found that where the school provides students with lockers and has control and access to the lockers, either by way of a master key or by way of retention of the combinations for the locks, a student's expectation of privacy is "at the lower end of the scale."[55] The Court of Appeal concluded that the evidence resulting from the search of a locker and the seizure of its contents was admissible, and that the student's Charter right had not been violated. The simple course of action for schools, then, is to dispel any notion of privacy by notifying students at the beginning of each school year that their lockers are school property and may be subject to search at any time.[56] Students have a right to know about the limits that a school places on their reasonable expectations of privacy.

In one Ontario case, after his conduct aroused the suspicion of police officers, a student was found with a gun in his backpack on school property. In response to questioning, the accused denied ownership of the bag in which his school work was found, along with the loaded handgun. The lower court held that the student had been "psychologically detained" without legal justification; that the police had failed to inform the accused of his right to legal counsel; and that, furthermore, the accused's privacy rights were breached because the police had no lawful authority to search the backpack, and his detention was therefore arbitrary in contravention of section 9 of the Charter. He was acquitted of the charges. The Court of Appeal overturned the acquittal, finding that the student had not been psychologically detained prior to the discovery of the gun and, further, that the lower court had made an error in excluding the gun as evidence on the basis of Charter violations. The court noted:

> [80] This case involves a loaded handgun in the possession of a student on school property. Conduct of that nature is unacceptable without exception. It is something that Canadians will not tolerate. It conjures up images of horror and anguish the likes of which few could have imagined twenty-five years ago when the *Charter* first came to being. Sadly, in recent times, such images have become all too common—children left dead and dying; families overcome by grief and sorrow; communities left reeling in shock and disbelief.
>
> [81] That is the backdrop of this case and in my view, it provides the context within which the conduct of the police should be measured.[57]

In essence then, the Court of Appeal took the position that school safety and the protection of other students were factors important enough to override the Charter rights of an individual student.

Dragnet Searches

The third type of search involves a situation in which authorities search a large group of students in order to discover one or two offenders; it is commonly referred to as a "dragnet" or "blanket" search. In the US case *Bellnier v. Lund*,[58] for example, an entire grade 5 class was strip-searched in order to find a student who had stolen $3.00. The court ruled this search unreasonable. In another US decision, *Jones et al. v. Latexo Independent School District*,[59] the court reinstated two suspended students and held that the "blanket search or dragnet is, except in the most unusual and compelling circumstances, anathema to the protection accorded citizens under the Fourth Amendment."[60]

Canadian courts have also had the opportunity to consider random or dragnet searches in the school setting. In *R. v. A.M.*,[61] the police conducted a search throughout a school using drug-sniffing dogs in response to a standing invitation from the principal, welcoming a search when the police were available. Students were informed of the search by the school principal via the public address system and were told to stay in their classrooms for the duration of the search. During the search, a dog focused in on a backpack in the school gymnasium. No students were present at the time. Upon searching the bag, the police found several forms of illegal drugs and drug paraphernalia.

The bag also contained A.M.'s wallet and identification. A.M. was charged with possession for the purpose of trafficking and other related offences. His legal counsel argued that the evidence against him should be excluded as the product of an unreasonable search. The court found that the principal had no information to suggest a reasonable belief that there were drugs in the school on this particular day. Accordingly, the court ruled that, in the absence of reasonable grounds for conducting it, the police search did not fall within the principles outlined in *R. v. M. (M.R.)* and the evidence was excluded. The court was clear that its decision was not meant to change the standard of "reasonable suspicion" in order to justify the use of drug-sniffing dogs, but that, in this case, the standard was not met.

Informational Searches

In today's school environment, students are frequently in possession of devices containing significant personal information. Smartphones, laptops, and iPads are just a few devices that can contain more personal information about students and their lives outside the classroom than would the same students' lockers, backpacks, or purses. The question of when schools can intercept and search such devices and what information they can take from them is a matter of increasing legal importance.

In one relatively recent American case,[62] school officials seized a student's cellphone. After taking possession, school administrators used the phone to determine if other students were violating the school's cellphone policy and, after accessing the student's texts and voice messages, found a message that implicated the student in dealing drugs. The court ultimately found that, although the administrators' seizure of the phone was justified because the student had violated school rules by using the phone, the search of the phone's contents was not justified in light of the absence of previous suspicion about the drug related activity.

Another American case took a different approach. In *J. W. v. Desoto County School District* ("*J. W.*"),[63] a student's phone was confiscated after he used it during school hours in violation of school policy. A subsequent search of the phone by a school official revealed a photo of another of the school's students with a BB gun. The school disciplined the owner of the phone because it took the position that the photo violated a school policy prohibiting students from displaying gang-affiliated messages (and the school took the position that the BB gun photo was evidence of gang activity). Although acknowledging that the school did not have suspicion of gang activity prior to the search of the phone, the court concluded that the student's rights (against unreasonable search and seizure) were not violated. The court cited the need for deference to the school's actions based on the principal's concerns about the student as a threat to school safety.[64]

It is unclear at this point whether Canadian courts will follow the American lead and, if so, which one of the above approaches. It is worth noting that such matters are always seen by the courts as contextual and fact-specific.

Questioning Students and the Admissibility of Statements

Persons in Authority

Questioning students is a widespread practice in Canadian schools, and can be a powerful tool in gathering evidence against young offenders. Section 146 of the YCJA sets the ground rules that must be followed before statements can be admitted as evidence. The first important feature of this section is that it applies to "persons in authority." In *Rothman v. The Queen*,[65] the Supreme Court of Canada determined that "persons in authority" are to be defined by means of a subjective test; therefore, if teachers are regarded as persons in authority by their students, they will be similarly regarded by the law. "Authority" is not used in its colloquial sense, but must involve a belief by the person who makes the statement that the person to whom it is made can influence the course of a prosecution.[66] In *R. v. H.*,[67] both the Alberta Youth Court and the Court of Queen's Bench agreed that teachers are persons in authority for the purposes of section 146(2).

In *R. v. Wells*,[68] the Supreme Court of Canada examined the factors to be considered in deciding whether or not a person is a "person in authority." Following *Rothman*, the court found the test to be subjective, from the viewpoint of the student, but it also required there to be a reasonable basis for the student's belief. People who are engaged in an arrest, detention, or examination, or whom the student reasonably believes are acting on behalf of the police or prosecutors—and may therefore be in a position to influence proceedings—are "persons in authority."

Because courts may consider school officials to be persons in authority, these officials must be aware of the requirements of section 146(2) if they wish statements given by students to be available for use in criminal proceedings. The first criterion, under section 146(2)(a), is that the statement be "voluntary." The term "voluntary" has a long and complicated legal history; however, it is sufficient for the purposes of this discussion to treat it as meaning that statements must be given "without fear of prejudice or hope of advantage exercised or held out by a person in authority."[69] In the school setting, threats of after-school detentions or promises that "things will go easier if you just tell the truth" may render statements inadmissible. In general, teachers should be cautious about conducting investigations in cases where there may be criminal consequences.

Informing Youths of Their Rights

The second criterion, set out in section 146(2)(b), is more problematic than the voluntariness criterion because it forces educators to act as police officers in informing students of their rights. Unlike the debate over informing students of their Charter right to instruct counsel once they are detained, the situation under the YCJA is clear: a student must be informed of her rights under section 146(2) if her statement is to be used as evidence against her. This requirement reflects a change in philosophy from that of the JDA because the YCJA emphasizes the need to protect the rights of children at every stage of the criminal process. It is important to note that the student is entitled to have her rights explained to her in a language that she understands. Studies in the United States have shown that children do not fully understand or appreciate their rights when they receive a *Miranda*-type warning.[70] It is, therefore, advisable for school boards to draft a plain-language document to be used in schools for advising students of their rights. Perhaps it would be even more appropriate to institute a policy of no questioning in cases where criminal consequences are clearly involved. In such cases, questioning is properly a matter for the police.

Consultation with an Appropriate Adult

Section 146(c) allows a youth to consult with a parent, counsel, relative, or "other appropriate adult" before making a statement. It may be difficult and time-consuming to contact one of these individuals; however, the youth must be allowed this opportunity as a statutory right.

A specific problem arises when a student chooses a teacher to be the "other appropriate adult." Section 146(9) of the YCJA indicates that persons consulted under section 146(2)(c) are not persons in authority for the purposes of this section.[71] Statements that a youth makes to a teacher acting in this capacity may therefore be admissible against him without the protection included in section 146(2)(b). Teachers should be particularly careful when asked to consult with a young person (within the meaning of s. 146(c)) so that they are not put in the awkward position of betraying their student's confidence. If the Crown subpoenaed the teacher to testify at the student's subsequent trial, the law would require the teacher to relate the entire contents of a conversation that the student may have thought was confidential. If the student consults a lawyer pursuant to section 146(2)(c), the conversation is protected by solicitor–client privilege (confidentiality). Similarly, parents are not required to testify against their children. There is no such teacher–student guarantee of confidentiality. Accordingly, we suggest that teachers not act as advisers under this section in cases where there is a potential for serious criminal consequences.[72]

Summary: Questioning Students

The questioning of students highlights the importance of differentiating between criminal and in-school investigations. Section 146 leaves little room for discretion on the part of educators; it comes into operation immediately if any of the statements made by a student are to be used as evidence against him.[73] The Supreme Court of Canada has determined that the requirements of section 146 are to be strictly adhered to, no matter how old or "street wise" a child may appear to be.[74] This reinforces the argument presented earlier that educators should develop different procedures when handling students who may be subject to possible criminal consequences than when enforcing school rules. In fact, we suggest that the difficulties of both questioning and searching students make it advisable to develop a working relationship with police officers and to use the resources of the police force to deal with situations involving criminal activity.

Citizen's Arrest

Because the minimum age of criminal responsibility is 12 years, the YCJA is relevant for elementary (up to grade 6) school teachers and principals only when they are investigating the actions of other young people over the age of 12, from outside their schools. There may be cases, for example, of children from a nearby high school vandalizing elementary school property or selling drugs to younger children. In these instances, an elementary school official should take appropriate action to stop the behaviour in question.

For the most part, school officials should consider the law governing searching and questioning discussed earlier, because the same rules apply to an elementary school teacher when dealing with a young offender. The primary issue occurs on the detention of a student: a high school student may choose not to voluntarily submit to being detained in an elementary school after being observed committing an offense. In cases where an offender will not cooperate with school authorities, it is possible to make a citizen's arrest. Adding further complication is that section 494 of the *Criminal Code* allows citizens to make arrests only when they find someone committing an indictable offence or when they believe an individual has committed a criminal offence and is being "freshly pursued" by the police.[75]

Indictable offences are generally serious offences under the *Criminal Code*, such as robbery, theft with violence or threat of violence, sexual assault, assault, vandalism, and the possession of or trafficking in illegal drugs (contrary to sections 4 and 5 of the *Controlled Drugs and Substances Act*).[76] If a school official witnesses one of these or similar offences, he or she has the lawful authority to place a student under arrest and deliver her to the police as soon as reasonably practicable. Because arrest is a highly intrusive act, any citizen should be cautious in exercising this power. There is a danger of civil liability for false imprisonment in cases where a citizen makes an arrest without lawful authority. For example, if a teacher was simply told about an offence and did not actually witness the event, she would have no power to arrest a student under section 494 of the *Criminal Code*. Furthermore, most citizens, including teachers, are not aware of which crimes are indictable and which are not.

A citizen can make an arrest by uttering words indicating that a person is under arrest and touching the person with a view to detention.[77] Once a person has been detained, he should be informed of the reasons for the arrest and his right to retain and instruct counsel (or a parent) without delay.

He should also be provided with access to a telephone. Section 494(3) of the *Criminal Code* states that the arrested person must be delivered to the police officer "forthwith"; therefore, there will ordinarily be no time for questioning. If, however, a young person is questioned, he should be informed of his rights under section 146 of the YCJA.

Student Records and the Youth Criminal Justice Act

An additional issue with regard to young offenders is the relationship between the school's duty to maintain a student record and section 110 of the YCJA, which prohibits the publication of a young offender's identity (with some exceptions). On a strict reading of section 110, it is unlawful for teachers to note on the student's record whether the student has been charged with or convicted of an offence under the YCJA because this would effectively "publish" the name of the offender.

This is a distressing development for two reasons. First, in cases where a student has been in custody as a result of her offence and, therefore, has been absent from school for three or four months, it may be vital for her future instruction to have the absence noted on her record. (In Chapter 6, Teachers as Social Welfare Agents, we discuss the school's role as a rehabilitative agency for young offenders after their custodial disposition, under the heading "Teachers as YCJA Rehabilitation Counsellors.") Second, most teachers would like to know whether they have a potentially violent child in their classroom—particularly if the child has come from another school or province, and her record contains no reference to the commission of a violent crime.

Perhaps an argument can be made that the restricted access to student records is sufficient protection for the young person, and that therefore the notation of a criminal offence on the record is not publication. In one Ontario case, however, the Supreme Court of Canada determined that a school board could not hold an expulsion hearing because the hearing would inevitably lead to the publication of the identities of the accused through their absence at school.[78] Following this case, the Supreme Court of Canada, in discussing publication under the YOA, stated in *Re F.N.*:

> The phrase "publish by any means any report" in s. 38(1) can therefore refer to something as formal as a government report or an article in a newspaper or as informal as court observers spreading gossip and innuendo.[79]

Given this broad definition of "publication," it is unlikely that courts will allow the notation of offences in a student record in the face of section 10 of the YCJA.

Competing Interests: Attempts at Resolution

Thus far, we have examined a teacher's role as an enforcer of rules under the Charter as an educational state agent and as an enforcer of the *Criminal Code* as a police agent under the YCJA. We now offer the following situations as an exercise in examining some of the difficult issues teachers and administrators face under the YCJA. In these cases, schools have taken disciplinary action through in-school mechanisms against students charged, but not yet convicted, under the YOA, the predecessor to the YCJA. The cases illustrate a classic dilemma between protecting a young person's Charter rights and maintaining a safe and orderly environment in the school. There are no clearly correct courses of action to reconcile all the interest involved in these cases.

The first case arose in a Saskatchewan school, where three students were charged and pleaded not guilty to allegations of sexual assault.[80] In response to the charges, the school placed the youths on "short bounds" restrictions, which required them to go immediately to their classroom on arrival at school and remain there for the duration of the day, except to attend physical education classes; in addition, they were to move through the halls only with the permission of a staff member. The parents challenged these restrictions. However, Justice MacLellan found them to be a valid exercise of the school board's powers to "exercise general supervision and control over schools" pursuant to section 91 of the *Education Act*.[81]

A second case occurred in Ontario, where four youths pleaded not guilty to charges of forcible confinement and sexual assault.[82] The principal of their school subsequently suspended them. The Peel Board of Education upheld the suspensions and moved to have the students expelled. It initiated an application to the Ontario Supreme Court to determine whether the proposed expulsion hearing would offend section 38 of the YOA, which prohibited the publication of the identity of a young offender. Justice Read held that the expulsion hearing could not proceed because it would inevitably lead to the publication of the identities of the accused and prematurely stigmatize them as guilty. Justice Read further stated:

> This comes distressingly close to condemnation without trial. The principal seems to have assumed that the students were guilty simply

because they were charged. That is wholly contrary to the fundamental principal of our system of justice. Everyone is presumed innocent until found guilty by due process of law. Had the principal not jumped to the conclusion that the students were guilty he would have no basis for ordering the suspension.[83]

A later Ontario case reached a different conclusion. In *G. (F.) v. Scarborough (City) Board of Education*[84] the guardians of two students brought an application before the court asking that the school board be prevented from holding an expulsion hearing pending the outcome of a related criminal trial. The three-judge panel in this case reached the opposite conclusion from the judge in the prior Ontario case, stating:

> [14] Conducting an expulsion hearing does not, by itself, constitute publication of a report that an offence, or an alleged offence, has been committed by a young person. Neither does a decision under s. 23(3) of the *Education Act* to expel a pupil constitute a conclusion that the student is also guilty of an outstanding criminal offence, given two sets of proceedings, different burdens of proof and a different purpose and focus to each.
>
> [15] The ordinary words to be ascribed to the words "publish" in s. 38(1) of the *Young Offenders Act* do not preclude holding a hearing under the *Education Act*. The Board may seek to hold the expulsion hearing in private, pursuant to s. 9 of the *Statutory Powers Procedures Act*, R.S.O. 1990, c. S.22. Section 207 of the *Education Act* empowers closed board hearings. Where a hearing is held *in camera*, confidentiality may be maintained.
>
> [16] In our opinion, the *Young Offenders Act* was never intended to deprive principals and school boards of the ability to enforce order and discipline in their schools. To interfere with the mandate of principals and school boards, in the exercise of disciplinary proceedings, would require very clear and concise language, which is nowhere to be found in the *Young Offenders Act*. In our view, it was never intended by parliament that the *Young Offenders Act* would be used as a shield against the enforcement of school discipline.
>
> [17] The Board has conducted itself in a manner that maintains confidentiality. It proposed to hold the expulsion hearing in private. For these reasons, we conclude that the *Young Offenders Act* does not preclude the Board from proceeding with the expulsion hearing.[85]

There are two important principles in conflict in these cases. The first principle is that school authorities should suspend students who are suspected of criminal conduct so that other students in the school are not put at risk. The second principle is that everyone has the right to be presumed innocent, and that children, in particular, should not be prematurely stigmatized as being guilty. Although the Ontario cases focus on protecting the identity of young offenders, the presumption of innocence is arguably the more significant issue. There are no simple answers to the questions that arise when a student is charged with a serious criminal offence. Section 7 of the Charter may protect the right of children to receive an education and not to be deprived of that right except in accordance with the principles of fundamental justice. Furthermore, section 11(d) of the Charter guarantees the presumption of innocence (although this is only true in the context of criminal or other serious offences). On the other hand, there are good public policy reasons for limiting these rights where school children are potentially at risk, and section 1 of the Charter allows school authorities to create reasonable limits.

We suggest that placing "short bounds" restrictions on students such as those used by the school in Saskatchewan may be an appropriate compromise, but it is far from being a definitive solution to all such situations. There are a number of variables to be considered in each case. These include the character of the students involved and the seriousness of the offence with which they are charged. Regardless of the manner in which the school deals with a particular case, it is recommended that school boards develop written policies for implementing discipline procedures, so that procedures can be more easily defended under section 1 of the Charter as limits that are "prescribed by law." School boards should also be sensitive to the need for protecting the identity of young offenders whenever possible. However, it is our contention that discipline procedures within the school need not be suspended until after the criminal process is finished.

The meshing of statutes, regulations, and policies were difficult even before the Charter's enactment. The additional challenges of the Charter in the discipline process have sent some educators scurrying for cover. There have, however, been relatively few actual Charter challenges with respect to the intersection of education and the criminal law. There is still time for educators to make proactive decisions before the courts require them to do so. Because classroom teachers are often in direct contact with many of these students, it is vital that they take an active role in the process. A careful in-school review of rules, procedures, and penalties may prevent legal action and give educators a greater sense of being in control of their own destinies. Action is better than reaction.

Summary

In this chapter we have discussed the interaction of police authorities with the school system and the varying investigative roles of school personnel. It is important to distinguish between a school investigation for breach of school rules and a police investigation involving criminal law. Drawing this line can be difficult given the overlap that can often occur between these two spheres. There is no dome of immunity for schools and the laws of the land must still be applied, albeit in a modified form. When teachers play a role as police agents, it must be one that is consistent with their primary roles as educational agents, including the promotion of a safe learning environment. Interaction with the police is an unfortunate necessity of modern school life. The question remains, however, what form and degree such interactions should take. The intersection between the schools and criminal law is an interesting and growing area that has an important impact on the lives of students and educators. Striking the proper balance between students' rights and maintaining order in schools is an ongoing challenge.[86]

NOTES

1 *Youth Criminal Justice Act*, S.C. 2002, c. 1.

2 For an example of this, see *R. v. M. (M.R.)*, [1998] 3 S.C.R. 393. This case was critiqued as well at the lower levels; see A.W. MacKay, "Don't Mind Me, I'm from the R.C.M.P.: R. v. M.R.M. Another Brick in the Wall Between Students and Their Rights" (1997) 7 C.R. (5th) 24.

3 For a discussion of the child-saving movement in the United States, see A. Platt, *The Child Savers: The Invention of Delinquency* (Chicago: University of Chicago Press, 1969); see also G. Parker, "American Child Saving: The Climate of Reform as Reflected in the National Conference of Charities and Corrections, 1875–1900" (1968) 18 *University of Toronto Law Journal* 371.

4 G. Parker, "Century of the Child" (1967) 45 *Canadian Bar Review* 741. The child-saving movement in Canada was represented by W.L. Scott and J.J. Kelso, who lobbied extensively for delinquency legislation, and consequently played a major role in drafting the JDA of 1908.

5 J. Leon, "The Development of Canadian Juvenile Justice: A Background for Reform" (1977) 15:1 *Osgoode Hall Law Journal* 71, at 81.

6 *Jowitt's Dictionary of English Law*, 2nd ed. (London: Sweet and Maxwell, 1977).

7 *Constitution Act, 1867* (U.K.), 30 & 31 Vict., c. 3, s. 91(27).

8 S.C. 1929, c. 46; S.C. 1932, c. 17; S.C. 1935, c. 41; S.C. 1936, c. 40; S.C. 1947, c. 37; S.C. 1949 (1st Sess.), c. 6.

9 Department of Justice, *Juvenile Delinquency in Canada: The Report of the Department of Justice Committee on Juvenile Delinquency* (Ottawa: Queen's Printer, 1965).

10 S. Reid and M. Reitsma-Street, "Assumptions and Implications of New Canadian Legislation for Young Offenders" (1984) 7:1 *Canadian Criminal Forum* 1, at 2.

11   P. Gabor, I. Greene, and P. McCormick, "The Young Offenders Act: The Alberta Youth Court Experience in the First Year" (1986) 5 *Canadian Journal of Family Law* 301. See also R. Corrado, "Juvenile Justice: From Creation and Optimism to Disillusionment and Reform," in R. Corrado, M. Le Blanc, and J. Trépanier, eds., *Current Issues in Juvenile Justice* (Toronto: Butterworths, 1983), 31-48; N. Boyd, "The Circularity of Punishment and Treatment: Some Notes on the Legal Response to Juvenile Delinquency" (1980) 3 *Canadian Journal of Family Law* 419. Boyd argues convincingly that the major problem with the rehabilitative ideal of juvenile institutions is the contradiction inherent in the goals of custody and treatment.

12   D.M. Steinberg, "The Young Offender and the Courts" (1972) 6 R.F.L. 86, at 87.

13   Supra note 4, at paras. 94 and 102.

14   N. Bala, "Diversion, Conferencing, and Extrajudicial Measures for Adolescent Offenders" (2003) 40 *Alberta Law Review* 991; see also R. Barnhorst, "The Youth Criminal Justice Act: New Directions and Implementation Issues" (2004) 46:3 *Canadian Journal of Criminology and Criminal Justice* 231.

15   *Safe Streets and Communities Act*, S.C. 2012, c. 1.

16   Barnhorst, supra note 14, at 233.

17   See Nova Scotia's *Children and Family Services Act*, S.N.S. 1990, c. 5, s. 22, which indicates that a child is in need of protective services when he has killed or seriously injured another person, caused serious property damage as a result of a lack of supervision by a parent or guardian, or when that parent or guardian refuses necessary services or treatment to prevent a recurrence of the behaviour.

18   *Youth Criminal Justice Act*, supra note 1, s. 4(c).

19   Ibid., s. 4(d).

20   Ibid., s. 10.

21   *R. v. M.S.S.* (1985), 23 C.C.C. (3d) 95 (Sask. C.A.); *R. v. J.D.B.*, summarized in 1 W.C.B. (2d) 344 (B.C.C.A.); and *R. v. D.W.H.*, summarized in 17 W.C.B. (2d) 180 (Alta. C.A.).

22   *R. v. W.W.W.* (1985), 20 C.C.C. (3d) 214 (Man. C.A.).

23   Adopted by the United Nations by resolution 44/25, November 20, 1989; ratified by Canada in December 1991.

24   A.W. MacKay, "Principles in Search of Justice for the Young: What's Law Got to Do with It?" (1995) 6:1 *Education & Law Journal* 181.

25   *R. v. P.D.F.* (1987), 57 C.R. (3d) 22 (Ont. Prov. Ct.).

26   *Youth Criminal Justice Act*, supra note 1, s. 42(2)(n).

27   J. Hackler, "The Impact of the Y.O.A." (1987) 29:2 *Canadian Journal of Criminology* 205, at 208.

28   *R. v. J. (E.A.)*, 2005 CarswellBC 502, 2005 BCPC 64.

29   See *R. v. Chernish* (1954), 109 C.C.C. 398 (Ont. C.A.) for a discussion of complicity in the context of aiding and abetting.

30   The Supreme Court of Canada has defined "assisting" as meaning encouraging the offence, facilitating its commission, or hindering its prevention. See *Dunlop and Sylvester v. The Queen*, [1979] 2 S.C.R. 881 (1979), 47 C.C.C. (2d) 93.

31   A.W. MacKay and L.I. Sutherland, "Making and Enforcing School Rules in the Wake of the Charter of Rights," in Y.L.J. Lam, ed., *Canadian Public Education System: Issues and Prospects* (Calgary: Detselig Enterprises, 1990), 65.

32 *R. v. J.M.G.* (1987), 54 C.R. (3d) 380 (Ont. C.A.); leave to appeal to the Supreme Court of Canada refused. For a stinging critique of this decision, see A.W. MacKay, "Students as Second Class Citizens Under the Charter" (1987) 54 C.R. (3d) 390.

33 For a detailed analysis of the "school as prison" analogy, see A.W. MacKay, "R. v. J.M.G. Case Comment: Students as Second Class Citizens Under the Charter" (1987) 54 C.R. (3d) 390. For an alternative view, see B.E. Thom and D.J. Thom, "School Order and Discipline Preferred Over Students' Rights: R. v. G. (J.M.)" (1990-91) 3:1, *Education & Law Journal* 105.

34 *Tinker v. Des Moines Independent Community School District*, 21 L. Ed. (2d) 733, at 737 (U.S.S.C. 1969).

35 *R. v. M. (M.R.)*, supra note 2.

36 Ibid., at para. 67.

37 *R. v. A.B.S.*, [1995] N.S.J. no. 535 (Q.L.) (Youth Ct.).

38 *Hunter v. Southam* (1984), [1984] 2 S.C.R. 145, 14 C.C.C. (3d) 97.

39 Ibid., at 159 (S.C.R.), 108 (C.C.C.).

40 Ibid., at 157 (S.C.R.), 106 (C.C.C.).

41 Ibid., at 167 (S.C.R.), 115 (C.C.C.).

42 *New Jersey v. T.L.O.*, 83 L. Ed. (2d) 720 (U.S.S.C.) ("*T.L.O.*"). For a critical comment on this decision, see S.M. Mooney, "New Jersey v. T.L.O.: The School Search Exception to Probable Cause" (1985) 21:2 *New England Law Review* 509.

43 R.V. Farley, "The Charter and Student Rights," in T. Wuester and A. Nicholls, eds., *Education Law and the Canadian Charter of Rights and Freedoms* (Vancouver: British Columbia School Trustees Association, 1986), 26, at 32.

44 *Safford Unified School District #1 v. Redding* (No. 08-479), 531 F.3d 1071 (U.S.S.C. 2009).

45 *R. v. M. (M.R.)*, supra note 2, at paras. 35-36.

46 Ibid., at para. 50.

47 L. Robinson, "The Charter and Searches and Seizures in Schools," in T. Wuester and A. Nicholls, supra note 43, at 96.

48 *Education Act*, S.N.S. 1995-96, c. 1.

49 *R. v. M. (M.R.)*, supra note 2, at paras. 52-54.

50 *R. v. Morrison* (1987), 35 C.C.C. (3d) 437 (Ont. C.A.).

51 *R. v. M. (M.R.)*, supra note 2, at para. 99.

52 Ibid., at para. 98.

53 *People v. Overton*, 229 N.E. (2d) 598 (C.A.N.Y. 1967). See also *T.L.O.*, supra note 42.

54 *R. v. S.M.Z.*, [1998] M.J. no. 587 (Q.L.) (C.A.) ("*S.M.Z.*"). See also *R. v. J.M.*, 2012 BCPC 126 (CanLII), where the BC Provincial Court considered the reasonableness of a search of a student's locker and jacket based on the smell of marijuana emitting from the locker.

55 *S.M.Z.*, ibid., at para. 21.

56 This approach was upheld in *Zamora v. Pomeroy*, 639 F.2d 665 (C.A.N.M. 1981), where school board regulations provided, "1. The school retains jurisdiction over lockers even though lockers are assigned to particular students. 2. The administration may inspect lockers at any time."

57 *R. v. B.(L.)*, 2007 ONCA 596.

58 *Bellnier v. Lund*, 438 F. Supp. 47 (N.D.N.Y. 1977).

59 *Jones et al. v. Latexo Independent School District*, 499 F. Supp. 223 (Dist. Ct. Texas 1980).

60 *R. v. M. (M.R.)*, supra note 2, at para. 97.

61 *R. v. A.M.*, 2008 SCC 19, [2008] 1 S.C.R. 569; affirming *R. v. A.M.* (2006), 79 O.R. (3d) 481 (Ont. C.A.); affirming *R. v. A.M.* (2004), 120 C.R.R. (2d) 181, 2004 ONCJ 98. The Supreme Court referred to Wayne MacKay's critique of the decision in *R. v. M. (M.R.)*, supra note 2, but only to disagree with the student rights emphasis or, more accurately, to emphasize school discipline and order as the primary concern. See also *R. v. Buhay*, 2003 SCC 30, [2003] 1 S.C.R. 631, which considered the reasonable expectation of privacy in a rented locker in a bus station.

62 *Klump v. Nazareth School District*, 425 F. Supp 2d 622 (E.D. Pa. 2006).

63 *J.W. v. Desoto County School District*, 09-Cv-00155 (N.D. Miss. 2010).

64 For an interesting discussion about student privacy rights in schools in the face of new technology, see S. Ratman, "Privacy Implications and Student's Rights with Regard to Device and Strip Searches: A Need to Reevaluate the Existing Search and Seizure Doctrine for Schools" (2012) [unpublished], archived at Schulich School of Law, Dalhouse University.

65 *Rothman v. The Queen*, [1981] 1 S.C.R. 640 (1981), 59 C.C.C. (3d) 30.

66 *R. v. A.B.* (1986), 50 C.R. (3d) 247, at 258 (Ont. C.A.). See also N. Bala, "Questioning of Young Suspects" (1986), 50 C.R. (3d) 260.

67 *R. v. H.* (1985), 43 Alta. L.R. (2d) 250 (Prov. Ct.); affirmed by unreported decision, June 26, 1986 (Alta. Q.B.).

68 *R. v. Wells*, [1998] 2 S.C.R. 517 (1998), 127 C.C.C. (3d) 500.

69 Bala, supra note 66. See also *Ibrahim v. The King*, [1914] A.C. 599, at 609 (P.C.) for the definition of "voluntary statements."

70 A.B. Ferguson and A.C. Douglas, "A Study of Juvenile Waiver" (1970) 7:1 *San Diego Law Review* 38. A Miranda-type warning requires that a suspect being taken into police custody be informed of the right to remain silent, the right to have an attorney present during questioning, and the right to have an attorney appointed if the suspect cannot afford one.

71 *Youth Criminal Justice Act*, S.C. 2002, c. 1, s. 146(9).

72 Teachers should also be aware that they have no duty to act as advisers; see L. Robinson, "The Young Offenders Act" (October 1984) *Canadian School Executive*.

73 In *R. v. H.*, supra note 67, four students confessed to having stolen a sum of money from a teacher. They were originally told that there would be no consequences if the money were returned; however, when the principal heard the confessions, he called the police, and the youths were charged with theft. The court excluded the confessions from evidence, and consequently acquitted the youths, because the principal had not informed them of their rights pursuant to s. 56 of the YOA.

74 *R. v. J. (J.T.)*, [1990] 2 S.C.R. 755, 59 C.C.C. (3d) 1.

75 *Criminal Code*, R.S.C., 1985, c. C-46, s. 494.

76 *Controlled Drugs and Substances Act*, S.C. 1996, c. 19, ss. 4 and 5.

77 *R. v. Whitfield*, [1970] S.C.R. 46, 9 C.R.N.S. 59.

78 *Peel Board of Education v. B. (W.)* (1987), 38 D.L.R. (4th) 566 (Ont. H.C.J.).

79 *F.N. (Re)*, 2000 SCC 35, [2000] 1 S.C.R. 880, at para. 24.

80 *H. et al. v. Board of Education of the Shamrock School Division No. 38 of Saskatchewan* (1987), 57 Sask. R. 188 (Q.B.).

81 The sole ground relied on by the parents was that the school board's actions lay beyond the powers granted by s. 91 of the *Education Act*. See *H. et al.*, ibid., at 190.

82 *Re Peel Board of Education et al.* (1987), 59 O.R. (2d) 654 (H.C.J.); overturned by *F.G. and J.M. v. Scarborough Board of Education (No. 1)*(1994) 28 O.A.C. (Ont. S.C.J.).

83 Ibid., at 661. See also J. Anderson, "Expulsion Hearing Contrary to Young Offenders Act," 7:4, *Canadian School Executive* 23, at 25.

84 *G. (F.) v. Scarborough (City) Board of Education* (1994), 68 O.A.C. 308 (Ont. S.C.J.).

85 Ibid., paras. 14-17.

86 W. MacKay and J. Burt-Gerrans, "Towards a Safe and Effective Learning Environment: The Delicate Balance of Rights and Order in Schools," in R.C. Flynn, ed., *In Support of Lifelong Learning* (Toronto: Informco, 2004), chapter 16, 230-250 (CAPSLE proceedings).

6
Teachers as Social Welfare Agents

This chapter examines how a teacher functions in the school environment as a social welfare agent. This is one of the emergent roles of teachers. It is the product of government's increased involvement in the welfare of children, as seen through more developed children's welfare agencies, and the passage of the *Young Offenders Act* (YOA) in the 1980s, replaced by the *Youth Criminal Justice Act* (YCJA)[1] in 2003. The teacher's role as social welfare agent is a complex mixture of a number of different roles, which draw on various areas of law. We examine each of these roles, and provide a brief description of the elements of each role. This chapter focuses on the identification of the roles, rather than on a thorough explanation of each role. In many cases, simply identifying the role is half the battle.

We begin by examining teachers as rehabilitative counsellors for young offenders in the school, and then look more generally at teachers, particularly guidance counsellors, as social workers. We examine teachers as child advocates both within the school and with agencies outside the school. In this external context, we focus on the teacher's role as coordinator of these outside agencies. Finally, we examine some of the family law issues that spill into the school environment and involve teachers as family mediators.

Teachers as YCJA
Rehabilitation Counsellors

The unique provisions of the YCJA place an additional burden on the school system to act in the rehabilitation of youthful offenders. The scheme of the YCJA provides for both punishment and rehabilitation. The legislation was enacted in an attempt to reconcile two competing views of youth crime. There was, and still is, a public perception that youth crime is increasing, and that the YOA, predecessor to the YCJA was "soft" on youth crime. Robert Weir reports that, in fact, Canada is tougher on young people convicted of criminal offences than most other countries with which Canada is commonly compared.[2] He points out that Canada has a higher incarceration rate for youthful offenders than any other Western country.

The YCJA attempts to have young persons who are involved in criminal activity take responsibility for their actions, while providing alternatives to incarceration for less serious offences. As we noted in Chapter 5, the Act allows for extrajudicial measures and sanctions as a means of diverting some young offenders away from youth court and possible incarceration. From the beginning, police must evaluate whether it is necessary to bring a youth into the judicial system. If the police choose to move the case into the system, prosecutors and judges can decide to apply extrajudicial measures and sanctions instead of incarceration or other traditional forms of punishment. Extrajudicial measures include apologies to victims, restitution programs that place the focus on accepting responsibility and making amends, and community service programs. Although the legislation does not specifically address the impact of extrajudicial measures on schools, it could affect the school that a youth attends. Often these measures involve specific, prescribed behaviours at school that require monitoring during school hours.

Historically, education has been seen as an important tool in the rehabilitation of youthful offenders. Egerton Ryerson, one of the founders of the education system in Ontario, worked toward crime prevention with juvenile delinquents.[3] One of the principal drafters of the *Juvenile Delinquents Act* (predecessor of the YOA), J.J. Kelso, also recognized the importance of education:

> Gradually we are coming to see that youthful offenders against criminal law cannot be reclaimed by force but must be won over to a better life by kindness, sympathy and friendly helpfulness; that we should substitute education for punishment and secure the hearty cooperation of the boy or girl in question in his or her own reclamation.[4]

The problem with using education as a tool for rehabilitation in the past was that there were no developed resources for dealing with difficult children, and special education was not a priority of school administrators. It is clear to most people who are involved in prosecuting young offenders that a significant percentage of these children have some type of special need, often emotional or cognitive, or are substance abusers.

Over the past four decades, however, there has been a general shift in the philosophy of educational professionals toward providing better services to children who are "specially challenged."[5] The ongoing debate over special education and inclusion illustrates the time and resources being spent on servicing "challenging" children. As these resources become more developed, the school system becomes more attractive to judges as a means of dealing with youthful offenders. Although students should not be sentenced to school, pre-emptive measures at school can prevent future clashes with the law. One benefit of welcoming disabled students within the school systems is the increased chance that these students will eventually contribute to society, rather than become a drain on it.[6]

As we have mentioned, the YCJA applies to young people aged 12–18. Children under 12 cannot be charged with a crime because it is assumed that they are too young to form criminal intent. Particularly violent, dangerous, or destructive children are usually dealt with under provincial child protection statutes.[7]

Unfortunately, children under the age of 12, as well as those between 12 and 18, sometimes engage in serious and disturbing acts of violence, both on and off school grounds. Indeed, the management of behaviour problems in schools has become a major source of stress for teachers and school administrators. Curbing violent and antisocial behaviour is an important objective that requires resources and expertise that are not always readily available in schools. Nonetheless, the teacher has come to be an important player in dealing with young children on the verge of criminal activity. This role is multifaceted and complex, and there are few guidelines for teachers.

Significant recent attention has been paid to the issue of cyberbullying as a growing concern. In 2011, the government of Nova Scotia established a task force to address increasing incidents of cyberbullying arising from elementary through to the high school setting.[8]

Identification of Young Offenders

One common complaint of school administrators is that the prohibition against the publication of the names of young offenders in section 110 of the YCJA makes it difficult to find out whether there are, in fact, any young offenders in their schools. This is also a major concern for teachers, who feel that they need to know this information to properly manage their classrooms.

In 2000, before the enactment of the YCJA, the Supreme Court of Canada addressed the issue of whether youth courts could distribute their dockets (schedule of individual appearances) to local school boards.[9] An accused young person applied for an order blocking the youth court from its routine distribution of the youth court docket to St. John's two school boards. (The boards were in the habit of providing the information to school psychologists and others on a need-to-know basis.) The Supreme Court of Canada found that the YOA did not allow for routine distribution of this information. The court objected to the fact that the information was not only delivered to the school of the accused in question, but to all schools across two school boards. It also noted that the information was being used for school purposes, and not for the purpose of administering justice.

The court stated that although disclosure to schools was possible under the Act, information could be disclosed only by certain persons, and disclosure was limited to the school that was directly dealing with the young person in question. The court found that the current practice of distributing the docket was overly inclusive, because the youth court sent the information to two school boards, when the young person was obviously not a student with both boards, and might not have been a student at all; moreover, the docket included the names of students who might not be a safety risk. The current practice was, at the same time, underinclusive because it failed to provide enough information for schools to determine whether the young person was a safety risk and additional action should be taken.[10] The court noted that the youth court judge would be in a good position to know whether any safety concerns needed to be communicated to the school board or school, and it could select an appropriate person (such as a youth worker or peace officer) to transmit this information in appropriate cases.[11]

What we can take from this case is that although schools may have a need for certain information, the method by which they receive this information ought to be individualized and carefully circumscribed to ensure that the identity of a young person is protected as much as possible. Reference to young people by their initials, rather than their names, in court cases also emphasizes the importance of protecting the identity of the young offender.

The YCJA specifically addresses the disclosure of information to schools and school boards. In section 125(6), the Act allows disclosure to schools and boards to (1) ensure compliance with a court order or reintegration program; (2) ensure the safety of staff, students, and others; or (3) facilitate the rehabilitation of the young person. This disclosure, however, is discretionary on the part of a youth worker, attorney general, or peace officer. In other words, the Act does not require these people to release this information.

If the courts are going to use schools as alternative rehabilitation facilities, school administrators must be brought into the rehabilitation team. The school, of necessity, will have to know when a youth is sentenced to three or four months in a custodial institution. Similarly, school administrators should be fully apprised of any and all probation orders affecting students in their schools. We recommend that administrators seek out their local youth court workers and build a team relationship. Schools and the justice system should be collaborators and not adversaries in dealing with young people in conflict with the law.[12]

The YCJA allows advisory groups or "conferences" to advise decision-makers (police officers, prosecutors, and judges) in determining consequences for a young person. The advisory group may involve parents of a young person, a victim, community agencies, and other professionals. This is a forum in which school administrators or counsellors may be able to improve the decisions made about a young person with information gleaned from the school setting. It is also a place in which they can raise concerns about keeping a young offender within a school setting. This is particularly important where a young person has a history of special needs or behavioural problems that could affect his success, and that of the rest of the class.

Teachers as Social Workers

In many areas of the school environment, teachers are expected to act as social workers for children under their care. This expectation is most prevalent among high school guidance counsellors—teachers who by their very description fit the social worker role. This role, however, is certainly not limited to guidance counsellors. Teachers often provide guidance to students on an informal basis. In some cases, teachers divide their time between teaching and counselling, thereby providing guidance on a part-time basis only.

It is the goal of many good teachers to gain the trust of their students and to help them develop as individuals, not simply as academics. Some teachers are more skilled at this than others, but most are involved to a certain extent in performing these child welfare functions. Perhaps the first warning for teachers who get involved in this caring aspect of their jobs is to be careful not to take on the problems of every child. Although it is essential that teachers "care about" the children they teach, teachers cannot be expected to "care for" all the needs of these children.

Examples of the difficulty in drawing this line can be seen in any school. Teachers often ask us about their liability for taking actions that involve the trust and confidence of a particular student. For example, what if a student comes to a teacher in possession of illegal drugs, is frightened, and does not know what he should do with them? He may have unwittingly fallen into possession of these drugs and now be caught in a dilemma. He comes to his teacher in confidence and expects the teacher's help as a caregiver. Many teachers who try to cultivate a trust relationship with their students would be tempted to tell him to throw the drugs away and never get involved with them again. Secure in her relationship with the student, a teacher may think she is in a safe position. Any teacher who has acted in this way, however, has come dangerously close to aiding and abetting a criminal offence. The proper course of action is to bring the student to the principal's office and work the situation out with the principal's assistance. In many cases, the student's parents should be informed. Needless to say, however, these actions may destroy the teacher's trust relationship with the student.

Students may come to a teacher they trust and say, "I need to tell you something, but you must promise me not to tell anyone." Many teachers will foolishly agree to this condition only to find themselves in an awkward position of breaching a confidence. If, for example, a student tells a teacher about abuse in the home, the teacher is under a statutory duty to inform the relevant authorities about any information received from the student. In short, a teacher should never make a promise of unconditional confidence to a student. The proper course is for the teacher to tell the student that he is more than willing to discuss any problem that the student has, that he is open to hearing what the student has to say, but that he cannot guarantee that he will not disclose the information to anyone. In most cases the student will proceed to discuss the issue with the teacher whether or not there is a promise of confidence.

A teacher's indiscretion in handling such a situation most often will not result in any criminal sanction, but it may result in an employment-related sanction. For instance, in *Singh v. Board of Reference and Board of School Trustees of School District No. 29 (Lillooet)*,[13] a secondary school teacher was a chaperone at a dance at which two workers took two female students from the school to a motel. The teacher followed and returned the girls to the school. After extracting a promise from the girls that this would not happen again, the teacher promised not to tell their parents. The teacher informed the vice-principal of the events. The next day, on learning of the incident, the principal gave the girls the option of telling their parents within a certain period of time or having him tell them. When the teacher found out about the principal's actions, there was a confrontation in the waiting area of the school office. The teacher shouted, "Leave her alone—go away—you have done enough damage." The board of reference found that this conduct, in addition to several years of various other incidents of misconduct, constituted just cause for dismissal.

The lesson to be learned here is that teachers must always be aware of potential employment hazards when dealing with students in a confidential setting. The question is: where do teachers' loyalties lie when offering guidance to students? Do they lie with the school board as employer, the parent of the student, or the student herself? The legal and ethical answers may vary depending on the circumstances.

Issues of confidentiality and identifying the client are particularly acute for school guidance counsellors and school psychologists. Their code of ethics may bolster the sense that their main duty is to the student rather than their employer school board. However, in legal terms, both the school board, as their employer, and the parent of the student may be legally entitled to certain kinds of information. This entitlement can arise through statutory language such as child welfare legislation, which mandates the reporting of suspected child abuse. If a student informs a guidance counsellor that she is pregnant and plans to have an abortion, there may be legal problems if the parents or guardians are not informed. The same could be said with respect to a student who is contemplating suicide.

In a 2005 judgment of the Ontario Superior Court, a judge ruled that a student had the right to expect that confidentiality of conversations with her school guidance counsellor would be respected.[14] The mother of the child brought a motion seeking an order from the court directing the school board to produce the girl's school record, including notes and reports written by the school's guidance counsellor, as part of a child protection case. While the court found the counsellor's notes and reports did not form part of the student record and were thus not statutorily protected by the *Education Act*, the judge found that the student had a common-law expectation of privacy. The main concern expressed by the court was that to allow such disclosure would effectively destroy the role of guidance counsellors, because students would be aware of the lack of confidentiality. The court noted that the circumstances of this case justified a finding that the communications between the student and the counsellor were confidential, but it did not go so far as to state that confidentiality would exist in every case.

In *R. v. O'Connor*,[15] the Supreme Court of Canada determined the procedure to be followed when seeking records in possession of a third party. The accused, a Roman Catholic bishop, was charged with numerous sexual offences allegedly committed in the 1960s against students at a residential school. He received a pretrial order for disclosure of the victims' medical, counselling, and school records. When the information was not fully disclosed, he obtained a stay of proceedings based on the argument that the lack of disclosure impeded his right to defend himself. The Crown successfully appealed to the Court of Appeal. The Supreme Court of Canada dismissed the bishop's appeal, and reviewed the two-part procedure for an application for the production of medical and counselling records in the possession of third parties. In order to begin the process, the accused must make an application to a court explaining why the records are relevant to his defence. Third parties in possession of the records and people whose privacy is affected (in this case, the victims) are then to be notified. The court will then subpoena the records, and a judge will examine them to determine whether they ought to be provided to the accused and whether failure to provide them will affect the accused's right to defend himself against the charges. It is the responsibility of the accused to convince the judge that the beneficial effects of releasing the records outweigh the negative consequences of their production.[16]

Teachers should be aware that since the *O'Connor* decision, some provinces have enacted legislation dealing with flow and access to personal health information;[17] however, this legislation does not change the principles in *O'Connor*. If the court subpoenas a teacher's records, she should seek guidance from school administrators before responding.

Another problem arises when a student admits to committing a crime or to intending to commit a crime. The admission may impose a duty on the teacher to inform the principal or other relevant authority so that any risks to the school population or the general public can be reduced. Failure to warn in a situation where a student announces a criminal or violent intent could be held to be an act of negligence within the principles discussed in Chapter 2 under the heading "Liability for Accidents at School." In the landmark US case of *Tarasoff v. Regents of the University of California*,[18] the California Supreme Court found that a psychologist with knowledge of a patient's intention to harm a specific individual had a duty to exercise reasonable care and warn the intended victim. Although *Tarasoff* has not been adopted in Canada, its principle of disclosure is generally followed where the harm is "serious and imminent." The ethical and legal lines to be drawn by guidance counsellors and teachers are complex, and we encourage discussion among colleagues.

In addition to questions of professional ethics, there may also be legal concerns about privacy and information flow in the student–counsellor relationship. These privacy issues can arise in respect to the school psychologist and the administration of tests. Wayne MacKay and Pam Rubin outline some of these concerns in their Ontario Law Reform Commission study on psychological testing:[19]

> If the examiner is a registered professional psychologist, he or she is professionally bound by that profession's code of ethics. These standards include confidentiality requirements as between a client and a psychologist, as well as the duty not to disclose test results directly to the client when, in exercising their professional judgment, a psychologist decides releasing data is not in the client's best interest. This latter "duty" [may be] in conflict with the access provisions of [freedom of information and protection of privacy legislation.][20] ...
>
> The role of guidance counsellors or school psychologists can be even more complicated by the range of people to whom they may owe duties. In terms of the code of ethics the student is the immediate client to whom a duty of confidentiality is owed. However, the counsellor or psychologist is employed by the school board and is accountable to it as an employee. There may also be ethical and/or school obligations to inform the parents on certain sensitive issues such as pregnancy, abortion or suicidal thoughts. Thus, people in these sensitive guidance positions are in particular need of clear legal guidance about the rules in respect to privacy.[21]

Reporting Child Abuse

One of the most obvious ways in which a teacher acts as a social worker can be seen in the reporting of child abuse. It is safe to say that most teachers are aware of their statutory obligations to report abuse; however, not all teachers are aware of the procedures they must follow. Many school boards have established specific protocols for the reporting of abuse, and we certainly advise all boards to have these types of policies in place. It may also be helpful, particularly for elementary teachers, to insist on a professional development session with local police authorities and child protection workers to clearly establish the appropriate lines of communication for reporting abuse. Some board protocols require teachers to bring the matter to the attention of the school principal and let her handle the reporting. Even if this is the protocol in a particular school, a teacher should still be aware of the actual process. Most reporting laws in Canada identify the individuals or authorities who must make the report, and some academics are of the opinion that the report must be made by the teacher, regardless of internal school procedures.

Clearly, provincial legislation takes precedent over school board policy. Some provinces have amended their legislation to address the question of whether a teacher can delegate his reporting obligation to another person, such as a school principal. The Ontario *Child and Family Services Act* now specifies that a teacher (or other professional) is obliged to report directly to the appropriate authorities, and cannot discharge this duty by delegating it to a school principal.[22] The Northwest Territories *Child and Family Services Act* also contains a clause prohibiting delegation.[23] It is perhaps advisable, in cases where a teacher feels it necessary to report an abusive situation, to report her suspicion first to the principal and then, in conjunction with the principal, to contact the appropriate authorities.

The first issue to be addressed with regard to abuse is what must be reported. Although the laws in each province differ with respect to this issue, each province's child protection statute contains a description of what constitutes a child "in need of protection."[24] Every teacher should obtain the provincial child protection statute in force in his province and review the definitions of "abuse," "neglect," and (in some cases) "child in need of protection" or "child in need of intervention." Because educators have a positive duty to report suspected child abuse, they should be familiar with how such abuse is legally defined.

Teachers are naturally reticent to involve outside authorities and initiate the trauma of a child abuse investigation. They are also concerned about the reaction of parents who are the object of suspicion. However, it is incumbent on teachers and other professionals to err on the side of caution when deciding to report. As one author states, "[S]topping child abuse can prevent irreparable physical and emotional damage and can often mean the difference between life and death."[25] Teachers should also be aware that most provinces have the ability to prosecute for failure to report suspected child abuse, although they rarely do so.[26] The consequences of conviction for failure to report can involve fines, probation, and even imprisonment; however, these penalties are rarely imposed.

The first component of any definition of "child abuse" is a definition of "child." In Manitoba, a "child" is a person under the age of majority; in New Brunswick, a child is a person actually or apparently under the age of majority; in British Columbia and the Yukon, a child is a person under the age of 19; in Prince Edward Island, Alberta, Ontario, and Quebec, a child is a person under the age of 18; and in Nova Scotia, a child is a person under the age of 16. Newfoundland and Labrador and Saskatchewan define a child as a person who is actually or apparently under the age of 16, and Saskatchewan refines this definition by stating that the person must be unmarried to qualify. In the Northwest Territories and Nunavut, a child is someone who is, or in absence of evidence to the contrary, appears to be under the age of 16.

The definition of "abuse" is slightly more abstract, and most of the statutes use broad and vague terminology to identify a range of specific behaviours and conditions that may constitute child abuse. There is general agreement that conduct that qualifies as child abuse can be divided into four major categories. W.F. Foster provides the following guidance in a useful article:[27]

1. *Physical abuse.* This includes "any physical force or action which results in or may potentially result in a non-accidental injury to a child and which exceeds that which could be considered reasonable discipline."[28]
2. *Emotional maltreatment.* This includes the acting out by those responsible for the welfare of a child of their negative or ambiguous feelings toward the child (through, for example, constantly chastising, blaming, belittling, ridiculing, humiliating, or rejecting a child or persistently displaying a lack of concern for the child's welfare), which results in some degree of emotional damage to the child.[29]
3. *Sexual abuse.* This includes "any sexual touching or sexual exploitation of a child and may include any sexual behaviour directed toward a child."[30]
4. *Physical or emotional neglect.* This includes "failure on the part of those responsible for the care of the child to provide for the physical, emotional or mental needs of a child to the extent that the child's health, development, or safety is endangered."[31]

A number of provinces have expanded their definition of what constitutes abuse for the purpose of child protection. In Nova Scotia, for example, section 22(2) of the *Children and Family Services Act* lays out an expansive definition of the types of abuse and neglect that may lead to a child being in need of protective services:[32]

> (a) the child has suffered physical harm, inflicted by a parent or guardian of the child or caused by the failure of a parent or guardian to supervise and protect the child adequately;
>
> (b) there is a substantial risk that the child will suffer physical harm inflicted or caused as described in clause (a);
>
> (c) the child has been sexually abused by a parent or guardian of the child, or by another person where a parent or guardian of the child knows or should know of the possibility of sexual abuse and fails to protect the child;
>
> (d) there is a substantial risk that the child will be sexually abused as described in clause (c);
>
> (e) a child requires medical treatment to cure, prevent or alleviate physical harm or suffering, and the child's parent or guardian does not

provide, or refuses or is unavailable or is unable to consent to, the treatment;

(f) the child has suffered emotional harm, demonstrated by severe anxiety, depression, withdrawal, or self-destructive or aggressive behaviour and the child's parent or guardian does not provide, or refuses or is unavailable or unable to consent to, services or treatment to remedy or alleviate the harm;

(g) there is a substantial risk that the child will suffer emotional harm of the kind described in clause (f), and the parent or guardian does not provide, or refuses or is unavailable or unable to consent to, services or treatment to remedy or alleviate the harm;

(h) the child suffers from a mental, emotional or developmental condition that, if not remedied, could seriously impair the child's development and the child's parent or guardian does not provide, or refuses or is unavailable or unable to consent to, services or treatment to remedy or alleviate the condition;

(i) the child has suffered physical or emotional harm caused by being exposed to repeated domestic violence by or towards a parent or guardian of the child, and the child's parent or guardian fails or refuses to obtain services or treatment to remedy or alleviate the violence;

(j) the child has suffered physical harm caused by chronic and serious neglect by a parent or guardian of the child, and the parent or guardian does not provide, or refuses or is unavailable or unable to consent to, services or treatment to remedy or alleviate the harm;

(ja) there is a substantial risk that the child will suffer physical harm inflicted or caused as described in clause (j);

(k) the child has been abandoned, the child's only parent or guardian has died or is unavailable to exercise custodial rights over the child and has not made adequate provisions for the child's care and custody, or the child is in the care of an agency or another person and the parent or guardian of the child refuses or is unable or unwilling to resume the child's care and custody;

(l) the child is under twelve years of age and has killed or seriously injured another person or caused serious damage to another person's property, and services or treatment are necessary to prevent a recurrence and a parent or guardian of the child does not provide, or refuses or is unavailable or unable to consent to, the necessary services or treatment;

(m) the child is under twelve years of age and has on more than one occasion injured another person or caused loss or damage to another person's property, with the encouragement of a parent or guardian of the child or because of the parent or guardian's failure or inability to supervise the child adequately.

If one considers the wording of the statute in combination with Foster's guidance as to the four types of abuse, a relatively clear picture emerges as to what a teacher should report. The decision of the Supreme Court of Canada in *Canadian Foundation for Children, Youth and the Law v. Canada (Attorney General)*[33] provides further guidance on the line between reasonable correction and child abuse. In this case, the court upheld section 43 of the *Criminal Code*, which provides a defence to assault charges for parents, teachers, and persons standing in the place of a parent who use reasonable physical force for purposes of correction. The majority judgment contains the following observations:

> [40] Generally, s. 43 exempts from criminal sanction only minor corrective force of a transitory and trifling nature.[34] On the basis of current expert consensus, it does not apply to corporal punishment of children under two or teenagers. Degrading, inhuman or harmful conduct is not protected. Discipline by the use of objects or blows or slaps to the head is unreasonable. Teachers may reasonably apply force to remove a child from a classroom or secure compliance with instructions, but not merely as corporal punishment.[35] Coupled with the requirement that the conduct be corrective, which rules out conduct stemming from the caregiver's frustration, loss of temper or abusive personality, a consistent picture emerges of the area covered by s. 43.

In addition to prohibiting the aspects of child abuse considered above, some of the statutes make specific reference to the perpetrator of the abuse as being relevant to the reporting requirement. In the Northwest Territories, Quebec, and Manitoba, the relationship of the abuser to the victim is applicable in only some forms of reportable abuse. In Alberta, Ontario, Prince Edward Island, Saskatchewan, and Nova Scotia, the relationship of the abuser to the victim is essential. Generally, for conduct to constitute abuse under the statute, an abuser must be a parent, guardian, or person who has care or charge of a child. Again, we recommend that teachers check the statutory provisions within their province as well as the school board regulations to determine the requirements that apply to the nature of the abuse and the identity of the abuser.

How much must a teacher know about a situation before she is obliged to report abuse? In British Columbia, Ontario, Prince Edward Island, Quebec, Manitoba, Nova Scotia, Saskatchewan, Alberta, and the Yukon, the teacher's duty to report arises when she has "reasonable grounds to believe," "reasonable grounds to suspect," or "reasonable and probable grounds to believe" that abuse has occurred or is occurring. These statutes use different language, but the common denominator is the word "reasonable." This word creates an objective standard to test whether a teacher should make a report in a given situation. The question a teacher must ask herself is whether a reasonable person, knowing all of the circumstances in question, would believe or suspect that abuse is taking place. If the answer is yes, then the teacher has a duty to report.

In contrast, the New Brunswick statute provides that the reporting requirement arises only when an educator personally believes or suspects that a child is a victim of abuse. This is a subjective standard: there is no test for whether the suspicion is reasonable; it is simply the judgment call of a particular teacher. In Newfoundland and Labrador, the Northwest Territories, and Nunavut, the requirement is stricter. Where a person has information that a child is or may be in need of protective intervention, the duty to report engages. This means there is no requirement that a teacher reasonably believe or suspect that a child is being abused. Rather, a teacher must report any information that indicates a need for protection of a child. Again, teachers are encouraged to involve their principals or other school administrators when they determine whether to report alleged or suspected abuse.

Note also that once the reporting duty arises, a report should be made as quickly as possible. Most of the statutes make reference to "forthwith" or "without delay," which indicates the need for an immediate reporting of all relevant information.

Most statutes protect the person reporting the abuse from legal action by the person who is the object of the report. This is true even if the suspicions of abuse eventually turn out to be unfounded. In the Nova Scotia statute, for example, a person making a child abuse report attracts legal liability only if he makes the report both falsely and maliciously.[36]

This is not to suggest that teachers should report based on vague suspicion alone. In one widely publicized case, a student at Memorial University in Newfoundland and Labrador wrote a paper for a social work course, to which she attached an appendix containing a first person accounting of an admitted child abuser.[37] The appendix did not have a proper footnote. The professor to whom the paper was submitted was concerned that the account was autobiographical and took her concerns to her department head. Without any consultation with the student, the department head made a "suspected ill treatment report" against the student to Child Protection Services (CPS). For several years, and without her knowledge, information circulated in the university, the social work community, and the RCMP suggesting that this individual was a child abuser. It would be, however, more than two years after the initial report before CPS made contact with her directly and laid out the accusation. The student was able to provide a copy of the textbook from which she had taken the accounting of child abuse, thus halting the investigation by CPS.

The student sued her professors and the university for negligence, and was awarded more than $800,000 in damages at trial. The award was overturned by the Court of Appeal, which found that her action was barred by the *Child Welfare Act* (as it was then), which provided that an action could not be properly brought "unless the making of the report is done maliciously or without reasonable cause." The Supreme Court of Canada accepted the case on appeal, and restored the decision of the trial judge. The court noted the importance of prudent decision making, stating:[38]

> [2] It is important that suspected child abuse be promptly reported. But, as this case illustrates, it is also important that persons in positions of authority (such as university professors in relation to their students) act responsibly and avoid unfounded and damaging reports of suspicion. Section 38(6) of the *Child Welfare Act*, R.S.N. 1990, c. C-12, requires there to be "reasonable cause" to make the report, thus striking an appropriate balance between the protection of children, the protection of third parties against unfounded allegations, and the protection of informants.
>
> • • •
>
> [34] ... While legislative and judicial policy mandates the quick reporting of information of suspected child abuse, it does not do so to the exclusion of consideration of the legitimate interests of the person named in the report, or the interests of informants. This is not at all to say that the respondents were obliged to conduct their own investigation of the suspected abuse. Informants are *not* required to have reasonable cause to believe abuse has in fact occurred before making a report. They are, however, obliged to have *reasonable cause to make a report to CPS*, i.e. to possess information that CPS reasonably ought to be asked to look into, even if it turns out to be misinformation. It is the absence of reasonable cause *even to make a report* that lies at the heart of the appellant's allegation of negligence.

The Supreme Court found that the professors acted on the basis of conjecture and speculation, falling short of the legal expectation of reasonable cause to make the report to CPS. The court noted that the professors did not seek an explanation from the student and, further, that there was no evidence that a child was currently in danger or in need of protection.

Clearly there is a balance to be struck in order to reach a reasonable cause to report and ensuring the safety of children, which is paramount.

School Attendance

Another aspect of the social work role of teachers is the effort made by school personnel to combat truancy. Although truancy was historically seen as simply a matter of rounding up delinquent children, in the modern educational environment, it is recognized as a much more complex issue.[39] A number of varying interpretations of truancy attribute its causes to a wide variety of factors, including the home environment, the socioeconomic position of the student, a student's unhappiness and inability to socialize, as well as the school environment itself.[40]

We do not propose in this book to delve into the complexities of truancy and the arguments over its causes and effects. Bob Keel explores these issues in his book *Student Rights and Responsibilities: Attendance and Discipline*.[41] It is safe to say that non-attendance is a prevalent problem, and that students clearly cannot succeed academically if they do not go to school. Teachers, although not the primary agents for enforcing school attendance, can serve a useful purpose in their social welfare role by identifying the causes of truancy in particular students and attempting to avert this behaviour before it starts. It is usually the classroom teacher who has the deepest understanding of students and the closest experience of them, particularly at the elementary level. These teachers are therefore in a good position to assess the signs of truant behaviour. The classroom teacher (or teacher assistants) may also have more access to parents than a principal or truancy officer. Particular attention should also be paid to more marginalized student populations, such as Aboriginal students, where schools may not be adequately accommodating particular cultural needs.

In the event that a teacher's intervention does not increase a student's attendance, teachers should be aware that most school boards have truant officers, sometimes called attendance counsellors. These counsellors provide support and counselling to high-risk students who might otherwise have attendance difficulties. Many schools also provide student counsellors, who attempt to contribute to the social and emotional growth of at-risk students. This is a positive trend toward seeking a proactive solution to truancy.

Some Ontario schools have implemented a program called supervised alternative learning for excused pupils (SALEP). This program is for students under 16 who wish to be legally excused from school because of negative school experiences. Counsellors can work with students and their parents to design work or home correspondence programs so that the students are not required to attend school for a limited period, after which they are encouraged to return to their school.

The legislative trend across Canada has been to put truancy into the arena of the family court, which also deals with cases arising from children's services legislation. In many provinces, a child who is consistently truant may be deemed to be a child in need of protection, and taken into the custody of a child protection agency. This is rare, however, since child protection advocates are reluctant to impose this sanction on a child and family, unless there is other evidence of the need for protection, such as neglect or abuse.

In Alberta, the courts have refused to interpret the section that requires every child between the ages of 6 and 16 to attend school as creating a legal duty that can result in punishment when it is not carried out.[42] The court reviewed legislation from other provinces and concluded that only Ontario and New Brunswick have created an offence for a truant child, and even then not in clear language. The court was persuaded by the legislative movement toward empowering family court to make orders for attendance, rather than punishment.

In some provinces, it is an offence for parents to allow their child not to attend school. These provisions have been challenged under the Charter as potentially violating the parents' freedom of religion, but the Supreme Court of Canada in 1986 ultimately upheld the requirement that children avail themselves of some form of provincially approved schooling.[43]

Teachers as Child Advocates

Having looked at the teacher as a rehabilitation counsellor and social worker, we now examine the teacher's social welfare role as an informal lawyer, or advocate, for students. Every individual in the care-giving professions who comes into contact with children feels a natural tendency to take on an advocacy role, particularly in relation to vulnerable children. It may be that a teacher simply acts as an advocate within the school system to achieve better services for a child, though she may also extend that role into seeking external resources, such as Children's Aid, the United Way, or Big Brothers/ Sisters, to name but a few. In the same way that educational systems have expanded and diversified, so too have the external government agencies that affect children. In earlier, simpler times, child advocacy was an easier task, given that the only resources that could be drawn on were those of the community in which the child lived. In today's more complex world, full of institutions established to help children, the child advocacy role becomes more complex. The range of services available on the Internet goes well beyond those in the local community.

Given the day-to-day contact of classroom teachers with their students, they are natural advocates for children with special needs. Often children of single-parent or low-income families need the help of an articulate advocate to obtain necessary services. Anyone who has dealt with the bureaucratic tangles that can be created by some child welfare agencies is well aware of this need. As any bureaucracy gets larger, the individuals within the system may focus too much on the delivery of service on a "macro" level and not enough on the "micro" needs of particular children and families. This is especially true in the age of government cutbacks, when every social welfare agency is struggling to justify its existence in obtaining government funding.

It is important to realize that advocacy is not necessarily adversarial. It is not always necessary for teachers to feel they must "take on the system," whether that is the education or the social welfare system. Often, the most effective form of advocacy is the simple co-opting and coordinating of support services. From an employment standpoint, it is also wiser to take a more subtle approach than to risk alienating individuals in the government hierarchy. This is especially true of internal advocacy within the school system. It may also be helpful in this regard for teachers as a group to encourage their school system to view child advocacy as a positive employment objective, and one that fits within the role of the teacher, rather than labelling teacher advocates as "disturbers."

One recent opportunity for teachers as advocates focuses on the role teachers can play in supporting student equality movements, such as gay–straight alliances.[44] In June 2012, Bill 13 received royal assent in Ontario, becoming the *Accepting Schools Act, 2012*.[45] This Act amended the *Education Act*, including placing an obligation on school boards to promote a climate of acceptance and inclusion, including but not limited to the support of students who want to create school-centred organizations to promote equality. It is obvious that teachers could play a significant part in such groups. The preamble to the Act specifically acknowledges the importance of a whole-school approach in the creation of a positive and welcoming school climate. The integral role of teachers as advisors for groups to support marginalized students was also noted by the Nova Scotia Task Force on Bullying and Cyberbullying in their 2012 report.[46]

Another good example of teachers acting as advocates for children in the school system is a breakfast program created by teachers in the Peel Board of Education. For some time, classroom teachers had noted that particular children were having difficulty concentrating in class and were consistently being disciplined for acting out. Finally, when the principal asked one of the children whether he had breakfast at home, the child stated that he was not usually able to have breakfast in the morning.

Over a number of months, the school implemented a program where each classroom teacher was instructed to keep a close eye on children who might not have been properly fed in the morning. Without singling the children out, teachers discretely sent them to the main office (often on the pretext of bringing the attendance record to the office). Once there, they were asked whether they had had breakfast and those that had not eaten were fed. The discipline problems in the school declined substantially as a result of this breakfast club, and numerous other schools have since adopted the program. This is an excellent example of classroom teachers and administrators identifying and solving a specific child welfare need. Clearly, the parents were not in a position to help, and it was not the kind of problem that could necessarily be solved through any traditional social welfare agencies. Although schools certainly cannot replace these agencies, this model of identifying problems and advocating solutions is an important and positive role for teachers in the school system.

In many instances, the advocacy role will involve the coordination of existing agencies rather than the creation of new programs within the school. Often, parents simply need to be directed to an appropriate agency and assisted by an advocate in negotiating with that agency in order to improve the welfare of their child. For instance, children whose parents are illiterate are certainly impeded by a lack of models at home to encourage and assist them in their studies. In this situation, a teacher can often be helpful by directing a parent to a community literacy program that would benefit both the parent and the child. Any such suggestion must, of course, be made with tact and sensitivity.

One particular problem with respect to teenage students mentioned earlier is the danger of a teacher acting as an advocate in young offender situations. Section 146(9) of the YCJA states that an adult consulted pursuant to section 146(2)(c) shall be deemed not to be a person in authority for the purposes of the admissibility of a statement under section 146. As we discussed in Chapter 5, Teachers as Agents of the Police, under the heading "Questioning Students and the Admissibility of Statements," section 146(2)(c) allows a young person to consult a parent or, in the absence of a parent, any other appropriate adult chosen by the young person, before giving a statement. Often, the individual of choice for a student is a teacher whom the student trusts. A teacher who takes on an advocacy role may be tempted to act in this advisory capacity when requested to do so by a student, particularly when the police are present and the student shows signs of fear. However, the danger in assuming this role is that, because the teacher is not required to give the student any warning that any statements the student makes are admissible as evidence in court, the student may be vulnerable to legal consequences as a result of any admissions he makes to the teacher.

Therefore, if the teacher consults with the student before formal questioning and the student confesses to having committed an offence, the Crown prosecutor may subpoena the teacher. The teacher will then be required, on the witness stand, to relate the statement made by the student. As advocates, teachers are not protected by the solicitor–client privilege that is enjoyed by lawyers. Therefore, if a teacher truly wishes to assist an accused young person in the absence of his parents, we recommend that the teacher direct the student to a local legal-aid service for advice. Teachers need to be aware that playing the role of legal adviser may create problems for the student further down the road.

Teachers as Family Mediators

The family as an institution in Canada (and elsewhere) is in a state of evolution, and the so-called traditional family is no longer the norm. Single-parent families, blended families, and families with same-sex parents are just a few examples of the evolving nature of the family.

The legal issues that can arise in respect to same-sex parent relationships have been explored in high-profile cases, including before the Supreme Court of Canada in *Mossop*,[47] a human rights case about equality for same-sex couples, and *Chamberlain v. Surrey District School Board No. 36*,[48] which addressed Charter issues. The Surrey School Board case dealt with classroom use of books that addressed same-sex parenting.

Given the large number of family breakups in today's society, teachers are often faced with difficult family law issues. Often a teacher may be trying to assist a child in dealing with the separation or divorce of her parents, while at the same time dealing with both parents. Provided that neither parent has been denied access to the child, both parents typically have general rights to participate in the child's education and to obtain their child's student records. These rights extend to the parent without physical custody as well as to the parent with whom the child lives. Perhaps more troublesome for teachers than parental participation in their child's education are the day-to-day custodial problems that arise when non-custodial parents arrive at the school to pick up their child. As well, the courts have awarded joint custody in divorce cases with increasing frequency, and thus there are sometimes two custodial parents. The *Criminal Code*[49] contains provisions that penalize anyone who wrongfully takes a child from someone with lawful care or charge of the child. In this regard, consider section 280:

280(1) Everyone who, without lawful authority, takes or causes to be taken an unmarried person under the age of sixteen years out of the possession of and against the will of the parent or guardian of that person or of any other person who has the lawful care or charge of that person is guilty of an indictable offence and liable to imprisonment for a term not exceeding five years.

(2) In this section and sections 281 to 283, "guardian" includes any person who has in law or in fact the custody or control of another person.

Section 282(1), which addresses child abduction in contravention of a custody order, reads as follows:

282(1) Every one who, not being the parent, guardian or person having the lawful care or charge of a person under the age of fourteen years, takes, entices away, conceals, detains, receives or harbours that person, in contravention of the custody provisions of a custody order in relation to that person made by a court anywhere in Canada, with intent to deprive a parent or guardian or any other person who has the lawful care or charge of that person, of the possession of that person is guilty of

(a) an indictable offence and is liable to imprisonment for a term not exceeding ten years; or

(b) an offence punishable on summary conviction.

Defences to the crime of abduction are set out in sections 284 and 286 of the *Criminal Code*. These defences provide that no one is to be found guilty of the offence of abduction if he can satisfy the court that he took the young person with consent of the legal guardian or if he can establish that the taking was necessary to protect the young person from danger or imminent harm. Section 286 states that the consent of the young person to the conduct of the accused person does not afford a defence. The defence of parental consent contained in section 284 raises interpretation problems. Who can consent to the taking of a child? Is it the parent who has temporary lawful custody, such as a father exercising his right of access, or the parent who has permanent custody, such as the mother? The Supreme Court of Canada clarified this section in *R. v. Dawson*, where Justice L'Heureux-Dubé stated:

I cannot accept the notion that a person who takes a child with intent to deprive the child's parent, or another person having lawful care or charge of the child, of possession of the child could escape liability by giving his or her own consent to the taking. Under the appellant's interpretation of s. 284, a babysitter or a teacher could take a child with intent to deprive the child's parents of possession of the child, and escape criminal liability ... simply by giving his or her own consent as a person having lawful possession of the child. Such an absurd result could not have been within the contemplation of Parliament in enacting s. 284.[50]

Many schools wisely require that a child's parent provide them with a copy of the current custody order at the beginning of each school year. This can provide school authorities with the information necessary for addressing complex and sensitive custodial issues. It is the responsibility of the parent who seeks changes to the custody order to provide the school with any changes to the order.

Physical Access to the Child at School

If a non-custodial parent wishes to pick a child up from school, the principal should contact the custodial parent (or parents) before allowing the child to leave. If a dispute seems likely, it may also be wise to notify the police, whose function is to ensure that court orders are obeyed. Ideally, the teacher or principal should obtain legal advice in situations where both parents claim the right to take the child, although this advice is not always quickly available. Having the custody order in hand may limit these types of disputes. Although teachers may be required to act as mediators in parental disputes over a child regarding education, educators should never attempt to adjudicate parental disputes over rights of custody or access.[51]

Decisions About a Child's Education

A parent who has been awarded exclusive or sole custody of a child has the right to make decisions that relate to the child's upbringing, including how and where the child will be educated.[52] However, under the *Divorce Act*, a parent with access to the child also has some rights to participate in the child's education.[53] A custody order usually grants the parent the right to give consent (medical or otherwise) on behalf of the child. A parent who does not have custody is not permitted to "interfere" in the child's upbringing even though she may have access to the child and the right to some degree of "participation" in decisions that affect the child. In today's custodial orders, joint custody has become more frequent. This means that both parents share custody of the child, although, typically, one parent is awarded day-to-day control. If there is any question about which parent is able to give permission for the child to participate in an activity or enrol in a course, the custody order should be reviewed to determine which parent can make that decision.

Access to Information About the Child's Education

There are always questions about if and how non-custodial parents may obtain information about their children. For several decades, courts have addressed the issue on an ad hoc basis. Often they have included a condition in a custody order requiring the custodial parent to ensure that the non-custodial parent is provided with information about the child, including medical records and school report cards. In 2002, the government introduced a bill to amend the *Divorce Act*. Suggested amendments to the Act included replacing the terms "custody" and "access" with the term "shared parenting," and the term "custody order" with "parenting order." As well, the bill included the following amendment, "[U]nless a court orders otherwise, any person with parental responsibilities is entitled to make inquiries, and to be given information, as to the child's health care, education, and religious upbringing."[54] These changes were based on the theory that shared parenting was a more child-centred approach than sole custody, and that having both parents involved in the child's life in a meaningful way was essential, unless that involvement was not in the child's best interests, which is the paramount concern of custodial orders. Amid significant debate from a number of public interest groups, Bill C-22 died on the floor in 2003. Thus, the proposed changes were never enacted, and the *Divorce Act* continues to reference "custody" and "access."

If the House of Commons had passed this bill, it would likely have resulted in significant changes to custody orders, with more information being available to parents who were characterized as "non-custodial." The effect would have been that more parents would have access to information from schools, because the presumption would have been that both parents are entitled to information about their child, unless it would be contrary to the child's best interests. Because the bill did not pass, it continues to be important that schools possess copies of custody orders so that they are aware of any restrictions or obligations with respect to access to information about students. Requests for custody orders should be general in nature so as not to single out divorced families. If there is no mention of access to information in the custody order, the legal presumption is that both parents have access. In most cases, it is in the best interests of a child for a teacher to make efforts to involve both parents to some extent in the education of their children.

Teachers as Paramedics

Although teachers are not typically trained to provide medical services, they are often called on to do so. In Chapter 2, Teachers as Parents, under the heading "Liability for Accidents at Schools," we discussed the role of the teacher in providing first aid when a student is injured in an accident. In our discussion about integrating students with special needs in Chapter 4, Teachers as Guardians of Equality, we identified the administration of medication as a service necessary to make schools truly accessible. In the past, this service has focused on special education classrooms. However, with the advent of inclusion, not to mention medications for attention deficit disorders (ADDs), allergies, and other health issues, it has become a matter of more general concern. Most school boards have policies that prevent teachers or school administrators, for example, from providing any non-prescription medications, such as headache relievers or antacids, to students.

Are teachers obliged to administer prescription medications? William Foster posits that a teacher's duty (or lack thereof) to provide medical services, including the delivery of medication, can be found in the collective agreements that govern teachers' working conditions, school board policy manuals, and government policies that relieve teachers of the obligation of providing certain types of medication.[55] Foster draws a distinction between long-term and emergency medication. An example of long-term medication is Ritalin, which a child may be scheduled to receive every day at lunch to manage symptoms of hyperactivity. This can be contrasted to an emergency medication, such as epinephrine, which a child may carry in an EpiPen in anticipation of an allergic reaction to peanuts or bee stings, for example. Many teachers' associations had, in previous years, maintained a position that their members should not be obligated to provide medication to students on an ongoing basis. This stance appears to have softened in recent years in most jurisdictions. A number of teacher associations now caution members that, although they may be obliged to administer medication to students, they should not do so without clear, written parameters in place to protect both the teacher and student.[56] School boards should ensure that there are clear policies or protocols on these important medication issues.

Foster notes that provincial education legislation contains little in the way of an express obligation to provide medical care, though most legislation notes that teachers may be called on by their school boards to perform duties in excess of those listed. Is there an implied obligation on the part of teachers to administer medication? The test created to determine whether an implied obligation exists was laid out in *Winnipeg Teachers' Association v. Winnipeg School Division No. 1.*[57] The case did not deal with teachers giving medication, but instead with teachers refusing to supervise lunch-hour activities. The Supreme Court of Canada held that, even though the duty was not contained in the collective agreement, teachers were under an implied duty to supervise the noon-hour activities of students. Chief Justice Laskin wrote the minority opinion (in which the majority concurred on this point). He pointed out that the fact that a collective agreement does not expressly impose a specific duty on teachers does not mean that the duty does not exist, because employers have the right to require employees to perform duties that are fair and reasonably related to the duties that they are required to perform in the ordinary course.

As well, Chief Justice Laskin noted that the mere fact that a teacher might be inconvenienced by the assigned duty did not necessarily make that duty unreasonable. On the basis of this decision, Foster argues that there are three steps to be considered in determining whether teachers are under an implied duty to administer medication to students. In short, he suggests that for an implied duty to exist,

1. there must be a clause in the legislation or collective agreement that contemplates the assignment of additional duties,
2. the administration of medication must further the role to which teachers are committed, and
3. the assignment to teachers of the job of administering medication must be fair and reasonable in the circumstances.[58]

Foster suggests that when one considers the issue of administration of medication by teachers in this light, it is

> not possible to reach the general conclusion that teachers' "job descriptions" can never include the administration of regular medication to pupils. Rather, the law on the issue, such as it is, suggests that a more appropriate conclusion is that teachers may legally be assigned the duty of administering such medication when it is fair and reasonable to so do.[59]

Foster provides a number of examples of factors that may come into play when deciding if it is fair and reasonable to require a teacher to administer medication, including the need for special training, the degree to which administering the medication interferes with the teacher's other mandated duties, and the number of students requiring medication in the class.[60] In today's world of ADD medication and inclusion, it is certainly possible that the amount of medication that various children require might make the job of administering it too onerous to be fair and reasonable for a teacher. Although the administration of medication might be left to teaching assistants, this solution does not solve the problems of safety or liability because these people may not have the necessary qualifications either. A school nurse may be an answer, but the funding for this position is often not available in a school's budget. The expertise required to administer medication is relevant to both the safety of students and the liability of the school.

Foster holds that a teacher's duty to administer emergency medication is not open to debate. He notes that every province has legislation requiring a person to render assistance to a person in peril when a "special relationship" exists, such as that between a teacher and student. He posits that it is clear that the general duty of teachers to exercise reasonable care and skill in attending to the health, safety, and comfort of their students includes the expectation that teachers will administer emergency medication as necessary.[61]

Wayne MacKay and Tonya Flood suggest that, although ideally the administration of medication should be left to the school nurse, it is a fact of life that many schools no longer have full-time nursing staff. As a result, teachers are often called on to deliver everything from hyperactivity to headache medications.[62] MacKay and Flood suggest that teachers who are required to deliver medication to students should ensure that their school boards have insurance coverage for dispensing drugs. If no such insurance exists, the safest route for teachers who want to avoid liability is to refuse to administer the medication. Overall, Flood and MacKay argue, the best solution is government and school board action in the form of the development of policies on drug administration and teacher training programs.[63]

In general, teachers who decide to administer medication to students should seek specific doctor's instructions from the parents. As well, teachers should seek training in dealing with students who are epileptic, diabetic, or subject to other physical disabilities. Schools and school boards need to develop clear rules and policies in this important area and provide the necessary medical supports for teachers. The present lack of clear guidance about a teacher's paramedical role causes anxiety for teachers and raises the possibility of liability for negligent conduct.

Who performs the necessary medical procedures for students with special physical needs, such as changing colostomy bags, removing fluid for children with cystic fibrosis, and feeding children by means of tubes? In many cases, educational assistants deal with these procedures. As with medication delivery, it is of the utmost importance that these individuals are properly trained to perform these procedures, because significant injury to a student could occur as a result of improper performance. The New Brunswick Department of Education specifies in its guidelines that teaching assistants may perform specific medical procedures, such as catheterization and administration of hypodermic needles to students, only after receiving "appropriate training."[64]

Several provinces have begun to acknowledge the issue of life-threatening allergies at governmental and administrative levels. In January 2006, the Ontario legislature brought in "Sabrina's Law," a statute intended to protect students with severe food allergies.[65] The law was named for a high school student who died of anaphylactic shock after eating cafeteria food that had come into contact with dairy products, to which she was severely allergic. Sabrina's Law requires schools to train staff and create procedures to address food allergy concerns and to develop individualized plans for every student in the school with anaphylaxis. In several provinces, individual schools have considered banning the sale of milk and milk products because of the severe allergy to dairy products of several students who attend the school.[66] Although not directly related to teachers' duties, these types of incidents show another area of concern for the teacher as paramedic. It is important for teachers to know which students in their class may have severe allergies so that they can do what is necessary to protect them from exposure to an allergen. School authorities may have an obligation, in both educational and legal terms, to make reasonable inquiries about the special health needs of the students attending the school.[67] Maintaining a safe school environment for all students is the responsibility of schools and their staff.[68]

Summary

This chapter discusses the different "social welfare" functions that may be performed by teachers. These include YCJA rehabilitation counselling, social work, family mediation, child advocacy, and paramedic assistance. Teachers perform many varied roles as social welfare agents. These roles are further complicated by the evolving nature of the family and changing societal expectations of teachers. Often, these roles arise simply as a result of teachers' constant and intimate contact with their students. In addition to providing their students with an education, teachers should at least be aware of opportunities to take action on behalf of their students in a social welfare context. They should also become familiar with the legal implications of adopting social welfare roles. This is one of the new and evolving frontiers in education law.

NOTES

1   *Youth Criminal Justice Act*, S.C. 2002, c. 1.

2   R. Weir, "What the Youth Criminal Justice Act Means to Your School" (2003) 12:4 *CAPSLE Comments*.

3   J. Leon, "The Development of Canadian Juvenile Justice: A Background for Reform" (1977) 15:1 *Osgoode Hall Law Journal* 71, at 81.

4   J.J. Kelso, "Delinquent Children: Some Improved Method Whereby They May Be Prevented from Following a Criminal Career" (1907) 6:3 *Canadian Law Review* 106.

5   T. Sussel and M. Manley-Casimir, "Special Education and the Charter: The Right to Equal Benefit of the Law" (1987) 2 *Canadian Journal of Law and Society* 45. See also A.W. MacKay and J. Burt-Gerrans, "Inclusion and Diversity in Education: Legal Accomplishments and Prospects for the Future" (2003) 3:1 *Education & Law Journal* 77; and A. Wayne MacKay, "Safe and Inclusive Schools—Expensive ... Quality Education—Priceless, for Everything Else There's Lawyers!" (2008) 18 *Education & Law Journal* 21.

6   MacKay and Burt-Gerrans, supra note 5.

7   See *Children and Family Services Act*, S.N.S. 1990, c. 5, s. 22, which indicates that a child is in need of protective services when he has killed or seriously injured another person, or caused serious property damage as a result of a lack of supervision by a parent or guardian, or when that parent or guardian refuses the services or treatment necessary to prevent a recurrence of the behaviour.

8   Wayne MacKay, "Respectful and Responsible Relationships: There's No App for That—The Report of the Nova Scotia Task Force on Bullying and Cyberbullying," February 29, 2012, http://cyberbullying.novascotia.ca/thereport.php.

9   *F.N. (Re)*, 2000 SCC 35, [2000] 1 S.C.R. 880.

10 Ibid., at para. 52.

11 Ibid., at para. 56.

12 A.W. MacKay, "Principles in Search of Justice for the Young: What's Law Got to Do with It?" (1995) 6:1 *Education & Law Journal* 181.

13 *Singh v. Board of Reference and Board of School Trustees of School District No. 29 (Lillooet)* (1987), School Law Commentary, Case File No. 3-5-8 (B.C.S.C.).

14 *Children's Aid Society of Ottawa v. N.S.*, [2005] O.J. no. 1070 (Q.L.) (S.C.).

15 *R. v. O'Connor*, [1995] 4 S.C.R. 411.

16 See *R. v. M.A.*, 2006 CanLII 37136 (ONSC), where the court refused to order disclosure of the Ontario Student Record to the applicant, a criminal defendant who was accused of sexual assault of his daughter; and *R. v. Maddison*, 2008 NSPC 82 (CanLII), where the court ordered disclosure of certain records of a particular student with certain personal details redacted, and denied access to other of the student's records.

17 For an example of this type of legislation, see Alberta's *Health Information Act*, R.S.A. 2000, c. H-5.

18 *Tarasoff v. Regents of the University of California*, S.F. 23042 (C.A.S.C. 1974).

19 A.W. MacKay and P. Rubin, *Study Paper on Psychological Testing and Human Rights in Education and Employment* (Toronto: Ontario Law Reform Commission, 1996).

20 See, for example, the *Municipal Freedom of Information and Protection of Privacy Act*, R.S.O. 1990, c. M.56.

21 MacKay and Rubin, supra note 19, at 163-164.

22 *Child and Family Services Act*, R.S.O. 1990, c. C.11, s. 72(3).

23   *Child and Family Services Act*, S.N.W.T. 1997, c. 13, s. 8(2).

24   See Saskatchewan's *Child and Family Services Act*, S.S. 1989-90, c. C-7.2, s. 11; Nova Scotia's *Children and Family Services Act*, S.N.S. 1990, c. 5, s. 22; Manitoba's *Child and Family Services Act*, C.C.S.M., c. C80, s. 17; and Prince Edward Island's *Child Protection Act*, R.S.P.E.I. 1988, c. C-5.1, s. 9.

25   R. Rosencrantz, "Rejecting 'Hear No Evil Speak No Evil': Expanding the Attorney's Role in Child Abuse Reporting" (1994-95) *Georgetown Journal of Legal Ethics* 327, at 331.

26   See Alberta's *Children, Youth and Family Enhancement Act*, R.S.A. 2000, c. C-12, as amended by S.A. 2003, c. 16, s. 9, or see New Brunswick's *Family Services Act*, S.N.B. 1980, c. F-2.2, s. 30(3).

27   W.F. Foster, "Child Abuse in Schools: Legal Obligations of School Teachers, Administrators, and Boards," paper presented to the national CAPSLE conference in Vancouver, British Columbia, April 29 to May 2, 1990.

28   T.L. MacGuire and D.S. McCall, *Child Abuse: A Manual for Schools* (Vancouver: EduServ, 1987), III-2. Also consider the reasonable discipline discussion in *Canadian Foundation for Children, Youth and the Law v. Canada (Attorney General)*, 2004 SCC 4, [2004] 1 S.C.R. 76, at paras. 36-40.

29   MacGuire and McCall, supra note 28, at III-5.

30   Ibid., at III-2.

31   Ibid.

32   *Children and Family Services Act*, S.N.S. 1990, c. 5, s. 22.

33   *Canadian Foundation for Children, Youth and the Law v. Canada (Attorney General)*, 2004 SCC 4, [2004] 1 S.C.R. 76.

34   See *R. v. Maddison*, 2009 NSPC 16 (CanLII), where the court found that an educational assistant who worked with a student with significant special needs had acted within the scope of section 43 in applying corrective force against the student either for purposes of ensuring compliance or to restrain aggressive behavior.

35   See, for example, *R. v. Burtis*, 2012 ABPC 12 (CanLII), where a special education teacher was convicted of assault for pinching a student's ears. The student was autistic, and repeatedly touched other people's ears; the teacher responded by pinching and pulling the student's ears and stating, "[T]here, how does that feel?" and "[Y]ou wouldn't like it if your friends did that to you." The court found that this was not corrective or objectively reasonable in nature. See also *R. v. Jonkman*, 2010 ABPC 245, where the court found a teacher guilty of assault for grabbing a 6th grade student by the arm and pulling him from his desk. See also *Ogg-Moss v. R.*, [1984] 2 S.C.R. 173, in which a counselor in a facility for adults with mental disabilities was charged with assault for hitting an adult resident in the face with a metal spoon.

36   *Children and Family Services Act*, S.N.S. 1990, c. 5, s. 23.

37   *Young v. Bella*, 2006 SCC 3, [2006] 1 S.C.R. 108.

38   Ibid. (emphasis in original).

39   D. Brown, "Truants, Families and School: A Critique on the Literature on Truancy" (1983) 35:3 *Educational Review*.

40   A. Dean, "The Attendance Board: An Alternative to Taking Truancy to Court," paper presented to the national CAPSLE conference in Vancouver, British Columbia, April 29 to May 2, 1990. See also G. Eastman, S.M. Cooney, C. O'Connor, and S.A. Small, "Finding Effective Solutions to Truancy: What Works," (2007) 5 Wisconsin Research to Practice Series (Madison, WI: University of Wisconsin–Madison/Extension).

41   R. Keel, *Student Rights and Responsibilities: Attendance and Discipline* (Aurora, ON: Canada Law Book, 1999).

42   *In the Matter of K.G.* (1987), School Law Commentary, Case File No. 2-1-6 (Alta. Prov. Ct.).

43   *R. v. Jones*, [1986] 2 S.C.R. 284.

44   Paul Clarke and Bruce MacDougall, "The Case for Gay–Straight Alliances (GSAs) in Canada's Public Schools: An Educational Perspective" (2012) 21 *Education & Law Journal* 143.

45   *Accepting Schools Act*, S.O. 2012, c. 5. The Report of the Nova Scotia Task Force on Bullying and Cyberbullying, supra note 8, also recommends that school boards and their staffs facilitate support groups for marginalized student populations.

46   Supra note 8. In the amended preamble to the Nova Scotia *Education Act* (amended by Bill 30 in June 2012), there is also reference to an inclusive and whole-school approach that combats bullying and promotes school safety,

47   *Canada (Attorney General) v. Mossop*, [1993] 1 SCR 554. In this case Justice L'Heureux-Dubé provided a compelling dissenting opinion in which she proposed an evolving model of the concept of "family."

48   *Chamberlain v. Surrey School District No. 36*, 2002 SCC 86, [2002] 4 S.C.R. 710.

49   *Criminal Code*, R.S.C. 1985, c. C-46.

50   *R. v. Dawson*, [1996] 3 S.C.R. 783, 1996 CarswellNS 420, at para. 30.

51   For an interesting discussion of the issues surrounding parental access and control, see C. Armsworthy, "Turning a Triangle into a Trapezoid: Custodial Disputes, Changing Families, and Redefining Parental Rights in Canadian Education Law" (2012) (unpublished, archived at Schulich School of Law Library).

52   L. Robinson, "Custody and Access," in E. Mendes da Costa, ed., *Studies in Canadian Family Law* (Toronto: Butterworths, 1972), 546.

53   *Divorce Act*, R.S.C. 1985, c. 3 (2d Supp.), s. 16(5).

54   Bill C-22, *An Act to Amend the Divorce Act, the Family Orders and Agreements Enforcement Assistance Act, the Garnishment, Attachment and Pension Diversion Act and the Judges Act and to Amend Other Acts in Consequence* (second reading February 25, 2003). This bill died on the order paper.

55   W. Foster, "Medication of Pupils: Teachers' Duties" (1995-96) 7 *Education & Law Journal* 45.

56   See Alberta Teachers' Association, "Administration of Medication: Rights and Risks," 2010, http://www.teachers.ab.ca/Publications/Other Publications/Teachers Guides/Pages/Administration of Medication.aspx.

57   *Winnipeg Teachers' Association v. Winnipeg School Division No. 1.*, [1976] 2 S.C.R. 695.

58   Foster, supra note 55.

59   Ibid.

60   Ibid.

61   Ibid.

62   A.W. MacKay and T.L. Flood, "Negligence Principles in the School Context: New Challenges for the 'Careful Parent'" (1999-2000) 10:1 *Education & Law Journal* 371.

63   Ibid.

64   New Brunswick Department of Education, Teacher Assistant Guidelines for Standards and Evaluation, http://www.gnb.ca/0000/publications/curric/teacherassisguide.pdf.

65   *Sabrina's Law*, S.O. 2005, c. 7, http://www.e-laws.gov.on.ca/html/statutes/english/elaws_statutes_05s07_e.htm.

66   "Edmonton School May Ban Sale of Milk," CBC News, May 31, 2005, http://www.cbc.ca/news/canada/story/2005/05/31/alberta-milk050531.html. See also, Isabel Grant, "Life, Liberty and Peanut Butter?" *The Globe and Mail*, November 26, 1997.

67   See, for example the BC government's document "Life-Threatening Food Allergies in School and Child Care Setting: A Practical Guide Resource for Parents, Care Providers and Staff," British Columbia Ministry for Children and Families, http://www.health.gov.bc.ca/cpa/publications/food_allergies.pdf.

68   The duties of teachers are usually laid out explicitly in the provincial legislation governing education. See, for example, the *School Act*, R.S.P.E.I. 1988, c. S-2.1, s. 98, or the *Education Act, 1995*, S.S. 1995, c. E-0.2, s. 231.

7
Teachers as Employees

This chapter deals with teachers' rights and responsibilities in the context of labour law. The preceding chapters have focused primarily on duties and responsibilities of teachers with regard to other people in the education system; in contrast, this chapter focuses on the teacher's own rights within the school system. Here we discuss the rights to freedom of religion, expression, privacy, lifestyle, and association as they relate to teachers in the school setting. We also examine teachers' rights and responsibilities under employment and labour law. In general, teachers are subject to a wide range of responsibilities that emanate from a number of distinct sources. It is noteworthy that the role and legal status of teachers in Canada has not, to date, been fully addressed by legislation.

Labour Law

In the field of labour law, recent rulings from the Supreme Court of Canada have changed the position of teachers with respect to their rights to bargain collectively. Originally, the public service nature of their work led to statutory restriction of teachers' rights to bargain collectively and to strike, because the Supreme Court of Canada's previous position was that the *Canadian Charter of Rights and Freedoms* did not protect the rights to strike or bargain collectively.[1] Teachers were left with traditional labour law remedies, such as filing grievances and arbitration.

However, that position changed drastically[2] with the Supreme Court of Canada's decision in *Health Services and Support—Facilities Subsector Bargaining Association v. British Columbia*,[3] where the court held that collective bargaining is protected by section 2(d) of the Charter, which guarantees freedom of association.

The *Health Services* decision was recently applied in a case involving a teacher's union in British Columbia.[4] In that case, elementary and high school teachers in the BC Teachers' Federation challenged provincial legislation that unilaterally overrode provisions of their existing collective agreements and prohibited collective bargaining on certain subject matter in the future, including matters involving restrictions on class sizes, class composition (the number of special needs children integrated into the classroom), ratios of non-enrolling teachers to students (teachers not assigned to classrooms such as librarians, counsellors, and special education teachers), workload, and days and hours of work.

The BC Supreme Court found that a majority of the challenged legislative provisions violated section 2(d) of the Charter. The legislation interfered with the collective bargaining rights of the teachers in a substantial way, which is the condition required by *Health Services* for finding such a violation. The court found that issues of class size, composition, non-enrolling ratios, workload, and hours and days of work are important issues to teachers and can greatly affect their working conditions. As a result, taking away the right to bargain with respect to these matters seriously eroded the bargaining strength of the teachers and increased the bargaining strength of the employer. The outcome of the legislation was a significant interference with the teachers' ability to come together and collectively pursue goals related to working conditions that were important to them. Moreover, the process of the interference with the collective bargaining rights of teachers also contributed to the Charter violation. The legislative changes were brought about without any consultation with the teachers' union; in fact, the government informed and sought advice only from the school board employer side of the bargaining table. The BC Supreme Court found that this lack of consultation sent messages to the teachers that whatever time, effort, and sacrifices they might put into the collective bargaining process, it could all be subject to a governmental decision to override the process without any consultation. This negated any process for voluntary good-faith bargaining, a fundamental requirement of collective bargaining upheld by section 2(d).

The court also disagreed with the government's argument that the provisions should be upheld according to section 1 of the Charter as valid restrictions on the Charter right in the name of educational policy decisions made for the public good. The court noted that public policy decisions of the government are similarly subject to the Charter, as is legislation, and that taking the issues out of the collective bargaining process altogether did not minimally impair the teachers' section 2(d) rights. The legislation was declared unconstitutional and invalid. The declaration of invalidity was suspended for a period of 12 months to allow the government to deal with the consequences of the decision.

The collective agreement between school boards and teachers is the guide for determining the rights and responsibilities of teachers, including when teachers can strike. One interesting development in this area is the courts' protection of teachers' right not to strike. For example, in *Forster v. Saskatchewan Teachers' Association*,[5] the court held that the teachers' unions were not entitled to discipline or suspend teachers who refused to partici-pate in strikes. The court stated that there was a distinction between a teacher as a teacher and a teacher as a union member. Teaching during a strike did not constitute professional misconduct or conduct unbecoming a teacher.

The other important matters arising from labour law are suspensions and dismissals. Case law suggests that school boards have the right to sus-pend teachers with or without pay,[6] although this may vary, depending on the provisions of the governing collective agreement. What constitutes just cause for the suspension or dismissal of teachers? Statutes sometimes provide guidance on the question, but judges and arbitrators frequently determine the matter on a case-by-case basis.[7] Another important issue is whether a teacher receives proper procedural protection before she is sus-pended or dismissed.[8] We discuss procedural protection below in the sec-tion entitled "Procedural Rights."

In terms of labour law, there is an additional danger for teachers lurking in the *Criminal Code*. If teachers are accused of an impropriety that also constitutes a criminal offence under the Code (particularly sexual interfer-ence or sexual touching), they can be dismissed for cause, even if they are acquitted of the charge by a criminal court. A school board, unlike a criminal court, is not required to be satisfied "beyond a reasonable doubt" before acting on its findings. Rather, it may dismiss a teacher by applying the civil standard of proof, which is generally known as the "balance of probabilities." Put simply, this means that if a school board is convinced that a teacher "more likely than not" was involved in an impropriety with students, it may dismiss the teacher.

An Alberta case, *Nand v. Edmonton Public School District No. 7*,[9] provides a good example of this process. In this case, the teacher was charged with the criminal offence of sexual assault against female students. The criminal proceeding ended in a mistrial, and the charges were ultimately stayed, which means, effectively, dropped. The board of trustees dismissed the teacher because of his criminal conduct. At issue was the type of proof necessary to sustain the board's decision. The teacher argued that the board did not allow him to make representations or call evidence in board hearings. Furthermore, the teacher argued that the board could not revisit the issue of sexual misconduct because the charges had already been stayed in the criminal court. The Court of Appeal sent the case back to the board. It stated that the board had applied the proper standard of proof in assessing the appropriate disciplinary action: the "high preponderance of probability," not proof "beyond a reasonable doubt." However, the court indicated that the board had erred in accepting the same character evidence that was used in the criminal proceedings. Because the board accepted this evidence at face value, it was required to allow the teacher to rebut the evidence against him by presenting evidence of his own.

In *Fountain v. College of Teachers (British Columbia)*,[10] the teacher was embroiled in an off-duty altercation with his two grown sons that ended with him firing shots above their heads to essentially scare them off his property. He was acquitted by the court of the charges regarding careless use of a firearm, but a panel of the College of Teachers determined that his actions amounted to professional misconduct. The BC Supreme Court noted that the appropriate standard of proof for professional misconduct at a disciplinary hearing is less than the criminal standard of beyond a reasonable doubt, but higher than the balance of probabilities, requiring proof "by a fair and reasonable preponderance of credible evidence."[11] The court found that the panel did not properly consider whether Mr. Fountain's off-duty conduct was enough to impair Mr. Fountain's ability to fulfill his responsibilities as a teacher or whether it would harm the education system. The court stated that not all off-duty conduct, even if it falls below the standard of the reasonable teacher, serves as a basis for discipline. Because the panel did not address the basis of their conclusion that this off-duty conduct was enough to attract disciplinary consequences, its verdict was unreasonable and the matter was remitted back to the College for reconsideration.

A Quebec case, *Cree School Board v. Northern Quebec Teaching Association*,[12] emphasizes the need for an arbitration board to consider all relevant evidence in dealing with the dismissal or suspension of teachers. In this case, a teacher was suspended for inappropriate sexual conduct at school. He filed a grievance, which resulted in a settlement, giving him a one-year leave of absence without pay. The following year, the board decided not to hire him, partly because of his misconduct in the past. A second settlement provided that he would be reinstated the next year. After the teacher's reinstatement, the board dismissed him again for sexual misconduct with his students. A third grievance ensued, in which the arbitrator ordered that the teacher be reinstated with full compensation. The board argued that the arbitrator failed to consider relevant evidence. The court agreed, and stated that arbitration boards must consider all relevant evidence in decisions relating to the dismissals of teachers. The court also noted that the board was not expected to apply a criminal standard of proof when assessing the evidence against a teacher. Therefore, the court held that the arbitrator's decision to reinstate the teacher was unreasonable.

The fact that cases like *Cree School Board* rely on evidence with a lower standard of proof against teachers indicates that teachers and all persons involved in the teaching and child-care professions are held to higher than average standards of conduct. Any unreasonable actions may be sufficient for dismissal or suspension. Conduct that might have called for suspension in the 1980s might well call for dismissal today because of these higher than average expectations.

In cases involving criminal conduct, some teachers who face dismissal may turn to their collective agreements or the courts for assistance. In a Saskatchewan case,[13] the Court of Appeal examined a situation in which a teacher was tried and acquitted on a charge under the *Criminal Code* of sexually touching some of her students. After the acquittal, the teacher applied for an extension of time to bring an action against the school board for wrongful dismissal. The court had the authority to hear the dismissal action because the teacher had no alternative remedy under the collective agreement or the *Education Act*.

On the other hand, in another Saskatchewan case,[14] the application by a teacher who applied to have her case regarding termination of her contract determined by the Saskatchewan Court of Queen's Bench was dismissed, because the court found that the school board had complied with the *Education Act* and the teacher had already unsuccessfully availed herself of the review procedures available to her. Accordingly, she was not entitled to impose a common-law obligation on the school division or individual defendants in relation to the termination of her contract by seeking other relief at court.

In another case, an ESL teacher was dismissed and her certificate of qualification was terminated when she engaged in a consensual sexual relationship with a 14-year-old student. She appealed the decision of the College of Teachers to the BC Supreme Court. After deciding that the student freely consented to the relationship, the court reduced the teacher's penalty from dismissal to a two-year suspension. In reducing the penalty, Justice Humphries stated:

The College is required, by its objects, to consider not only the public interest but the professional interest of its members. It did not do so here when it failed to give any analysis or consideration to the many mitigating factors specific to this case, in particular, failing to consider the uncontradicted evidence that the appellant will not re-offend, poses no risk to the public, and in view of her unblemished record since these long-past events, is not in need of rehabilitation. Its decision cannot stand and the appeal is allowed.[15]

The ramifications of sexual misconduct do not necessarily end at dismissal from a particular school board. This sort of misconduct may also result in a permanent revocation of a teacher's licence to teach.[16] In *Hansen v. The Disciplinary Hearing Subcommittee of the College of Teachers and the Council of the College of Teachers*,[17] the BC Supreme Court reviewed a decision of the discipline committee that found a teacher guilty of misconduct for inappropriately touching several students. The court declined to interfere with the decision of the discipline committee, whose findings were largely based on the credibility of witnesses, because the members of the committee, who heard the testimony, were in a better position than the reviewing court to assess credibility. The legislation that governs the teaching profession in every province entitles discipline committees to make findings of misconduct in cases where these findings are warranted.

The online era creates more risks for teachers with respect to sexual misconduct. In British Columbia, one teacher was stripped of his right to teach for at least 15 years following an investigation by the RCMP where links to Internet pornography with titles including references such as "teacher" and "coach" were discovered on his laptop. The RCMP's investigation was begun when the teacher hooked his laptop up to a projector for a lesson at school, and a student noticed a link onscreen titled "schoolgirl porn."[18] A second BC teacher lost his right to teach for five years following an exchange of personal Twitter messages, texts, and emails regarding love and a future together with a 17-year-old high school student whom he was tutoring in English.[19]

It is obvious from the case law that teachers must avoid any sexual contact with students. Even if a teacher is not charged with a criminal offence, as in the *Mitchell* case, school boards have frequently taken the position that dismissal is the appropriate disciplinary measure in these cases, and the courts have consistently upheld this position.

Obviously, any criminal conviction involving sexual misconduct can also result in dismissal at the discretion of the board. Courts have consistently upheld the right of school boards to dismiss teachers who have been convicted of a criminal offence.

Convictions for offences that do not involve sexual activity have also resulted in the dismissal of teachers. Most education statutes provide that a criminal conviction may be cause for dismissal where the circumstances of the offence render it inadvisable to continue the employment of the teacher. In Manitoba, a teacher pleaded guilty to 11 charges of theft and 1 charge of public mischief. The criminal acts were admittedly the result of a mental illness suffered by the teacher. The teacher had an exemplary and unblemished record for 13 years with the school board; however, the school board elected to dismiss the teacher on the basis of the criminal convictions. An arbitration board accepted mental illness as a reason for the abnormal conduct and overturned this dismissal. The Manitoba Court of Appeal overruled the arbitration board and reinstated the dismissal. The Court of Appeal decided that the school board had cause for dismissal and that in the circumstances the arbitration board should not substitute its opinion of the proper discipline for that of the board.[20]

Stress: The Inclusive Classroom and Other Challenges

There are many sources of stress for teachers in today's educational environment. Classrooms almost always include students with special needs, and with these additional needs come increased challenges for teachers, including concerns related to occupational safety and risk management. These concerns also relate to the school population at large, as do the challenges posed by behaviour management and growing school violence.[21] This has been further exacerbated in recent years by harassment from either students or, with increasing frequency, parents. These problems are partially the result of underfunding of inclusive classrooms and the failure to provide the resources needed to properly accommodate the diverse needs of modern students.

Stress Generally

Today, many teachers' unions, as well as many school boards, are concerned about the rising incidence of teachers using sick time, as well as short- and long-term disability plans, to cope with job stress. A study of urban teachers in Saskatchewan by University of Regina professors Ron Martin and Rod Dolmage found that 61 percent of teachers had reported becoming ill due to work-related stress, almost 40 percent had to take time off work because of stress, and 51 percent stated that they would leave teaching if they found a viable career alternative.[22] Kenneth Leithwood notes the following:

Teachers who experience burnout are less sympathetic towards students; less committed to and involved in their jobs, have a lower tolerance for classroom disruption, are less apt to prepare adequately for class, and are generally less productive.[23]

Robert Smol suggests that, in his experience as a teacher, it is the most highly motivated and committed teachers who undergo the most stress. He quotes Professor Martin from the University of Regina who states that "[b]urnout is more common in the young, highly motivated, energetic, hard-working teacher. The people who burn out are the people who pour everything into it without balance."[24] Thus it is often the most effective and valuable teachers who are lost to the system because of stress and burnout.

Leithwood also suggests that, at any given time, the number of teachers feeling stressed is 15 to 45 percent.[25] There are a variety of factors that may cause or contribute to the stress that teachers feel every day. Leithwood suggests that emotional exhaustion is a frequent problem, which can result from larger class sizes, more teaching periods, and teaching outside a familiar subject area.

The expectation of the omnicompetent teacher is a major source of stress. There are a number of steps teachers can take to reduce stress, whether at home or in the workplace, including availing themselves of numerous online resources and the services of local agencies. Nonetheless, there are many demands on the modern teacher, including the numerous diverse roles they are expected to play in the changing Canadian society.

Occupational Safety

Including children with special needs in a regular classroom may raise a number of concerns about occupational health and safety for classroom teachers. These include, but are not limited to, injuries from the physical demands associated with a physically disabled student and injuries incurred in attempts to prevent self-injury or aggression from students who exhibit behavioural difficulties. In *Kendal v. St. Paul's Roman Catholic Separate School Division No. 20,*[26] an elementary teacher of special needs students sued her employer school district after she was injured while attempting to restrain a student with Asperger's syndrome. The student had a lengthy history of violence and aggression. The teacher claimed that the school district was negligent in failing to exercise the duty of care it owed to her as an employee.

The trial judge found that the school district did owe the teacher a duty of care, but the question at issue was whether having the student in the school was an unreasonable risk within that duty of care. He found that the teacher had failed to prove that the school division had created an unreasonable risk in choosing to keep the student in the school. He noted that the value of education for children with special needs outweighed the risks associated with the inclusion program. The Saskatchewan Court of Appeal dismissed the teacher's appeal, agreeing with the trial judge's decision that the school district had recognized the relevant risks and taken adequate steps to address them.

Brian Nolan, Jennifer Trépanier, and Brian Ellerker discuss the intersection of education of students with special needs and teacher safety.[27] They focus on the rights of Ontario school personnel to a safe working environment and discuss the collision between collective agreements, the *Education Act*,[28] and the *Occupational Health and Safety Act*.[29] The authors found that, in a number of cases, special needs assistants, educational assistants, and teachers have refused to work with special needs students because of concerns about their own safety. Their refusals stemmed from their rights under occupational health and safety legislation. Although this legislation appears to focus on physical working environments, rather than on people with whom an employee is required to interact, the authors note that Ontario Ministry of Labour investigators have made orders against school boards based on this legislation.[30] This is problematic for a number of reasons.

Nolan, Trépanier, and Ellerker argue that this legislation was not intended to apply to these circumstances. They base this assumption on the fact that teachers are exempt from the *Occupational Health and Safety Act* by virtue of the *Education Act* and its regulations. As well, they note that teacher assistants at the university level are exempt, but elementary and secondary school educational assistants are not exempt. Further, they argue, the occupational health and safety regulations do not apply when the safety concerns are "inherent," a "normal condition of the worker's employment," or "when the worker's refusal to work would directly endanger the life, health or safety of another person."[31] Thus, the authors argue, there is a basis on which teachers should be able to refuse to work with special needs students. They suggest that educational assistants, who are not exempt from the provisions of the occupational health and safety legislation, function in an analogous role to other exempt workers—teachers. Nolan, Trépanier, and Ellerker also note that, in all other areas, school boards are required by law to take every reasonable precaution to protect employees. This includes providing safety apparel as necessary.[32]

The authors also discuss the possibility of human rights complaints from parents and students as a result of work refusal by school personnel. A teacher's or an assistant's refusal to work with a student could result in the student being unable to attend school, leading to a viable complaint that the school board has not provided the appropriate accommodation to allow the student an education.[33] From a human right's perspective, this could be seen as discrimination based on disability. Any refusal to work pursuant to a school board directive could result in severe employment consequences as well.

Teachers should be frank with their school administrators about perceived safety risks. They can note their concerns by carefully documenting incidents of behaviour, including the date; time; information about what was going on in the classroom when the outburst occurred; and details about the response, its effectiveness, and the consequences. Teachers should keep the school updated about their concerns and note whether and how the school deals with the issues. Ultimately, it is the school board's responsibility to develop policies to address safety issues and consider appropriate placement for students; it is the teacher's responsibility to implement these policies. All schools should have a policy for reporting and following up on staff injuries. As well, school boards should provide training for teachers in crisis prevention and behaviour management to limit the number of physical incidents that arise. Teacher training programs should also be offering more instruction on both the challenge of the inclusive classroom and strategies and techniques for behavior management.[34] Teachers should also consult their unions, as well as their employers, on the issues of occupational health and safety.

Risk Management

Many teachers have expressed concerns about their ability to physically manage children with aggressive behaviours in a regular classroom. They worry about injury to other students and their own legal liability in the event of injury. It is our opinion that teachers need not worry excessively about personal liability because the school board, as employer, would be vicariously liable for any student-to-student aggression that occurred in the course of a teacher's employment. However, on a day-to-day level, behavioural problems in schools and growing violence raise challenging issues.[35]

Parental Harassment

As teachers become more accessible to parents via email and classroom telephones, and as some parents become more demanding with respect to their children, the risk for harassment of teachers increases. Monika Reed suggests there are a number of reasons for the increase in parental harassment incidents.[36] She cites poor coping skills, poor communication skills, language barriers, mental health problems, family breakdown, and poor parenting skills as only a few of the issues that create situations of harassment of teachers by parents.[37] Reed distinguishes between criminal harassment, which involves a victim's fear for his safety, and civil harassment, which is typically based on emotional distress caused by inappropriate (though not overtly threatening) behaviour. She defines harassment as "offensive behaviour, which is persistent, notwithstanding that the person acting has been made aware that it is inappropriate and unacceptable."[38]

With respect to intervening, Reed has a number of suggestions gleaned from the former Calgary Board of Education's HEART team. HEART stood for harassment education and advocacy resource team. The team was made up of specially trained volunteers who worked with school employees to address situations of harassment. Members of the team provided a number of services to board employees, such as coaching them in strategies for dealing with parents and providing mediation services where the school had unsuccessfully attempted to address the situation on its own. In more serious situations, where a parent presented a possible threat to a teacher and refused to be involved in mediation, HEART suggested a no-trespass letter, which barred the parent from being on school property or making contact with the teacher. If necessary, it suggested that a restraining order or peace bond be obtained by the school.

Reed maintains that when relationships between teacher and parent have disintegrated to the point of harassment, the situation has become one of abuse and teachers should not attempt to deal with it on their own. Instead, school administrators and the board should be involved to protect teachers and devise projects, such as the Calgary board's HEART, to maintain a safe and supportive environment within the school community.[39] A comprehensive legal review of the issues of parental harassment can also be found in Bob Keel and Nadia Tymonchenko's book on this topic.[40] Fundamentally, school boards have primary authority in shaping the school environment, and parents are allowed on school premises entirely at the school's discretion. It is a privilege that can be revoked. As we have discussed, education is a state-related activity and does not involve rights derived from parental delegation.

Defamation as a Response to Harassment

As an example of the degree to which parental harassment can occur, we offer the case of *McKerron v. Marshall*.[41] In this case, a father removed his son from class during the school year, and informed the principal that he would not return the child to school until a number of changes were made. The principal refused to make these changes. The father then met with the principal, the school superintendent, and a school trustee and presented them with documents that questioned the teaching abilities of his son's teacher. One of the documents was a letter from himself and his wife demanding the removal of the teacher. The school representatives told him that they would not remove the teacher, but they would conduct an investigation. Unhappy with this response, the father appeared at the teacher's school one morning with a banner on his car stating that the teacher was unstable and demanding her removal. The father was informed that he was not to appear at the school anymore.

When he defied this demand, he was charged and convicted of violating a court order. He then filed complaints against the teacher with the local board of education and the Ontario College of Teachers. His complaints of incompetence and abuse were investigated and determined to lack merit. The teacher requested and received a transfer to another school district, but the father appeared at her new school and complained to the principal. The teacher obtained an interim injunction against the father, ordering him to refrain from defaming her, which he ignored. The father was then charged with contempt of the order and a further order was issued to carry him through to the trial.

At trial, the court found that he libelled the teacher on two occasions and ordered him to pay her the two years' salary that she lost because she was unable to work because of depression. In addition, he was required to pay $100,000 for defamation, $20,000 for intentional infliction of mental suffering, $150,000 for aggravated damages, and $5,000 for punitive damages. The court noted that he had not been able to prove any of his allegations of incompetence or abuse, and had pursued his claims for self-aggrandizement.

From this case, it is clear that courts are not willing to accept parental harassment of a teacher that goes to this extreme. It is important to understand, however, that most cases will neither be this extreme nor result in such large awards. It is certainly preferable to reach a solution to harassment cases through the use of systems such as Calgary's HEART before resorting to litigation to prevent unnecessary expenditure of time and money and avoid considerable personal hardship. Teachers have the right to, and a legitimate expectation of, respectful treatment by parents, students, and others.

The Internet has provided another medium through which teachers may experience parental harassment, because parents are able to easily, widely, and, if they chose, anonymously, disseminate their views and criticisms of the teacher through cyberspace.[42] Three recent Canadian defamation cases have involved parental harassment of teachers over websites. In *Newman et al. v. Halstead et al.*,[43] the parent of a child in the Comox District School Board in British Columbia created a website called GAFER (Growing Advocacy for Educational Reform) and then used the site to post the names and photos of educators, school board members, and parents along with allegations of wrongdoing. One particular teacher, Newman, was targeted on the website with statements that he was being investigated by the RCMP following an assault in a parking lot. The court awarded Mr. Newman significant damages, considering the extent of the broadcast of the defamatory publications, the teacher's position of standing in the community, and the degree of harm to him and others on the site. The judge stated: "Not only students, but the community as a whole suffers when those involved in education are unfairly and unnecessarily publicly maligned. ... Each is entitled to his or her well-deserved good reputation."[44]

Angle v. LaPierre[45] is an Internet defamation case from Alberta. Denis LaPierre established a website titled Schoolworks! Inc., where he published correspondence between school officials and parents in two different Alberta communities who were engaged in persistent complaints, demands, threats, and allegations related to the treatment of their children by two different teachers. Along with the correspondence, LaPierre, a former principal, posted additional commentaries that portrayed the plaintiffs as uncaring bullies. At the Alberta Court of Appeal, LaPierre, Schoolworks! Inc., and the parents all argued that the publications and comments made by them were protected by "qualified privilege," which is premised on the value of informed public debate of significant public issues. The qualified privilege argument was defeated because the Supreme Court of Canada had previously found that it does not apply where the dominant motive for publishing is actual or express malice, or when the limits of the duty or interest have been exceeded.[46]

In *Ottawa Carleton Catholic District School Board v. Scharf*,[47] the parent and advocate of a child with Down's syndrome were involved in a dispute with the principal and superintendent of the Ottawa-Carleton District School Board and published defamatory statements on a website as well as sending them by email to school board members, principals, and elected members of the provincial legislature and the Parliament of Canada. After the court found in favour of the school officials, the defendants, as well as being required to pay damages to the principal and superintendent, were ordered to remove all defamatory material from any website over which they had control and were required to publish a public apology and retraction of the comments at their expense in an Ottawa newspaper. A permanent injunction against future defamatory statements about the educators was issued. The judge noted that the wide reach of the Internet exacerbates the potential for harm from defamation.[48]

In a recent article by Ruth Broster and Ken Brien regarding the cyberbullying of educators,[49] following a discussion of the above three cases, the authors comment that courts are not taking parental harassment of educators via the Internet lightly, although they must acknowledge parental Charter-protected freedom of expression in their determinations. The authors conclude with respect to parental defamation via the Internet:

> These three cases indicate that courts are recognizing the seriousness of defamatory statements made against educators through the Internet. At the same time, courts are still careful to protect the *Charter* rights to freedom of expression of students and parents. With rapid changes in technology, the challenge for educators and policy makers, and for lawyers and judges, is to maintain valued legal principles while developing appropriate and effective policies and practices that preserve the safe and orderly learning environment that is required and expected in schools.[50]

Accusations levelled against teachers by students and reinforced by upset parents can have severe consequences; Jon Bradley, an associate professor of education at McGill University, notes that the number of these accusations that turn out to be false is on the rise. He found that parents are often too quick to point fingers, and though teachers are usually cleared of the false accusations, this is not always the end of the matter for the teacher. In one case, a teacher accused of physical assault committed suicide, even after the student had recanted and the teacher had been cleared of the charges.[51]

Legal Rights of Teachers

The legal rights of teachers in Canada are conferred primarily by the Charter, provincial education statutes, provincial human rights codes, and labour law (both case law and statutes). Just as teachers are subject to scrutiny under the Charter in their handling of students, so are teachers' employers under the scrutiny of the Charter when dealing with teachers' rights and freedoms in the context of employment.

Teachers' rights issues usually unfold within the framework of the Charter; however, some cases that involve discrimination based on disability, family status, ethnicity, race, sex, or other grounds are decided by human rights tribunals. There is some overlap between the protection afforded by human rights codes and that afforded by the Charter. Teachers may have the option of choosing the forum in which to raise their claims. There are generally three procedural forums: arbitration boards in union grievance procedures, the human rights commission, and the court system.

Choosing one forum does not necessarily prevent a teacher from also proceeding in another. Although the principles are similar, the dispute resolution system and the remedies available through human rights legislation are radically different from those available under the Charter. Human rights legislation conciliates and mediates problems, and the government of each province pays the costs of having a human rights officer investigate and mediate. Only as a last resort will a tribunal be set up to adjudicate a human rights complaint in an adversarial setting.[52] The remedies available most often involve monetary compensation[53] and directions for appropriate behaviour in the future.[54]

The Charter, on the other hand, is the supreme law of Canada. As we have discussed, it contains more powerful remedies than human rights legislation. It also has the advantage of being able to set precedents that are national in scope.[55] Teachers and teachers' associations are therefore more likely to use the substantial powers of the Charter than human rights legislation to challenge a school board's actions when they wish to set a useful precedent for the future.[56] However, the costs of pursuing a Charter remedy through court action are much higher than using the human rights commission process.

Freedom of Religion

Religious freedoms are protected by section 2(a) of the Charter. Although there is a lot of discussion about separate or denominational schools and the religious rights of students, there has been little legal commentary about the religious rights of teachers in Canada. A related issue arose when the BC College of Teachers (now the BC Ministry of Education Teacher Regulation Branch) refused to certify graduates of Trinity Western University, a private Christian institution, on the basis of its concern that Trinity Western graduates would be intolerant of gay and lesbian students.[57] When matriculating at Trinity Western, students were required to sign a code of conduct agreement stipulating that they would not engage in any biblically prohibited conduct, including homosexuality. The Supreme Court of Canada ruled that although the College of Teachers was entitled to consider whether the university had breached equality rights in its certification assessment, the college acted unfairly in denying Trinity Western graduates teaching certificates. The court found no evidence to support the college's suggestion that the graduates were more likely than other teachers to discriminate against homosexual students when they began to work in the public school system.

We have recently seen an attempt by the government of France to prevent students from wearing religious symbols, including hijabs, yarmulkes, and crosses. The long-term effects of this decision remain to be seen. A different reaction to the presence of religious symbols at school is apparent in Canada, thanks to the emphasis on tolerance, freedom, and equality contained in the Charter. In 2006, on an appeal from the decision of a school board in Quebec to ban the wearing of the kirpan, a religious object resembling a dagger and made of metal, by Sikh students at school, the Supreme Court of Canada declared such a ban unconstitutional[58] in what has been called a "ringing defence of religious freedom."[59]

Religious Holidays for Teachers

Religious holidays have been an issue in the educational environment. In *Commission scolaire regionale de Chambly v. Bergevin*,[60] the Supreme Court of Canada considered the case of three Jewish teachers who chose to take leave from their teaching positions to celebrate Yom Kippur. The school board agreed to allow the teachers to take the leave as unpaid time. The teachers filed a grievance and an arbitration board found that they had been discriminated against and not properly accommodated by the school board. The case was ultimately appealed to the Supreme Court of Canada. The court found that the school calendar was discriminatory against Jewish teachers, because the majority of teachers had their religious holidays recognized by the school calendar. The court found further that it was reasonable for the school board to pay Jewish teachers for the Yom Kippur holiday.

Freedom of Expression

Section 2(b) of the Charter guarantees everyone freedom of thought, belief, opinion, and expression. This section has received broad interpretation by the Supreme Court of Canada. Freedom of expression has both content and form, and includes any "activity which conveys or attempts to convey meaning."[61] Further, the purpose of this guarantee is to permit "free expression," as well as to "promote truth, political or social participation, or self-fulfillment."[62] It therefore includes expression through conduct and dress, as well as through speech. For teachers, freedom of expression breaks down into two categories: expression within the school and expression outside the school.

School boards have relied on the reasonable limits exemption in section 1 of the Charter to curtail teachers' freedom of expression rights. They will continue to use it to require teachers to conduct themselves in a manner that is consistent with a positive school environment. Because teachers are regarded as role models and exemplars of positive social values, there are greater limitations on their speech than on others in Canada. One aspect of this positive school environment is that it be free of discrimination. The Supreme Court of Canada raised this issue in *Ross v. New Brunswick School District*,[63] which dealt with a teacher who published anti-Semitic writings and made racist comments on public television. Although the disciplinary action against the teacher was found to infringe his Charter rights, the Supreme Court held that the infringement was justified under section 1 of the Charter. In delivering its decision, the court stated that public school teachers "must be seen to be impartial and tolerant."[64]

More difficult issues arise where, for example, a teacher places an anti-abortion poster on his door or wears unorthodox clothing. Usually, the Charter protects these activities; however, there may be limits, depending on an activity's disruptive potential. The "material and substantial disruption" test from the US case of *Tinker v. Des Moines*,[65] as discussed in previous chapters, was referred to in *British Columbia Public School Employers' Assn. v. B.C.T.F.*,[66] where a teacher wore a black armband and told students that she was "silently protesting" certain standardized tests at the school. She explained to students why she was wearing the armband, and the students responded with cheering and a discussion of the situation. Her employer ordered the teacher to remove the armband, and the union filed a grievance that such direction was contrary to section 2(b) of the Charter. The BC Arbitration Board upheld the direction, finding that, although it was an infringement of section 2(b), under section 1 of the Charter it was minimally impairing to the teacher's rights, because the teachers were free to express themselves as long as they were not engaging students at the elementary school in their protest.

Recently, teachers in Prince Rupert, BC and their school board have gained national attention from the media in both the *Vancouver Sun* and the *Huffington Post*.[67] The confrontation occurred during the province-wide "dark day for education" organized by the BC Teachers' Union to protest the 11th anniversary of Bills 27 and 28, which stripped away teachers' rights to bargain class size and composition and which came into force in late January 2012. In order to protest these bills, teachers took to wearing black shirts.

This was not the problem, however. Three teachers from Prince Rupert decided to put the words of section 2 of the Charter (free speech and association) on their black shirts. They were ordered to remove or cover these shirts by their school board. The poignancy of restricting the teachers' freedom of expression by actually disallowing them from wearing the words of the Charter enshrining freedom of expression cannot be missed. However, the chair of the district's board of education disagreed, saying that it is political messaging, something that was banned in an arbitration decision in 2011 (see the *Vancouver Sun* article). This provides a thought-provoking illustration of the differences between freedom of expression in the population at large and freedom of expression granted to teachers in schools. It is also an example of how something that would be innocuous or even encouraged in Canadian society, such as the words of our Charter, may be considered inappropriate in a school setting.

Canadian courts have also placed limits on hate speech in the context of academic freedom. In *R. v. Keegstra*, a high school teacher was charged under section 319(2) of the *Criminal Code* with unlawfully and wilfully promoting hatred as a result of numerous derogatory and inflammatory statements he made to his students about Jews.[68] His students were expected to reproduce his views on exams and papers or their grades would suffer. He challenged the constitutionality of the criminal charge, arguing an infringement of his section 2(b) Charter right to freedom of expression. The Supreme Court of Canada found that the charge did violate his right to freedom of expression, but the violation was justified under section 1 as a reasonable limit in a free and democratic society.

School boards will encounter greater opposition in attempting to demonstrate reasonable limits on the freedom of expression outside the school because this sort of expression involves a less direct impact on the school environment. However, where a published expression is seriously controversial, teachers can be subjected to censorship or dismissal. In the *Ross* decision,[69] the New Brunswick Human Rights Board of Inquiry held that a teacher who published a number of anti-Semitic books, as well as letters to the editor claiming that the Holocaust was a myth, violated human rights legislation. The teacher in question taught mathematics and therefore did not have occasion to air his views directly in the classroom. Although he did not advocate these views in school, the Human Rights Board of Inquiry found that his writings had impaired his ability as a teacher. The school board was ordered to put him on immediate leave of absence without pay for a period of 18 months and attempt to find him a non-teaching position. If a non-teaching position was not available or not accepted, his employment was to be terminated. Initially, the board imposed a "gag order" prohibiting the teacher from producing anti-Semitic materials; the New Brunswick Court of Queen's Bench struck the order down, but the Supreme Court of Canada ultimately upheld it.[70]

In contrast, some courts have held that teachers enjoy a significant amount of freedom of expression and that, if a teacher is "attempting to communicate certain information and opinions that would stimulate discussion and challenge his students," his expression is protected. This was the conclusion in *Morin v. P.E.I. Regional Administrative Unit No. 3 School Board*,[71] where the teacher was allowed to show a controversial video for purposes of class discussion and education. Of course, there are limits, as indicated by *R. v. Keegstra.*

In Chapter 4, Teachers as Guardians of Equality, we discussed the "teachable moments" case, in which a Manitoba teacher was denied the right to reveal her lesbianism to her junior high school students.[72] An arbitration board refused to accept jurisdiction on the issue. Clearly, school districts may continue to attempt (often successfully) to place limits on their teachers' rights to address certain subjects. School boards and provincial governments, for better or worse, are responsible for curriculum. These authorities must balance the free speech rights of teachers against the perceived needs of students and the related limits on curriculum.

A common problem both inside and outside the school is the freedom to express criticism of employers and fellow teachers. Criticism of employers can put teachers in a vulnerable position because if a teacher's comments are construed as "insubordination," the teacher can be suspended. This is particularly true in cases where a teacher makes critical comments within the school setting.[73] It is more difficult to make out a case for disciplining a teacher who makes comments outside the school,[74] unless the comments are so critical and inflammatory that they impair the teacher's ability to teach, or lead to a public perception of inability to teach.[75] Criticisms of fellow teachers are restricted by statute or regulation in most provinces as well as in the various codes of professional conduct.

In *Cromer v. British Columbia Teachers' Federation*,[76] a teacher was charged with violating the federation's code of ethics because of her criticism of a teacher-counsellor at a public meeting. The teacher's son was a student at the school in which the teacher-counsellor worked. In the course of her duties, the teacher-counsellor developed lists of questions regarding teenage sexuality and distributed them to students. Many parents complained about the distribution, and it was decided that the issue would be addressed at a parents' advisory committee meeting. The meeting became heated, and a number of exchanges occurred between the parents and the teacher-counsellor, who was attempting to defend her position.

During the meeting, there was a confrontation in which the teacher made personal attacks against the character and teaching ability of the teacher-counsellor. On discovering that the teacher worked at another school in the same town, the teacher-counsellor complained to the teachers' federation. An investigative committee of the federation decided that the complaint was proper and could proceed. The teacher then brought the issue to the Supreme Court of British Columbia on an application for judicial review, arguing that several of her rights were violated. She was unsuccessful. On appeal, she argued only that her right to freedom of expression had been violated. She contended that her professional code of ethics should not apply when she spoke as a parent, and not as a teacher. The BC Court of Appeal rejected this argument, stating:

> I do not think people are free to choose which hat they will wear on what occasion. [The teacher] does not always speak as a teacher, nor does she always speak as a parent. But she always speaks as [the teacher]. The perception of her by her audience will depend on their knowledge of her training, her skills, her experience and her occupation, among other things. The impact of what she says will depend on the content of what she says and the occasion on which she says it.[77]

The court then considered whether the teacher's right to freedom of expression should override the code of ethics. The court found that if she had spoken out regarding the teaching of human sexuality, then her right to freely express her opinion on that subject should have overridden the code of ethics. However, the court found that because her comments were personal criticisms of the teacher-counsellor, and not addressed to the subject matter of the meeting, her speech was not protected by section 2(b) of the Charter. She was therefore bound by the code of ethics at the time she made the statements about the teacher-counsellor.

Personal Views and Lifestyle

The private lives of teachers may cause difficulty with employers and consequently lead to court challenges. As we saw in *Ross*, the "teacher as role model (in and out of class)" theory leads to less privacy for teachers than for many other workers. In an article entitled "Freedom of Expression and Public School Teachers," Allison Reyes noted:

> Teachers are a significant part of the unofficial curriculum because of their status as "medium." In a significant way the transmission of prescribed "messages" (values, beliefs, knowledge) depends on the fitness of the "medium" (the teacher).[78]

Two young high school teachers at Churchill High School in Winnipeg produced a colourful and racy example of violating teacher role-model standards. In February 2010, the two teachers, one male and one female, engaged in a fully clothed lap dance in front of one hundred students at a "spirit rally." The students ranged from grades 9 to 12 and some students were as young as 13. The very graphic dance was captured by a student with a cellphone and uploaded to the Internet, quickly becoming a sensation on YouTube and other Internet venues. Parents and others in the community were outraged and called for action. Most of the students witnessing the event cheered and made positive comments about their "cool" teachers, but even some of the students felts that the teachers had gone too far.

The school board that employed the teachers was neither amused nor cheering. After sending the young teachers home without pay and giving consideration to firing them, the teachers were disciplined.[79] This case raises a number of interesting issues about the limits of teachers' free expression. Although the desire to be cool and relate to their students is understandable, teachers must exercise great caution. This is even truer in the age of social media, where momentary lapses in judgment can be captured online for all time. What might at the time be considered a private or at least a limited audience situation, can go viral on Facebook or YouTube within a few moments.

Although lap dances in front of a school assembly seem an obviously dubious choice, even less problematic behaviour may be found to fall short of the expected standard for teachers. The consequences for teachers' reputations, and even their continued employment, can be devastating. This is a cautionary tale for teachers, especially in the Internet age.

The Charter arguments advanced in the teacher lifestyle cases involve the protection of "liberty" and "security of the person" under section 7 and "freedom of expression" under section 2. Teachers are under constant scrutiny in their communities because parents are extremely sensitive about who is setting an example for their children. This was brought to light recently in *Kempling v. British Columbia College of Teachers*.[80] In this case, a high school teacher and counsellor wrote and published an article and a series of letters to the editor expressing his views on homosexuality as aberrant behaviour. His writing proved to be highly controversial, drawing heated responses from readers, many of whom found the statements discriminatory against homosexuals. The College of Teachers' review panel began a disciplinary investigation, found the teacher guilty of professional misconduct, and suspended his teaching licence for one month. Despite the fact that the teacher's conduct occurred outside the school and there was no evidence of a poisoned school environment, the panel believed that the teacher's actions would adversely affect the learning environment. The teacher appealed to the BC Supreme Court, which upheld the panel's decision. The court held that the teacher's Charter rights were not infringed and that the suspension was reasonable. The BC Court of Appeal also upheld the panel's decision.

As discussed earlier in this chapter, another restriction on the lifestyle of teachers is the fact that most collective agreements allow school boards to dismiss teachers who are convicted of a criminal offence. In serious cases, such as sexual assault, the basis of dismissal is obvious and the dismissal is relatively easy to justify.[81] However, it is more difficult to justify dismissal in cases such as possession of marijuana[82] or impaired driving. The test generally is whether the subject matter of the offence is inconsistent with a person's continued duties as a teacher.

One colourful example of the limits on teachers' privacy and lifestyle rights is the case of *Abbotsford School District 34 Board of School Trustees v. Schewan*.[83] In this case, two teachers, a married couple, were suspended for misconduct by the school board that employed them. The husband photographed his wife nude from the waist up, and the photo was published in *Gallery Magazine*. When the board learned of the publication, it suspended both teachers for six weeks. The teachers' appeal to a board of reference was allowed, with the board finding that the teachers, although lacking in judgment, were not guilty of misconduct. The school board appealed to the BC Supreme Court. The court determined that the key question in adjudicating the teachers' misconduct was whether the conduct fell within the moral standards of the community in which they taught. The court reduced the teachers' suspensions from six weeks to four. On appeal, the BC Court of Appeal found that the main issue was the meaning of the word "misconduct" in the *School Act*. The court found that the word included the conduct of a teacher off school premises because

> a teacher holds a position of trust, confidence, and responsibility. If he or she acts in an improper way, on or off the job, there may be a loss of public confidence in the teacher and in the public school system, a loss of respect by students for the teacher involved, and other teachers generally, and there may be controversy within the school and within the community which disrupts the proper carrying out of the education system.[84]

The court went on to hold that the question in this case was not whether the photograph was obscene, but whether the publication of the photograph would negatively affect the education system. After finding that *Gallery Magazine* was designed to exploit sex, the court went on to hold that, by allowing the photograph to be published in such a magazine, the actions of the teachers were bound to have an adverse effect on the education system of Abbotsford. The court upheld the school board's right to suspend the teachers. In the end, the school board did not object to the lower court's reduction of the suspension to four weeks. Ultimately, the standard adopted by the BC Court of Appeal was not a national standard, but at most a provincial and more likely a localized community standard. This opens the door to different standards in different parts of the country. For example, a court in Quebec could choose to apply a different standard than a court in Prince Edward Island. Indeed, in Quebec, a teacher who appeared nude on the cover of a nudist magazine was not subject to any sanction.

In one instance in the United States, a prospective teacher was actually denied her teaching degree because of her personal life choices. Just days before commencement, campus officials viewed the MySpace page of Stacy Snyder, of Millersville's School of Education, University of Pennsylvania, and discovered a photograph of her drinking from a plastic cup and wearing a pirate hat, with the caption "Drunken Pirate." The administrators called the photograph "unprofessional" and refused to award the education degree and teaching certificate to Ms. Snyder, instead issuing a degree in English. Ms. Snyder has since filed a federal lawsuit seeking her education degree, teaching certificate, and $75,000 in compensatory damages.

Privacy in the Internet Age

The example of Stacy Snyder, above, raises the question of the privacy rights of teachers with respect to their online information. In California, legislation was recently passed restricting employers from demanding social media accounts or login credentials from their employees.[85] Eric Goldman notes that, although this legislation appropriately protects employees' online privacy, the blunt drafting creates problems. Because "social media" isn't definable, the law covers more than anyone expects, effectively governing all digital content and activity both on the Internet and stored in local storage devices. Furthermore, Eric Goldman notes that it's not always clear when social media accounts are "personal"; some are business-related, and in such a context it is entirely appropriate for employers to demand the login credentials. However, it may be difficult to draw the line between a personal and business-related social media account.

In Canada, the trend in human resources (HR) departments is toward using social network searches to "weed out" prospective employees, and it may be that asking for login credentials is a logical next step in this process.

In the absence of a regulatory framework, it may be difficult to keep employees' privacy from being invaded. Until limits are legislated, employees' may find their online privacy being invaded, and it is wise to be aware of that fact.

A recent Supreme Court of Canada decision involving a teacher considered the rights provided to employees in terms of the privacy they can expect on workplace-issued devices. In *R. v. Cole*,[86] a teacher's school-owned laptop was seized by the principal after pornographic images involving children were discovered on it in a routine scan. Although the court found that the school was within its rights to seize the laptop, it also noted that, in handing the computer over to the police, the school board and police breached Mr. Cole's Charter rights by proceeding with a warrantless search of the device. In spite of the breach of rights, the court allowed the evidence to be used against Cole in the criminal case, because it determined that a failure to allow the information could bring the administration of justice into disrepute within the meaning of section 24 of the Charter. The court left for another day specific commentary on an employer's ability to limit an employee's expectation of privacy.

The legal challenge is to strike a proper balance between the privacy rights of teachers and the legitimate interests of an employing school board in ensuring that teachers provide a proper role model for students. The role of teachers as moral exemplars in the community is not only a public expectation but also a part of the statutory definition of the duties of a teacher.[87] The nature of teaching places limits on the public conduct of teachers. In Charter terms, the question is: "What limitations on the free expression and liberty of teachers can be justified as reasonable in light of their professional duty to act as role models for their students?" Another question is: "What private conduct is relevant?" In the modern electronic age, the scope of everyone's privacy is shrinking; this is particularly true for teachers.

Freedom of Association

Freedom of association is protected by section 2(d) of the Charter. In at least one respect it can raise issues of lifestyle because teachers may be subject to censure if they associate with a group that is frowned on by their school board. This can certainly become a problem if the teacher is employed in a particularly conservative community, because, as the *Kempling* case[88] indicated, local community standards would apply when evaluating whether an activity adversely affects a school environment. As yet, there have been few courtroom confrontations in this area, and the possible restrictions on association are open to speculation.[89]

In 1970, the government of British Columbia passed an order in council stipulating that provincial educational institutions would not employ teachers who advocated the policies of the Front de libération du Québec (FLQ) or those who supported the overthrow of governments by violent means. In *Jamieson et al. v. Attorney General of British Columbia*,[90] several university professors and a welding instructor from a vocational school sought a declaration from the court that the order was outside the authority of the province because it interfered with freedoms provided by the federal government, including the freedoms of association and expression. None of the plaintiffs had actually advocated the policies of the FLQ or the overthrow of a government. The defendant province brought a motion asking the court to dismiss the case, arguing that the plaintiffs were not entitled to bring the case to court because they had not suffered any losses as a result of the order in council. The court found that the interest of the plaintiffs, although genuine, was hypothetical. It suggested that, for these plaintiffs to be heard in court, they would need to suffer a loss as a result of the order in council—for example, being fired for advocating the policies of the FLQ. Because this had not happened, the court refused to hear their case. It may be significant that this case predates the Charter.

This raises interesting questions regarding possible situations in which a teacher could find herself. What if a teacher wished to be a member of an extremist religious organization that advocated terrorism? Given the Supreme Court of Canada rulings discussed earlier with respect to freedom of expression, such as *Ross*,[91] it appears likely that membership in a gay rights group is acceptable, although membership in extremist organizations may not be. Unlike gay rights organizations, extremist organizations do not espouse the virtues of tolerance and acceptance expected of a teacher in the public school system. The Elementary Teachers' Federation of Ontario is a member group of the Coalition for Lesbian and Gay Rights in Ontario.

A more concrete problem for some teachers is the freedom "not to associate." In every province, teachers' contracts are regulated through collective bargaining legislation, and the profession is very much a "closed shop." In Ontario, for example, there are a number of different teachers' federations. Every teacher is a member of the Ontario Teachers' Federation, and the bylaws of this federation mandate that members join one of the affiliate organizations for different classes of teachers. There are four affiliate groups: the Elementary Teachers' Federation of Ontario (ETFO),[92] the Ontario English Catholic Teachers' Association (OECTA), the Ontario Secondary School Teachers' Federation (OSSTF), and l'Association des enseignants Franco-Ontarians (AEFO).

One of the former affiliates involved in this mandatory division of teachers was challenged under section 6 of the Ontario *Human Rights Code*.[93] Two female teachers complained that they did not wish to be designated as members of the Federation of Women Teachers' Associations of Ontario (FWTAO) because they were opposed to belonging to the single-sex federation. Their complaints related to the fact that women were not permitted to join the Ontario Public School Teachers' Federation (OPSTF) because of a bylaw that required them to join the FWTAO. Female teachers were considered voluntary members of the OPSTF. The Ontario Human Rights Commission agreed with the teachers. The Ontario High Court of Justice upheld the commission's decision, stating that the bylaw constituted discrimination under section 6 of the Ontario *Human Rights Code* and was not justified under section 14(1) of the Code. A previous complaint based on the same issue was launched under the Charter;[94] however, this complaint dealt only with violations of the *Human Rights Code*.

The freedom "not to associate" may also become an issue when a teachers' federation takes a political stance outside the realm of education. For example, the OSSTF has adopted policy statements on nuclear disarmament and globalization. What if it adopts a resolution on abortion? Would a teacher be forced to pay union dues to an organization that used the money to advocate causes that the teacher did not support? The Canadian Supreme Court has upheld a decision involving the Ontario Public Service Employee Union that the use of union dues is a private matter and beyond the reach of the Charter.[95] The court's reasoning could easily be applied to teachers' federations as well.

Equality Rights

Section 15 of the Charter guarantees equality and prohibits discrimination on the basis of a number of enumerated grounds.[96] Some of these grounds, such as age, physical disability, and sex, are particularly relevant for teachers. The Supreme Court has stated:

> It may be said that the purpose of section 15(1) is to prevent the violation of essential human dignity and freedom through the imposition of disadvantage, stereotyping, or political or social prejudice, and to promote a society in which all persons enjoy equal recognition at law as human beings or as members of Canadian society, equally capable and equally deserving of concern, respect and consideration.[97]

Discrimination on the basis of sexual orientation, though not specifically prohibited under section 15, is prohibited under human rights legislation, and can be of particular concern to teachers. Sexual orientation has also been held by the courts to be an unlisted ground of discrimination in section 15 of the Charter.[98]

Age

The prohibition against age discrimination has been used to challenge mandatory retirement policies in a number of cases involving university professors with differing results. In a series of rulings,[99] the Supreme Court of Canada held that mandatory retirement policies violated section 15 of the Charter. However, the court upheld these policies as a reasonable limit pursuant to section 1. More recently, human rights tribunals and courts have struck down mandatory retirement policies,[100] which then led to legislative changes abolishing mandatory retirement in human rights and labour and employment laws.[101] The provinces also followed the federal pattern. At the time of publication, only New Brunswick still allowed employers to enforce mandatory retirement in the context of a "bona fide retirement or pension plan."[102]

Physical Disability

Section 15 protects teachers with physical disabilities by requiring school boards to accommodate physical disability provided that it does not have a negative impact on a bona fide work requirement. The Supreme Court of Canada has outlined the test for this requirement:

> To be a bona fide occupational qualification and requirement a limitation ... must be imposed honestly, in good faith, and in the sincerely held belief that such limitation is imposed in the interests of the adequate performance of the work involved with all reasonable dispatch, safety and economy, and not for ulterior or extraneous reasons aimed at objectives which could defeat the purpose of the [Human Rights] Code. In addition it must be related in an objective sense to the performance of the employment concerned, in that it is reasonably necessary to assure the efficient and economical performance of the job without endangering the employee, his fellow employees and the general public.[103]

This matter has not arisen often in the school setting, but presumably the court's reasoning will apply to require reasonable access for teachers with physical disabilities.

The Supreme Court of Canada has more recently deemed that an apparently discriminatory standard can be a bona fide occupational requirement if it meets three tests:

1. The employer adopted the standard for a purpose that was rationally connected to the performance of the job.
2. The employer adopted the standard in an honest belief that it was necessary to the fulfillment of that work-related purpose.
3. The standard itself is reasonably necessary. To show this, the employer must demonstrate that it is impossible to accommodate individual employees who share a claimant's disability without creating undue hardship for itself.

This test did not originate in the educational context, but rather as the result of a challenge to the physical testing of firefighters in British Columbia. In this case, a female firefighter argued that an aspect of the physical test to qualify as a firefighter was inherently discriminatory against women.[104]

Another politically sensitive issue in the area of physical disability is the presence in the classroom of teachers who are HIV-positive or have AIDS (acquired immune deficiency syndrome). The legal trend, both in Canada and the United States, is to classify persons with the HIV virus as "disabled" and, therefore, subject to human rights protection.[105] In Nova Scotia, the issue was brought to the fore in a rural community, where a young teacher was found to be carrying the HIV virus. He was initially reassigned to non-teaching duties (under the threat of a boycott by parents) but was eventually appointed to a provincial task force on AIDS to diffuse the situation.[106] School boards and provincial governments across the country are faced with the challenge of educating the public about HIV and AIDS, and formulating policies that respect the rights of individuals living with HIV/AIDS.[107]

Sex

Discrimination on the basis of sex has been tested in the courts in the past and is likely to be the object of further discussion. In a 1985 case, *Nevio Rossi v. School District No. 57*,[108] a male teacher applied for a job teaching physical education to female students. The school board refused his application because it claimed the job required a female instructor. The BC Human Rights Council held that the school board could not prove that being female was a necessary requirement for the job and awarded damages to the teacher. In a later case, *Wall v. Kitigan Zibi Education Council*,[109] a female complainant alleged that she was dismissed from her teaching position because she became pregnant. The Canadian Human Rights Tribunal dealt with this case as an issue of discrimination based on sex. The tribunal concluded that there was insufficient evidence to support the allegation of discrimination. It considered the fact that the education council had generally been flexible in accommodating parenting needs. The evidence suggested that the teacher had chosen not to return to work.

The outcome of *Wall v. Kitigan Zibi Education Council* supports the view that discrimination on the basis of pregnancy amounts to discrimination on the basis of sex. This is an interesting development because, surprisingly, an early Supreme Court of Canada decision based on the *Canadian Bill of Rights* held that distinctions based on pregnancy did not constitute sex discrimination.[110] Since the Charter, and an increased emphasis on human rights statutes, courts and other judicial decision-makers have extended the protection of pregnant women in the workplace.[111] In addition, some human rights legislation specifically includes the right to protection from discrimination on the basis of pregnancy.[112] These additional protections for pregnant women are as applicable to teachers as to any other employees.

Another aspect of sexual discrimination that tests the limits of section 15 is the use of affirmative action in hiring policies. Traditionally, in Canada, upper administrative levels of education were dominated by men. Many school boards may therefore wish to offer superintendent positions and principalships to women on a preferential basis. Justification for doing so is provided in section 15(2) of the Charter.

> 15(2) Subsection (1) does not preclude any law, program or activity that has as its object the amelioration of conditions of disadvantaged individuals or groups including those that are disadvantaged because of race, national or ethnic origin, colour, religion, sex, age or mental or physical disability.

To date, school boards have not needed to rely on section 15(2) because women have been able to fill administration positions on the basis of merit alone. Affirmative action policies could also be used to hire more teachers from visible minorities and the First Nations without running afoul of the Charter equality guarantees. The Supreme Court of Canada recently set out a test for section 15(2) of the Charter in *R. v. Kapp*,[113] so that a particular affirmative action program does not violate the section 15 equality guarantee if the government can demonstrate that the program has ameliorative or remedial purpose and it targets a disadvantaged group. In such a case, a government program is protected by section 15(2) and will not violate the equality guaranteed by section 15.

Sexual Orientation

The issue of sexual orientation as a ground of discrimination arose in *Vriend v. Alberta*.[114] In *Vriend*, a laboratory worker was dismissed from his position at King's College in Edmonton when his employer became aware that he was gay. The college thought it was entitled to dismiss him because the Alberta human rights legislation, the *Individual's Rights Protection Act*, did not include sexual orientation as a prohibited ground of discrimination. There had been numerous attempts to include sexual orientation as a ground, but the government had deliberately chosen to omit it from the Act. The teacher argued that the college had violated his section 15(1) Charter right to equality.

The Supreme Court of Canada considered whether the Alberta legislature had the right to omit sexual orientation as a prohibited ground of discrimination and determined that it did not. The court deemed that from that time forward, the Act should be read to include sexual orientation as a prohibited ground of discrimination. Discrimination on the basis of sexual orientation is now a prohibited ground of discrimination in all provinces, based on both human rights codes and the Charter.

In *Willow v. Halifax Regional School Board*,[115] a female teacher was accused of acting improperly toward a female student when two other teachers saw them standing together in a changing room. While police investigated, no charges were laid and no basis was found for the complaint. Ms. Willow, the teacher, brought a complaint to the Nova Scotia Human Rights Board of Inquiry alleging discrimination on the basis of her sexual orientation. The Human Rights Board agreed, finding that the suggestion that Ms. Willow was engaged in a sexual relationship with her student was not gender-neutral, but arose from a stereotype that homosexuals are more likely to seek out young people than are heterosexuals. The board found discrimination against Ms. Willow on the basis of sexual orientation and chastised Ms. Willow's school principal, the teacher who reported the incident, and the school board for acting on this homophobic stereotype.

Dismissal for Denominational Cause

The unique denominational school structure in various provincial education systems raises difficult questions about the denominational rights of teachers. Alberta, Saskatchewan, and Ontario have maintained a system of denominational (separate) schools. Quebec has organized schools along English and French, rather than religious, lines. New Brunswick, Nova Scotia, Prince Edward Island, Newfoundland and Labrador, Manitoba, and

British Columbia treat separate schools as private schools. These private schools may receive some government funding, but are also required to charge attendance fees. Denominational schools within the meaning of section 93 of the *Constitution Act, 1867* are publicly funded.

The rights of teachers in denominational schools provide a prime example of the blend of Charter issues, human rights statutes, and labour law in the field of education. Simply stated, the problem arises when a teacher employed by a denominational school board violates some aspect of the prevailing religious faith. The majority of cases have involved Roman Catholicism. Denominational school boards have traditionally claimed the legal authority to dismiss teachers whose conduct contravenes their religious tenets, because they feel these teachers undermine the underlying purpose of their schools.

In legal terms, dismissing teachers for denominational cause is a battle between two constitutional standards. The first is contained in section 93 of the *Constitution Act, 1867*, which protects the rights of the province to establish a separate school system.[116] This section is fortified by section 29 of the Charter, which states that nothing in the Charter derogates from any of the rights in the Constitution respecting denominational schools. In *Casagrande v. Hinton Roman Catholic Separate School District No. 155*,[117] the school board dismissed a teacher for engaging in premarital sex that resulted in a second pregnancy outside of marriage.

The teacher was pregnant when she was hired, but did not notify the school board of this fact. After discovering her pregnancy, the school board warned the teacher that it would dismiss her if she engaged in any further premarital sex. Upon notifying the school of her second pregnancy and requesting maternity leave, the teacher was dismissed. She was granted a hearing with the board of reference, but her dismissal was upheld. The board held that her dismissal was not discriminatory on the basis of her sex because it was not a result of her pregnancy. Rather, it was a result of her engaging in premarital sex, conduct prohibited on religious grounds for both male and female teachers. The court failed to note that the results of premarital sex can be more obvious (in the form of pregnancy) for women. The Alberta Court of Queen's Bench dismissed her appeal. The court held that a school board holding the right to establish denominational schools also holds the right to dismiss teachers for not maintaining the "denominational character" of the school.

These principles were followed by the Newfoundland Supreme Court in *Hogan v. Newfoundland School Boards*.[118] The Newfoundland court made it clear that once a school board explicitly states that adherence to the basic tenets and philosophy of a particular denomination governs a school, the school is constitutionally protected in upholding these tenets. The Supreme Court of Canada has also provided some guidance for determining what aspects of the school system are central to its denominational character.[119] Matters such as curriculum, the hiring of teachers, and the selection of students were considered vital to the denominational character of the school.

The other side of the issue is that teachers are entitled to freedom of conscience and religion as provided by section 2(a) of the Charter, and the equivalent provisions in human rights legislation. The Supreme Court of Canada has recognized the balancing necessary when dealing with these inherently contradictory rights, but has leaned toward protecting the distinct nature of denominational schools:

> [V]iewed objectively, having in mind the special nature and objectives of the school, the requirement of religious conformance including acceptance and observance of church rules regarding marriage is reasonably necessary to assure the achievement of the objectives of the school.[120]

The basic principle derived from this decision is that, where the actions of a teacher in a denominational school (even one not protected by section 93 of the *Constitution Act 1867*), can reasonably be seen to undermine the religious objectives of the school, the teacher may be dismissed for just cause.[121] In the past, section 136(1) of the Ontario *Education Act* prevented school boards from taking into account the religious affiliation of teachers who applied for jobs as long as the applicants agreed to respect the philosophy and traditions of the denominational school. In 1999, the Ontario Court of Appeal held that section 136(1) could adversely affect the right of school boards to dismiss teachers for denominational cause.[122] It therefore found that section 136(1) was a violation of section 93(1) of the *Constitution Act, 1867*, which preserves the rights and privileges that denominational schools had at the time of Confederation. The Court of Appeal upheld the lower court's ruling that section 136(1) was of no force and effect. The western provinces and Newfoundland and Labrador, which joined Canada after 1867, incorporated denominational rights in their respective terms of union. The government of Newfoundland and Labrador recently reduced the extent of denominational rights by a constitutional amendment.

Overall, teachers in denominational systems must be particularly careful about their conduct, both in and out of school. Teachers who are employed by denominational school systems obviously face significant restrictions on privacy and lifestyle rights. These restrictions can be even greater than those faced by teachers in the public school system.

Procedural Rights

Thus far, we have concentrated on the substantive rights of teachers; however, no less important are their procedural rights. Procedural rights apply to the manner in which teachers are treated by their employers and professional organizations. They usually arise in the context of disciplinary action, and involve questions of whether a teacher has been given an adequate opportunity to be heard and to respond to prejudicial evidence. Procedural protections have traditionally been grounded in the principles of administrative law. More recently, however, they have also been derived from section 7 of the Charter.

Procedural Safeguards in a Disciplinary Context

Administrative law requires that government officials and their delegates provide certain procedural safeguards to individuals when decisions are made that affect these individuals. Because the government regulates education, these protections must be extended to teachers. This means that teachers are entitled to receive a fair hearing in accordance with the rules of natural justice and fairness when they are suspended or disciplined. Natural justice issues may also arise where certification is at issue. In *Barrow v. Manitoba (Minister of Education and Training)*,[123] the court held that, although the minister of education had the right to suspend a teacher convicted of assault, the minister could not take this action until the convicted teacher had a reasonable chance to respond to a review committee's recommendation of suspension. Although the court did not comment on the committee's recommendation, it strenuously objected to the fact that the teacher was not informed of it.

Barrow indicates that some degree of protection is offered to teachers in suspension and dismissal situations. Generally, school boards are required to develop evaluation procedures that contain teaching guidelines; provide for notice in cases where problems arise; provide for warnings and an opportunity for improvement; and, finally, provide some form of meeting with the employer before a teacher can be suspended. Sometimes the minimal procedural safeguards are set out in the governing education statutes. These protections are often further enunciated in regulation and policy.

In *Haché v. Lunenburg County District School Board*,[124] a teacher was acquitted of several criminal charges of sexual assault but convicted of six others. On appeal, the court set aside the six convictions and ordered a new trial. However, the Crown never proceeded to a new trial, so ultimately the teacher was never convicted on any charges. Notwithstanding the lack of criminal convictions, the school board discharged the teacher on the basis of allegations of inappropriate sexual contact with students. The teacher appealed his discharge to the board of appeal, which upheld the decision of the school board. He then applied for judicial review to the Nova Scotia Supreme Court and was successful in having the decision of the board quashed, because the judge found that the teacher had not received proper notice of the complaint on which his dismissal was based.

The school board appealed to the Nova Scotia Court of Appeal, which upheld the decision of the lower court, albeit for different reasons. The court noted that acquittal in criminal court does not generally prevent the same issue from being relitigated in an employment situation. As noted earlier, there is a lower standard of proof in the employment context. In this situation, however, the judge found that the evidence of one of the victims on which both the criminal and employment case depended was not believable. The Court of Appeal held that, because of this, the evidence given by that witness did not meet any standard of proof and could not be relied on. In practical terms, this means that school boards should carefully analyze any evidence they plan to use to ensure that it, at a minimum, meets the lower balance of probabilities standard.

If a teacher is eventually dismissed, the rules of procedural fairness require that a further appeal be available through the grievance process in the collective agreement. In *Lebelle v. Yellowknife Public Denominational District Education Authority*,[125] the court found that section 57 of the *Education Act*, although not intended to give all teachers an absolute right to arbitration, was intended to secure that right for dismissed teachers. Teachers' associations also have a responsibility to meet similar standards when dealing with their members, because employment is conditional on membership in the association.

In *Yorke v. Northside-Victoria District School Board*,[126] a teacher who was dismissed because of suspected alcohol abuse challenged his dismissal by a school board. He was successful in having the dismissal quashed by a board of appeal, and was reinstated on a two-year probationary contract. On appeal to the Nova Scotia Court of Appeal, he was successful in obtaining reinstatement with a full contract. The court found that the board of appeal had no authority under the *Education Act* to reinstate the teacher under a probationary contract. As a result, the teacher was never properly discharged, so his permanent contract remained in effect, subject only to dismissal for just cause or because of a drop in enrollment. The court ruled that a probationary contract should not be used as a disciplinary measure, unless the governing statute and the collective agreement authorized this use.

Procedural Rights Under the Charter

Two older court decisions have provided opportunities for protecting the procedural rights of teachers by means of section 7 of the Charter. In the early years of case law involving the Charter, section 7 was interpreted as not protecting economic or employment rights. Therefore, a teacher whose employment was affected through suspension or dismissal enjoyed no protection under this section. Soon after the Charter came into effect, the Supreme Court of Canada had an opportunity to evaluate the scope of section 7. In *Robert Olav Noyes v. Board of School Trustees, Dist. No. 30 (South Caribou)*,[127] a 1985 case, a teacher was suspended without pay after he was charged with a criminal offence, but before he was tried. The teacher claimed that his suspension violated section 7 as well as section 11(d) (presumption of innocence) of the Charter. The court held that the words "life, liberty and security of the person" in section 7 did not include employment. The court further held that the suspension did not presume guilt on the part of the teacher, and therefore it upheld the school board decision. Five years later, the Supreme Court of Canada reiterated its opinion that section 7 did not protect employment rights in a case known as the *Prostitution Reference*.[128]

Some courts, including the BC Court of Appeal, have held that section 7 of the Charter may be interpreted to protect employment rights within the meaning of the term "liberty."[129] This case arose when the provincial medical services commission placed restrictions on doctors, and the court decided that these restrictions unduly fettered the doctors' rights to pursue their profession.[130] In another 1989 decision, the Supreme Court of Canada commented on the evolution of section 7, and indicated that the scope of the phrase "life, liberty and security of the person" is broad enough to protect economic rights in a suitable case.[131] This holding has yet to be tested in a teacher dismissal case.

Duty of Fair Representation

Yet another important procedural right of which teachers should be aware is the "duty of fair representation" that is required of teachers' unions or associations. Section 74 of the Ontario *Labour Relations Act, 1995* states:

> A trade union or council of trade unions, so long as it continues to be entitled to represent employees in a bargaining unit, shall not act in a manner that is arbitrary, discriminatory or in bad faith in the representation of any of the employees in the unit, whether or not members of the trade union or of any constituent union of the council of trade unions, as the case may be.[132]

In *Dionne v. C.A.W., Locals 199 & 1973*, the Ontario Labour Review Board examined the scope of the duty of fair representation, and concluded:

> The duty of fair representation applies to the way in which the union represents employees in their relationship with their employer. Because the employees cannot bargain on their own, the union must represent them fairly. However, section 69 [now 74] does not regulate the relations of employees to each other, or to their union as an organization. It does not regulate internal union affairs.[133]

Although this case was not about a teachers' union, teachers may take from it that their union must act in a fair manner. This does not mean, however, that teachers can always expect the union to act in a way that protects the best interests of individual teachers. Sometimes a union will need to act in a way that protects the interests of the entire union and not particular individuals. Courts have upheld the right of unions to balance individual with group needs, provided that they do so without improper motives after considering all relevant issues.[134]

Sexual Misconduct in Schools

Sexual misconduct has no doubt been occurring in schools for many decades;[135] however, it is now common for people to voice their complaints about it. In Canada, sexual harassment is dealt with through the human rights codes and the relevant tribunals in each province. The case law has determined that sex discrimination includes sexual harassment, and the conduct of employers has been subjected to review on the basis of that interpretation. However, modern human rights codes are being amended specifically to address the problem of sexual harassment. Section 5(2) of the Nova Scotia *Human Rights Act* prohibits sexual harassment, and section 3(o) defines "sexual harassment" to mean

> (i) vexatious sexual conduct or a course of comment that is known or ought reasonably to be known as unwelcome,
> (ii) a sexual solicitation or advance made to an individual by another individual where the other individual is in a position to confer a benefit on, or deny a benefit to, the individual to whom the solicitation or advance is made, where the individual who makes the solicitation or advance knows or ought reasonably to know that it is unwelcome, or
> (iii) a reprisal or threat of reprisal against an individual for rejecting a sexual solicitation or advance.

This provision and others like it, make it clear that "vexatious sexual conduct" or unwelcome sexual comments are prohibited by law and subject to censure by human rights tribunals.

Teachers also have the right to inform a school board of unwelcome sexual conduct by a fellow teacher or a school principal and request that the offending individual be disciplined. The Supreme Court of Canada has held that employers are liable under human rights codes for the human rights violations of their employees, particularly with regard to sexual harassment.[136] This reasoning has been adopted and applied by the courts in relation to universities, and there is no reason to believe that the same reasoning would not also apply to school boards. Consequently, school boards have a crucial interest in eliminating sexual harassment from the school environment and in taking appropriate action when a complaint is brought to their attention.[137] We recommend adopting preventive measures against sexual harassment. If a school board's actions are inadequate, a complainant has the option of seeking a remedy through a provincial human rights commission.

In *Avalon North Integrated School Board v. The Newfoundland Teachers' Association*,[138] a school board took action to address a complaint brought by two teachers against the principal of their school. The teachers stated that the principal put his arms around them, and touched the breast of one of the teachers. One teacher also related that the principal pushed his body against her, pressing her up against the wall, and that she was forced to push him away. The school board determined that a penalty of one year's suspension and counselling was the appropriate discipline in the circumstances. The arbitration board held that the principal's behaviour was culpable and deserving of a major suspension; however, it reduced the length from one year to eight months. The arbitration board was mildly critical of the school board for not having an explicit policy on sexual harassment in the workplace.

The issue of sexual harassment is always a difficult one for the person faced with the harassment. It is often a traumatic and disturbing situation. All teachers should be aware that there are avenues for redress in cases where objectionable conduct warrants a harassment complaint. A teacher may bring the complaint directly to the school board or to the local human rights commission. It is certainly advisable for school boards to develop policies and procedures on sexual harassment in the workplace, and for teachers to take part in this process so that these situations can be avoided if possible, and dealt with expeditiously when they arise.

Clearly, sexual harassment is not the only type of harassment met by today's teachers. Issues of race, disability, sexual orientation, and religion are other possible avenues for harassment. Proactive school boards should make it clear that no form of harassment is acceptable.

Summary

In this chapter we have shifted the spotlight to focus on the rights of teachers as employees. This includes fundamental rights such as freedom of expression and religion along with traditional labour and employment rights. It is clear that the rights and responsibilities of teachers are constantly evolving, particularly in areas involving the Charter. It is up to the courts to determine the extent to which the Charter affects established practices, and how much weight is given to court interpretations under the various provincial human rights codes. One thing is clear: the law can be used to advance the rights of teachers as well as to enforce their responsibilities with respect to employers, parents, and students.

NOTES

1   *Delisle v. Canada (Deputy Attorney General)*, [1999] 2 S.C.R. 989; *Reference Re Public Service Employee Relations Act (Alta.)*, [1987] 1 S.C.R. 313; *RWDSU v.* Saskatchewan, [1987] 1 S.C.R. 460.

2   Constitutional scholar Peter Hogg has called it a "180-degree shift" (Peter W. Hogg, *Constitutional Law of Canada*, 5th ed. (Toronto: Carswell, 2007) (looseleaf), ch. 44 at 44-6).

3   *Health Services and Support—Facilities Subsector Bargaining Assn. v. British Columbia*, 2007 SCC 27, [2007] 2 S.C.R. 391.

4   *B.C.T.F. v. British Columbia*, 2011 BCSC 469, [2011] B.C.W.L.D. 5218.

5   *Forster v. Saskatchewan Teachers' Federation*, [1992] S.J. no. 85 (Q.L.) (C.A.).

6   *Ontario Secondary School Teachers' Federation, District 9 v. Greater Essex County District School Board (Bondy Grievance)*, [2001] O.L.A.A. no. 561 (Q.L.) (Arb. Bd.). In this case, the arbitrator stated that, despite the grievor's excellent teaching record, his actions in searching students warranted a suspension without pay.

7   *Frontenac County Board of Education v. Ontario Public School Teachers' Federation (Wolff Grievance)*, [1998] O.L.A.A. no. 704 (Q.L.) (Arb. Bd.). In this case, the arbitration board decided that although a school board may suspend a teacher without pay, it may be required to help the teacher find suitable employment opportunities.

8   *Bhaduria v. Toronto Board of Education* (1999), 173 D.L.R. (4th) 382 (Ont. C.A.); leave to appeal refused [1999] S.C.C.A. no. 212 (Q.L.). In this case, the Court of Appeal reiterated the importance of a full arbitration and grievance process before a teacher's employment can be terminated.

9   *Nand v. Edmonton Public School District No. 7*, [1994] A.J. no. 675 (Q.L.) (C.A.); leave to appeal refused [1995] S.C.C.A. no. 8 (Q.L.).

10 *Fountain v. College of Teachers (British Columbia)*, 2007 BCSC 830, [2007] 11 W.W.R. 281.

11 Ibid., at para. 45, citing *Jory v. College of Physicians & Surgeons (British Columbia)*, [1985] B.C.J. no. 320 (B.C.S.C.), at para 14.

12 *Cree School Board v. Northern Quebec Teaching Association*, [1997] Q.J. no. 1444 (Q.L.) (S.C.).

13 *Kearl v. Ile-v-à-la-Crosse School Division No. 112*, [2003] S.J. no. 534 (Q.L.) (C.A.).

14 *Mitchell v. Gilpin*, 2004 SKQB 311, 250 Sask. R. 246.

15 *Mitchell v. British Columbia College of Teachers*, [2003] B.C.J. no. 3056 (Q.L.), at para 37 (S.C.).

16 Ibid.

17 *Hansen v. The Disciplinary Hearing Subcommittee of the College of Teachers and the Council of the College of Teachers* (1991), School Law Commentary, Case File No. 6-1-5 (B.C.S.C.).

18 "B.C. Teachers Suspended Over Porn, Twitter, and Sleepovers," CBC News, July 21, 2012, http://www.cbc.ca/news/canada/british-columbia/story/2012/07/17/bc-teachers-porn.html.

19 Ibid.

20 *Greenway v. Seven Oaks School Division No. 10*, [1991] 2 W.W.R. 481 (Man. C.A.).

21 A.W. MacKay and J. Burt-Gerrans, "Toward a Safe and Effective Learning Environment: The Delicate Balance of Rights and Order in Schools," in R.C. Flynn, ed., *In Support of Lifelong Learning: Proceedings of 2002 CAPSLE Conference* (Toronto: Informco, 2004), 206-227.

22 Robert Smol, "Teacher Stress Is Killing My Profession," September 4, 2009, CBC News, http://www.cbc.ca/news/canada/story/2009/09/04/f-vp-smol.html.

23 K. Leithwood, "School Leadership in Times of Stress" (2003) 30:1 *Orbit Magazine*.

24 Smol, supra note 22.

25 Leithwood, supra note 23.

26 *Kendal v. St. Paul's Roman Catholic Separate School Division No. 20*, [2004] S.J. no. 361 (Q.L.) (C.A.).

27 B.P. Nolan, J.E. Trépanier, and B. Ellerker, "When Special Needs Education and Safety Collide: Occupational Health and Safety Implications of the Education of Special Needs Pupils in Ontario" (2005) 15:1 *Education & Law Journal* 235.

28 *Education Act*, R.S.O. 1990, c. E.2.

29 *Occupational Health and Safety Act*, R.S.O. 1990, c. O.1.

30 Nolan, Trépanier, and Ellerker, supra note 27, at 237.

31 *Occupational Health and Safety Act*, supra note 29, ss. 43(1)(a) and (b).

32 Nolan, Trépanier, and Ellerker, supra note 27, at 239.

33 Ibid., at 241-242.

34 This was one of the recommendations made by Wayne MacKay in "Connecting Care and Challenge: Tapping Our Human Potential—Inclusive Education: A Review of Programming and Services in New Brunswick," New Brunswick Department of Education, January 2006, http://www.gnb.ca/0000/publications/mackay/MACKAYREPORTFINAL.pdf).

35 E. Roher, *An Educator's Guide to Violence in Schools*, 2nd ed. (Aurora, ON: Canada Law Book, 2010).

36 M. Reed, *Parental Harassment* (Toronto: CAPSLE, 2002), 245.

37 Ibid.

38 Ibid.

39 Ibid.

40 R. Keel and N. Tymonchenko, *Parental Harassment* (Aurora, ON: Canada Law Book, 2004).

41   *McKerron v. Marshall*, [1999] O.J. no. 4048 (Q.L.) (S.C.).

42   R. Broster and K. Brien, "Cyber-Bullying of Educators by Students: Evolving Legal and Policy Developments" (2010) 20 *Education & Law Journal* 35.

43   *Newman et al. v. Halstead et al.*, 2006 BCSC 65.

44   Ibid., at para 303.

45   *Angle v. LaPierre*, 2008 ABCA 120.

46   See *Botiuk v. Toronto Free Press Publications Ltd.*, [1995] 3 S.C.R. 3, at paras. 79 and 80.

47   *Ottawa Carleton Catholic District School Board v. Scharf*, 2007 CarswellOnt 5017 (ONSC); affirmed 2008 CarswellOnt 1107 (ONCA); leave to appeal refused 2008 CarswellOnt 7193 (SCC).

48   Ibid., at para 28 (ONSC).

49   Broster and Brien, supra note 42.

50   Ibid.

51   Mark Gollom, "False Abuse Accusations Against Teachers 'On the Rise,'" April 24, 2012, CBC News, http://www.cbc.ca/news/canada/story/2012/04/23/teachers-falsely -accused.html; see also "Tweets About Teachers Get 9 Brampton Students Suspended," November 22, 2012, CBC News, http://www.cbc.ca/news/canada/toronto/ story/2012/11/22/toronto-brampton-twitter-students.html, which discusses the discipline imposed on nine students from a Brampton high school who were suspended for making inappropriate comments about several of their teachers on Twitter.

52   For further discussion of this complex topic, see B.J. Bowlby, D. Michaluk, and J. Wootton Regan, *An Educator's Guide to Human Rights*, 2nd ed. (Aurora, ON: Canada Law Book, 2009).

53   In some rare cases, a defendant has been ordered to comply with the Act in a more substantive fashion. For example, in *Re Saskatchewan Human Rights Commission et al. and Canadian Odeon Theatres Ltd.* (1985), 18 D.L.R. (4th) 93 (Sask. C.A.), a theatre was ordered to make better space available for patrons in wheelchairs.

54   For a more complete discussion of the workings of human rights tribunals, see the Ontario Human Rights Commission, Teaching Human Rights in Ontario: An Educational Package for Ontario Schools (Publications Ontario, 2001), http://www .ohrc.on.ca/sites/default/files/teaching%20human%20rights%20in%20ontario_ accessible.pdf.

55   There is a *Canadian Human Rights Act*, R.S.C. 1985, c. H-6, whose application is limited to employees in an area over which the federal government has exclusive control—for example, national defence.

56   W. MacKay, in "The Marriage of Human Rights Codes and Section 15 of the Charter in Pursuit of Equality: A Case for Greater Separation in Both Theory and Practice" (2013) 10 *Journal of Law and Equality* [forthcoming], cites *Moore v. British Columbia*, 2012 SCC 61 as an example of a human rights challenge producing a landmark ruling. This is now more common.

57   *Trinity Western University v. College of Teachers (British Columbia)*, [2001] 1 S.C.R. 772. Recently, Trinity Western College has displayed interest in opening a law school. In an editorial on the *Globe and Mail* website, a writer expressed the opinion that a law school with an effective ban on lesbian and gay students should not be allowed in Canada. This was because the writer believed that it would be in direct contradiction with law in Canada, with "[e]quality at its heart" and that the training of lawyers needs to be "untainted by discrimination" as a principle. See "No Gay-Free Law School

Should Stand in Canada," *Globe and Mail*, February 7, 2013, http://www.theglobeandmail.com/commentary/editorials/no-gay-free-law-school-should-stand-in-canada/article8356107.

58 *Multani v. Commission scolaire Marguerite-Bourgeoys*, 2006 SCC 6, [2006] 1 S.C.R. 256.

59 For further discussion, see W. Smith, "Private Beliefs and Public Safety: The Supreme Court Strikes Down a Total Ban on the Kirpan in Schools as Unreasonable" (2006) 16 *Education & Law Journal* 83.

60 *Commission scolaire régionale de Chambly v. Bergevin*, [1994] 2 S.C.R. 525.

61 *Irwin Toy v. Quebec (Attorney General)*, [1989] 1 S.C.R. 927.

62 *R. v. Zundel*, [1992] S.C.R. 731, at 732.

63 *Ross v. New Brunswick School District No. 15*, [1996] 1 S.C.R. 825.

64 Ibid.

65 *Tinker v. Des Moines*, 21 L.Ed. 2d 733 (U.S.S.C. 1969).

66 *British Columbia Public School Employers' Assn. v. B.C.T.F.*, [2011] B.C.W.L.D. 6210 (Arb. Bd.).

67 See Mike Hager, "Teachers' Charter Rights T-shirts Deemed Too 'Political' for Prince Rupert Classrooms: Superintendent Rules Fundamental Rights Enshrined in Charter Create Improper Attire," *Vancouver Sun*, January 28, 2013, http://www.vancouversun.com/business/Teachers+Charter+rights+shirts+deemed+political+Prince+Rupert+classrooms/7885109/story.html; Danielle S. Laughlin, "Should Teachers Wear Their Politics on Their Sleeves?" *Huffington Post*, February 5, 2013, http://www.huffingtonpost.ca/danielle-s-mclaughlin/teachers-charter-tshirt-banned_b_2623284.html.

68 *R. v. Keegstra*, [1990] 3 S.C.R. 697.

69 *Ross*, supra note 63.

70 Ibid.

71 *Morin v. P.E.I. Regional Administrative Unit No. 3 School Board*, [2002] P.E.I.J. no. 36 (Q.L.) (C.A.). In this case, a teacher attempted to show a religious fundamentalist video to his class for discussion purposes. Mr. Morin was awarded $75,000 in damages at the appeal court level, a much larger sum than the $15,000 awarded at the original trial: see "Large Damage Award for Freedom of Expression Case" (2005) 3:3 *Edu-Law Newsletter* 2. Freedom of speech for teachers was also affirmed in a decision involving the discussion of class size and composition (*British Columbia Public School Employers' Association v. British Columbia Teachers' Federation*, 2005 BCCA 393), a case that dealt with controversial collective bargaining issues: see "Teacher's Right of Free Speech Affirmed," *Edu-Law Newsletter*, ibid., at 1.

72 "Disclosure of Sexual Orientation" (1998) 12:6 *School Law Commentary* 1.

73 *Pentek v. St. Paul County No. 19 (Board of Education)* (1987), 81 A.R. 43 (Q.B.). In this case, the court held that a teacher's intemperate words in a letter of complaint to a superintendent alleging misconduct in the administration of school affairs warranted sanction, but not dismissal. The teacher was suspended for one year without pay.

74 *Eggerston v. Alberta Teachers' Association*, [2002] A.J. no. 1358 (Q.L.) (C.A.). In this case, a teacher criticized her child's teacher at a parent–teacher meeting. The child's teacher claimed that this amounted to unprofessional conduct. The court disagreed. It held that the teacher's status as a parent required balancing her parental role with her professional responsibilities. She was not reprimanded for her criticisms.

75 *Toronto Board of Education v. Ontario Secondary School Teachers' Federation, District 15*, [1997] 1 S.C.R. 487. A teacher who makes threats of violence against his employers is not only guilty of misconduct; he also adversely affects the public's perception of the school's ability to teach. See also S. Stushnoff, "The Freedom to Criticize One's Employer," in W.F. Foster, ed., *Education and Law: A Plea for Partnership*, proceedings of the 1990 CAPSLE conference, Vancouver (Welland, ON: Éditions Soleil, 1992).

76 *Cromer v. British Columbia Teachers' Federation and the Attorney General of British Columbia*, [1986] 5 W.W.R. 638 (B.C.C.A.).

77 Ibid., at para. 56.

78 A. Reyes, "Freedom of Expression and Public School Teachers" (1995) 4 *Dalhousie Journal of Legal Studies* 35. This quotation was cited with approval by the Supreme Court of Canada in *Ross*, supra note 63.

79 Steve Lambert, "Teachers May Be Fired Over Pretend Lap Dance," *The Chronicle Herald*, February 24, 2010; Sarah Boesveld, "Teachers Disciplined for Doing Lap Dance at School," *The Globe and Mail*, February 25, 2010.

80 *Kempling v. British Columbia College of Teachers*, [2004] B.C.J. no. 173 (Q.L.) (S.C.); affirmed [2005] B.C.J. no. 1288 (Q.L.) (C.A.); for academic commentary on this case, see P. Clark, "Understanding Kempling v. British Columbia College of Teachers Through Multiple Discourses on Freedom of Expression" (2007) 17 *Education & Law Journal* 1.

81 See, for example, *Peterborough County Board of Education v. Ontario Public School Teachers' Federation (Peterborough District)*, [1998] O.J. no. 3149 (Q.L.) (C.A.). In this case, a teacher's dismissal was upheld by the court because he was convicted of sexually assaulting students.

82 In a pre-Charter case, *Beckwith and Allen v. The Colchester-East Hants Amalgamated School Board* (1977), 23 N.S.R. (2d) 268 (T.D.), two teachers were dismissed because of their conviction for possession of marijuana.

83 *Abbotsford School District 34 Board of School Trustees v. Schewan* (1987), 21 B.C.L.R. (2d) 93 (C.A.).

84 Ibid., at para. 15.

85 Assembly Bill 1844, described in Eric Goldman, "Big Problems in California's New Law Restricting Employers' Access to Employees' Online Accounts," September 28, 2012, http://www.forbes.com/sites/ericgoldman/2012/09/28/big-problems-in-californias-new-law-restricting-employers-access-to-employees-online-accounts.

86 *R. v. Cole*, 2012 SCC 53.

87 See, for example, the provisions of the Nova Scotia *Education Act* and the Ontario *Education Act*, set out in Chapter 3, Teachers as Educational State Agents, under the heading "State Agent Defined."

88 *Kempling*, supra note 80.

89 The sexual orientation of teachers is a matter of concern to many school boards and parents. Under many human rights codes, discrimination on the basis of sexual orientation is forbidden. In *Vriend v. Alberta*, [1998] 1 S.C.R. 493, the Supreme Court of Canada stated that college employees are protected from dismissals based on sexual orientation.

90 *Jamieson et al. v. Attorney General of British Columbia* (1971), 21 D.L.R. (3d) 313 (B.C.S.C.).

91 *Ross*, supra note 63.

92   This is a relatively new affiliate, created on July 1, 1998, by the coming together of the Federation of Women Teachers' Associations of Ontario (FWTAO) and the Ontario Public School Teachers' Federation (OPSTF).

93   *Tomen v. Ontario (Human Rights Commission)*, [1995] O.J. no. 1818 (Q.L.) (Div. Ct).

94   *Re Tomen and Federation of Women Teachers Association et al.* (1987), 61 O.R. (2d) 489 (H.C.J.). Justice Ewaschuk held that the Charter did not apply to the situation because the bylaw could not be characterized as a government action. Although the *Teaching Profession Act* required membership in the parent organization (OTF), the bylaw in question was developed through the internal organization of the OTF and was too far removed from government to be protected by the Charter.

95   *Lavigne v. Ontario Public Service Employees Union et al.*, [1991] 2 S.C.R. 211.

96   See the discussion of section 15 in Chapter 4, Teachers as Guardians of Equality.

97   *Law v. Canada (Minister of Employment and Immigration*, [1999] 1 S.C.R. 497, at para. 51.

98   *Egan v. Canada*, [1995] 2 S.C.R. 513.

99   See *McKinney v. University of Guelph et al.* (1990), 118 N.R. 1 (S.C.C.).

100   See *Nilsson v. University of Prince Edward Island*, 2010 CarswellPEI 50, 2010 C.L.L.C. 230-019 (P.E.I.H.R.T.).

101   The federal government struck out the mandatory retirement provisions of the *Canadian Human Rights Act* and *Canada Labour Code*, effective in 2012.

102   New Brunswick *Human Rights Code*, R.S.N.B. 1973, c. H-11, s. 1; S.N.B. 1985, c. 30, s. 3.

103   *Ontario Human Rights Commission v. Etobicoke*, [1982] 1 S.C.R. 202, at 208.

104   See *British Columbia (Public Service Employee Relations Commission) v. B.C.G.E.U.*, [1999] S.C.J. no. 46 (Q.L.). This is commonly known as the *Meiorin* case.

105   In Canada, *Pacific Western Airlines v. Canadian Airline Flight Attendants Association* (1987), 28 L.A.C. (3d) 291, and *Centre D'Accueil and Sainte-Domitille v. Union des Employees de Service Local 298*, cited in (1989), School Law Commentary, Case File No. 4-1-1. In the United States, *Chalk v. U.S. District Court Central California*, 840 F.2d 701 (9th Cir. 1988). For a detailed discussion of AIDS-related discrimination and employment, see D.J. Jones and N.C. Sheppard, "AIDS and Disability Employment Discrimination in and Beyond the Classroom" (1989) 12:1 *Dalhousie Law Journal* 103.

106   For a more thorough description of the chronology of events in this case, see Jones and Sheppard, supra note 105, at 103-104.

107   See, generally, J. Mosoff, "Is the Human Rights Paradigm 'Able' to Include Disability: Who's In? Who Wins? What? Why?" (2000) 26:1 *Queen's Law Journal* 225.

108   *Nevio Rossi v. School District No. 57* (1985), 7 C.H.R.R. Decision 511 (BC Human Rights Tribunal).

109   *Wall v. Kitigan Zibi Education Council*, [1997] C.H.R.D. no. 6 (Q.L.).

110   *Bliss v. Canada (Attorney General)*, [1979] 1 S.C.R. 183.

111   *Floyd v. Canada (Employment & Immigration Commission)* (1992), 93 C.L.L.C. 17,008 (Canadian Human Rights Tribunal). See also *Brooks v. Canada Safeway Ltd.*, [1989] 1 S.C.R. 1219, which overturned *Bliss*, supra note 110.

112   See, for example, the Newfoundland and Labrador *Human Rights Act*, S.N.L. 2010, c. H-13.1, which specifies in s. 9(2): "Where this Act protects an individual from discrimination on the basis of sex, the protection includes the protection of a female from discrimination on the basis that she is or may become pregnant."

113   *R. v. Kapp*, 2008 SCC 41, [2008] 2 S.C.R. 483, 2008 CarswellBC 1312.

114 *Vriend v. Alberta*, supra note 89.

115 *Willow v. Halifax Regional School Board*, 2006-NSHRC-2, 56 C.H.R.R. D/157.

116 The Ontario Court of Appeal, in *Re Essex County Roman Catholic School Board and Porter et al.* (1978), 21 O.R. (2d) 255, stated that because the Constitution allows for denominational schools, and schools generally can dismiss for cause, then denominational schools can dismiss for denominational cause.

117 *Casagrande v. Hinton Roman Catholic Separate School District No. 155*, 51 Alta. L.R. (2d) 349.

118 *Hogan v. Newfoundland School Boards*, [1997] N.J. no. 154 (Q.L.) (S.C.T.D.).

119 See *Greater Montreal Protestant School Board v. Quebec (Attorney General)*, [1989] 1 S.C.R. 377 for more specific information on this issue.

120 *Re Caldwell et al. and Stuart et al.* (1984), 15 D.L.R. (4th) 1 (S.C.C.). In this case the dismissal of a teacher for marrying outside the Roman Catholic faith was held not to be a human rights violation. The school in question was religious in nature, but not a section 93 denominational school.

121 In *Ontario English Catholic Teachers' Assn. v. Dufferin-Peel Roman Catholic Separate School Board*, [1999] O.J. no. 1382 (Q.L.), the Ontario Court of Appeal reaffirmed the decision made in *Caldwell and Stuart*, supra note 120, by stating that if a policy is necessary to the preservation of denominational education, it is a bona fide occupational requirement. See also *Greater Montreal Protestant School Board v. Quebec (Attorney General)*, supra note 119, for more specific information on this issue.

122 *Daly et al. v. Attorney General of Ontario* (1999), 44 O.R. (3d) 349 (C.A.); leave to appeal refused [1999] S.C.C.A. 321.

123 *Barrow v. Manitoba (Minister of Education and Training)*, [1992] M.J. no. 384 (Q.L.) (Q.B.).

124 *Haché v. Lunenburg County District School Board*, [2004] N.S.J. no. 120 (Q.L.) (C.A.).

125 *Lebelle v. Yellowknife Public Denominational District Education Authority*, [2001] N.W.T.J. no. 81 (Q.L.) (S.C.).

126 *Yorke v. Northside-Victoria District School Board*, [1993] N.S.J. no. 149 (Q.L.) (C.A.).

127 *Robert Olav Noyes v. Board of School Trustees, Dist. No. 30 (South Caribou)* (1985), 6 C.R.D. 400 (B.C.S.C.).

128 *Reference re ss. 193 and 195.1(1)(c) of the Criminal Code (Man.)*, [1990] 1 S.C.R. 1123. This case is commonly known as the *Prostitution Reference*.

129 *Wilson v. Medical Services Commission of British Columbia*, [1989] 2 W.W.R. 1 (B.C.C.A.); leave to appeal refused.

130 Ibid.

131 Although some Supreme Court decisions, such as *Irwin Toy*, supra note 61, are important in assessing the scope of section 7 in terms of economic rights, Chief Justice McLachlin stated in *Gosselin v. Quebec (Attorney General)*, [2002] 4 S.C.R. 429, at para. 81: "Nothing in the jurisprudence thus far suggests that s. 7 places a positive obligation on the state to ensure that each person enjoys life, liberty or security of the person. Rather, s. 7 has been interpreted as restricting the state's ability to deprive people of these. Such a deprivation does not exist in the case at bar."

132 *Labour Relations Act*, 1995, S.O. 1995, c. 1, Sched. A.

133 *Dionne v. C.A.W., Locals 199 & 1973*, [1994] O.L.R.B. Rep. 532, 1994 CarswellOnt 1423, at para. 46.

134   See *Van Uden v. C.U.P.W.*, 1998 CarswellNat 1882 (C.L.R.B.), and also *Davison v. N.S.G.E.U. (sub nom. Davison v. Nova Scotia Government Employees Union)* (2004), 694 A.P.R. 365, 220 N.S.R. (2d) 365, 22 C.C.L.T. (3d) 236, 31 C.C.E.L. (3d) 209, [2004] N.S.J. no. 36 (Q.L.), 2004 CarswellNS 38, 2004 NSSC 29.

135   For a more detailed discussion on this topic, see R.G. Keel and N. Tymochenko, *An Educator's Guide to Managing Sexual Misconduct in Schools* (Aurora, ON: Aurora Professional Press, 2003).

136   *Robichaud v. Canada (Treasury Board)*, [1987] 2 S.C.R. 84 (1987), 40 D.L.R. (4th) 577.

137   Ibid.

138   *Avalon North Integrated School Board v. The Newfoundland Teachers' Association* (1990), School Law Commentary, Case File No. 5-2-1 (Nfld. Arb. Bd.).

8

The Role of Technology in the Classroom and Beyond

Introduction

This chapter begins with a general discussion of emerging issues around copyright and technology. It is hard to believe that 20 years ago, when we wrote the first edition of this book, there was no email, let alone Internet, social media, online piracy, Facebook, and Twitter, among other things we take for granted in our technology-driven society. Even when we think back to 2006, when the second edition of this book was published, Facebook was not yet open to the wider public (that happened in September 2006), and it was certainly not ubiquitous until 2008. The absence of social media is hard to imagine today, and one can only wonder what we will face when we sit down to write the fourth edition of this book. This chapter is called "The Role of Technology in the Classroom and Beyond," but it is the "beyond" part that causes us most concern. As we pointed out in Chapter 4, Teachers as Guardians of Equality, in our discussion of bullying, student use of technology reaches far beyond the classroom, but has a profound impact within it.

The second section of this chapter discusses copyright in some detail because we have a brand new *Copyright Act* (as of November 7, 2012) with significant changes. The third section outlines ownership of the original materials teachers create.

Information Technology: Social Media and Electronic Communication

There has been a flurry of activity and writing on the subject of social media, electronic communication, and "cyberconduct" over the past five years and we suspect that this will continue for the next several years.[1] The most important piece of advice we can provide is to stay current, and openly and often discuss the use of technology, both personally and professionally, with colleagues. Here we discuss the most common social media and communication tools currently in use, but we recognize that these could be completely outdated two or three years from now.

Use by Teachers

We have divided this topic into those issues facing teachers and those affecting students. Within these two separate areas we examine both social media issues and communication issues.

Social Media

Most teachers working today have been given the admonishment "Do not 'friend' students or their parents on your Facebook page," and this logic applies equally to other social media outlets, such as Twitter, Instagram, and similar sites. With technology, it is critical to determine whether you are using a broad spectrum social media site like Facebook, where the content is widely available, or whether your use is confined to individual communication, like email. The obvious problem with broad social media is that it is difficult to limit who can see your information. Although you may think you are using it properly, you do not control the web designers, and privacy settings can change frequently without your knowledge. What you think is a harmless photo of yourself on vacation in Mexico can turn into an inappropriate communication when accessed by the wrong pair of eyes. We discuss several examples of this in Chapter 7, Teachers as Employees. (Recall the infamous "lap dance" uploaded to YouTube.) It is not only students whom teachers need to be concerned about, but also current or future employers.

This doesn't mean that a teacher can't personally maintain a Facebook page, but it is important to select each friend carefully and ensure that you avoid "friending" a student or parent at your school. In England, the National Association of Schoolmasters Union of Women Teachers (NASUWT) published a helpful guideline for using Facebook and controlling your privacy and security settings. At a minimum, NASUWT recommends the following:

Privacy setting	Recommended security level
Send you messages	Friends only
See your friend list	Friends only
See your education and work	Friends only
See your current city and hometown	Friends only
See your likes, activities, and other connections	Friends only
Your status, photos, and posts	Friends only
Bio and favourite quotations	Friends only
Family and relationships	Friends only
Photos and videos you're tagged in	Friends only
Religious and political views	Friends only
Birthday	Friends only
Permission to comment on your posts	Friends only
Places you check in to	Friends only
Contact information	Friends only

- Always make sure that you log out of Facebook after using it, particularly when using a machine that is shared with other colleagues/students. Your account can be hijacked by others if you remain logged in—even if you quit your browser and/or switch the machine off. Similarly, Facebook's instant chat facility caches conversations that can be viewed later on. Make sure you clear your chat history on Facebook (click "Clear Chat history" in the chat window).
- Employers may scour websites looking for information before a job interview. Take care to remove any content you would not want them to see.[2]

In addition to these common-sense guidelines, most provincial teachers' unions produce a guidebook or handbook each year that includes a section on cyberconduct and social media.[3] Unfortunately, there are often circular references to school board policies or "attending professional development" sessions. This is not entirely helpful when you are looking for specific direction. If you have similar guidelines in your province, seek out the specific school board or provincial policies and stay current on changes.

This does not mean that you must keep social media and online communication out of the classroom. Schools have websites and teachers are often invited to create and maintain their own web page. This can be a lot of work, but rewarding for everyone and a great way to stay connected to your students and parents on a professional platform. Another option is to create a Facebook profile for your classroom ("Mrs. Smith's Grade 7 Class—Like us on Facebook!") and invite the students to participate in its maintenance and updating. It could also have its own linked Twitter feed. The point is to avoid making your personal Facebook available to a broad base. A note of caution: if you "friend" your classroom Facebook page you will provide a link to your own Facebook profile, so we recommend not doing so or creating a professional profile separate from your personal profile (use your work email rather than personal email) and maintaining your personal friends separately. As time passes, there will no doubt be tech-savvy teachers who have grown up with Facebook and Twitter (and whatever else comes along); with this more widespread use and comfort, we will perhaps see more innovations on how to use social media.

In their CyberTips for Teachers[4] brochure, the Canadian Teacher's Federation published a useful summary of guidelines that relates specifically to social networking. Some highlights include:

- Do not post anything on a social media site that you would not post on the bulletin board outside your classroom.
- Establish professional boundaries. Do not share any of your personal information with students.
- If you are going to "chat" with students online, make sure you have downloaded the appropriate software applications to record a transcript of the chat and establish "office hours" so that there is an appropriate time and time limit for the chat.
- Never post criticism of or share confidential information about a colleague or student online.

Parents and teachers have always faced problems in their shared role of educating students in relation to new technology. In 1992, when the first edition of this book came out, only a few schools had computers for student use and there were no policies on students bringing laptops to school—there were no laptops, or cellphones. We cannot deny the existence of these innovations in the school environment. We are therefore left with the task of adopting the new technologies and trying our best to teach children how to effectively and appropriately use them. How does a student know when it is appropriate to turn off his phone? You have to teach him. What kinds of photos are inappropriate for a student to post on Facebook? You have to teach her. What kind of Internet and social media communication constitutes cyberbullying? We have to teach everyone. The tendency to keep teachers away from social media denies students an opportunity to learn from their teachers how to use social media in a responsible manner.

The Member's Guide to the BC Teachers' Federation[5] sets an appropriate tone for allowing teachers individual autonomy when using technology with the following statement:

> 51.C.03 [T]he professional autonomy of teachers includes deciding ... whether using information and communications technology is the most appropriate method of communication with parents.

We may see more attempts in future to carve out a similar discretion for teachers as provincial governments and school boards become more comfortable in this arena.

Electronic Communication: Email, Texting, and Cellphones

In addition to broad-based social media such as Facebook and Twitter, teachers also have the opportunity for targeted electronic communication to students and parents through both email and texting. This is far less dangerous for teachers because it is less likely to be taken out of context or fall into the wrong hands. Email is currently the most common communication tool in schools and we encourage its use. It has several advantages for everyone:

- it maintains a record of conversations in case of misunderstandings;
- it can ensure clarity of communication;
- it provides flexibility in terms of communication between parents and teachers, as opposed to restricting access to the telephone during school hours; and
- it allows for several individuals to be copied at once—for example, the parent, student, and principal.

Email is really just another way for a teacher to "send a note home" with a student or for a parent to send a note to the teacher, but without the high risk of the note being lost or crumpled in the bottom of a backpack. Used properly, email can be an asset; however, like everything else, if you are not careful, email can be harmful. This is not only true for teachers, but for all of us who use email, whether for personal or business purposes. Everybody has a list of email etiquette rules (if you Google "email etiquette" you will find thousands), but here are a few of our favourites to keep in mind:

- Read before sending; check your tone and fix your mistakes.
- Do not email when you are angry.
- Beware of hitting "Reply All" unless you mean it.

- Keep messages brief and to the point.
- Be mindful of tone—sarcasm does not travel well by email.
- Generally avoid criticism in email—it also travels poorly.
- Don't write in ALL CAPS—it looks like yelling.
- Remember that emails to students and parents are not private.
- Use English—leave the OMGs and LOLs out of the conversation.

Find a way to store your emails in subfolders so that you can keep a record for at least one or two years. This is simply a matter of creating a folder in your inbox called, for example, "School Email 2014" and moving emails into that folder. Sent items can be more difficult to manage because it is a nuisance to search through all of them to find relevant ones but, unfortunately, the most important email you want to keep is often one that you wrote yourself and sent to a parent or student. You can manage sent items by either copying yourself on these emails or by archiving your sent items in subfolders by calendar year so that, should you need to find one, it is available to you by searching through just one year. Search engines are so good and storage capacity so vast that this is relatively simple.

The second direct communication tool is texting. For many of us with teenagers of our own, texting is an invaluable tool for communicating not only with our children but also with friends, family, and colleagues. However, in our view, and as expressed by the Canadian Teachers Federation, texting crosses the line of "establishing professional boundaries." It is hard for us to imagine a situation where it is appropriate for a teacher to text a student or parent. Of course, in a medical or other emergency, you need to communicate in any and all ways you can. However, generally there is no reason for parents and students to have that kind of access to you nor is there any reason for them to have your personal cellphone number. There is also the danger of long-term storage of text messages, which are more difficult to track and store and therefore harder to defend if there is a problem. Text messaging also tends to be truncated and abrupt, which may create a higher risk of being misunderstood. Even the notion of the "special access" to your personal cellphone could be misunderstood. Given all these difficulties, it is our position that you reserve your cellphone number and texting solely for private use.

When teachers have come into conflict with either the criminal law or their employers, it is often because of an initial lack of judgment or poor personal conduct on the teacher's part. A teacher who behaves inappropriately with a student can expect to see evidence of the relationship in text messages, on Facebook posts and chats, or in emails, but these are merely symptoms of underlying bad judgment. Technology does not create the problem; it is simply a tool used as part of it. It would be a shame for the vast majority of teachers to deny themselves the full and robust use of technology because a few teachers with poor behaviour or judgment have clouded the issue. We are always primarily concerned with the teacher who may fall into a bad situation unwittingly. If you follow some of the guidelines above and those developed by your union and school boards, we think you can have a healthy and productive relationship with technology in the classroom.

Use by Students

Students do not have the same developed sense of "established professional boundaries" between school and the rest of their lives. To most students, life is one big jumble of academic work, social interaction, personal relationships, communication, activity, and conflict. To students, technology simply presents itself on a broad-based social media platform and a targeted communication platform, and is as integral to their days as breathing.

Social Media

The most important issue relating to students and social media is cyberbullying and the misuse of technology in that area. We have discussed this issue extensively in Chapter 4, and there is no need to repeat the discussion here. Bullying is bullying, whether you throw a rock at someone or a tweet. However, short of actual bullying, social media conduct can be inappropriate and ill-advised, and teachers must be open to working closely with parents to manage this behaviour. The Nova Scotia Teachers Union offers a comprehensive statement on the kind of cooperation required by everyone to create a healthy and "bully-free" environment:

> The NSTU believes the following Guiding Principles should inform the approach adopted by all education partners concerning the appropriate use of the Internet and communications technology:
>
> (a) Safe and caring schools that promote healthy workplaces for members and healthy learning environments for children and youth should be a provincial priority.
>
> (b) Collectively, society shares the responsibility for creating positive learning environments that include cyberspaces which foster respect and understanding, and are free from inappropriate cyberconduct including cyberbullying.
>
> (c) Individual rights to freedom of information, thought, belief, opinion and expression, should be balanced with the rights and responsibilities of parents, guardians and the education community. These include the right to guide individuals in the responsible use of information and communication technology.

(d) Any response to cybermisconduct and/or cyberbullying should focus on protection of students, members, and the school community.

(e) Cybermisconduct, including cyberbullying, negatively influences student learning and member workplaces and should be viewed as a significant occupational health and safety issue.

(f) Cybermisconduct that originates from the school or from the community-at-large, which ultimately has a negative impact on the school climate and/or culture, warrants action by the school board, including the imposition of sanctions, when appropriate on the offender or offenders.

(g) Swift, decisive action is necessary to effectively respond to cybermisconduct and/or cyberbullying. Varied strategies and responses are required to address this complex, multifaceted problem.[6]

Technology has to a large extent removed the boundary between home and school, and the two are now difficult to separate. Even though school staff has no jurisdiction outside school boundaries in the strictest sense, technology is "everywhere all the time" and items that have been posted at home can become relevant in school the following day. We all carry our digital imprint around with us in a very real sense, and students are no exception. As discussed in Chapter 4, we are seeing the birth of lawsuits in which a school board and its personnel are being sued for failure to adequately intervene in cases of bullying, and it is an open question whether this may apply in other uses of technology. What if the case involves a young girl who posts inappropriate photos on her Facebook page and is then the target of a stalker? If the school personnel are aware of the behaviour and do nothing to notify the parents and intervene, is there potential liability if the girl suffers harm as a result?

It is still too early to tell, but good judgment and caring for the welfare of your students remains the golden rule. Provided you take the care of a reasonable and prudent parent in handling these situations, you will be absolved of liability. More important, the role of the school is not to avoid liability but to provide an encouraging and productive learning environment. This means educating students about appropriate behaviour in the digital world with regard to both themselves and others. This will largely be done at the provincial and school board policy level and not in the courts.

Electronic Communication: Email, Texting, and Cellphones

It has become increasingly common for students to have phones at a relatively young age and this trend shows no sign of slowing down. The sooner good phone habits can be introduced, the better for everyone involved. For the most part, this is not a legal question, but simply a change in the school environment. When a teacher monitoring the playground sees a student walk up and punch another student in the face, it is a simple matter to reprimand him and waltz him to the principal. Now that same student may be hunched over his phone in a corner of the playground posting negative and derogatory things about another student to the same (or significantly worse) effect, but without your knowledge.

We must leave the use of phones and texting to school policy because this is primarily a question of controlling the school environment, which is clearly under the school's jurisdiction and discretion pursuant to the education acts of most provinces. There may be parental conflict where parents want their children to have access to their phones—for scheduling appointments, sports, and day-to-day issues that may arise—but this is again fully within the discretion of the school during school hours. We have reviewed a number of policies across Canada and it seems that schools are finding various ways to balance and manage the new digital intruder in the classroom.

Unfortunately, smart phones and tablets can be used not only to contact your parents about your orthodontist appointment but also to cheat on tests. Students can text message questions to one another and receive answers back. They can also use cellphones to take pictures of questions on exams, send them to other students, and wait to receive an answer. Teachers are often at a loss as to what can be done about these issues, though in many cases there are simple solutions, such as requiring students to place any smart phones under their desks or at the front of the room during exams. In 2010, the Canadian Council on Learning produced an excellent survey on the issue, "Liars, Fraudsters and Cheats: Dealing with the Growth of Academic Dishonesty."[7] The council reported that technology played a major role in modern-day cheating and in the attitudes toward cheating. High-speed Internet allows students to access information quickly and easily and the chances of getting caught are low. They further cited a US national survey of students in grades 7 through 12, which found that more than half (52 percent) admitted to some form of Internet-enabled cheating. Nearly 38 percent had "cut and pasted" material from websites and submitted it as their own work, 32 percent had searched the Internet for teacher manuals to find solutions to problems in their textbooks, and 21 percent had downloaded papers from the Internet and submitted them as their own work.[8]

In recent years, teachers, particularly those in high schools and middle schools, have seen an increase in plagiarism, as students purchase term papers from Internet-based clearing houses—such as papers4less.com, cheathouse.com, and schoolsucks.com—and submit them as their own work. Some school districts have responded by subscribing to online plagiarism prevention sites, such as turnitin.com. These sites allow teachers to check papers submitted by students against all information available in the site's database. In many cases, schools openly admit to using these sites in the hope that the warning alone will encourage students to produce their own work.

Many teachers feel that cheating is a moral and societal issue they cannot solve alone; however, it is an issue that teachers must at least attempt to manage. Like many of the issues relating to technology, the evil is not necessarily the device itself but the manner in which it is used, whether for cheating or bullying. A key part of every curriculum in the 21st century must now include our relationships and attitudes toward technology and the digital environment.

Copyright

One relevant component of the digital environment is copyright law. For years we had an outdated and ineffective copyright law in Canada, dating back to 1924. With the onslaught of digital formats for both audio and visual products and the pirating of these products, the federal government was under pressure to update copyright law. This was finally accomplished on November 7, 2012. Although a comprehensive review of copyright law is beyond the scope of this book, any discussion on teachers and the law would be incomplete without it.

What Is Copyright?

Essentially, copyright is the right to copy—or, as section 3(1) of the *Copyright Act* elaborates,

> the sole right to produce or reproduce the work or any substantial part thereof in any material form whatever, to perform the work or any substantial part thereof in public or, if the work is unpublished, to publish the work or any substantial part thereof.[9]

The goal of copyright is to strike a balance between the following two separate interests: promoting the public interest of accessing works and ensuring that creators are rewarded for the creation of works.[10] A work refers to any original literary, dramatic, musical, or artistic work, which is original and has been expressed in some material form by a creator.[11] A work must have the following requirements to have copyright:

1. skill and judgment
2. expressed in tangible form.[12]

Copyright covers economic and moral rights. Economic rights are the ability of the copyright owner to profit from his work. This includes the right to produce or reproduce the work in any form. This category also includes the right to sell, license, or assign certain aspects of the copyright to others. Moral rights protect the unique relationship between a creator and her work. These rights prevent others from distorting or modifying the work in a way that prejudices the author. These rights are the exclusive domain of the creator and they cannot be sold or licensed; they can, however, be waived.[13]

Who Owns Copyright?

The creator and the owner of the work are two different concepts in copyright. The creator is the person who created the work, while the owner is the person who holds the economic rights in the work.

Generally, the creator is the first owner of the copyright.[14] However, employees who create works in the course of their employment do not typically get first ownership of the copyright in these works.[15] For example, if someone works as a staff writer for an online magazine, the magazine is the owner of the articles written during the employee's tenure. This exception extends only to works employees create as part of their regular duties.

The test of whether the creator completed the work as an employee or an independent contractor is:

1. Who owned the tools used to create the work?
2. Who controlled or directed the creation of the work?
3. Who assumed the financial risk in creating the work?
4. How significant is the author's role as an employee?

Moreover, employment contracts may stipulate that the employer is the owner of copyright of any works produced during the course of employment.

If there are more than one creators of a work, each person has equal ownership of the copyright in the work. There is still only one copyright in the work, but it is held jointly by all of the creators. Each creator's contribution to the work does not need to be equal in terms of quantity or quality for joint ownership. Each contribution has to be substantial; minor input or editing does not qualify for authorship. All of the creators' contributions must have a common design in order for joint ownership to exist.

In a collective work, several creators create a work together, but each creator has a distinct part within the final work. For example, encyclopedias and dictionaries can be collective works.[16] Each author owns copyright in his or her individual contribution to the collective work. However, the person who arranges the collection has copyright in the entire collection.

How Is Copyright Infringed?

Copyright infringement is the unauthorized use of the protected original expression.[17] The *Copyright Act* describes the following activities as copyright infringements:

1. sell or rent out the work without authorization;
2. distribute to such an extent as to affect prejudicially the owner of the copyright;
3. expose or offer for sale or rental, exhibit in public, or distribute by way of trade;
4. possess for the purpose of doing anything referred to in the three previous points; and
5. import to Canada with the purpose of doing anything referred to in points 1 to 3.[18]

The most common method of infringing copyright is the unauthorized reproduction or distribution of a work. A popular example is the illegal downloading of copyrighted music on the Internet.

In order to demonstrate that copyright has been infringed, the owner must show proof of ownership in the copyright; that there is sufficient similarity between the owner's and the infringer's work; and that the infringer had access to the copyrighted work. Access is presumed if the copyrighted work was widely distributed—for example, posted online. The reproduction must be of a substantial part of the work.

Simply copying someone else's ideas or information in one's own words does not infringe copyright, because copyright protects *the way* that information is expressed, not the idea itself. However, when using someone else's ideas, citation is essential. Some works are considered to be in the "public domain." This means that the works can be copied and used without the permission of their creator and without paying royalties. A work usually comes into the public domain because the author has died and the copyright has expired. The general rule is that a work comes into the public domain at the end of the 50th year following the death of its author. However, in some jurisdictions (for example, the United States and the European Union), it can be as much as 70 years or 95 years, depending on when the work was created.[19]

Are There Exceptions to Infringement?

The main defence to infringement is fair dealing. Fair dealing gives anyone the ability to use copyrighted material provided that the use is fair and for a valid purpose.

The *Copyright Act* includes the following broad categories of valid fair dealing:

- research,
- private study,
- criticism,
- review,
- news reporting,
- education,
- parody, and
- satire.[20]

Even if the use falls within one of these categories, it could still be deemed unfair, depending on a number of criteria. In the Supreme Court of Canada decision *CCH Canadian Ltd. v. Law Society of Upper Canada*,[21] the court clarified six criteria used for evaluating fair dealing:

1. *Purpose:* Does the purpose fit into one of the categories listed in section 29 of the Act?
2. *Character:* How many copies are made and how widely are they distributed—that is, to large or small groups of people?
3. *Amount:* How much of the work is used?
4. *Alternatives:* Is the dealing reasonably necessary to achieve the goals of the person using the material and is it possible to use non-copyrighted material to achieve that goal?
5. *Nature:* Is the original work published or unpublished?

6. *Effect:* How does the unauthorized use affect the original work's market?[22]

There are additional exceptions to infringement covered within the *Copyright Act*. In the next section we examine exceptions that apply to educational institutions.

Exceptions to Copyright Infringement for Educators

Copyright infringement in educational institutions became a significant issue with the arrival of the photocopier, but it extends into other common classroom practices. This is particularly true as the Internet has become a significant resource for teachers and students. Any communication, distribution, or performance of works in the classroom raises potential issues of copyright infringement. Happily, there are many exceptions to copyright infringement that benefit educators, especially with the amendments to the *Copyright Act* in 2012.

As noted above, it is not an infringement to use a work for the purposes of research, private study, criticism, review, news reporting, education, parody, or satire as long as the dealing is fair.[23] Whether a dealing is fair depends on the overall circumstances. Essentially, fair dealing allows particular uses of copyright material for social benefits that are deemed important enough to exceed the rights of copyright holders.

In *Alberta (Education) v. Canadian Copyright Licensing Agency (Access Copyright)*,[24] a 2012 case, the Supreme Court of Canada examined the concept of fair dealing in relation to photocopying materials for educational purposes. In this case, teachers had made photocopies of short excerpts of books for their students. Access Copyright, the major Canadian copyright collective responsible for collecting licensing fees (tariffs), wanted a fee for this activity under the *Copyright Act*. All of the provincial departments of education as well as a large number of school boards objected to the tariff. They claimed that the act of making these small copies should be deemed "fair dealing" and exempt from paying any licence fees or tariffs. The Copyright Board and the Federal Court of Appeal decided that it was not fair dealing and a tariff (licensing fee) should be paid. The Supreme Court of Canada disagreed. It stated: "Teachers have no ulterior motive when providing copies to students."[25] According to the Supreme Court, however, the copying was permitted without implementation of a tariff because it was deemed to fall within the exception of fair dealing for the purposes of research or private study in the *Copyright Act*.

You may be wondering why the Supreme Court of Canada included this exception under "private study" as opposed to "education" from the list of broad categories of fair dealing. This decision was released in July 2012, before "education," "parody," or "satire" were included in the amendments of November 2012. Given that, as result of this case, some classroom photocopying is exempt under the category of "private study," it seems obvious that the court would also likely exempt similar use under the new category of "education" as specifically listed in the new *Copyright Act.* It is also fair to assume that the court will continue to interpret "fair dealing" broadly.

This decision means that educators may reproduce and share short excerpts from a copyright-protected work without infringing copyright. A "short excerpt" could be a chapter from a book, a magazine article, or an entry from an encyclopedia, but it's definition depends on the work itself, and substantial copying is not permitted. In the past there were a number of agencies that operated as copyright collectives. These agencies provided licences to copy (for a fee) and compensated the author of the work with the fees collected. Most school districts across Canada (with the exception of those in Quebec who deal with the Quebec collective, "Copibec") had Access Copyright licences. Parties licensed by Access Copyright could copy, within prescribed limits, without seeking permission from the work's creator.

With the July 2012 Supreme Court of Canada decision in *Alberta (Education)* and the new educational-purpose exemption passed into law in November 2012, many school districts, provinces, and universities began asking themselves whether they still need to pay for a licence. This has set off a shock wave through the world of copyright collectives and it remains to be seen what will happen. In January 2013, the Ontario Library and Information Technology Association passed a resolution (along with several other library associations across Canada) rejecting the use of current Access Copyright licence agreements and calling on all educational institutions to cancel their existing licences. Part of the reasoning behind their opposition to Access Copyright is as follows:

> [T]he addition of "education" to the fair dealing categories, and the broad support for fair dealing in the Supreme Court's pentalogy rulings of July 2012 provide further support for the position that the Access Copyright license does not provide any additional value to institutions beyond their existing rights.[26]

At this point, Access Copyright is objecting vehemently to the mass exodus of licensed institutions, but it appears it has very little legal basis left to challenge the clear educational-purpose exemption.

In addition to photocopying, educators may reproduce works for the purpose of education or training in order to display them in an educational institution.[27] For example, educators may copy a work onto a white board or project a work onto a screen using a digital projector. This exception does not apply, however, if there is a copy of the work commercially available in the appropriate medium.

It is permissible for educators to play sound recordings, radio, or television for students, as long as the performance:

- takes place on the premises of an educational institution;
- is for educational or training purposes;
- is for an audience consisting primarily of students, instructors, or anyone directly responsible for setting curriculum; and
- is without any "motive of gain."[28]

The above exception applies only to television or radio programs at the time they are being transmitted—that is, live radio or television—or to copies of news programs made at the time they were being transmitted.[29] "Motive of gain" means that the educational institution cannot recover costs, including overhead costs, other than those associated with playing the programs.[30]

A further exception allows an educator at a non-profit educational institution to make a single copy of broadcast programs, other than the news, where the copy is made at the time of transmission. The educator then has 30 days to decide whether to share the copy on the premises of the educational institution for an educational purpose. If the copy is shown at any time, or if it is not erased within the 30-day period, the educational institution must pay a royalty payment for the program.[31] As well, the educational institution must record information related to the making and erasing of the copy, as well as any public performances of the copy.[32]

With the rapid dissemination of information in all areas of our lives, educators must be aware of copyright issues at play in the workplace. Many acts that would infringe copyright outside educational institutions may now be covered by exceptions within the *Copyright Act*.

What's New in the Copyright Act?

After many years of proposed changes, the government has enacted new sections with the aim of modernizing copyright in Canada to meet the demands of the digital age. Before these amendments, the *Copyright Act* had not been changed since the 1990s.

As you read above, one of the changes was the expansion of fair dealing to include "education," "parody," and "satire." By adding "education" to the list of acceptable exceptions to infringement, the government is seeking to promote broad, affordable access to literary materials for students and teachers to encourage a vibrant learning environment. Other changes that the government reports as its goals with the amendments to the *Copyright Act* include:

- implementing the rights and protections of the World Intellectual Property Organization (WIPO) Internet treaties;
- giving copyright owners the tools they need to combat piracy;
- clarifying the roles and responsibilities of ISPs and search engines;
- encouraging innovation in the private sector through exceptions for technical computer processes;
- providing legal protection for businesses that choose to use technological protection measures or "digital locks" to protect their work as part of their business models; and
- giving consumers the ability to, among other things, record their favourite TV shows for later viewing, transfer music from a CD to a digital device, or to create a mash-up to post online.[33]

One of the most important aspects of copyright law in the classroom is for teachers to lead by example by showing a respect for copyright and the rights of creators generally. That means discouraging illegal downloads of music and visual media as well as software. What a teacher does privately in his or her own home is up to the teacher, but in the classroom it is important to reinforce these values.

Intellectual Property in Materials Prepared by Teachers

A related area of law deals with ownership of materials developed by teachers. Teachers have long assumed that they own the lesson plans they have created. Over the past few years teachers have become more involved in curriculum development and the creation of materials for which there is a commercial market. As school districts struggle to make money to stretch their increasingly underfunded budgets, they are examining this potential source of revenue with interest. The main issue is whether individual teachers own the materials they have created, or whether their employer school boards own the materials as works created "in the course of employment."

The issue arises in this manner because of section 13 of the *Copyright Act*, which states:

> (1) Subject to this Act, the author of a work shall be the first owner of the copyright therein. ...
>
> (3) Where the author of a work was in the employment of some other person under a contract of service or apprenticeship and the work was made in the course of his employment by that person, the person by whom the author was employed shall, in the absence of any agreement to the contrary, be the first owner of the copyright, but where the work is an article or other contribution to a newspaper, magazine or similar periodical, there shall, in the absence of any agreement to the contrary, be deemed to be reserved to the author a right to restrain the publication of the work, otherwise than as part of a newspaper, magazine or similar periodical.[34]

In a 2001 article,[35] Rod Dolmage and Paul Clarke suggest that one reason for the interest in this topic is that computer technology has made it possible for almost any teacher to create materials of commercial quality. The authors also note that the Internet has provided a place for quick and inexpensive distribution of their work, and many teachers are developing online classes for their school districts. At the university level, administrators and professors have been debating the ownership issue for some time. Dolmage and Clarke note that although ideas vary among Canadian universities as to who owns the material, the issue is generally governed by collective agreements.

The same cannot be said for the public school system. If a collective agreement does not clearly delineate ownership, disputes will be settled by an adjudicator or, in some cases, the courts. Dolmage and Clarke acknowledge that teachers have generally been presumed to own the copyright in the materials they prepare. However, they argue that in the "contemporary context," the presumption of ownership ought to be reversed in favour of school boards. After an analysis of section 13 and a consideration of whether or not teachers meet the definition of "professionals," Dolmage and Clarke conclude that teachers are professionals working under contracts of service with their employing school boards. From this, they suggest that teacher-created materials that clearly relate to the teacher's position with the board are owned by the board.[36] However, they also note that school boards should carefully consider before enforcing these ownership rights because the significant legal costs of enforcement are likely to result in little revenue.[37] Finally, Dolmage and Clarke argue that the involvement of the board should be for the benefit of students and the public at large, rather than for the benefit of their own budgets.

It is clear from the lack of case law and the ongoing disagreements among legal analysts[38] that this issue is not likely to grow. The new *Copyright Act* clearly has a specific purpose to protect the creators of copyright and it is possible that the theory of potential board ownership originally advanced by Dolmage and Clarke has now simply fallen away. Teachers are not compensated in current contracts for the creation and addition of copyrighted works to the "asset base" of the school board and it would be difficult for a court to find a reasonable bargain there, considering all the budget cutbacks in recent years and restrictions on salary increases for teachers across Canada.

Summary

There have been many changes in the law since the second edition of this book, but likely none as dramatic as the changes in technology and copyright law. Teachers now have to contend with a social media universe in addition to their classroom environment. They have new tools for interacting with students and some of these tools can be dangerous if handled improperly. Students have exciting new ways of interacting with the world around them and they need an abundance of help and support to learn how to do so in a healthy way, particularly in relation to cyberbullying and appropriate behaviour in the digital universe. Finally, copyright law has seen one of the biggest changes in the past 50 years and, most important, an error has been rectified (in the opinion of many observers) to reinstate an exemption for copying when it comes to educational purposes. This is a positive development for schools, teachers and students.

NOTES

1   See, for example, "Professional Advisory—Use of Electronic Communication and Social Media" (February 23, 2011), Ontario College of Teachers, http://www.oct.ca/ resources/advisories/use-of-electronic-communication-and-social-media; "Cybertips for Teachers" (2011), Canadian Teacher's Federation, www.ctf-fce.ca/Documents/ Resources/en/cyberbullying/2011/CYBER2011_Brochure_EN_PRINT.pdf.

2   National Association of Schoolmasters Union of Women Teachers, "Social Networking—Guidelines for Members" (2012), http://www.nasuwt.org.uk/ InformationandAdvice/Professionalissues/SocialNetworking/NASUWT_007513.

3   See, for example, "NSTU Guidebook 2012/2013" (2012), at 71, http://www.nstu.ca/ images/pklot/Guidebook2012Jan13NEW.pdf; "Member's Guide to the BC Teachers' Federation" (2012), at 160, http://bctf.ca/uploadedFiles/public/AboutUs/ MembersGuide/guide.pdf.

4   "Cybertips for Teachers," supra note 1.

5   "Member's Guide to the BC Teachers' Federation," supra note 3, at 161.

6   "NSTU Guidebook," supra note 3, at 72.

7   Canadian Council on Learning, "Liars, Fraudsters and Cheats: Dealing with the Growth of Academic Dishonesty" (2010), http://www.ccl-cca.ca/CCL/Reports/ LessonsInLearning/LinL20100707AcademicDishonesty.html.

8   Common Sense Media, "Hi-Tech Cheating: Cell Phones and Cheating in Schools: A National Poll" (2009), http://www.commonsensemedia.org/hi-tech-cheating, as cited in Canadian Council on Learning, supra note 7.

9   *Copyright Act*, R.S.C. 1985, c. C-42, s. 3(1).

10   *CCH Canadian Ltd. v. Law Society of Upper Canada*, 2004 SCC 13, [2004] 1 S.C.R. 339, at para. 10.

11   *Copyright Act*, supra note 9, s. 5.

12   *CCH Canadian*, supra note 10, at para. 16.

13   *Copyright Act*, supra note 9, ss. 14.1 and 14.2.

14   Ibid., s. 13(1).

15   Ibid., s. 13(2).

16   Ibid., s. 2.

17   Ibid., s. 27(1).

18   Ibid., s. 27(2).

19   The term of copyright used to be life plus 50 years in the United States and was extended by the "Sonny Bono Copyright Term Extension Act" (1998), Pub. L. 105-298. The Walt Disney Company exerted a lot of pressure to ensure that Mickey Mouse did not fall into the public domain 50 years after Walt Disney's death. (Walt Disney died in December 1966 so, without this amendment, Mickey Mouse and other characters would be public property in 2016.)

20   *Copyright Act*, supra note 9, s. 29.

21   *CCH Canadian Ltd.*, supra note 10.

22   Ibid.

23   *Copyright Act*, supra note 9, s. 29.

24   *Alberta (Education) v. Canadian Copyright Licensing Agency (Access Copyright)*, 2012 SCC 37.

25   Ibid., at para 23. The copying was permitted because it was deemed to fall within the exception of fair dealing for the purposes of research or private study in the *Copyright Act*.

26   OLITA Resolution, January 25 2013, Inside OLITA, http://www.accessola2.com/olita/ insideolita/wordpress/?p=58235.

27   *Copyright Act*, supra note 9, s. 29.4.

28   Ibid., ss. 29.3 and 29.5.

29   Ibid., ss. 29.5 and 29.6.

30   Ibid., s. 29.3.

31   Ibid., s. 29.7.

32   Ibid., s. 29.9.

33 Government of Canada, Balanced Copyright, http://balancedcopyright.gc.ca/eic/site/ crp-prda.nsf/eng/h_rp01153.html#amend.

34 *Copyright Act*, supra note 9, s. 13.

35 R. Dolmage and P. Clarke, "Copyright Ownership of Teacher-Prepared Materials: An Examination of the Issues in a Contemporary Context" (2002) 11 *Education & Law Journal* 321, at 323.

36 Ibid., at 340.

37 Ibid.

38 See K. Kindred, "Copyright Ownership of Teacher-Prepared Teaching Materials: A Response to Dolmage and Clarke" (2003) 13:2 *Education & Law Journal* 299, where the author, a Halifax-based labour and employment lawyer, criticizes Dolmage and Clarke's conclusion regarding the ownership of teacher-prepared materials. Kindred suggests that, in general, copyright laws support teacher ownership, and that on the basis of that ownership teachers and school boards should be able to come to some agreement as to the fair use of these rights. Kindred's ownership argument is based on teachers' "high degree of personal contribution to the work and the lack of employer control of teaching methodology."

EPILOGUE
Concluding Thoughts on New Challenges Facing the Modern Teacher

Teachers play many different roles in modern society and their complex relationships with students, parents, fellow teachers, and school administrators have been further complicated by legal rules. In the days of the one-room schoolhouse, a teacher was, in a very real sense, the delegate of the parents and, in a fairly direct way, their employee. The school trustees, who were parents in the community, would hire and fire the teacher and set the terms of employment. The range of jobs that the teacher was expected to perform included janitorial tasks, such as keeping the fire going; medical tasks, such as checking for contagious diseases; administrative supervision of the school; and, of course, teaching students in a range of grades. Even in those less complicated days, teachers played many different roles—a fact that is reflected in some of the older education statutes.[1] However, there were very few laws that intruded into the daily working life of a teacher.

Today's modern teacher is expected to play a wide variety of roles: parent, educator, equality promoter, police agent, social worker, and paramedic, to name but a few. There are also many different legal rules that structure and define the roles of teachers in the modern school. As emphasized in the preceding chapters, the legal rights and responsibilities of a teacher depend on the role that he happens to be playing at a particular time. The *in loco parentis* role that a teacher plays has now been diminished. Instead, teachers more commonly act in various capacities as agents of the state. Because the *Canadian Charter of Rights and Freedoms* regulates state agents, teachers and other educational professionals have been swept into the intricacies of constitutional law. This, coupled with the growth of statutory law and regulations, has plunged teachers into the legal dimensions of the educational process. Teachers sometimes feel as though they have parachuted into a foreign land.

Another growing aspect of this foreign land is ever-expanding technology and a revolution in forms of communication in terms of social media. Teachers, along with the rest of us, live in a world of texting, tweeting, and Facebook. In these domains the students are generally more knowledgeable and adept than their parents and teachers. The gap between youth and adults in respect to both technology and social media is a large one, and the challenge of bridging that divide falls to teachers. The expanding dimensions of the new challenges of technology and social media are emphasized by the references throughout the book to the problems of cyberbullying and a separate chapter on teachers and technology (Chapter 8). The rapidly evolving law on related matters of privacy, data control, freedom of information, and the Internet add yet another layer of complication.

Although the arrival of the Charter in 1982 has been the major force in judicializing education, it is certainly not the only factor. Education statutes and related regulations have become more detailed with every passing year, and new laws regulating employment, medical practices, technology, and child guidance have emerged. Judges and lawyers have become much more involved in educational policy-making, and there is a growing consciousness of the legal implications of being a teacher. As students and parents become increasingly aware of their legal rights, they look more expectantly to the courts to solve educational problems.[2] This does not mean, however, that the courts are running Canadian schools. The tradition of judicial deference to local school boards and political authorities is still alive and well in Canada. However, it is clear that the law has become a more significant aspect of education, crucial to an understanding of the roles of the teacher and the expectations placed on her. Some understanding of the legal framework within which schools operate is essential to being a good teacher.

Debate continues about whether the growing role for lawyers in Canadian education is a good thing.[3] Whatever the resolution of these debates, Canadian society is increasingly regulated by laws, and teachers, like everyone else, cannot escape this reality. Rather than decry this state of affairs, teachers are well advised to learn about the legal implications of their job.

In previous editions of this book, the predominant legal issue was the impact of the Charter on education. In the 21 years that have passed, it is clear from the case law cited here that the Charter's impact has been growing. This situation will continue as case law on the Charter evolves; but other issues have also come to the forefront and these too will have a significant impact on teachers, the education system in general, and the law.

Bullying (and its insidious relative, cyberbullying), religious accommodation, and appropriate education for students with special needs are three such emerging issues. These issues are examples of areas in which society's expectations of the omnicompetent teacher are growing. Further challenges for teachers and the school system include the ever-expanding world of technology and its impact on education, as well as the effect of social media insofar as it creates the "multitasking" student. All of these issues are also examples of areas where the law will add to the challenges experienced by today's teachers in modern classrooms. The role of the teacher continues to be demanding as well as rewarding.

As the preceding chapters reveal, it is not possible to write about teachers and the law without also discussing the rights and responsibilities of other actors in the field of education. In order to examine the rights of teachers in the workforce, we explored the rights and duties of school boards and administrators in their role as employers. Only by understanding the rights of parents and students is it possible to comprehend the legal role of teachers in the school. Because the role of the teacher has expanded so dramatically, it is necessary to have at least a passing familiarity with the role played by the police, social agencies, and medical professionals. Of course, it is also vital to re-examine the meaning of education and teaching.

The school is a microcosm of society, along with its inherent value disputes. Long before the Charter, conflicts involving language, religion, and culture were being played out in the schools. These conflicts have new dimensions in an increasingly diverse and multicultural Canada. Denominational education has been entrenched in the Canadian Constitution since 1867 and, as we have seen, has limited the human rights of many Canadian teachers in its systems. Minority language educational rights were entrenched in 1982 in section 23 of the Charter, but the emotional debates about this issue have much deeper roots. The education of Aboriginal children in residential schools, a national disgrace, has only recently begun to get the attention it deserves. There is also a growing awareness that when educators impose Judeo-Christian values in schools, they are, in effect, pursuing a policy of cultural assimilation. This awareness is particularly important for teachers in recognizing the historic claims of First Nations groups, as well as the contributions of Canadians from many different ethnic, religious, and cultural backgrounds. The multicultural reality of Canada is ever-increasing. Indeed, one of the most difficult challenges for teachers is the continuing fight against the pernicious influences of discrimination in Canadian society.

In addition to facing these broad societal and national challenges in a public forum, teachers are ultimately responsible for the education of children. Contrary to some bad press about individual teachers, most teachers are dedicated to their profession and care deeply about their students. In some cases, the law appears to interfere with this expression of care, as is dramatically emphasized by the loosened evidentiary requirements and the stringency of the laws relating to sexual interference. Hugging a child can be an appropriate expression of care in the proper context and is not always an inappropriate expression of sexual interest. In other cases, the law imposes a legal duty of care with respect to negligence. To some teachers, the law and its complex rules are the enemies of education and harmonious teacher–student relations. We do not agree. Lawyers and teachers can, and must, work together to provide a better education for all students. Understanding the legal framework for schools is an important aspect of forming a constructive partnership that will serve the interests of all Canadians. Effective and professional teachers cannot ignore the law that has become as much a part of the school environment as the air they breathe.

NOTES

1   See, for example, *Education Act*, R.S.N.S. 1967, c. 81, s. 54.

2   A.W. MacKay, "The Rights Paradigm in the Age of the Charter," in R. Ghosh and D. Roy, eds., *Social Change and Education in Canada*, 3rd ed. (Toronto: Harcourt Brace Jovanovich, 1995), 224.

3   A.W. MacKay, "The Judicial Role in Education: Promise or Threat?" (1988) 1:1 *Education & Law Journal* 127 and A.W. MacKay, "Safe and Inclusive Schooling—Expensive ... Quality Education—Priceless, For Everything Else There are Lawyers" (2009) 18 *Education & Law Journal* 21. The debates explored in these articles are even more relevant today.

Table of Cases

Index